MODELLERS
2
DATAFILE

THE HAWKER
HURRICANE

A COMPREHENSIVE GUIDE FOR THE MODELLER

Richard A. Franks

SAM Publications

Front cover:
The cover artwork depicts a Hurricane Mk IIC, BE581, JX•E of No. 1 Squadron and was created exclusively for this publication by Michelle Marsan.
A limited (2000) number of prints are available. Please write to SAM Publications for more details.

Modellers Datafile No.2
The Hawker Hurricane

by Richard A. Franks

First published in Great Britain, 1999 by SAM Publications
4 Princeton Court
Pilgrim Centre
Brickhill Drive
Bedford MK41 7PZ
England

ISBN 0 9533465 1 X

Typesetting and repro by DMZee Marketing Limited, 4 Princeton Court, Brickhill Drive, Bedford MK41 7PZ England
Designed by Simon Sugarhood
Printed and bound in the United Kingdom by Printhaüs, 2 North Portway Close, Northampton NN3 8RQ England

The Modellers Datafile Series

Acknowledgements
A word of thanks must go to the following people and organisations, without whose help and encouragement this title would never have happened: The Department of Information Services, Royal Air Force Museum, Hendon; The Aircraft & Exhibits Department, Royal Air Force Museum, Hendon; The Photographic Department, Royal Air Force Museum, Hendon; Royal Air Force Museum, Cosford; Rolls-Royce Heritage Trust, Derby; Trevor Snowden, Airfix Ltd; Neil Robinson, AirGen Publications; Neil Burkill, Paragon Designs; Gaston Bernal, AeroMaster Products; Michael Payne; Jim Roeder; Rudy Binneman.

Contents

Contents

Preface

'Cawnpore I', a Mk IIC
(BE500, LK•A) of No. 87
Squadron in flight *(© C.E. Brown)*

Welcome to this, the second in our Modellers Datafile series. This series of books has been conceived from the outset with the static scale model maker in mind, although I am sure that they will prove as popular with aviation enthusiasts and historians. In the past there have been a number of titles which looked at a specific subject, but they only offered historical and technical information. The Modellers Datafile series has been created to offer the modeller information which will be of use when building the type. Each title will contain a short historical text describing the design's evolution, technical data, scale plans, colour interior drawings, black and white sketches, details of how to make all versions in all scales, a list of all known kits of the type, accessories and decals for the type and finally a comprehensive bibliography to help the reader decide on other suitable titles should he wish to do further research.

The choice for this second title is, once again, a purely personal one. My great admiration of the Hurricane is due, I think, to that fact that it does not have the glamour of its opposite number in the RAF, the Supermarine Spitfire. As a strong and stable gun platform the Hurricane could not be surpassed and the type was used in greater number than the Spitfire at the beginning of the war. For this reason, coupled with the obvious strength and purposeful nature of the design, it makes the type irresistible to an ugly old work horse like me!

Richard A. Franks

Photographs

A great number of the photographs used in this title have come from the Royal Air Force Museum's (RAFM) extensive collection. Each picture can be obtained from the RAFM, using the 'P' prefixed number shown in brackets at the end of each caption.

For more details and an up-to-date price list contact the Photographic Department of the RAFM on (44) 0 181 205 2266.

Royal Air Force Museum
HEND☉N
Britain's National Museum of Aviation

Glossary

No. 111 Squadrons Mk Is undergoing servicing at Northolt in 1938
(© RAF Museum P002635)

AA .... Anti-Aircraft
A&AEE ..... Aeroplane & Armament Experimental Establishment
AACU .... Anti-aircraft Co-operation Unit
AASF .... Advanced Air Striking Force
Air Cdre ..... Air Commodore (RAF)
ACM .... Air Chief Marshal (RAF)
AFC .... Air Force Cross (RAF)
AFDU .... Air Fighting Development Unit
AI .... Airborne Interception (radar)
Air Mshl .... Air Marshal (RAF)
ASC .... Air Support Control
AVG .... American Volunteer Group
AVM .... Air Vice Marshal (RAF)
BAFO .... British Air Forces of Occupation
BEF .... British Expeditionary Force
BS .... British Standard
BSDU .... Bomber Support Development Unit
Capt .... Captain
CMF .... Central Mediterranean Force
CO .... Commanding Officer
Do .... Dornier
DFC .... Distinguished Flying Cross
DFM .... Distinguished Flying Medal
DSO .... Distinguished Service Order
DTD .... Directorate of Technical Development
FAA .... Fleet Air Arm
FEAF .... Far East Air Force
Fg Off .... Flying Officer (RAF)
Flt Sgt ...... Flight Sergeant
Flt Ltn ...... Flight Lieutenant
FRU .... Fleet Requirements Unit
FS .... Federal Standard
FTS .... Flying Training School
GLO .... Ground Liaison Officer
Gp Capt ..... Group Captain (RAF)
HAL .... Hawker Aircraft Ltd.
HF .... High-Altitude Fighter
HMS .... His/Her Majesty's Ship
HQ .... Headquarters
IFF .... Identification Friend or Foe

kg .... Kilogram
KG .... Kampfgeschwader (Luftwaffe)
JG .... Jagdgeschwader (Luftwaffe)
lb .... Pound
LDV .... Local Defence Volunteers
LF .... Low-Altitude Fighter
L.G. .... Landing Ground
lt .... Litre
Lt Cdr ..... Lieutenant Commander (Royal Navy)
Lt Col ..... Lieutenant Colonel
MAC .... Mediterranean Air Command
Maj .... Major
MAP .... Ministry of Aircraft Production
Me .... Messerschmitt (also Bf)
Mk .... Mark
ML .... ML Aviation Ltd.
MU .... Maintenance Unit (RAF)
NF .... Night Fighter
No. .... Number
NCO .... Non-commissioned Officer
NEAF .... Near East Air Force
OTU .... Operational Training Unit
PFF .... Pathfinder Force
Plt Off ..... Pilot Officer (RAF)
PR .... Photographic reconnaissance
PRU .... Photo-reconnaissance Unit
RAAF .... Royal Australian Air Force
RAE .... Royal Aircraft Establishment
RAF .... Royal Air Force
RATO .... Rocket Assisted Take-Off
RAuxAF ..... Royal Auxiliary Air Force
RCAF .... Royal Canadian Air Force
RNAS .... Royal Naval Air Station
RP .... Rocket Projectile
SAAF .... South African Air Force
SBC .... Small Bomb Container
SCI .... Smoke Curtain Installations
Sgt .... Sergeant
Sqn .... Squadron
Sqn Ldr ..... Squadron Leader (RAF)
T .... Trainer
TI .... Target indicator
UK .... United Kingdom
USAAC ..... United States Army Air Corps
USAAF ..... United States Army Air Force
USS .... United States Ship
VC .... Victoria Cross
VE-Day ..... Victory in Europe Day
VJ-Day ...... Victory in Japan Day
Wg Cdr ..... Wing Commander (RAF)
W/O .... Warrant Officer
/G .... Suffix letter added to aircraft serial number denoting that it carried special equipment and was to be guarded at all times

A Monoplane Fighter

To understand the factors which shaped the Hurricane's design, you must look at the design of fighters prior to this time. With the end of the First World War, military planners in the UK believed that the Ten Year Rule would apply; namely that ten years warning of another war would provide sufficient time to prepare. Therefore, with the Royal Air Force's policing actions in Iraq and the North West Frontier Province, the Air Staff considered that general purpose and army co-operation types would suffice and this remained the case throughout the 1920's and early 1930's. There was another factor that restricted the growth of a new generation of fighters, namely that some members of the Air Staff still had a very negative attitude to the monoplane designs that were coming into vogue at this time, based on a number of fatal accidents with monoplane designs before WWI. Also, to be fair, there were no bombers that could not be dealt with by the current fighter types in service. The fact that the RAF only derived any tactical knowledge of their fighter's effectiveness by annual exercises may seem logical, but when you realise that the bombers which they were tested against were also from the RAF, this should give you some idea of the insular environment in which the RAF's long term planning was done at this time. With such a small annual budget (just £10,000,000), the RAF had little capital to fund any research and development of monoplane designs.

The Hurricane design can trace its lineage not just to the Fury, but to the predecessor of that design, the Hawker Hart. This aircraft was developed from an Air Ministry specification issued in 1926 and, when during military exercises in 1930 this bomber proved to be faster than all current RAF fighters, the need for a new breed of fighter was obvious, even to the Air Staff. The advance made with the Hart had been appreciated by the Chief Designer at H.G. Hawker Engineering Co., Ltd., Sydney Camm. To this end he had initiated a development, as a private venture, of the Hornet (later called Fury) design. The appointment of ACM Sir John Salmond as the Chief of the Air Staff in 1930, soon saw added urgency regarding to the whole concept of a new fighter. Of all of the front line fighters of the day, the Bristol Bulldog was the fastest at 174mph, then the Siskin (156mph) and then the Gamecock (155mph). This should however be compared with the new Hart bomber which had a top speed of 184mph! Combine this with the fact that there was no radar for interception, and that all the fighters were armed with two rifle-calibre machine guns, it was very unlikely that the fighters would, even if perfectly positioned during the bomber's flight across them, be able to get off more than a fleeting burst of gun-fire.

The Air Staff decided to overcome this situation via a few simple criteria: increased speed that would be offered by the new V12, in-line Rolls Royce Kestrel, then coming into service in the Hart and Hornet, and increased armament. This latter was not easily acheived, as the current Vickers Mk III machine gun, although offering 1,000rpm, still suffered with stoppages that meant that the guns had to be in reach of the pilot. The

Hawker Fury, K8238 of the Central Flying School, Upavon, 1938 *(© C.E. Brown)*

high rate of fire also meant that ammunition storage had to be within the fuselage. Not withstanding this, the Air Ministry issued one of the most advanced specifications of the time: F.7/30. This design called for faster, better performing and more manoeuvrable aircraft than any existing type, with a top speed of at least 250mph, and to reduce additional development costs, this design also had to be capable of being a night-fighter. Although events soon overtook this specification, Gloster's design became the famous Gladiator, while Hawker's design was the P.V.3, which was basically a Fury with a Goshawk engine. Many of the aerodynamic elements of this design were fitted to the Intermediate Fury (G-ASBE) and the High Speed Fury (K3586).

Birth of the Hurricane

By 1933 the F.7/30 specification had shown the Directorate of Technical Development (DTD) that the designs being submitted to meet this requirement were only going to be stop-gaps. The biplane design had reached the zenith of its development, and the increasingly dangerous political situation in Germany meant that the need for a new breed of monoplane fighter was dawning. In August of this year Sydney Camm spoke with the DTD about future fighter requirements for the RAF and the development of the existing Fury design as a monoplane. By October 1934, the initial designs for this had been created and were shown to the Air Ministry. The design utilised the Goshawk powerplant, which as yet had not shown its inherent coolant-system weakness, and basically the aircraft looked like the High Speed Fury with one wing, a revised upper decking to include an enclosed canopy, a fixed and spatted undercarriage and the steam-evaporation system

The Hawker 'High Speed' Fury (K3586) in flight
(© RAF Museum P002651)

installed in a ventral unit, similar to a standard radiator. Air Ministry interest was high, as the type would easily meet the 275mph speed requirement. In 1934 however the troublesome Goshawk was replaced by the new P.V.12, which was a developed version of the Rolls-Royce 'R' engine so sucessfully used by the Schneider Trophy racers. This engine did away with the need for the steam cooling system and also offered a 40% increase in take-off power and a 60% increase in power at service altitude when compared with the latest Kestrel (Mk V). From now on the new design, having few links with the Fury, was referred to as the 'Monoplane Interceptor'. With detail design and testing of the base design under way, the next

A group shot of members of the Hawker staff along with a foreign deligation viewing the Fury. To the extreme left of the group can be seen John Hindermarsh and Flt Lt P.W.S. 'George' Bullman
(© RAF Museum P008773)

change to affect the design was the utilisation of a fully retractable undercarriage. Fitting this undercarriage to the Hawker design had been made easier by the centre of gravity requirements moving the radiator 18 inches aft due to the increased weight of the new P.V.12 engine. This therefore left the forward interspar centre-section area unobstructed, and a retractable undercarriage was installed. Even at this early stage Camm saw the need to give his design a wide-track undercarriage and low pressure tyres. This meant that each leg had to retract inward and that they were inclined forward once extended. Retracting this leg into the spar bay resulted in a break in the oleo and the use of a radiusing link to orientate the unit into the bay during the retraction sequence.

Armament

Development of suitable armament was another factor and the new Armament Research Division of the Air Ministry sponsored evaluation of various machine guns at the end of 1933. Firms entering this evaluation included Vickers, Lewis, Colt, Madson, Spandau, Kiraleji, Darne and Hispano, and after extensive testing the Colt example proved superior. This weapon however used 0.300in rifle-calibre rimless ammunition, so the Air Ministry undertook discussions with the Colt Automatic Weapons Corporation to see if the gun could be modified to accept 0.303in ammunition. Once this was found to be feasible (in early 1934), the specifications were passed out to the British aircraft industry, although due to the huge amount of money the British Government owed the USA from the First World War it was highly unlikely that they would obtain the license agreement. With the new Colt weapon a realistic proposition, the Air Ministry issued a full specification (F.5/34) for a fighter equipped with six or eight of these guns.

Hawker undertook additional design work adapting the Monoplane Interceptor design to the new F.5/34 specification, but at the same time they also continued with the four-gun installation in the design. This four-gun machine was produced as a 1/10th scale model and tested in the National Physics Laboratory, Teddington reaching an equivalent speed of 350mph by August 1934. This design was put forward to the Air Ministry and resulted in F.36/34 being issued to cover the type. Both F.36/34 (Hurricane) and F.37/34 (Spitfire) were issued to bring both of these designs in line with overall specification S/34, instigated by Sqn Ldr R.S. Sorley of the Air Ministry Operational Requirements Branch, who convinced both Sydney Camm and R.J. Mitchell that this was essential. The Monoplane Interceptor now became the 'F.36/34 Single-Seat Fighter - High Speed Monoplane' and by the 17th November 1934 drawings were with the Experimental Shops for preparation of the first jigs. A full wooden mock-up of the design was created by the Experimental Department to study all the problems associated with the production of such a modern and complex type. By the 10th January 1935 a conference was held about this mock-up in Canbury Park Road, Kingston and although the design utilised four machine guns Air Cdre L.A. Pattinson of the Armaments Research Division stated that unless a license agreement could be reached with Colt, the design would be unlikely to have eight guns installed. Hawker's staff had already undertaken design work to convert the design to an eight-gun layout though.

On the 21st February 1935 the first performance data was released for the design. This indicated that the maximum level speed would be 330mph (15,000ft) at 4,480lb. Service ceiling was envisaged as 32,500ft with a maximum ceiling of 34,800ft. On this day Hawker received the Air Ministry manufacturing contract for one prototype, registered K5083, but still no final decision on the armament layout! Six weeks later it was agreed that no guns, just ballast, would be fitted to the prototype and that the ballast would equate to two Vickers Mk V guns in the fuselage (either side of the engine) and one Colt (Browning) machine gun in each wing. This all changed with the license agreement between Colt and BSA (Birmingham Small Arms) in July 1935, so the prototype contract was amended to show the installation of eight Browning machine guns in the wings (although the Vickers guns still remained as 'alternatives'?).

Work now started on actually creating the prototype.

The Beginning

The F.36/34 prototype under construction, with the Merlin 'C' installed and one of the proposed fuselage-mounted Vickers machine guns installed

The design of the Hurricane was based very much on the technology that had existed previously, insofar as the aircraft used many of the elements of the previous Hawker Hart and Fury. Basically the F.34/36 (or Hurricane as it was to become), was the Fury, with the upper wing removed and its area added to the lower one, an enclosed canopy and the spatted wheels replaced with inward retracting examples.
To be fair this is too simple a look at the F.34/36 design, but the basic idea is there as the Hawker F.34/36 used a Warren truss construction, with swaged wire bracing and fabric covering. The fuselage used four stainless steel longerons, with steel panels and duralumin tubes that were fixed with plates and bolts. The use of such a structure may seem old fashioned when compared to the other F.36/34 competitor (the Spitfire), but this extremely strong, yet lightweight, construction was to serve the type well during the early stages of World War II.

August 1935 saw the prototype (K5083) structurally complete and this included the installation of the Rolls-Royce P.V.12, which was now renamed the Merlin. The guns were not available for fitment, so ballast for these and additional fuel tankage was installed. The airframe was loaded onto trucks at the Canbury Park Road plant and taken to the assembly shed at Brooklands on the 23rd October. Once assembled, the aircraft (now also 'weighted' with 200lb ballast for the radio equipment) was weighed, then a series of ground-running and taxying trials commenced with Chief Test-Pilot Flt Lt P.W.S. 'George' Bulman at the controls. It was in his hands that the prototype took to the air for the first time on the 6th November 1935 from the grass strip at Brooklands. This first flight took place even though the Merlin 'C' engine failed to pass the 50-hour provisional civil certificate of airworthiness! The 2nd flight took place on the

11th November, with the 3rd on the 23rd November and the 4th on the 26th November. Trouble with the engine did occur after eight test flights, and by the flight on the 5th February 1936 the engine had been changed from the 11th to the 15th version of the 'C'. Test flying was undertaken by George Bulman, as well as Philip Lucas and John Hindmarsh, although George was responsible for the development of this new fighter. Initial flights showed that the canopy framework needed additional

This picture shows the prototype nearing completion in September 1935

The prototype Hurricane (K5083) in its initial form (single canopy stiffener) flying near Martlesham Heath in 1937
(© C.E. Brown/RAF Museum 5684-1)

With K5083 in the background, the Hawker Chief Draughtsman hands over the clearance certificate to the Flight Commander of Martlesham Heath in 1937
(© C.E. Brown/RAF Museum 5684-16)

fighter would be issued a production contract lead Hawkers to to go ahead with work to production standard. In March 1936 the Production Drawing Office started work on the drawings and the Production Planning Department created draft schedules envisaging a potential production output of 1,000 machines. This was to prove very fortunate, as on the 3rd June 1936 Hawker received a contract (527112/36) from the Air Ministry for 600 aircraft. By the 8th June the manufacturing drawings were with the Production Shop and on the 27th June the name Hurricane was accepted by the Air Ministry.

By the time the order was placed with Hawkers, Rolls-Royce had done sufficient development on the 'C' to cure most of the problems so far encountered, and this new version was initially know as the 'F', although it later went into production as the Merlin I. The prototype gained its armament in August and it continue to undertake service development work. A trial installation of the TR.9B transmitter/receiver was undertaken in April 1937, and the prototype continued with service trials at

strengthening, the tailplane struts were not necessary and engine cooling problems were caused because that the radiator was too small. By the flight on the 7th February 1936 all these modifications had been made and Bulman was satisfied that these problems had been addressed and that the aircraft was suitable for service evaluation by the Royal Air Force. The airframe was therefore delivered to the Aircraft and Armament Experimental Establishment at Martlesham Heath. Testing was undertaken between the 18th and 24th February 1936 and the evaluation was slowed by problems with the Merlin 'C'. Failure of the supercharger bearings resulted in another change from the 19th to the 17th 'C', although further problems with the valve spring and automatic boost-control capsule all occurred during this period. This all proved to be academic though, as development of the Merlin 'C' was not going to be continued. A maximum speed of 315mph at 16,200ft was achieved, with a service ceiling of 34,500ft and an absolute ceiling of 35,400ft. The airframe was now returned to Brooklands for further development work, although it also went to Rolls-Royce to rectify minor faults on the Merlin 'C' (No. 19). The worsening international situation (this was the time of the Abyssinian Crisis) and the strong rumours that the F.36/34

A beautiful shot of K5083 undergoing undercarriage retraction tests at Martlesham Heath in 1937
(© C.E. Brown/RAF Museum 5684-10)

the A&AEE. Detail work on the production versions was now undertaken at Hawker, but early in July 1937 the prototype was flown by Sqn Ldr Anderson of the A&AEE to the Royal Air Force Pageant, Hendon, where it was shown to the public for the first time. Initially the prototype had a flap section under the lower fuselage, forward of the radiator, but this was thought to have caused radiator over-heating (where in fact the real reason was insufficient capacity in this unit) and it was locked shut (Note: all production examples had this centre-section flap deleted). In this new form George Bulman flew the prototype on the 15th July 1937. At last, during August, the eight Browning machine guns were installed in the prototype, and with the old Merlin 'C' engine the aircraft flew on the 17th of that month. Actual trial firing of the armament was undertaken in October and these trials highlighted the need for some form of heating for the guns. Modifications were made to K5083, channelling hot air from the engine to the gun bays. Throughout September and

carburettor intake area, which was increased, and the glycol header tank, which had to be repositioned.

By the time that K5083 had returned to Brooklands for spinning trials, the first production Merlin II engine had been delivered to Hawkers. This was installed in the first production Hurricane (L1547) on the 19th April. By the end of November this year no fewer than seven production airframes were flying and service acceptance began.

Flt Lt P.W.S. "George' Bulman in the prototype, K5083, at Martlesham Heath in 1937 (© C.E. Brown/RAF Museum 5684-13)

October the prototype continued service handling and performance trials at Martlesham Heath. where it achieved 318mph at 15,500ft. It returned to Brooklands on the 20th October, after the completion of these trials, and it started to undertake spinning trials in the capable hands of George Bulman on the 6th November. Developments also continued with the powerplant, as the Merlin I (Merlin 'F') had been discontinued and the new Merlin II (Merlin 'G') was envisaged for the production Hurricane. Revisions to the rocker box flanges of this engine required the revision of the nose cowling contours on the Hurricane. Other modifications included the

Into Service

In 1935, Lord Swinton, Secretary of State for Air, had set up the dispersed 'shadow factory' production scheme and in July 1936 the Air Defence of Great Britain became Fighter Command under ACM Sir Hugh Dowding. All of these factors were to be of great importance to the development of the Royal Air Force during the period leading up to the Second World War. Production Scheme F of 1936 stated that 500 Hurricanes (and 300 Spitfires) were to be in service by March 1939. Earlier expansion of the RAF had been achieved with older biplanes such as the Hind, Hart, Fury, Demon, Gladiator and Gauntlet. By January 1937 Fighter Command had (or was creating) twenty-six regular and auxiliary fighter squadrons. Of these, No. 111 (Fighter) Squadron at Northolt had received the first Hurricanes around Christmas 1937. The first four machines at this unit were L1548 to L1551 and these were joined by twelve more (L1552-L1561, L1563 & L1564) before the end of February 1938. During this initial work up on the type, the Squadron, lead by Sqn Ldr John W. Gillan, suffered a few accidents, some of which were fatal. Trying to instill confidence in his men for the Hurricane, Gillan undertook a high-speed flight from Northolt to Turnhouse and back on the 10th February 1938. Even though he encountered high headwinds on the flight out, he was able to return the same day and use the tailwind to cover the 327miles in 48minutes at an average speed of 408.75mph. The second squadron, No. 3 at RAF Kenley, received the Hurricane by early April and their first machines included L1565-L1573, L1576-L1580, L1582, L1586-L1588.

An in-flight study of Mk I, L1683 in 1938
(© RAF Museum P002590)

Modifications continued on the Hurricane, as the production version tested by Hawker and at Martlesham Heath showed that the rudder's effect during a spin recovery was slightly deficient. To overcome this L1547 was fitted with a 3 inch extension at the base of the rudder. A strake on the lower fuselage was added to match the revised rudder lower profile and the tailwheel was

A pilot of No. 111 Sqn, at Northolt in 1938, boards his Mk I (© RAF Museum P002630)

Pilots of No. 111 Squadron standing in front of Mk I, L158? at RAF Northolt in 1938
(© C.E. Brown/RAF Museum 5797-2)

fixed. These modifications were incorporated in production machines from the 7th March 1938. Installation of Rolls-Royce ejector exhaust stacks on the production test airframe (L1547) showed a 2mph increase over the 'kidney' type currently used. These new ejector stacks were fitted to all subsequent production aircraft, and retro-fitted to all existing machines. All the production examples so far had had the fixed-pitch Watts Type Z3890 wooden propeller, but in 1938 trials began with the de Havilland Hamilton two-pitch three-blade metal propeller. Installation of this propeller on L1562 allowed a pitch of 30.5 degrees for take-off and 42.5 degrees for flight and this resulted in an increase in rate of climb. Fitment to production aircraft of this propeller began with L1780 in January 1939 and involved some modifications, as the type's settings were related to engine speeds, and therefore existing Merlin II engines had to be modified with a revised special propeller shaft. From the 2,907th Merlin II a new 'universal' shaft was installed, and this resulted in the Merlin III, which was fitted to Hurricane L1909 onwards. Fitment of the D.H. variable-pitch three-blade propeller was standard on production examples from L1980.

Production of the Hurricane was to be improved with the building of a new factory at Langley (Parlaunt Park Farm). This was achieved thanks to the formation of a Trust by T.O.M. Sopwith in July 1936 which allowed Hawker to buy shares of the Siddeley Development Company. The increased capital offered by this purchase allowed a loan to be issued which lead to the construction of the Langley factory. By mid-1938 the factory was well on the way to completion and with the increased funding available to the Government after the Munich Crisis, a further order for 1,000 Hurricanes was placed on the 1st November that year. A big blow to development and production testing occurred on the 6th September when John Hindmarsh was killed in the crash of L1652. Joining the team after this was R.C. Reynell and he was followed later by J. Grierson. With the arrival of the Bf 109D and its cannon armament on the scene, discussions were undertaken regarding to the armour plating fitted to the Hurricane. The first scheme (Scheme A) called for just a piece of armour plate forward of the cockpit, while Scheme B called for the installation of bullet-proof windscreens to all production machines within three months and the fitment of armour plate aft of the pilot's seat by September 1939.

The variable-pitch propeller had bestowed benefits on the Hurricane, so when Rotol Ltd (formed by Rolls-Royce and Bristol) started development of the hydraulically-operated constant-speed three-blade propeller, Hawkers were keen to utilise it on the Hurricane. With the purchase from the Air Ministry of an old No. 56 Squadron Mk I (L1606), trials began with the new Merlin III and the 10ft 6in Rotol three-blade propeller. This machine was registered as G-AFXX and Lucas first flew the machine on the 24th January 1939. Within a few days this machine achieved 328mph at 16,200ft and got to 15,000ft in just 6.2 minutes.

The use of stressed metal wings had been considered right at the beginning of the Hurricane design, as the fabric wings were not considered able to survive battle damage, which would lead

The first tropicalised Hurricane, L1669. This machine later went to the Middle East and it features the early style of tropical filter unit

to 'ballooning' of the material and possible loss of large areas of fabric. The actual metal wing of the Hurricane was identical to that envisaged for the Henley in its dive-bomber role. The first Hurricane with metal wings (L1877) was flown (by Lucas) on the 28th April 1939. Initial production of these wing sets was slow, and only a dozen more were available by August. By September production was stepped up for all production machines and the last fabric-wing machines left Brookland in March 1940. Cannibalising scrap aircraft began in February

Accidents with the new Hurricane were common, as seen in this view of Mk I, L1869 of No. 501 Sqn which crashed near Filton in 1939 (© RAF Museum P001861)

A Mk I, L1577 operated by No. 3 Squadron is seen here at their base, RAF Kenley in late 1938 (© Michael Payne)

Ex-No. 56 Squadron Mk I L1606 was purchased by Hawkers and registered as G-AFXX; used for trials with the new Rotol three-blade constant-speed propeller

1940 and this allowed the fitment of the metal wings to all older machines. The existing TR.9B radios installed in the Mk Is had been found to 'fade', and their range was somewhat restricted. therefore the improved TR.9D was introduced in early 1939. This installation resulted in the introduction of a new aerial mast, revised in layout from the older 'pole' type, and an aerial lead running from the top of the mast to the top of the rudder.

Tropicalising the Hurricane was considered as early as February 1939 by the Air Staff. If war occurred with Germany, sympathies in Italy would threaten British interests in the

Middle East. To overcome this, a suitable fighter must be converted to operational capacity in the desert environment. Because the Spitfire was wanted for home defence, the Hurricane was the prime candidate for the task. Hawker already had experience with operating their types in this environment, and as the Turkish and Persian Air Forces had expressed interest in the Hurricane pre-war, they had already undertaken some preliminary conversion studies. Working with C.G. Vokes Ltd, Hawker created the multi-vee chin intake for the type and this was first installed in L1669, which was flown by Lucas on the 17th May 1939. The installation of increased armament in the Hurricane did not begin until much later, but there was a trial conducted with a Hurricane on the new 20mm Hispano Mk I cannon. Two of these 20mm cannon were installed in L1750 at the request of A&AEE Initially though this installation was only for the benefit of the new Westland Whirlwind fighter, as the A&AEE wanted to achieve test-firing experience with the new cannon.

The Hurricane had continued to equip a number of RAF squadrons during this time as the situation in Europe worsened. In March 1939 Germany occupied Czechoslovakia and in April Italy marched into Albania. To cover the increased demands being put on the RAF, the Secretary of State for Air, Sir Kingsley Wood, submitted an estimated budget of £205 million, the largest ever. By September 1939 497 Hurricanes had been delivered, it was now ready to go to war...

To War

Mk I, AL•? of No. 79 Sqn with groundcrew using the tailplane as a table for their lunch at Biggin Hill
(© RAF Museum P002649)

With the outbreak of war on the 3rd September 1939 there were eight squadrons of Hurricanes in the Royal Air Force. The French Cabinet had demanded ten fighter squadrons from Britain, but ACM Dowding would not release the Spitfire from Home Defence duties and the onus therefore fell on the Hurricane. Two elements were called for: the first was the Advanced Air Striking Force (AASF) and the other was to offer fighter cover for the British Expeditionary Force (BEF). Only four squadrons were released for this task and therefore Nos. 85 and 87 Squadrons were used for the BEF fighter cover and Nos. 1 and 73 for the AASF. At a later date Nos. 607 and 615 RAuxAF Squadrons joined Nos. 85 and 87 Squadrons. No. 1 Squadron moved to Le Havre on the 8th September, on to Cherbourg on the 10th and then to Vassincourt on the 15th. No. 73 flew to Caen on the 10th September. On the 30th October Plt Off Mould in L1842 attacked and shot down a Do 17 near Toul, the first victory for the RAF in France. Two days later No. 73 Squadron joined the action with their first victory being claimed by Fg Off E.J. Kain and by the end of 1939 twenty enemy aircraft had been claimed by the squadrons. In early 1940 No. 1 Squadron started to receive the new Merlin III powered Mk I's. These machines also had the new de Havilland variable-pitch propellers and by March the entire Squadron had re-equipped.

During February 1940, the radio system installed to the Hurricane was upgraded. The TR.9D radio was replaced with the VHF TR.1133, improving overall ground-to-air

communication and the installation of this radio resulted in the removal of the aerial lead from the aerial mast, and the fitment of aerial leads from each tailplane to the fuselage sides. The installation required that existing machines were replaced with those fitted with the TR.1133. No. 17 Squadron was the first to receive these new machines by March 1940, and the inclusion of the TR.1133 was achieved after the 100th example built by Glosters. The TR.1133 radio equipment was also combined with the Rotol three-blade propeller, and the first machine built in this manner was P2682.

Here, an unknown Hurricane Mk I is seen having crashed somewhere in Belgium during the 'Phoney War' period
(© R. Binneman)

Mk I, UZ•O of No. 306 Sqn, at a snowy RAF Ternhill in the winter of 1940/41
(© RAF Museum P011467)

No. 601 Squadron Mk I's being re-armed at RAF Tangmere in 1940 (© C.E. Brown)

Norway

On the 9th April 1940 Germany attacked Norway. Initially Gladiators of No. 263 Squadron and Hurricanes of No. 46 Squadron were to be sent to Norway aboard HMS Glorious, although only the Gladiators were able to base themselves there as the Hurricane's base was not ready. In May, No. 46 Squadron returned to Norway, although three were damaged on landing at Skaanland and therefore the remaining machines joined the Gladiators at Bardufoss. The squadron had its first victory on the 28th May, but by the 3rd of June the evacuation of the British forces from Narvik had started. This evacuation had been completed by the 7th and although the original plan was to destroy the Hurricanes on the ground (as the pilots had no experience of deck landing), Sqn Ldr K.B.B. Cross (the C.O of No. 46 Squadron) asked for permission to try and land the aircraft on HMS Glorious. All the pilots of the squadron 'volunteered' to do deck landings and each was successful, although it was all for nought as history shows that Glorious was caught by Scharnhorst and Gneisenau and sunk. Of all the No.

46 Squadron crews on Glorious (many were on M.V. Arandora Star), only Sqn Ldr Cross and Flt Lt Jameson survived.

The Low-countries

On the 10th May 1940, the Germans began their invasion of Holland, Belgium and Luxembourg. Holland was attacked on the 14th and by the next day it had capitulated. The air component (Nos. 85, 87, 607 and 615 Squadrons) was reinforced with Nos. 3, 79 and 504 Squadrons after the first attack on Belgium on the 10th May and the AASF had also been reinforced with No. 501 squadron. Now the Hurricane strength in France was ten squadrons, the amount originally demanded by the French Cabinet, although the squadrons were heavily outnumbered by the Luftwaffe. The pilots and machines were in constant action and they often found themselves landing at new bases, as their original ones were overrun by the German forces. As the German offensive moved towards the French ports, the AASF moved south-westwards to Troyes and although thirty-two more Hurricanes were sent on the 13th May, ACM Dowding now called a halt to any further machines being released. In the north the air component was suffering and by the 17th May only three squadrons remained at full operational strength, so on the 21st May the air component returned to England. To protect the retreating BEF the home-based Spitfire and Hurricane squadrons were ordered into battle. No. 32 was the first into action on the 19th May. No. 79 Squadron, which had moved to France in early May, returned to Biggin Hill, although a number of their pilots were dead and their aircraft had been burnt at Merville. Both of these squadrons were now stood-down and moved north to re-equip, while their place was taken by No. 213 and 242, who continued to cover the BEF. On the 26th May the Dunkirk evacuation started and on the 28th No. 213 Squadron saw action over the beaches destroying a number of German aircraft that were strafing and bombing the troops. For nine days the evacuation continued and throughout this period

Hurricane squadrons had between five and six missions a day over the beach. With the Dunkirk evacuation complete, there was still two weeks of action before the Battle of France ended. During this period the AASF operated from a large number of temporary bases near Paris. On the 3rd June the remaining aircraft of the AASF were withdrawn to six bases south-west of Paris. With just the Hurricanes remaining in France, their task was to cover the ports being used to evacuate troops. To help the limited number of Hurricanes, Nos. 1, 17 and 242 Squadrons were temporarily sent from the UK to cover the ports of Nantes, Brest and St. Nazaire. By the 18th June all remaining Hurricanes were ordered back to the UK, although many were destroyed on the ground in France as they were unserviceable. Of the 261 AASF Hurricanes sent, 75 were shot down, 120 were destroyed on the ground due to unserviceability or lack of fuel and just 66 were flown back to the UK. In all 477 fighters had been lost in this campaign. The loss of these machines was a blow, but they could be replaced. However, experienced pilots could not. And now the RAF was to face its greatest test, the Battle of France was over and the Battle of Britain was about to begin.

The Battle of Britain

It must never be underestimated just how bad things were for Britain during the June and July 1940 period. During the Battle of France the RAF had lost a huge number of aircraft and pilots and although ACM Dowding had resisted the depletion of his fighter squadrons, of the fifty-two fighter squadrons seen as the minimum required to defend Britain, just thirty-six were combat ready on 7th June.

Obviously the manufacture of new airframes was paramount and on the 12th May the production planning department of the Air Ministry had been formed into an autonomous body, the Ministry of Aircraft Production (MAP). Guidance of this department was from Lord Beaverbrook and during the seven month period up to August 1940, 1,373 Hurricanes were produced against a target of 1,045. Fighter Command also worked up, equipping all the badly depleted squadrons and forming new ones. The demand on Hurricanes was such that even old fabric-winged Mk I's on Station Flights were recalled and issued to front-line squadrons. By the time the Battle of Britain occurred however, most of these old machines had been replaced with the newer Mk I's.

Before going into detail about the battle, it would be nice to clarify why the Hurricane went for the bombers, leaving the

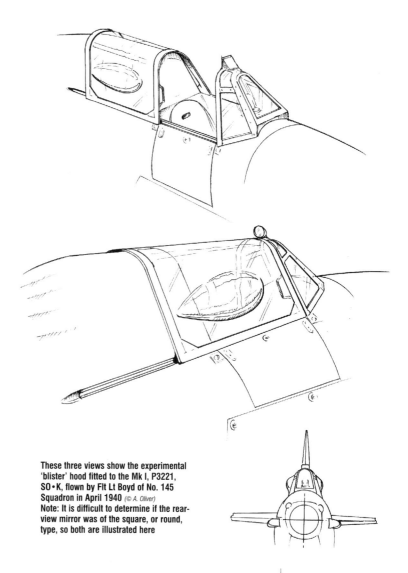

These three views show the experimental 'blister' hood fitted to the Mk I, P3221, SO•K, flown by Flt Lt Boyd of No. 145 Squadron in April 1940 (© A. Oliver)
Note: It is difficult to determine if the rear-view mirror was of the square, or round, type, so both are illustrated here

Spitfire to go after the fighters. It is not true to say that the Hurricane was equal to the Bf 109, but at its own rated altitude (15,000ft) it was at least a match. If the Bf 109 had a height advantage, or dived away, the lesser drag of the type meant that the Hurricane could not attempt to pursue it. Getting combined Hurricane and Spitfire interception of bomber and fighter formations was not possible. Therefore, once it was apparent that if the German fighters were brought into action early they

Mk I, V71??, VF•V of No. 601 Sqn, with Fg Off Whitney Straight and groundcrew standing in front, RAF Northolt 1940/41
(© RAF Museum P002622)

Mk I, L2124, SD•H of No. 501 Squadron *(© RAF Museum P019139)*

would soon be low on fuel and have to return to their bases, the Spitfires would climb to entice the Bf 109's into combat. Once they had turned back to their bases, the bombers were left open to attack by the Hurricanes.

Even with the AASF in France, the Luftwaffe had started limited attacks on the south-eastern coast of England, on the 5th June. During July however Luftflotte 3 were in a position to mount attacks in daylight against British convoys in the English Channel. Standing patrols over the convoys by Fighter Command did offer protection, but these groups were often jumped by large numbers of German fighters while the shipping was attacked by Ju 87's. The effect of this action throughout July and into early August was to see 186 enemy aircraft destroyed for the loss of forty-six Hurricanes and thirty-two Spitfires.

By the beginning of August the Luftwaffe had completed planning for the assault on Britain and the great Adlerangriff

Mk I, YB•S of No. 17 Sqn, showing the damage to the trailing edge of the starboard wing following combat on the 19th May 1940 *(© RAF Museum P010057)*

(Eagle Attack) was set for August 10th. Operations actually began on the 8th August, when Ju 87's and Bf 110's attacked a convoy off the Isle of Wight. The Hurricanes of No. 145 Squadron intercepted them and it was to the Hurricane that the honour of firing the first shot during this historic battle went. At the same time Luftflotte 2 squadrons attacked Dover and a coastal convoy heading for the Thames Estuary and were met by Hurricanes of Nos. 32, 56, 85, 151, 501 and 615 Squadrons. Bad weather on the 10th August stopped the actual Adler Tag (Eagle Day) assault, but attacks on Dover did happen on the 11th,

seeing the Hurricanes of Nos. 1, 17, 32, 56, 85 and 111 Squadrons in action against it. A very heavy raid was launched against Plymouth and Hurricanes of Nos. 2 87, 213 and 238 Squadrons were sent up to face them. Now the Luftwaffe turned its attention to the radar chain (Chain Home) along the coast, probably because of the speed with which their attacks were intercepted during these initial raids. On the 12th the Ventnor towers on the Isle of Wight were attacked, putting it out of action until the 23rd. The same group attacked Southampton and Portsmouth during the day, although they were intercepted by Hurricanes of Nos. 32, 43, 145, 238 and 601 Squadrons. At the same time the airfields at Manston, Lympne and Hawkinge were attacked by squadrons of Luftflotte 2, and damage to each was substantial. On the 13th the raids were far-ranging, and although No. 56 Squadron's base at Rochford was targeted, it escaped undamaged. That evening the Luftwaffe started night attacks on aircraft factories, with the Nuffield site at Castle Bromwich being damaged. On the 15th the weather was at last fine, so all three Luftflotten could launch a combined attack. It was believed by the high-ranking Luftwaffe commanders that the response to their attacks had been achieved with the use of fighters from the north of England, and therefore they expected little defence when the bombers from Norwegian airfields attacked. They were to be (rudely) disappointed! Nos. 605 and 73 Squadrons were in action for these northern raids, and they inflicted severe damage on the Luftflotte 5 groups that attacked. In the south, raids were launched against Martlesham Heath and Rochester and during the large number of engagements with these formations, about thirty aircraft were shot down. By early evening a formation of three-hundred enemy aircraft headed towards the Hampshire and Dorset coast, and were intercepted by Hurricanes of Nos. 87, 213, 238 and 247 Squadrons. Raids against Croydon were also mounted and No. 111 and No. 32 Squadrons went up to meet them. Damage was caused to a number of factories in this raid, and one of the companies effected was Rollasons, who were repairing Hurricanes. On the 16th the raids continued, with three heavy ones. The first was against airfields in Kent, the second against Hampshire and it was here that Hurricanes stored at No. 8 MU, RAF Brize Norton were destroyed. The final attacks of the day were in the early evening and consisted of a number of raids over the Suffolk area to the Isle of Wight area. It was of course during the second raid that Flt Lt J.B. Nicholson of No. 249 Squadron was to be awarded the Victoria Cross. Based at Boscombe Down the squadron had been sent up against the incoming enemy aircraft, and set up patrols between Ringwood and Poole. Whilst looking for

"STEVENS + HIS POP-EYE"

Bf 109's over the Southampton area, Nicholson's section was bounced by Bf 110's and his aircraft was hit by 20mm cannon fire. Two shells penetrated the cockpit and the other hit, and ignited, the reserve fuel cell. With the aircraft on fire, and suffering severe burns, Nicholson was about to bail out when his attacker overshot and as the Bf 110 flew into his sight, Nicholson squeezed the fire button on the control column and opened fire, shooting the Bf 110 down! He then extracted himself painfully from the stricken Hurricane and descended to earth by parachute. Unfortunately LDV forces managed to shoot him in the buttocks as he descended, but he was taken to the Royal Southampton Hospital where he made a recovery and was later informed that he had been awarded the coveted Victoria Cross, the only Fighter Command recipient of the award.

The sheer number of attacks were such at this time that raids were getting through to their targets simply because the fighters could not be everywhere at once. On the 18th the airfield at Kenley was attacked and the bombers destroyed every hangar bar one, even though the Hurricanes of No. 111 and Spitfires of

No. 64 Squadrons had intercepted them.

During this period the Hurricane underwent some modifications to make it more battle-worthy, using the experience so far gained in the European and Battle of Britain periods. The addition of nearly 52lb of armour plate was made to protect the pilot, and this was later supplemented with another 50lb of plate to protect the pilot from attacks from behind. The fuel tanks were made self-sealing with Linatex

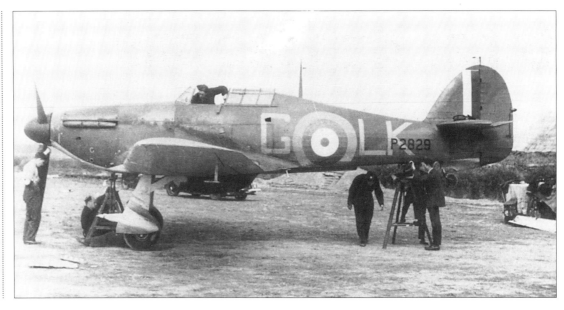

Mk I, P2829, LK•G flown by 'Watty' Watson of No. 87 Squadron seen at RAF Exeter in September 1940
(© Michael Payne)

Flt Lt I.R. Gleed of No. 87 Squadron seen in his Hurricane P2798, LK•A. Note Gleed's personal marking 'Figaro' on the edge below the cockpit sill
(© Michael Payne)

The Hurricane Mk I, V6632, UF•L flown by Sgt Frank Jensen of No. 601 (County of London) Squadron, RAuxAF
(© Michael Payne)

covers and the firewall aft of the engine was completely sealed. Revisions were also made to the propeller during this period, with the new Rotol RX/2 coming into use. This unit could not be fitted to the Merlin III initially, as the 'universal' shaft in that engine was not totally 'universal'. As a result, from Merlin III No. 5606 a truly universal shaft was installed and this allowed the installation of the Rotol RX/2 propeller on all new aircraft from that date.

Returning to the battle, the first real casualty in the Luftwaffe inventory during the Battle of Britain was the Ju 87, which had proved to be highly vulnerable to the Hurricane and Spitfire, so their role was taken by the Bf 110. On the 1st September 1940, No. 1 (RCAF) and No. 303 (Polish) Squadrons, flying the Hurricane, entered the battle to bolster the heavily depleted Hurricane forces of the RAF. Depletion of aircraft and pilots within Fighter Command was such that during this month, Lord

Dowding instigated the 'Stabilisation Scheme'. This scheme stated that all squadrons be graded into three classes. The A Class included No. 11 Group and the Middle Wallop and Duxford sectors in No. 10 and 12 Groups. The B Class were the remaining squadrons in the No. 10 and 12 Groups. These were kept at full strength, if at all possible, to act as reinforcements for the A Class squadrons. The final class, C, was made up of the groups in the north and west, and these trained the pilots and were therefore only partially operational. During the raid of the 4th September, Hurricanes and Bf 110's fought a huge battle over the Hawker's factory at Brooklands, with No. 249 and 253 Squadrons taking part. By the beginning of September (7th) the Luftwaffe turned its attention to London and the raids of that day along with those on the 9th, 10th, 11th, 12th and 13th were all directed at the capital. This allowed a new, more flexible, method of operation for the fighter squadrons. As all the attacks were on the capital, the fighter squadrons could be moved about to meet the threat, simply attacking the formations and then using one of the bases around the capital to re-arm and refuel. The zenith of these attacks is agreed to be those that occurred on the 15th September and during this day Sgt R. Holmes of No. 504 (County of Nottingham) Squadron, based at Hendon, shot down two Do 17's using up his ammunition, so he used his Hurricane to ram a third. I am sure that many have seen the images of the tailless (and wingless) Do 17 plumetting to earth, crashing onto Victoria Station. Holmes actually baled out and landed on the roof of a house in Chelsea, sliding down it and landing in a dustbin! German losses on the 15th were 56 machines in comparison to those of Fighter Command which were 26, and Hitler's patience had been exhausted, so on the 17th he cancelled the planned sea-borne invasion (Operation Sealion) of England. Although the Luftwaffe continued to bomb the capital, their raids moved more and more towards the cover of night. The Battle of Britain was over. After the 15th September the Luftwaffe no longer achieved the successes it had in the past and from this day on the losses experienced by the RAF were fewer than the replacements they received.

The Hurricane and Spitfire had broken the concept of Blitzkrieg which had so effectively over-run most of Europe, and the 'few' had achieved victory over superior numbers at a time of greatest pressure.

Other Nations and Operations

Chapter 5

Yugoslavia

The first nation to order the Hurricane was Yugoslavia, due to the direct relationship that this country had enjoyed with Hawkers since 1931, when both supply and licensed production of a large number of Hawker Furys and Hinds had been undertaken. Early in 1938 an order was placed for twelve Hurricane Mk I's, and they all came from the initial Air Ministry ordered production batch. The first aircraft, '205' (ex-L1751) was flown from Brooklands to Belgrade on the 15th December 1938. A second order for a further twelve machines followed and these were also taken from an Air Ministry contract (N2718 to N2729) and deliveries commenced in February 1940. These machines differed from the first batch, as they were Merlin III powered, had D.H. three-blade propellers and metal wings.

The Yugoslav government had also successfully negotiated a license agreement and so an initial order for forty machines was placed with P.S.F.A.Z Rogozarski at Belgrade. A follow-on order of another sixty was placed with the Zmaj (Fabrika Aeroplana I Hidroplana) factory at Zemun. Engines for these machines were shipped directly from Rolls-Royce in England and although a high production rate from these two factories had been envisaged, Germany invaded Yugoslavia on the 6th April 1940 and all production ceased. At the time of the invasion less than twelve license-built Hurricanes had been produced. The Royal Yugoslavian Air Force had a force of some thirty-eight Hurricanes at the time of the invasion, eighteen being with the 51st Fighter Squadron, 2nd Regiment at Sarajevo, fourteen with the 33rd Fighter Squadron, 4th Regiment based at Zagreb and the rest with the 34th Fighter Squadron, 4th Regiment also at Zagreb. For a week after the

An excellent study of an early Hurricane in Yugoslavian Air Force markings being test flown by Flt Lt P. Lucas

A Belgium Hurricane (H-33) after a wheels-up landing prior to WWII *(© R. Binnemans)*

February 1939.

As the clouds of war gathered, the British government realised how vulnerable the aircraft factories in the UK would become, and how advantageous it would be to have production of aircraft types such as the Hurricane undertaken in Canada. To this end the Air Ministry set up a specification with the Canadian Department of National Defence for the production of Hurricanes in Canada. A contract was placed with the Canadian Car & Foundry Co., Ltd. at Montreal and a pattern aircraft (L1848) was dispatched on the 2nd March 1939. Within a year the first forty aircraft ordered under this agreement reached the UK, and from 1940 onwards a combined production of some 1,451 aircraft were built for both the RAF (under the Ministry of Aircraft Production contract) and RCAF (under the Canadian Department of Munitions & Supply contract).

Persia

After an official visit by a delegation from Middle Eastern countries in 1939 and 1940, the Persian government placed an order for eighteen Mk Is. Only one aircraft, L2079, was delivered before war broke out, and this was followed by another (P3720) in 1940. The remainder of the contract was held in abeyance, and completed after the end of the war.

Belgium

In April 1939 the Belgium government ordered twenty Mk I's. For further production a license agreement was set up between Hawkers and Avions Fairey (Société Anonyme Belge) for the licensed production of Hurricanes in Belgium. During the same month the first machine, L1918, left Brooklands and this was followed by the remaining nineteen aircraft. It seems likely however that the last five of these machines did not reach Belgium before the German invasion in the Spring of 1940.

License production was to have started with eighty machines being produced by Avions Fairey at their Gosselies factory. These machines differed from British-built examples by having four 12.65mm (0.5") machine guns in the wings and only two were completed by the time of the German invasion, with one more complete but without engine at the factory.

Poland

The French and British governments had agreed to supply Poland with aid for defence in March 1939, and the Polish government asked for the supply of one Hurricane (L2048) for evaluation, plus an option on nine more. Only the evaluation machine reached Poland by the time of the German invasion, and the remaining nine aircraft, although already dispatched,

invasion these machines were in constant use, but by the 14th April 1940, due to deteriorating weather and the proximity of the German ground forces to their base, most of the aircraft had been destroyed on the ground.

South Africa

In November 1938 the South African government asked the Air Ministry to release seven Mk I's for use by the South African Air Force (SAAF). These aircraft came out of store at No. 36 MU and were dispatched to South Africa during November and December of that year. They arrived at Durban, where they were assembled and then flown to Pretoria. Here they joined the Hawker Furys of No. 1 Squadron SAAF.

Rumania

At about the same time as the South African government started negotiations, the Rumanians also requested twelve machines after a visit of King Carol to inspect the Hurricanes at Odiham. Organising the production of these machines took a considerable time, and the first was eventually dispatched just a week before war was declared. Whether or not these machines were actually used by the Rumanian Air Force when they became involved in the war in 1941 is not really known.

Canada

The Canadian government ordered twelve Hurricane Mk I's in the autumn of 1938, and these were released and shipped to Montreal right after the Munich agreement. Each aircraft was assembled at Vancouver, with six being completed by

A line-up of Hurricane Mk I's of the Belgium Air Force (with H-21 in the foreground) prior to WWII *(© R. Binnemans)*

The Belgian Air Force only operated two early Hurricanes fitted with three-blade propellers, both being ex-RAF machines which had landed in error in that country, and here you see one of them. No confirmation of their original, or subsequent identity is known (© R. Binnemans)

were diverted to Gibraltar for RAF service. However, the ship carrying them was apparently sunk and they never saw service.

Finland

When Finland was attacked by Russia late in 1939 they had no real allies, but there were a number of nations that were sympathetic to their needs. The British government did not want to supply arms directly, in fear that it might result in Russia attacking Britain, however this was overcome by the government selling twelve Hurricane Mk I's to Gloster Aircraft Company, who then resold them to Finland. There seems to be some confusion as to the actual source of these twelve machines, as some state they were part of an order for Poland, while others state they came from stocks held at No. 19 and No. 20 MUs. Whichever is the case these machines were in standard RAF camouflage and by early 1940 they were delivered to Finland. This was to be of little assistance to Finland, as they were only available for six weeks before fighting ceased and a peace treaty was signed with Russia on the 12th March 1940.

On the 25th June 1941 however, the Finnish government decided to declare war on Russia (just days after Germany attacked them), and as a result became an enemy of the allies. This period was known as the 'Continuation War' and during it the remaining Hurricanes flew alongside Bf 109's supplied by Germany on Finnish attacks against Russia.

Iceland

After the retreat from Norway in May 1940, Hurricanes moved to Iceland to protect this area and stop any German advance in this direction. Based at Kaldadarnes was No. 98 Squadron, who flew the Fairey Battle, and in July 1941 four Hurricane Mk IIA Series 2s (Z4037, Z4045, Z4048 and Z4049) were sent from storage at No. 47 MU. They were only operated for a short while in this role, as on the 7th July 1941 it was announced that United States troops would be responsible for the protection of this island henceforward. No. 98 Squadron stood down and departed for Britain in July. One Flight remained at Reykjavik, and this became No. 1423 Flight, which in August was reinforced with five more Hurricane Mk IIAs (Z4607, Z4617, Z4631, Z4639 & Z4702). Standing patrols were soon set up, and although there were a number of overflights by German aircraft, no claims were ever made in relation to these machines being shot down. The garrison stood down at the end of the year, with No. 1423 Flight being disbanded on the 19th

December. All of the Hurricanes were crated and returned to the UK and storage at No. 41 MU on S.S. Crane.

Middle East

The four million square miles of the Middle East Command were, in June 1940, covered by just 300 aircraft. Of these 18 of the 29 squadrons were equipped with types such as the Gladiator and Blenheim, plus Lysander and Sunderland. The remainder were made up of antique types, including a number of old Hawker designs.

The first Hurricane in this area, L1669, had been shipped to the Sudan at the end of 1939 for trials with tropical filters fitted.

Mk I, Z4271, 'G' of No. 260 Sqn, with pilots and groundcrew in front, 1941
(© RAF Museum P014386)

By July 1940, Air Cdre Collishaw ordered this machine into action. Unfortunately its guns had long since become useless thanks to the dust and sand, so the aircraft was flown from airfield to airfield on the front to give the enemy the impression that modern fighters were in the area! Collishaw urgently requested Hurricanes, and although some of those ordered by Poland were diverted to the area, these were lost when the ship carrying them was sunk. In June however, four Hurricanes were diverted to Malta, which was currently receiving great attention from the Italian Air Force (Regia Aeronautica). Along with the three (or four) Gladiators on the island, these Hurricanes took on the might of over 200 Italian aircraft based in Sicily. To allow

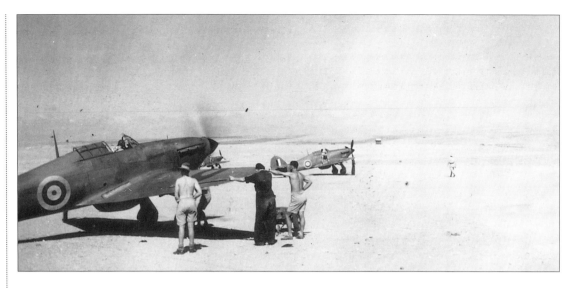

Mk I, 'V' of No. 260 Sqn, taxying at Amman in June 1941 *(© RAF Museum P014382)*

Mk I, V7566 of No. 73 Sqn, on its nose after crashing during a ferry flight from Takoradi to Cairo in December 1940 *(© RAF Museum P005093)*

these machines to operate from the short and bomb-scarred airfields on Malta, they had only six Browning machine guns fitted to reduce the all-up weight. To keep them serviceable various bits from other types were used and there are photographs of the Gladiators fitted with Blenheim propellers. Malta was of such strategic importance that, on the 2nd August, HMS Argus was sent to the island. On board were twelve Hurricane Mk I's, which were launched 200 miles away from the island and all arrived safely. The next attempt, on the 17th, resulted in disaster, as the aircraft were launched at their absolute range and although they all took off safely, only four Hurricanes reached the island, the rest crashing in the sea after running out of fuel.

To ease the supply of aircraft into the Mediterranean theatre, Takoradi on the Gold Coast was set up as a sea terminus. Under the command of Gp Capt H.K. Thorold, this unit was established on the 24th August 1940. On the 5th September the first shipment of six Hurricanes (without tropical filters) arrived along with six Blenheim IV's and were uncrated and assembled. On the 19th they started their air ferry flight and arrived (all bar one) seven days later and were allocated to No. 274 Squadron. The lack of air filters meant that these aircraft were so worn out by the shipping and ferry flight, that they were returned to Abu Sueir for new engines. On the 6th September HMS Argus had arrived with twelve filter-equipped Hurricanes, which then made their way to No. 274 Squadron. No. 73 Squadron was moved from the UK to the Middle East on the 6th November, and the pilots and thirty-four Hurricanes arrived at Takoradi aboard HMS Furious. The next squadron in the area to receive the Hurricane was No. 208 (Army Co-operation) Squadron. This squadron had operated the Lysander in the Middle East since 1939, but in December 1940 they received one of the first Hurricanes (now re-engined), which had been fitted with a forward facing camera and was thereafter referred to as the Tac R Mk I. During the end of 1940 these Hurricanes were used in support of the land offensives, and by January 1941 all the Hurricanes had tropical filters fitted.

Although the land army was sweeping forward in the Middle East, the situation in Greece dictated that Air Cdre Longmore release six Hurricanes for the defence of the island.

Greece

It must be understood that by the time of the invasion of Greece, the Luftwaffe had reinforced the Italian forces and with that came the end of any hope of a quick conclusion to action in this theatre.

Greece was attacked by Italy via Albania on the 28th October 1940 and although Allied forces were not initially deployed to the area, by the end of the year a number of squadrons equipped with Gladiators and Blenheims were sent. The Greek army soon pushed the Italian forces back into Albania, as did the RAF squadrons to the Regia Aeronautica. This situation could not continue and when Germany invaded Bulgaria on the 1st March 1941 more support was drained from the Middle East Command. This however had the knock-on effect of allowing the axis forces to counter-attack in Libya and soon over-run the Allied forces due to their depleted status. The situation in Greece was reinforced in January 1941 when three Gladiator squadrons

(33, 80 and 112) were transferred into the area. These squadrons were to be re-equipped with the Hurricane as soon as possible, and on the 7th February Hurricanes were allocated to No. 80 Squadron, becoming B Flight under the command of Flt Lt M. St. J. Pattle. The aircraft soon went into action and on the 28th February a big air battle with Hurricanes and Gladiators of Nos. 33, 80 and 112 Squadrons resulted in twenty-seven enemy aircraft being shot down, five of them by Pattle himself.

On the 6th April Germany attacked Yugoslavia on five sides. By this time all the Gladiators in Greece had been replaced by Hurricanes Mk I's, but due to the sheer number of forward Axis forces, they were withdrawn to the Athens area on the 17th April. By the 19th twenty-two Hurricanes remained serviceable and the situation was worsening. By the 20th three more Hurricanes had been lost and on the same day a large attack was made on Piraeus by the Luftwaffe. This attack was met by Nos. 33, 80 and 208 Squadrons with fifteen remaining Hurricanes and the flight was led by Sqn Ldr Pattle (now the CO of No. 33 Squadron) and during the ensuing air battle fourteen enemy aircraft were destroyed, but with the loss of five Hurricanes, one of which was Pattle's. One of the great aces had been lost; in just four months he had achieved 24 victories over German aircraft, plus approximately 11 more whilst flying a Gladiator against Italian aircraft in the Western Desert. On the 22nd and 23rd all British aircraft (except the Hurricanes) were ordered back to Crete or Egypt. The Hurricanes remained around Argos, and some replacements were also received, but they were not to last long as an attack of Bf 110's on the airfields the same day resulted in just seven Hurricanes being left intact and two days later these were ordered back to Crete.

Crete

The speed of events in the Greek campaign was such; that planning for the defence of Crete was not possible. As a result of

this there were just fourteen aircraft available to defend the entire island. Of these, seven were Hurricanes. During the next few days of attack, four of the other machines were destroyed, plus two Hurricanes. Seven more Hurricanes arrived from Takoradi, giving twelve in all and it was with these machines that the Allied forces awaited the inevitable invasion.

Fighting always went very much in favour of the Axis forces, and by the 19th May just four Hurricanes and three Gladiators remained serviceable. These machines were therefore ordered back to Egypt. With no real fighter protection for the island, the Germans launched their attack the following day. Only at Maleme were the airborne troops successful. Here they set up a base and over a week thirty thousand troops landed there. The RAF tried to base Hurricanes once more on the island, and although the first task force was captured, Heraklion was chosen for a second attempt. The airfield was chosen to receive twelve Hurricanes via Egypt, but during the delivery flights some were shot down by Naval gun positions, others crashed on

Mk IIB, BP166, KC•J of No. 238 Sqn in North Africa
(© RAF Museum P008450)

landing and all those that actually survived were destroyed by a bombing raid on the airfield before they could even be refuelled. Some Hurricanes with 44 gallon fuel tanks did operate over the island from bases in Egypt, but by the end of May Crete had fallen, even though about half of the Allied troops had been evacuated.

Iraq

The defence of Iraq had been in effect since the Anglo-Iraqi Treaty of 1934 and the RAF had a big presence in the area with a large base at Habbaniyah. In April 1941 however the base

Hurricane Mk I's being uncrated at Takoradi in 1941

included a training school and seventy antique aircraft. On the 30th April power in Iraq was seized by paid Axis sympathiser Rashid Ali, and Habbaniyah found itself surrounded by the Iraqi Army! To defend themselves the RAF personnel adapted the antique Audax and Oxford aircraft to carry bombs. The next six days saw the Iraqi forces, including their air force, attacking the base, albeit ineffectively, and by the 5th May the Iraqi forces had lost interest and moved away towards Baghdad. German aircraft were now seen in Northern Iraq and when Habbaniyah was attacked by Luftwaffe He 111's on the 16th May the decision was made to send No. 94 Squadron. They arrived on the 17th May, comprising nine Gladiators and four Hurricanes. Operations showed that the German bases were beyond the range of the Hurricane, so two were sent equipped with 44 gallon fuel tanks. These machines undertook attacks on the German bases, and although one was lost, they were reinforced with four more machines on the 21st. On the 24th a Tac R Mk I Hurricane was allocated to No. 94 Squadron and this machine undertook reconnaissance missions straight away. This soon indicated that the uprising had been squashed and that the situation had stabilised. On the 1st June the Regent was returned to the capital and the revolt in Iraq was at an end.

Syria

The German aircraft flying to Iraq in May 1941 were staging through Syria, utilising the pro-Vichy regime of the Syrian government. It became apparent to Allied powers that defence of areas such as the Suez Canal would become extremely difficult if this situation was allowed to continue unchecked. On the 25th of May a force was assembled to eliminate any threat Syria offered, and in this force were one squadron and a flight of Hurricanes. No. 80 Squadron had recently withdrawn from Crete and were now re-equipped with Hurricanes fitted with tropical filters. The Flight was part of No. 208 (Army Co-operation) Squadron, equipped with Tac R versions. The ground assault started on the 8th June and the aircraft were confronted with quite modern French types such as the Dewoitine D.520 and Morane Saulnier MS.406. The Hurricanes fared well against these, but the Naval Fulmars that were also operating in this area were no match, and a number were lost. After the capture of Damascus the Vichy forces started to resist much harder and with the change in the overall war situation, No. 260 Squadron was sent to the area with its Hurricanes. By the 10th July the Allied forces had the Vichy forces trapped and had total air superiority. On the 14th the Vichy forces surrendered.

Evolution

Hurricane Z3663, HP•E of No. 247 Squadron. This unit arrived at Exeter to co-operate with Turbinlite Havocs and had to change their codes to 'ZY', as the Gunnery Research Unit at Exeter already used the 'HP' code *(© O,Brien via M. Payne)*

With the end of the campaigns in the Middle East, the front-line use of the Mk I had come to a close. The proposal to install four cannon in a fighter had been put forward in 1935 and because at this time the Hurricane had fabric wings and a wooden propeller, the loss in speed (reducing it to 270mph) was considered too great by the Air Ministry, so the project was stopped. Hispano cannon had been trial-fitted into a Mk I (see Chapter 2), but this was to gain air-firing experience with the weapon before it was used in the Westland Whirlwind (the design which met the 1935 cannon-armed fighter requirement). An improvement in power, along with the adoption of the metal skinned wings did allow for increased armament to be a real possibility once again. A Mk I, L1856, had been fitted with the Rolls-Royce R.M.3S (Merlin VIII) engine and test flown in July 1939 and L2026 had the Merlin XII installed at the same time. Hawker's own machine (G-AFXX that had tested the de Havilland propeller) was used to test the Rolls-Royce R.M.4S (Merlin 45) engine in June 1940. On the 11th June 1940, P3269 was fitted with the Merlin XX and Rotol R.X.5/2 constant-speed three-blade propeller. This machine's engine offered a two-stage supercharger that resulted in a power output of 1,185hp and this allowed it to reach 348mph in the hands of Philip Lucas, the fastest speed ever achieved by the Hurricane. Modifications were required to increase the coolant circulation and radiator size and this resulted in the top speed of this aircraft, now called the Mk II, dropping to 342mph.

Increased armament was proposed by Hawker in January 1940. An additional four guns, two in each outer metal wing panel, was logical, but due to other concerns (the losses in France and the Battle of Britain), the Air Ministry made no decision. With the adoption of the Merlin XX into the existing Mk I airframe with little modification, Hawker had introduced the Mk II without any interruption in production. The first examples of these machines were not, however, fitted with the new twelve-gun wing and therefore the first 120 Mk II's were

delivered to the RAF from the 4th September 1940 in this format, designated the Mk IIA Series 1. The Mk IIA Series 2 was fitted with all the connections to allow the fitment of the eight- or twelve-gun wing and provision for the installation of the new 44 gallon drop tanks (initially these were used on the Mk I {See Chapter 5}, and were not jettisonable), and its production was introduced at Langley and Brookland in October 1940. It was also in this version that an additional bay was added forward of the cockpit front frame, increasing the overall length of the Hurricane by seven inches. The twelve-gun wing was introduced in November 1940 and this version became the Mk IIB. As well as development of the drop tanks, Hawker had looked into the carriage of bombs by the Hurricane. A Mk I (P2989), had been fitted to carry two 250lb bombs, and flew for the first time at Boscombe Down on the 18th April 1941. The first Mk IIB fitted with this equipment was Z2326 and although testing showed that removal of the outer two guns in each wing made it easier to access the associated wiring etc for the carriers, it was not always done in service, and many 'Hurri-Bomber' squadrons retained all twelve guns.

The next variant was without doubt the most important, as it was the Mk IIC of which 4,711 were built. The four-cannon fighter proposal was first made in 1935 by Sqn Ldr R.S. Sorley for Spec. 10/35. This specification was changed into a requirement for a twin-engined fighter (Westland Whirlwind), but Hawker decided to continue with their own research of the cannon installation in the Hurricane's wing. Official permission was gained to fit a pair of Oerlikon cannon in the wing of a damaged Hurricane and this initial installation was followed by a similar one in the wings of a Mk I for flight trials. The first flight of this machine took place on the 7th June 1940 and air firing trials continued until the aircraft was issued to No. 151 Squadron at North Weald on the 19th August for service trials. With this experience under their belt, Hawker obtained 30 pairs of wings (all damaged in the armament bays) and these were

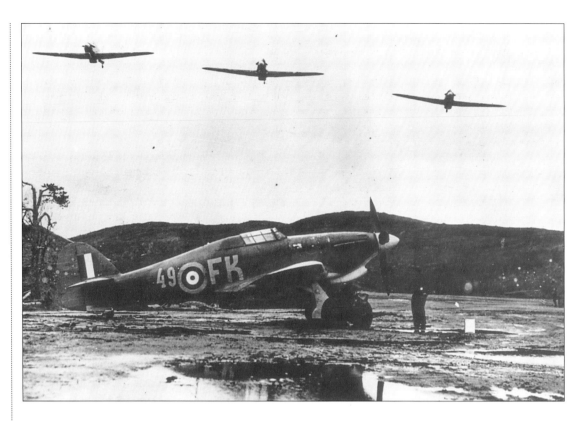

Mk IIB, Z3768, FK•49 of
No. 81 Sqn, Vaenga, Russia
in 1941

sent to the Experimental Shop at Canbury Park Road in
November 1940. The first Hurricane to fly with the new cannon-
wing installation was V7360 on the 5th December, followed by
W9314 and V7260. With the Merlin XX-powered Hurricanes on
the production line at this time it was decided to fit the hand-
built cannon wings to this new version. The first cannon-armed
Mk II, V2461, (the prototype Mk IIC) was flown on the 6th
February 1941 and differed from the earlier version in having
the Chatellerault belt ammunition feed in place of the Oerlikon
drum feed. During production of the Mk IIC, problems with the
supply of the Chatellerault feed meant that both belt and drum
feeds were installed, the newly-built cannon wings being
introduced into the production line from May 1941.

The next version of the Mk II was to see the installation of the
40mm cannon, resulting in the Mk IID. In 1939 both Rolls-
Royce and Vickers had been developing quick-firing anti-tank

weapons of 40mm calibre. These weapons were light and
although designed for ground troops, the Air Ministry saw they
were suitable for fitment to an airframe. In May 1941 the Air
Ministry approached Hawker and asked if two Vickers Type 'S'
cannon could be fitted under the wing of the Hurricane. Within
two months the drawings were complete and the first weapons
were with the Experimental Shop at Kingston. These weapons
were fitted to Mk II Z2326 and first flown in this configuration
on the 18th September. Having installed the Vickers weapon and
passed the aircraft to Boscombe Down for service trials, they
were asked to adapt the design to accept the Rolls-Royce Type 'R'
belt-feed 40mm guns. This was achieved in Z2326 also, and
although the first service examples of the new Mk IID had the
same armour as the Mk IIA/B, later examples had an added
368lb of armour plate fitted. When the Mk IID was issued to
front line units nearly all of them went overseas, operating with

Mk IIC, FT•?, 'RP De Deken'
of No. 43 Sqn with Plt Off J.
Daniels in the cockpit, Drem
(© RAF Museum P008004)

great success in the Middle and Far East.

At the same time as cannon were fitted to the Mk II, work also progressed on the installation of rockets. Six three-inch rocket projectiles (RP's) were to be used and the first aircraft to get this installation was a Mk IIA (Z2415). This machine had already been involved in terminal velocity trials and therefore featured a strengthened main spar. With full gun armament and attachment points for the RP's, this machine flew for the first time on the 23rd February 1942 and was then passed on to Boscombe Down for trials. Initially the rudimentary rockets were simply a 40lb cast-iron head mounted onto a 3in tube, in which was a solid propellant. The tail was three finlets bolted to the tube and due to the burning of the propellant (from the rear of the rocket forward), the initial trials showed the weapon to be very difficult to aim. Producing a central exhaust pipe up the inside of the tube and burning the propellant from the front to the back helped and the introduction of a cruciform tail and a 60lb head was also instigated. Trials at A&AEE continued, with two tropical airframes converted to the task (BN583 and BN902), and the number of the new rockets was increased to eight.

the wing up to heights of 30,000ft on a regular basis throughout the whole of the Middle East theatre.

Mention now should be made of the final two versions of the Hurricane: Mk IV and V. In early 1941 proposals were made to the M.A.P. that the Hurricane should be modified for ground-attack ('close-support') work in North Africa. Initially it was intended just to introduce a 'universal' wing, which would be capable of meeting all the requirements of the fighter, fighter-bomber and reconnaissance versions. This wing was intended to have just two Browning machine guns, but be internally wired for all installations. By the time work had progressed on the Mk IIE (as this version was originally known), the Mk IIC with cannon armament and the Mk IID with rocket armament had arrived, so complicating the 'universal' wing further. Extra armour protection was also called for in a ground-attack machine and this included armour plate around the engine, and a totally revised radiator unit. As well as a revision in cooling intake capacity to meet the demands of a desert environment, the entire unit had to be armour plated, resulting in a completely revised profile. As you will see, the type now had little in common with the Mk II airframe and by the time the prototype

Mk IIC, BP389 (GO•E), BP387 (GO•J), HL85? (O•P), HL735 and others of No. 94 Sqn, in flight, North Africa in 1942

The whole of the Mk II series were capable of a great number of tasks and as well as those already covered the type was used in a number of close-support roles. To achieve this many modifications were incorporated throughout the rest of the type's service. The ability to carry two 500lb bombs greatly increased the destructive capacity of the 'Hurri-Bomber' and the type could also carry Small Bomb Containers (SBC's) or two Smoke Curtain Installations (SCI's). The type was also adapted to the reconnaissance role, although almost solely in the Middle East. The Mk IIA, B & C airframe was used and retained its armament, but this was supplemented with a forward-facing F.24 in the starboard wing root or two oblique F.24 cameras in the rear fuselage. For high-level reconnaissance work the type had all armament removed and three (one oblique, two vertical) cameras in the rear fuselage. Extra fuel was carried in additional tanks fitted into the redundant armament bays in each wing (increasing total fuel capacity to 194 gallons). The type was also used until 1945 for Meteorological Calibration work, carrying a psychrometer strut-mounted onto

was nearing completion (January 1943) the decision was made to redesignate the type as the Mk IV. The prototype, KX405, flew for the first time on the 14th March 1943 and a second, KZ193, followed on the 23rd March. Production began in mid-April and they were produced alongside the Mk IIB, C & D on the production line. KZ193 was soon fitted with an improved Merlin 32 driving a four-blade Spitfire-type Rotol propeller (Dia. 10ft 9in.) and this became the Mk V. This machine was later joined by another converted Mk IV (NL255) and although they both undertook extensive service trials at Boscombe Down, the ground-boosted Merlin engine proved prone to overheating and eventually both airframes were reverted to Mk IV configuration and the Mk V never reached serial production.

The later marks at war

With the end of the Battle of Britain in September 1940, Fighter Command was able to take stock of it's squadrons, re-equip and re-organise. During the Battle of Britain period a large number of European pilots had swelled the ranks of the

Mk IIB, HL795, 'V' of No. 274 Squadron (© RAF Museum P019144)

RAF and in October 1940 the first all-American squadron was formed. This squadron, referred to as 'Eagle Squadron' was No. 71, and it formed with the Hurricane Mk IIB at Kirton-in-Lindsey on the 8th October 1940. By November the Blitz was well under way and it was during the winter of 1940/41 that Hurricanes were used as a form of night fighter, although all interception was attempted by dint of 'night vision', moonlight or searchlights. Success, as you would expect in these circumstances, was rare and it was during this period that Wg Cdr W. Helmore came up with the idea of a powerful airborne searchlight. This was to be fitted to a twin-engine radar-equipped night fighter and was to operate alongside a Hurricane. The 'Turbinlite' installation was made in the Havoc,

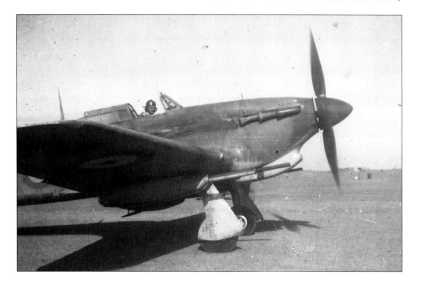

Mk IID of No. 6 Sqn on the ground at Shandur in December 1942 (© RAF Museum P013260)

as well as a few Beaufighters and a Mosquito and ten flights were soon established to operate the type. Little success was made with these machines and the concept was soon abandoned. In late 1940 and early 1941 the Hurricane was used to act as bomber escort to light bombers that were attacking shipping in the French and Belgian ports. This was a task the type was unsuited for and until the Hurricane was equipped with the 44 gallon fuel tank, it would remain so. The type was also used for cross-channel offensive operations in the form of 'Rhubarbs'. These were low-level bombing raids in Europe by Hurricanes, in the hope that this would lure up Luftwaffe fighters, so that the top-cover Spitfires could attack them. By May 1941 there were twenty-nine squadrons of Hurricanes participating in regular attacks in Europe.

Russia

When the German attack on Russia commenced on the 22nd June 1941, Churchill pledged support for any man or state who fought Nazism and, in so doing, undertook to support the Russians in their fight against Germany. To offer air cover over the ports that would receive this military aid, two squadrons (No. 81 and No. 134) were formed as No. 151 Wing at Leconfield on the 12th August under the command of Wg Cdr H.N.G. Ramsbottom-Isherwood. Thirty-nine Mk IIB's were collected for the squadron and of these twenty-four were flown aboard HMS Argus and the remainder packed for shipment at the same time. The convoy (including all the groundcrew etc) set sail on the 21st August, and arrived at Murmansk on the 28th. The Hurricanes flew off and landed at Vaenga, but the rest could not be unloaded, due to enemy air activity, and were diverted some 400 miles east! Even without the environment to assemble the aircraft, the groundcrew and Russians managed to get the aircraft together and flown out to join the rest within a few days. The Wing got into action very quickly, although there were initial problems with weapons and lubricants and by the end of September No. 81 Squadron had twelve victories (and one loss) to No. 134 Squadron's four kills. During the quiet period of October, as the winter set in, the British crews trained their Russian counterparts to use, service and fly the Hurricane and by the end of November, the British personnel returned to the UK. No. 151 Wing's machines became the 72nd Regiment of the Red Naval Air Fleet (commanded by Capt Safonov). Further shipments of Hurricanes were sent to Russia, 2,952 being supplied in total.

The Channel

In 1942 the Hurricane was able to fully undertake the tasks of cross-channel offensive operations, with anti-shipping, bomber escort and intruder roles. The role of intruder was a difficult one, but one to which the Hurricane was well suited. No. 1 Squadron was well versed in the intruder role and Flt Ltn K.M. Kuttlewascher (a Czech) was the squadron's best exponent. Going out at night, these Hurricanes would cross the channel, move into France and find a suitable target, then attack. The targets were usually airfields, and here the Hurricane's stable gun platform meant that the pilot could pick off returning German bombers as they approached for landing. The Dieppe raid on the 19th August 1942 involved a large number of Hurricanes and the first were those of No. 43 Squadron. The landing was a disaster for the British troops and, as the Germans had been warned of the assault, flak was also intense.

A number of pilots were lost in this first raid, and all aircraft over the beaches sustained quite serious damage.

The Mediterranean

It was during the Spring of 1941 that the first Mk IIA's and Mk IIB's started to arrive at the MU's in the Canal Zone. Action against the Italian forces in East Africa saw the successful use of the Hurricane by No. 41 Squadron (SAAF), and by November 1941 all the pockets of Italian resistance in the area had surrendered. The setting up of the Desert Air Force ended the need for Army Co-operation squadrons, as the air and ground forces now worked in unison. Operation Crusader (to relieve Tobruk) opened on the 18th November with the Hurricanes of Nos. 33 and 208 Squadrons providing air support. After an initial surge back by German forces, the combined assault of the Desert Air Force made them withdraw to the west, and Tobruk was relieved. As the Germans moved back towards Gazala, the Luftwaffe tried to offer cover and during this period Hurricane squadrons again provided both offensive and reconnaissance cover for the ground troops. No. 2 Photographic Reconnaissance Unit had been formed at Heliopolis in June 1941, with three locally-modified Hurricane PR Mk I's. The unit moved to Tobruk in November and started to operate the Hurricane in five-hour flights of over 11,000 miles to collect tactical information. By mid-December the German front at Gazala had been breached and the ground forces moved forwards once more. The advance stopped at El Agheila, and with the entry into the war of Japan on the 7th December 1941, a situation outside this theatre was once again to have a dire effect upon it.

In January 1942 Rommel counter-attacked and for two days the Hurricanes and Kittyhawks of the Desert Air Force were unable to take-off due to severe floods which had affected their airfields. Moving to Msus, Nos. 1 (SAAF), 30, 94, 238 and 274 Squadrons were able to fly a mass of operations in response to the enemy attack, despite appalling weather. The Germans kept on advancing and the British withdrawal was to stop at the previous German defensive line at Gazala. The Hurricane units were starting to re-equip and No. 6 Squadron was given six of the new Mk IID's for their new role as an anti-tank squadron. After an attack by the Germans in early June, the British forces

had withdrawn into Egypt, although during this period the Mk IID's of No. 6 Squadron were used to good effect for the first time. Top-cover offered by the Hurricanes etc. enabled the British troops to withdraw with little enemy attack. By the end of June the German advance had been halted by the Eighth Army at El Alamain.

Malta

The role of Malta has already been covered in a little detail, however the position of this island within this theatre is such that is deserves further coverage. The massive attacks on Malta had initially been held off by three Gladiators, however with the arrival of a mixed-bag of Hurricanes on the island, No. 261 Squadron was formed for its defence. With the sheer level of attacks aimed at the island it was soon decided that bomber operations could no longer take place from it. Without the ability to strike at the German shipping, enemy interest in the island seemed to abate, and in the respite the Maltese squadrons were re-equipped. In early April 1941 twelve Mk II's were delivered to No. 261 Squadron and as these machines had a better performance and climb ability than the Mk I's, they were able to get up to the bombers faster. The result of this was that the enemy bombers operated at a higher level, and this reduced the success of their raids. With the daily bombardment somewhat reduced, the Wellingtons returned to the island to resume bombing raids on German shipping. Arrival of more Hurricanes by sea on the 27th April and 8th May resulted in there being

Mk IIA Series 2 (Gloster-built) BG766, seen here in a publicity shot taken on Malta, is armed with two 250lb bombs for an offensive sweep over Sicily

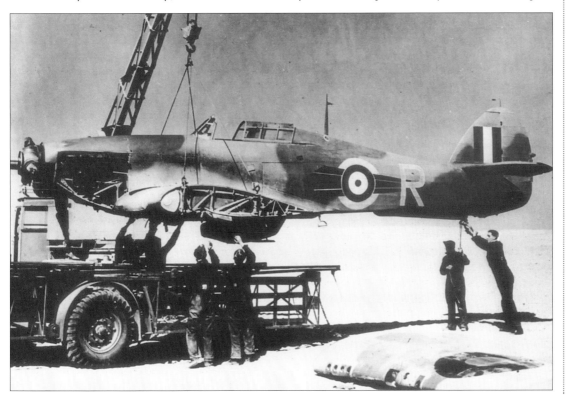

The fuselage of Mk IIB, BD930, 'R' of No. 73 Squadron being loaded onto a trailer after crashing in the desert

Flt Lt Lister of No. 43 Sqn, by the nose of a Mk IIC at Maison Blanche in November 1942 (© RAF Museum P008016)

forces stopped and dug in. For months the situation was stagnant, although the Luftwaffe units based in the Balkans and Crete were able to undertake attacks in the Canal Zone. No. 73 Squadron undertook the defence of Cairo against this action and elsewhere in the area No. 208 Squadron undertook reconnaissance sorties and No. 218 moved to El Alamain for defence work over the dug-in troops. By October 1942 the Eighth Army was ready for the assault, as was the Desert Air Force. The bombardment began on the night of the 23/24th October and the Hurricane squadrons were involved from the beginning. During the 23rd October to 8th November period six of the Hurricane squadrons claimed 39 tanks, 212 lorries, 26 fuel trucks, 42 guns and over 200 other small vehicles for the loss of eleven pilots. The German and Italian forces broke on the 4th November and by the 6th they were in disorganised flight. This offered superb targets for the Hurricanes, especially the Mk IID's. On the 8th November British and American troops landed on the French Moroccan and Algerian coasts under 'Operation Torch'. This combined force was covered by units of the RAF, FAA, SAAF and USAAF, and Hurricanes were included in these groups. Once the airfield at Maison Blanche had been captured, eighteen drop-tank equipped Mk IIC's of No. 43 Squadron arrived from Gibraltar. By the end of December five Hurricane squadrons were based at Souk el Arba, Bone, Souk Ahras and Youk Les Bains.

With the German forces still in retreat, the Eighth Army captured Tripoli and such was the speed of the Allied forces movement, that Hurricanes were actually landed behind the retreating enemy and were then used to attack them from the direction of their own lines! No. 6 Squadron was based at Castel Benito and from here it flew the Mk IID against the German forces facing the Eighth Army and Free French troops at Zamlet el Hadid with great success. By May 1943 the Axis forces were trapped and although attempts were made to airlift in fuel and supplies, these met with failure and by the 13th May all enemy action stopped in Tunisia.

Now it was time for attention to turn to Sicily with the re-deployment of twenty Hurricane squadrons within the Near and Middle East prior to the landings in Sicily, although the Order of Battle for the invasion only lists one Hurricane squadron, and that was in reserve. By this time the Hurricane had been relegated to second-line duties and would have been deleted from the Middle East Command had it not been for the arrival of two new weapons: the 40mm cannon and the 3in rocket projectile. No. 6 Squadron had pioneered the use of the 40mm cannon and in early 1944 it converted from the Mk IID to the Mk IV. These machines armed with the 3in rockets were used for the first time operationally on the 29th March 1944, when a suspected German HQ was attacked near Durazzo, Albania. The situation in Yugoslavia (with 1 million Yugolsav partisans active) lead to the creation of the Balkan Air Force and No. 6 Squadron with its Mk IVs was attached to it, based at Grottaglie. By October 1944 they were joined by No. 351 (Yugoslav) Squadron who were also equipped with the Mk IV. Here, and at other remote sites, the Hurricanes made rocket and cannon attacks in support of the partisans. Anti-shipping operations were also undertaken as well as knocking out bridges, enemy columns and even pin-point locations. Such was the situation in the Balkans that No. 6 Squadron remained in this area right up until the end of the Second World War, and was the last Hurricane squadron to continue the fight against the Axis forces. No. 351 Squadron also remained in the area, and in June 1945 they became part of the re-constituted Yugoslav Air Force.

about fifty Mk IIA and IIB's on the island. A new squadron, No. 185, was formed on the 12th May from the machines in No. 251 Squadron and No. 1430 Flight. It was during May that German attention turned to Russia, and as a result the Luftwaffe group was removed from the area. In this 'quiet' period Malta was able to restock and repair the damage and on the 21st May No. 126 Squadron came to the island. In June the first cannon-armed Mk IICs arrived and were passed out to all three Hurricane squadrons. In December 1941 Luftflotte 2 moved from Russia to Rome and during the first week the Luftwaffe undertook 600 sorties against the island. Once again the Wellingtons were withdrawn under this intense bombardment. During February 1,000 tons of bombs were dropped on Malta, in March it was 2,000 tons and in April it was 6,700. In March the first Spitfires reached the island, and as the Luftwaffe bombers were now escorted by the Bf 109F, the Hurricane found itself out-classed. Only 18 Hurricanes remained by the end of April, although forty-seven Spitfires arrived on USS Wasp and a further eighty more arrived in May. With the depletion of the Hurricanes on the island it is not surprising to find that the type was replaced in all three squadrons by the end of July

The Mediterranean once more
Because of the situation in Malta, reinforcements to Rommel's troops in North Africa had continued and this lead to the withdrawal of British troops to El Alamain as stated earlier.

With the Eighth Army dug in at El Alamain, the German

Sea Hurricane

Sea Hurricane W4C of No. 760 Sqn on the ground at Yeovilton with officers under instruction standing around the cockpit
(© C.E. Brown/RAF Museum 5946-14)

Having been a little slow in developing a specialised ship-borne interceptor in the inter-war period and with the war clouds gathering in 1938 the answer was seen to be in the adaptation of our latest fighter, the Gloster Gladiator, to the role.

The situation in Norway in April 1940 highlighted the fact that the RAF had no means of supporting an expeditionary force from its bases in the UK. The successful landing of the No. 46 Squadron Hurricanes on the carrier deck for their movement to Norway, and back, proved that the use of such a modern fighter from a ship was possible. The situation in 1940 was such that the loss of shipping was so high that measures had to be considered to assist against the long-range German reconnaissance aircraft that plagued the British fleets. With the loss of the carriers Courageous and Glorious in the Norwegian campaign there was no quick way to replace them and this meant that a stop-gap measure had to be considered. To that end the concept of launching Hurricanes off the fo'c'sle of a merchant ship was initiated. The Directorate of Research and Development (Air) approached Hawker in October 1940 to see if it was feasible to fit the necessary catapult equipment to the airframe. On the 19th January 1941 a decision was made to go ahead with the idea and an order was placed for twenty sets of this equipment from Hawker by the Admiralty. With their usual far-sightedness, Hawker started work on a naval Hurricane and converted a repaired Hurricane with a Vee-frame arrester hook and catapult spools. This machine was passed to RAE Farnborough in March 1941 for evaluation. In the meantime work started on the conversion of fifty Hurricanes to Sea Hurricane Mk IA's. The conversion on these machines saw the

fitment of additional strengthening to the airframe to soak up the shock of the rocket-assisted take-off (achieved in just 80 feet). The catapult spools were added on the rear spar, under each wing and either side of the radiator. Shackles were fitted to the front spar of each side of the centre-section to allow the airframe to be hoisted onto the ship, while tie-down eyelets were added under each wing tip to allow the aircraft to be lashed-down during bad weather and in high seas. A special headrest

A nice under-surface view of Sea Hurricane Mk IB, Z4039 of No. 762 Squadron in flight
(© C.E. Brown)

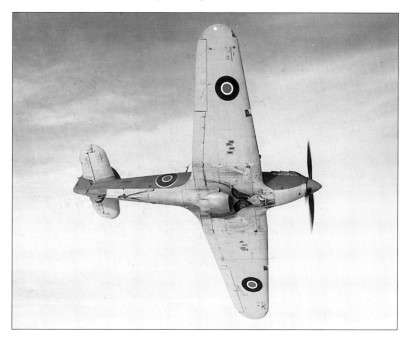

Sea Hurricane Mk IC, V6741, April 1943 (© Real Photographs)

was added to soak up the energy of the rocket-assisted take-off and the RAF radio was replaced with a TR.1147 unit. Under a directive from Churchill thirty-five merchant ships at various locations were to be converted to 'catapult aircraft merchantman' (CAM-ships), while five were converted as 'fighter catapult ships' and the converted Hurricanes became know as 'Hurricats' (Hurricane-catapult). The launch of a Hurricat from a CAM-ship would allow the convoy to protect itself against the roaming Fw 200 Condors, but after engaging the enemy the pilot was basically left with the option of ditching his machine near the

Sea Hurricane Mk IB, Z4039 of No. 762 Squadron in flight, 1943 (© C.E. Brown)

convoy and hoping to be picked up, as there was no method of returning the aircraft back to the merchantman. This was not a popular option with the pilots and therefore the first such were volunteers from the Fleet Air Arm (FAA).

Initial trials with this launch system were undertaken from the Empire Rainbow off Greenock and these were followed by similar trials by the FAA on the first CAM-ship, Michael E. in Bangor Bay during the Spring of 1941. This ship was to set sail on the 27th May 1941, but unfortunately was torpedoed and sunk before its Hurricat could be launched. Of the remaining

Fighter Catapult Ships, HMS Patia was sunk by bombs before its Hurricats were embarked, HMS Springbank and Ariguanu operated the Fulmar before they too were sunk. HMS Pegasus also only ever had Fulmars on board, and this ship was returned to the Clyde for catapult training duties before any Hurricats embarked on it. This left just HMS Maplin to operate Hurricats, and it was used in eight convoys. The first was in June 1941, and on the 18th the Hurricat was launched to chase a snooping Fw 200, although this was shot down by the convoy's guns before the pilot could bring his guns to bear. During another convoy in June, Lt R.W.H. Everett managed to shoot down an Fw 200, although in the ditching of his Hurricat, the radiator struck the water violently and Everett found himself some thirty feet below the waves before he could get out of the aircraft. For this action he was awarded the DSO, and in future all Hurricat pilots were told to tighten their harness, release the emergency escape hatch, slide back the canopy, and ensure the ditching was undertaken with both flaps and wheels retracted.

All the Fighter Catapult Ships except Maplin were withdrawn during 1941 and all Hurricat operations had been undertaken by the CAM-ships. The first operation use was from Empire Foam on the 1st November 1941 with Plt Off G.W. Varley at the controls. By this time all the FAA pilots had been replaced by RAF pilots and the Hurricats now carried 44 gallon jettisonable fuel tanks. Four shore bases were established at Belfast, Mersey, Clyde and Bristol, where a CAM-ship needed for a convoy would acquire its complement of Hurricats prior to setting out to join the convoy. Three main routes were used for these convoys (Atlantic, North Africa and Russia), the Atlantic route was covered by RCAF airfields in Nova Scotia, while the North Africa route utilised the fighters based on Gibraltar. Only the Russian route required the CAM-ships as their only protection, and the

Sea Hurricane Mk IIC, NF717, April 1943 (© Real Photographs)

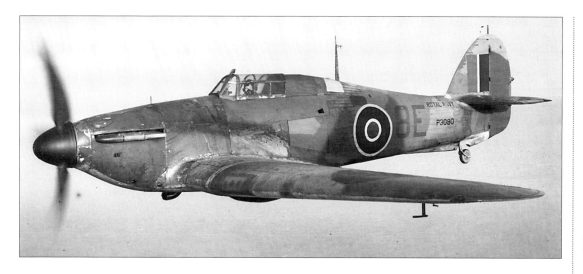

Sea Hurricane (P3090)
in flight (© C.E. Brown)

first such convoy set out on the 26th April 1942 with the Empire Morn CAM-ship. During the return of this convoy a Bv 138 was driven off, and a Ju 88 shot down, although the pilot of the Hurricat bailed out too low and was killed. Improvements arrived in early 1942 with the fitment of the Type K single-man dinghy and the special seat-pack Model A Mk II designed for use in the Hurricat. These increased the survivability of a ditching in all bar the northern waters, and things were improved further with the installation of electrical sockets for the pilot's electrically heated flying suit and gloves, plus some RCAF cockpit heaters in the Hurricats based on Canadian-built Hurricanes.

This scheme was short lived, as the loss of the aircraft and the inflexible nature of the operation lead to the setting up of another system. This was to convert merchant ships (usually grain ships or tankers) to small escort carriers. These vessels became known as MAC-ships (merchant aircraft carriers) and with the removal of the superstructure and off-setting of the bridge, a basic flight deck could be installed on which Hurricanes or Swordfishes could operate. No hangers were available on these vessels, so the aircraft stayed on deck all the voyage, resulting in a small number of flying hours being achieved before the salt water rendered the airframes useless. The Sea Hurricane Mk IB was developed for MAC-ship operations (those on the CAM-ships being referred to as the Sea Hurricane Mk IA), having the Vee-frame arrester hook and catapult spools tested by Hawkers previously (Note that the twenty-five Mk IIA's converted to Sea Hurricanes in this manner were referred to as Sea Hurricane Mk IB's, even though they were Mk II airframes).

The first convoy to receive the protection of these ships was PQ18, which had HMS Avenger with twelve Sea Hurricane Mk IB's on board from No. 802 & No. 883 Squadrons. Having sent up its Hurricanes on a number of occasions HMS Avenger moved off to protect PQ14, leaving PQ18 under the protection of CAM-ship Empire Morn.

Sea Hurricanes equipped Nos. 801, 806, 880, 885 and 803 Squadrons of the FAA by the end of 1941 and along with the Mk IB came the cannon-armed Mk IC. The first of this version joined No. 811 Squadron in January 1942, but they later equipped Nos. 801, 802, 803, 880, 883 and 885 Squadrons. Conversion of standard Mk IIC's into Sea Hurricanes began with the order of seventy conversion sets by the Admiralty in March 1942 and these were followed by further examples converted by General Aircraft Ltd. In total 185 such Mk IIB's and IIC's were thus converted but, because they retained all RAF radio equipment etc and were serviced in accordance with the RAF AP's, they are not true Sea Hurricanes and are best thought of as 'Hooked' Hurricanes.

In May 1942 Hawker undertook the first true Sea Hurricane Mk IIC conversion on BD787 and in mid-1942 conversion sets for this version were made available, General Aircraft Ltd undertaking the work. During early 1942 the number of Hurricanes required on the MAC vessels was reduced, as the number of aircraft carriers escorting convoys increased. At the time that these Hurricanes were coming off the MAC ships they were going onto the carriers. The use of these carriers to protect the convoys was to prove invaluable, especially when you consider the effect of the convoy that reached Malta in early 1942 and the fact that the previously-unprotected convoys to Russia could now have the presence of a carrier and its Sea Hurricanes. The Sea Hurricane's days were soon over however, as the type was outclassed by mid-1942 and being replaced by the Seafire. From March to June 1942, No. 883 and 885

A Sea Hurricane Mk IA (V6756) on the catapult of a CAM-ship in 1940

Squadrons were based at Peterhead and Cranwick, operating under RAF Fighter Command. In January 1943 No. 804 Squadron operated from Ouston for fighter patrols on the eastern coast. Sea Hurricanes were used during Operation Torch, where they carried US star insignia to identify them to the American ground forces, and HMS Biter's and Dasher's aircraft were to achieve mixed success against the Vichy Dewoitine D.520 and Morane Saulnier M.S. 406. Throughout 1944 and 1945 the Sea Hurricane was used less and less in Naval operations, as it was phased out in favour of the Seafire, Wildcat and Corsair, but they were used on a number of protective air patrols and anti-submarine operations. These operations were undertaken by the Mk IIC, with both cannon and rocket projectiles being used, but by the beginning of 1945 the Sea Hurricane had been totally replaced in the Naval inventory by the types previously mentioned.

Final Service

Chapter 8

A Mk IIC of No. 20 Squadron being serviced at Akyab

In this final chapter about the history of the Hurricane it is necessary to look at the other area in which the type was to see great service, namely the Far East, and also to consider its use by other countries both pre- and post-war.

The Far East

The first operation in this area was during the period leading to the fall of Singapore. By the time fifty-one Hurricanes arrived at Singapore on the 3rd January 1942, the Japanese forces were less than one hundred miles away. To make matters worse these vital aircraft remained in their crates until the 19th. These machines' first action was impressive, but when the Japanese bombers returned the next day they were escorted by Mitsubishi A6M Zeros and the table was turned. The problem was that although the Hurricane was superior to the Zero above 20,000ft, the Japanese pilots preferred to engage in combat below that level and thus the Hurricanes were completely outclassed. Such was the situation that by the 28th January only twenty of the fifty-one Hurricanes remained. These machines continued to operate until the 10th February, when the remaining seven withdrew to Sumatra. On this island No. 226 (Fighter) Group was formed with the remaining aircraft and thirty-three Mk IIAs that had been flown off HMS Indomitable. On the 14th February the Japanese attempted an assault on the island and this was beaten off by Hudsons and Blenheims escorted by Hurricanes. The Hurricanes did manage to make attacks on the Japanese bases, but instantly the Japanese made paratroop drops on one of the main Allied bases on Sumatra and over-ran it. The situation was now such that the other base on the island had to be abandoned and the Hurricanes retreated to Java, leaving all their spares behind. By this time (18th February) only twenty-five aircraft remained and these were operated by No. 232 and No. 605 Squadrons. By the 28th February the number of Hurricanes was such that the aircraft from No. 232 joined No. 605 as one squadron. The squadron retreated once more on the 2nd March and by the 7th March just two machines remained. With no fuel or ammunition these machines were destroyed on the ground and the crews tried to make their way to Australia.

Java

One part often forgotten in Hurricane history is the use of the type by the Dutch Java Air Force. After the fall of Singapore twenty-four Mk I's were sent to Java and handed over to the Dutch Java Air Force. In less than two weeks these men had accounted for thirty Japanese aircraft for the loss of eighteen Hurricanes. More Hurricanes soon arrived at Batavia harbour and of these twenty-four were passed to the Dutch. By the 27th February these machines were allocated to Tjililitan, Tasikmalaja and Ngoro, where they set about attacking the

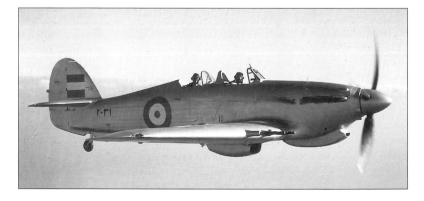

The Mk IIc (Dual Control) for the Iranian Air Force in flight
(© Hawker Siddeley)

A Mk IIC of No. 1662
Conversion Unit, with LF513
in the background, at RAF
Lindholme in 1945
(© RAF Museum P016751)

invading Japanese forces. This was not to last however, as the Japanese launched a series of heavy raids on the bases of the Allied forces and within two days nearly the entire force had been destroyed.

Burma

The Japanese attack on Burma began on the 23rd December 1941 and the defence of the entire country was in the hands of sixteen Brewster Buffaloes of No. 67 Squadron and twenty-one P-40's of the American Volunteer Group (AVG). Against this were ranged 500 combat aircraft of the Imperial Japanese forces. A batch of thirty Hurricanes was diverted from Singapore and initially these flew alongside the well-worn Buffaloes of No. 67 Squadron. These were joined at Ceylon by a further two squadrons of tropical Mk IIB's, also diverted from Singapore.

By early February the situation was worsening, and Moulmein airfield was captured. By the 11th there were just 15 serviceable Hurricanes left and by the 5th March, just six. Even in this situation the combined forces of the Hurricanes, Buffaloes and P-40s were able to retain air superiority. When Rangoon fell on the 8th March 1942, the main supply artuary was cut and AVM D.F. Stevenson ordered the remaining aircraft to move back. From rough strips cut in the jungle the aircraft operated against the Japanese columns, although not without loss. By the 12th March the remainder of No. 67 flew to Akyab, an island off the coast of Burma and here they re-equipped with Mk IIA's from Ceylon.

In central Burma No. 17 Squadron operated the remains of No. 221 Group's Mk IIA's from Magwe. On the 20th March Japanese troops landed 200 miles to the south of Magwe and on the following day Hurricanes and Blenheims took off to attack

Mk IIC, PZ865 'Last of the Many' under construction at Langley in 1944
(© Hawker-Siddeley)

Mk IIC, LF363, ground running at Langley prior to delivery to the RAF in 1944
(© RAF Museum P002613)

the Japanese force. They were extremely successful in this attack, but before they could attack again in the afternoon, the Japanese attacked Magwe. During the next twenty-five hours of attack the Hurricanes managed to shoot down a few aircraft, but the entire base was destroyed and only five of the Hurricanes remained. These machines were therefore moved back to Akyab and the Japanese forces attacked on the 23rd, 24th and 27th March. The No. 17 Squadron crews moved back to Jessore via Myitkyina to re-equip with the Mk IIB. Defence of Burma had come to an end and the remaining parts of the 'Burwing' moved into China and the ground forces into India.

By mid-1942 replacements were making their way into India and Ceylon at a rate of more than 50 machines a month. By June there were eleven re-equipped or formed Hurricane squadrons. The squadrons were No. 17, No. 30, No. 67, No. 79, No. 135, No. 136, No. 146, No. 258, No. 261 and No. 681. The latter of these had formed from the remains of No. 3 Photographic Reconnaissance Unit at Pandaveswar. All of these squadrons were under No. 224 Group and were equipped with Mk IIA Series 2 and Mk IIB machines. These were backed up in August with the important 44 gallon drop tanks, which would allow the Hurricanes to support the group troops up to 400 miles away from their base.

Back in Burma No. 261 and No. 30 Squadrons were moved into the airfields at Ratmalana and Trincomalee off of HMS

Indomitable in April 1942. By the time of the Japanese attack on the 5th there were about fifty serviceable Hurricanes to respond. No. 30 and No. 258 Squadrons were the first to intercept the Japanese and four days later Hurricanes of No. 261 Squadron were in action. Although outclassed by the Mitsubishi A6M Zero fighter, the Hurricane did inflict a large number of losses on the other types operated by the Japanese Army and Navy Air Forces. By the latter part of 1942 the Japanese were poised at the threshold of India, and in December they launched a number of raids on Calcutta. Defence of this city was the job of No. 17 and No. 79 Squadrons and with their Hurricanes they were able to turn back the Japanese attacks. In the west of Burma the ground forces, supported by No. 28, 261 and 615 Squadrons, made an assault starting in December 1942 and although the troops made good progress they were soon stopped, and ultimately forced to retreat in May 1943. By June there were sixteen Hurricane squadrons in the area and these included the first Mk IID equipped unit (No. 11 Squadron at Baigachi), offering a total of 670 machines. At this time a number of these aircraft were handed over to the Indian Air Force equipping No. 6 Squadron (IAF) at Trichinopoly in August 1943. In November 1943 the second assault was undertaken by XV Corps and once again this ground push was heavily supported by Hurricanes, although by this stage Spitfires and Thunderbolts had started to arrive in the theatre. Unfortunately once again the assault was

PZ865 'Last of the Many' was used in the early transition trials of the Hawker P.1127 due to its wide speed range
(© Hawker-Siddeley)

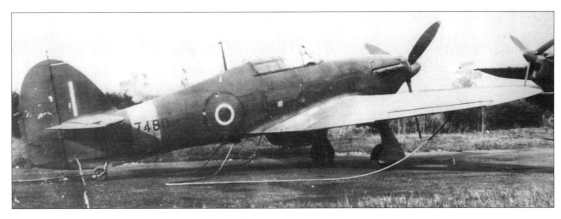

Hurricane Mk I V7480 was one of the aircraft involved in the towing trials by Flight Refuelling at Staverton

halted in February 1944, but this was partially due to a Japanese attack into India, against Calcutta, at the same time. By March the Japanese forces had attacked across the Kabaw Valley, severing an important supply route and by the 16th they had advanced on the Minipur Plain and laid siege to Imphal. The Hurricane squadrons of Nos. 34, 42, 113, 11 and 28, plus No. 1 Squadron (IAF) fought in this campaign and through good communication with ground forces were able to reduce the effects of the Japanese ground attacks. Throughout the entire siege, Imphal was reinforced entirely by air, as the Japanese still did not have air superiority in the theatre. The Mk IIC's of No. 1 Squadron (IAF) were equipped with a camera inboard of the starboard cannon and these machines were used to make tactical-reconnaissance sorties over the entire battle area, resulting in a number of assaults being discovered, and swiftly dealt with by other cannon-armed Hurricane squadrons. In India too the Mk IID was to make a name for itself, as No. 20 Squadron equipped with the type and was in action throughout the second assault. It was not just as an attack aircraft that the Hurricane proved of great use. After the relief of Imphal, the 14th Army moved into the Kabaw Valley, the most malaria-infected area in the world, and it was here that the SCI installations under the outer wings of the Hurricane were used to spray DDT along the entire length of the valley and along all roads. This resulted in a greatly reduced number of casualties for our ground forces, but it must be remembered that this operation was carried out at the height of the monsoon season, with over 175 inches of rain falling in Northern Burma, and the Hurricanes flying at ground level! The second Chindit expedition in May 1944 was the real start of the relief of Burma. The Hurricane squadrons of Nos. 79, 123, 134, 135, 146, 258 and 261 were now withdrawn to re-equip with the Republic P-47D Thunderbolt. The six Hurricane squadrons in No. 221 Group were joined by No. 60 Squadron (168 Wing) using the Mk IV from their base at Silchar and the remaining Hurricane units in the campaign were No. 20 Squadron (Mk IV), No. 4 & No. 6 Squadrons, IAF (Mk IIB/C) and No. 9 Squadron, IAF. The 14th Army moved into central Burma as the 1944 monsoon season began, but the ground forces with considerable input from the ground attack squadrons, were able to make good progress and by November had captured the important 'Vital Corner'. The XV Corps made progress in the Arakan, and once the Japanese left Akyab, the Allied forces were able to use this as a base for a series of coast-hopping assaults. With the capture of the Shwebo Plain in central Burma, Hurricanes were able to base themselves at Shwebo, Onbauk and Monya and the machines of No. 60 and 113 squadrons were able to take part in the assault on the Japanese stronghold at Gangaw. The pattern of assaults was now set and the Hurricanes were at the front as they supported the ground troops' surge forward. By the 20th March, such was the speed of the advance that Mandalay fell, and by the 3rd May the 26th Indian Division entered Rangoon.

Fighting continued until the Japanese agreed to unconditional surrender on the 14th August 1945 and throughout all of the campaign in this theatre the Hurricane had been at the front. Unlike many types the Hurricane had served from day one of the war in Europe to the final day of the conflict in the Far East.

Other duties

As well as those tasks we have already covered in the previous chapters, it must be remembered that the versatile Hurricane also fulfilled a number of other tasks throughout the war.

Meteorological Duties

Meteorological Flights were set up in August 1943 for the new air routes to the Far East and in August 1943 the first Hurricanes were used for this task by No. 1413 Flight at Lydda. Initially tired old tropical Mk I's were used for this task, but later Met Mk IIC's were used. The other flights involved in this task were No. 1412 at Khartoum, No. 1414 at Mogadishu and Eastleigh and No. 1415 at Habbaniyah and their work continued until September 1945 when No. 1413 and 1415 Flight were re-equipped with Spitfires and the other flights were disbanded.

'624' of Esquadrilha de Caca 1 at Espinho was one of a number of Mk IIC's operated by the Portugese Air Force until 1954 (© Hawker-Siddeley)

Calibration Squadrons

The Hurricane was also used once the special calibration squadrons were set up in 1941. These squadron were used to calibrate the various searchlight and gun defenses around the UK and as the crews needed an understanding of the equipment they were helping calibrate, No. 116 (Calibration) Squadron was set up at RAF Hendon. This squadron also helped calibrate the Type I radar equipment, the P.P.I. searchlight radar, and later even helped with the calibration of the mobile radar units used by the invasion forces after D-Day. No. 527 Squadron was also set up for calibration work at RAF Hornchurch in 1943, but was specifically designated to calibrate the Type I radar. By mid-1945 the range of new radar equipment was such that all calibration work was being carried out by twin-engine types.

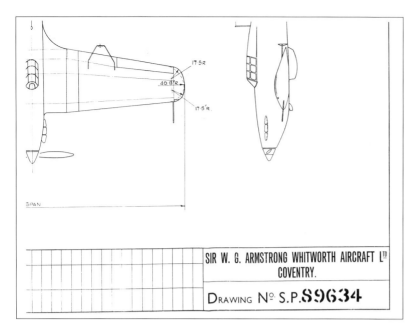

SIR W. G. ARMSTRONG WHITWORTH AIRCRAFT Lᵀᴰ
COVENTRY.

Drawing Nᵒ. S.P.S9634

One of the experiments often noted for employing the Hurricane was the laminar-flow wing testing work carried out by the RAE for Armstrong Whitworth after the war. There are a number of photographs still in existence about this machine, but to date no details of the modifications undertaken have ever been shown. Shown here is the original drawing by Armstrong Whitworth Aircraft Ltd of the modifications made to that machine's outer wing. The starboard wing was identical, but lacked the test frame aft of the trailing edge or the pitot tube. Note that no change in the overall span of the wing was made, just the modifications to the tip profile (original tip profile shown in dotted line).

Training, Co-operation and Communication Squadrons

The Hurricane, once removed from a front-line duty, was also used in a great number of training and conversion units throughout the war. Training pilots for co-operation work was also a task the Hurricane was used for when No. 516 (Combined Operations) Squadron was formed from No. 1441 Flight at DunDonald on the 28th April 1943. This squadron trained pilots to lay smoke-screens, deliver rocket attacks and do tactical reconnaissance during a number of combined assault exercises along the Scottish coast and by March 1944 the squadron was

The last Hurricane on RAF charge was Mk IIC LF363
(© Hawker-Siddeley)

using Tac R Mk IIC's for tactical reconnaissance training prior to the D-Day invasions. By June 1944 the squadron had moved south and been re-equipped with North American Mustangs.

Base defence and communication work was also done by a number of Hurricanes, as No. 267 Squadron operated at least one at their base at Heliopolis in April 1942, and No. 95 Squadron at Sierra Leone had another up until September 1942. One of the most impressive records for Hurricanes was with No. 680 (Photographic Reconnaissance) Squadron. This

squadron set out to survey much of southern Europe and it was the PR Mk IIs of the squadron that flew over one million miles delivering the photographs to the rear bases of the RAF Middle East Command and HQ MAC (Mediterranean Air Command), without a single accident.

Peacetime service and sales abroad

Royal Air Force
By the end of the Second World War most of the Hurricanes in RAF service had been relegated to second line duties. The last squadron to officially operate the Hurricane was No. 6 Squadron, who flew the Mk IV and operated from Palestine until October 1946.

Indian Air Force
The Indian Air Force continued to operate the Hurricane in the North West Frontier Province until 1946. It is believed that a Canadian-built Mk XII remained airworthy until 1953.

Irish Air Corps
During the war the Irish Air Corps acquired a number of Hurricanes including a Mk I (P5176) that crash-landed in early 1942 and was later bought by the Irish government. This first machine was numbered 93 in Irish Air Corps service and it was soon joined by another two, 94 (ex-Z2832) and 95, both of which had also crash-land in Eire. In July 1943 these latter two examples were returned to the British government in exchange for three Mk I's. These became 103, 104 and 105 (ex-V7540) and they were soon joined by a fourth (106, ex-Z4037). Until the end of the year a further seven Mk I's and six Mk II's were delivered and these all remained in service until 1947.

Experiments and modifications
In this section on the history of the Hurricane are considered some of the various modifications and experimental work the type was used for.

Daimler-Benz Hurricane
Fearing that the war would stop the supply of Merlin engines for their Hurricanes, the Yugoslavian Air Force installed a Daimler-Benz DB601A into one airframe in 1941. This conversion was done by a party from the Ikarus company at Zemun and they installed the new engine, built the revised engine bearers and cowlings and modified the coolant system. This machine was later evaluated alongside a standard Merlin powered Hurricane Mk I, and Yugoslavian pilots preferred the Daimler-Benz powered examples.

As far as is currently known, this was the only airframe to be converted in this manner.

Trials in the UK
One Hurricane Mk II was used to test the Rotol Jablo four-blade propeller that was due to be used on the production Typhoon and Tornado series. During 1941 Rotol Ltd used Mk IIs Z2321 and Z2322 for a series of trials relating to propeller behaviour during diving and landing.

A Mk II was delivered to the RAE at Farnborough in 1941 for trails with rocket-assisted take-off trials. These trails were not designed for launching the Hurricane from carriers, but were in regard to take-off in an overload configuration from short airfields. No evidence has been found to show that these RATO bottles were ever used operationally by the RAF.

Four Mk IICs were passed to Flight Refuelling at Staverton for towing trials behind a Vickers Wellington. The idea behind this was to allow the bomber streams to tow their own fighter cover

into action, as the fighters at that time were woefully deficient on operational range. A number of towing trials were undertaken at Staverton, but because of the prolonged periods at altitude, the Hurricanes suffered severe icing and this often prevented the aircraft starting up once it was cast-off. This trouble was to plague the trials, and in the end it resulted in the whole idea being dropped.

Along the same lines as the above system, Short Bros. Ltd, were asked to design a cradle so that a Liberator could carry the Hurricane 'piggy-back' fashion. By the time design were was complete, the icing problems with the towed examples were known, and so this idea was also dropped.

Post-war sales

Portugal
Some fifty aircraft that had been in store were to be supplied to this country in 1945-6. A number of these, approximately forty, were reconditioned by Hawker Aircraft Ltd and the remainder were dismantled and supplied as spares. All of these machines and parts were delivered to Portela de Sacavem at Lisbon. These machines were operated at Aerial Base No. 3, Tancos and with the Defence of Lisbon Fighter Squadron until 1951. It was in this final year of service, that these machines were flown back to the UK for use in the film 'Angels One Five'.

Persian Air Force
An order for sixteen Hurricanes had been placed by this government in 1939, but only two of these were ever delivered. Another ten are believed to have been left behind by No. 74 Squadron during the war, and these too were operated by the Persian Air Force.

As with the Portuguese examples, those sent to Persia postwar were ex-RAF examples. They were Mk IIC's and they were supplied without cannon, and the resulting holes faired over. These machines were used as fighter-trainers and they were delivered to the Advanced Group of the Persian Fighter Training School at Dosham Teppeh.

A single two-seat example was also supplied. This machine

was a conversion of KZ232 and it became 2-31 in Persian service. Initially this conversion had both cockpits exposed, but after testing the rear position was given a modified Tempest canopy and in this form the aircraft was delivered to Doshan Teppeh in 1947.

The last Hurricanes
Two of the most famous Hurricanes both lay claim to being the 'last' Hurricanes! The first was the last example on RAF charge and the other was the last built.

LF363, a Mk IIC, was built at Langley and delivered to the RAF in January 1944. It was issued to No. 309 (Of Province Ziemia Czerwienska) Squadrons, operating as 'F' with this squadron. In 1945 this machine went to No. 41 Operational Training Unit, where it was earmarked for issue to Portugal. By 1950 however it was on charge with Station Flight at RAF Waterbeach in flying condition.

PZ865, a Mk IIC, was the last Hurricane built and was never issued to the RAF, being bought back by Hawker Aircraft Ltd. This machine, named 'Last of the Many', was later registered as G-AMAU and with guns removed it was painted blue with gold trim. In 1950 this machine was entered by H.R.H. Princess Margaret in the King's Cup Race, where it was placed second. In 1951 it was once again racing and in this year it starred in two films alongside LF363 and Portuguese examples. In 1960 it was decided to return the aircraft to its original wartime colour scheme and it was continued to be used for such tasks as 'chase plane' for the target-towing trials with the Sea Fury and for the same role during transitional trials with the P.1127.

Both of these machines are now operated by the Battle of Britain Memorial Flight, RAF Coningsby, Lincolnshire. The former (LF363) has only recently been returned to flying condition having crash-landed at RAF Wittering a number of years earlier after an in-flight fire. PZ865, no longer being the only example the MOD operates, has now (1999) been sent for a total refurbishment at RAF St. Athan and it is hoped that both will be seen once more together in the skies over UK and Europe at the dawn of the new millennium.

The Basics

As you would expect with such a famous type, there have been a great number of kits produced of the Hurricane. Most of these were in 1/72nd scale, but there have also been a couple in 1/48th scale, plus single examples in 1/144th, 1/32nd and 1/24th. In the past few years these have been supplemented by a number of new toolings released in both 1/72nd and 1/48th scales.

The Hurricane in 1/144th Scale

Revell: Mk I

This kit was originally issued in 1973. It was re-issued in 1992, although it is currently unavailable. There is one decal option in this kit and although it is unidentified in the instructions, the subject is a machine from No. 32 Squadron, RAF Biggin Hill.

Even after twenty-six years this kit is still the only example in this scale. Overall the dimensions are good, with the wing span correct and the length slightly under-scale. The shape of the fuselage is not good however, as the nose tapers too gently and the shape of the rear fuselage is too thin, tapering too sharply towards the rudder. The aft decking behind the canopy is poorly represented and the top contour of the engine cowling is too flat. The shape of the rudder is incorrect, not having enough curvature at the rear and the ventral strake is much too small. The shape errors in the fuselage width and profile also lead to an inaccurate canopy. For some reason the undercarriage bays are oversized and the carburettor intake and radiator are poorly represented.

Verdict
Overall, this is not the best representation of the Hurricane, but it is the only example in this scale. Corrections can be made to this kit and the small scale make this task not too onerous.

The Hurricane in 1/72nd Scale

Airfix: Mk IV

This kit was originally issued in 1961 and is long since out of production. There was just one decal option and although unidentified in the instructions the aircraft offered is of No. 164 Squadron, RAF Fairlop.

The span in this kit is 2.5mm short, the fuselage length is 3.5mm short and the nose is 2mm too narrow. The wings themselves are quite good although in comparison to many other kits the tips are far too rounded. Once again the nose contour is too gentle, but in this kit the rear fuselage is well represented. The front of the vertical fin is incorrect and is 2mm short, while the lower ventral strake is too small.

Many have made comments about the exaggerated wing-root fairing, which is moulded with the fuselage halves. This approach to this complex area of the kit makes it look too thick, and unfortunately, due to the way in which it is tooled, it is impossible to correct. Detail errors include the spinner, which is too short, the undercarriage which in this kit is very crude (an indication of the age of the original tooling) and finally, the incorrect radiator for the Mk IV. This mark of the Hurricane had a very heavily armoured radiator bath. The example in this kit looks like a standard example without the 'stepped' armour common to the Mk IV. Biggest omission from the kit is the carburettor intake under the nose/wing, which is totally absent! The kit does include the rocket projectiles for each wing, but these are very crude and would be best replaced.

Verdict
Once again a unique kit, as this is the only Mk IV ever produced in any scale. The kit has been out of production so long now that it can only be considered as a curio since Airfix released a new tooling in 1973.

Revell: Mk I

This kit was first issued by Revell in 1963. It has since been reissued in 1975, 1978, 1982, 1992 and is currently available. It has also been issued by Advent (1979-80), Storia (1973 & 1977/8), Lincoln Industries (Revell/New Zealand - late 1970's) and Revell/Mexico (1990's).

The following colour options in the above examples were:

1963	– Unidentified Battle of Britain example	
1975	– Three options:	• No. 73 Squadron, Battle of France
		• No. 303 (Polish) Squadron
		• No. 85 Squadron
1982	– No. 85 Squadron	
1992	– Two options:	• No. 303 (Polish) Squadron
		• No. 253 Squadron

The overall dimensions in this kit are good, with the span and length being slightly underscale. Many details are incorrect though, with the wing chord too wide, the outer wing panel surface detail incorrect and the tailplane too thick with the elevators incorrectly defined. The fuselage is an oddity, being too wide at the cockpit, too tapered towards the tail and having too gentle a taper on the engine cowling? Overall, this results in an 'odd' looking model. The usual problems around the nose and cockpit exist, the rudder is not bad in profile, but the ventral strake is once again too small. The undercarriage bays are oversized and incorrectly shaped and the undercarriage legs are crude. Finally, the radiator is completely the wrong shape and much too big.

Verdict
Overall another kit that is best left on the shelf. The original

issue is of interest to the collector, but the others will only result in an 'odd' looking model. With the new example from this source now available, this tooling would be best sent into store.

FROG: Mk IIC/Sea Hurricane

This kit was first released in 1967 and it remained under the FROG label until 1977, by which time 520,000 units were produced. The kit was also issued by AMT (1967), Bienengraber (early 1970s), Hema (1969), Humbrol (1973-4), Minicraft (1972), Minix (1968-9), Remus (1977-8) and Tashigrushka (early 1980's). The kit was also issued under the Novo label (1979) and it was planned for release by NOVOEXPORT in 1982, but this never happened.

The colour options in the kit we have are:

- Mk IIC, JX•E of No.1 Squadron
- Unidentified Sea Hurricane (Note: These markings are for a Mk IC, not a Mk IIC as offered in the kit)

Both length and span are about 2mm (6" in scale) short and the tailplanes are too narrow. The nose profile is once again incorrect, although better than the early Airfix and Revell examples. The curvature of the upper decking, aft of the cockpit to the vertical fin is far too pronounced. The area aft of the cockpit also suffers with an odd 'concave' effect, that totally spoils the overall look. The cockpit canopy has too shallow a forward section and is too wide at the base of the main (sliding) section.

Omissions from the kit include the anti-glare guards for the No. 1 Squadron example (not on the box art either). The radiator is crude, as are the bombs and rockets that are included. As the kit offers a Sea Hurricane option, there is a separate insert for the tail-hook cut-out on the rear fuselage. Unfortunately there is no actual tail-hook included and the decal option offered is not for a Mk IIC as depicted in this kit.

Verdict

Overall this kit was good for its time, but thirty years down the line it is now out-classed. The inclusion of the Sea Hurricane was a nice touch, although the omission of the hook and the wrong decals make it a bit of a waste. The early boxed examples of this kit stated that a twelve-gun version could be built, but this is only possible with all the necessary conversion work being undertaken by the modeller!

KeilKraft: Mk IIC

This kit dates way back to 1958, and this was the only WWII era subject produced by this English firm.

There was only one decal option offered in this kit and it was:

- Mk IIC, PZ865, 'Last of the Many'

Like the Frog kit, this one is 2mm (6" in scale) short in length and span. The elevators are too far (2mm) inboard and the landing light (which for PZ865 correctly only offers one on the port side) is too far inboard. The cannon fairings moulded into the wings are different lengths, when they should be identical. The fuselage has a good nose profile, but is a bit too thick overall and does suffer from a very thick vertical fin. Unfortunately after all that good work the canopy is 5mm (1' 6" in scale) too long, being positioned too far forward, the upper decking aft of the fuselage is totally wrong and the trailing edge of the rudder is too flat. The undercarriage is designed to be retracted and is anyway very crude and oversized.

Verdict

Another one for the collector I feel.

Airfix: Mk I and Mk IIB

This kit was originally issued as the Mk IV RP (see elsewhere) and it was revised to this version by Airfix in 1972. This tooling has been issued in 1984, 1988-9 ('Aircraft of the Aces' series) and 1990. The kit was also included in a 50th Anniversary set for the Battle of Britain in 1990 and was announced in 1984 within the 'Day One' series, although it was never actually released in it. This model is currently available.

In New Zealand the kit was issued in the Toltoys range in the late 1970's and in America MPC issued it twice; 1972-7 and 1977.

There were two options offered in this kit and they were:

- Mk I, P3069, RF•C of No. 303 (Polish) Squadron, RAF Northolt
- Mk IIB, BE417, AE•K of No. 402 Squadron, RCAF, at RAF Warmwell

This kit offers the early and late style of Rotol propeller, two 250lb bombs and racks, two 40mm 'S' cannon and eight 3in rocket projectiles. Dimensionally the span is just 0.5mm (less than 3" in scale) short. The length is a little short with the early spinner, by nearly 2mm (6" in scale) short with the later style spinner. The rear fuselage profile is good although the effect is a little too thin at the tail and the slope aft of the cockpit starts too soon. The nose profile is good, although it starts to slope too soon resulting in a somewhat skinny looking front end. The fuselage overall is too thin in planform and this also results in the canopy being 'squashed' to accommodate the narrow cross-section, but correct depth. The undercarriage bays are too big, but doors for both extended and retracted options are included. A few amendments should be made to the propeller and spinner, although the Mk II version looks too pointed. The mass of ordnance is a real treat, although the quality is a bit mixed. The bombs and rockets are quite good, the drop tanks look too rounded, but the 'S' cannon are excellent. All of these will be of great benefit to those making other kits, especially the Heller and new Revell examples.

Airfix 1/72nd scale Hurricane Mk IIB

Verdict

Overall this is a good kit. The changes from the totally inaccurate Mk IV to this version have resulted in a sound, albeit basic, kit. The attempt to make the Mk I and Mk II is a bad idea, as the difference in their lengths means that this kit cannot be accurate for both and is best used as a basis for the Mk I.

Matchbox: Mk IID/Mk IIC

This kit was released in 1974 and has been included in the 'Classic WWI Fighters' box set in 1986. The kit is not current within the Matchbox range. In the USA this kit was issued by AMT in 1979.

There were the following two options in the kit:

- Mk IID, BP188, JV•V of No. 6 Squadron, RAF LG. 89, Western Desert, July 1942
- Mk IIC, BE500, LK•A, 'United Provinces - Cawnpore I', No. 87 Squadron, RAF Warmwell, 1941

This kit is 1mm too big in span and a little bit under in length. The fuselage is not bad, having the engine cowling a little too shallow and the decking aft of the canopy being inaccurate in profile and section. This results in the canopy once again being 'squashed' and is made worse by the fact that it is also 1.5mm too long. Both options in this kit should have the exhaust shields, although these are not included in the kit. The undercarriage is a little basic, although the bay is about right and boxed in. The carburettor is oversized but the radiator unit is correct in size and profile. Final points to note are that the propeller blades are 1.5mm too long, the spinner needs a bit of flattening and the rudder and vertical fin are some 2mm short.

Matchbox 1/72nd scale
Mk IID/Mk IIC

Verdict
Overall this is a good, basic kit. It is no worse, or better, than the Airfix example, although the fabric effect and child-like nature of the tooling mean it is not really for the enthusiast modeller.

Airfix: Mk I
This kit was originally released in 1978 and has since been re-issued in 1980-1 and 1983 and is currently available.

Originally this kit was issued with just one option:

• Fg Off Clowes of No. 1 Squadron, RAF Wittering

This kit has also been issued in the 'Aircraft of the Aces' series with the markings of Bob Stanford-Tuck's machine.

This kit is dimensionally accurate in both span and length. The engine cowl is good, although the extreme front taper is not pronounced enough. The rear fuselage is excellent, with even the extreme taper shown correctly. All the other areas that cause problems, e.g. fuselage contours, lower engine cowling, canopy rails and cockpit shape, are correct in this kit. The undercarriage bays are poor, with little interior detail and are a bit oversized. The undercarriage doors are moulded with the oleo legs and this makes them a bit crude. The radiator bath and air intake are also well represented.

Airfix 1/72nd scale
Hurricane Mk I

Verdict
This is Airfix's third attempt at the Hurricane in this scale. The model is a bit basic, especially in the cockpit interior, but overall the outline is accurate.

Academy: Mk IIC
This kit was issued in 1998 and is purported to be based on the old Frog tooling, albeit revised.

It offered the following two colour options:

• ZB464, QO•Z of No. 3 Squadron, RAF in 1941
• HL684, LK•? of No. 87 Squadron, RAF in 1942

If this kit is based on the old FROG kit there are no great similarities in the two. The kit is accurate in span but the fuselage is 3mm too long. The tailplanes are completely incorrect in shape and chord, looking as if they have come from a Curtiss P-40! The biggest problem is the cross-section of the fuselage, which is totally inaccurate. The whole fuselage is too thin, resulting in the entire model looking 'skinny' when viewed from the front. This has also resulted in the canopy being too narrow. Note that the code offered for the first colour option, ZB464 is

Academy 1/72nd scale
Mk IIC

not correct, as this series was issued in the 1980's and is more appropriate to types such as the Panavia Tornado! BZ464 seems a likely option, but this serial was allocated to a Boston IV. It is therefore likely that the serial should be Z*464 where * is a number between 1 and 9 e.g. Z2464, Z3464 or Z4464.

Verdict
When first announced we all thought we would have an accurate kit of the Hurricane at last, however the reality was something different. This kit is certainly '90's technology, but the excessive dimensional inaccuracies make it one which is best left alone. The new Revell offering is a far better option.

Heller: Mk IIC
This kit was originally issued by Heller in 1978, then again from 1979-85, 1986-1992 and is not currently available. It was also specially packed for the Norwegian market in 1991. It was released in 1990 under the Airfix label within the 'Battle of Britain 50th Anniversary' set and has also been issued under the SMER label in 1988. This tooling is currently available from SMER.

The Heller version offered the following two options:

• Mk IIC of No. 253 Squadron
• Mk II of the Ground Attack Training Unit, India, 1945

The span is 0.5mm short and the fuselage is 2mm too long. The nose cowling is 2mm too deep at the leading edge and the outer wing panels are too broad. Once again the upper engine cowling curve is too shallow, but the rear fuselage profile looks right. Because the canopy is moulded to be posed open, the upper decking aft of the cockpit is too low and if you close the canopy this area has to be built up. The landing lights are too far inboard, while the Hispano cannon ports are too far outboard! The undercarriage is poor, but has the correct style of wheel hub detail, even if one of the retraction struts is missing from each oleo. The radiator is two-piece, with an interior, and is of good shape. The carburettor intake and tropical filter are not bad, although the latter needs a bit of reprofiling. The final details needing attention are the propeller blades, which are too broad.

Verdict
It has its faults, but this is one of the better kits. By using the unwanted ordnance from the Airfix kit you can make up the options actually offered on the decal sheet in this kit.

Hasegawa: Mk I 'Douglas Bader'
This machine was issued in 1998 and is a simple amendment to the standard Mk I kit with the inclusion of the following decal option:

• Mk I, V7467, LE•D of No. 242 Squadron flown by Sqn. Ldr. Douglas R.S. Bader

This kit is accurate in span and length. The model could have been made using the excellent Arthur Bentley scale plans, as it matches them in every respect. The nose profile is perfect and as this kit has been moulded with the entire nose as separate parts, this is a kit that can claim to make both Mk I and Mk II versions. Carefully examine the lower wing panel and you will see that the outer cartridge ejector chutes for a twelve gun wing are included; fill these for any Mk I version. The radiator bath is the correct length, but a bit thin. The upper decking aft of the canopy shows the flat, then sloped shape of this area and the canopy is correct in both profile and section, although it is not positionable. The wheel

Hasegawa 1/72nd scale
Hurricane Mk I
'Douglas Bader'

wells are excellent and boxed-in with good detail and depth. The undercarriage legs and doors are separate and can only be posed in the extended position. The wheels also include good reproductions of the spoked hubs of this type. Both the pointed and blunt Rotol spinner are included, although only one is required in this kit. The exhaust stacks are separate and well moulded.

Verdict

Well the only bad point about this kit is the fabric effect on the rear fuselage, which is over-accentuated for this scale. Some primer and a rub-down will reduce this and the end effect is an accurate and well detailed reproduction of the Hurricane in this scale.

Hasegawa 1/72nd scale
Hurricane Mk I (Late)
'Battle of Britain'

Hasegawa: Mk I 'Late Type' Battle of Britain

This kit is the same as the one reviewed above and only differs in the following two colour options:

- Mk I, V6864, DT•A of No. 257 Squadron, flown by Sqn. Ldr. Robert R.S. Tuck
- Mk I, P3395, JX•B of No. 1 Squadron, flown by Arthur Clowes

Hasegawa: Mk IIC 'The Last of the Many'

This kit was released in 1997 and is based around the same tooling as the Mk I reviewed earlier. This kit includes the following colour options:

Hasegawa 1/72nd scale
Hurricane Mk IIC
'Last of the Many'

- Mk IIC, PZ865 'The Last of the Many' as flown by Hawker Aircraft Limited
- Mk IIC, BD869, QO•P of No. 3 Squadron, 1941

The kit has the same overall accurate dimensions as the Mk I. The separate nose section allows the longer fuselage to be achieved in this version. The entire wing is different, as it has the 20mm cannon moulded integrally with each wing panel. The correct ejector ports and upper wing blisters are also present. All other comments made about the Mk I apply here and the instructions do point out that the starboard landing light should be painted out for PZ865.

Hasegawa: Mk IIC 'Yugoslav Air Force'

This kit is identical to the one reviewed above, although it comes with special markings for the following option:

Hasegawa 1/72nd scale
Hurricane Mk IIC
'Yugoslav Air Force'

- Mk IIC, LB886 of the Yugoslavian Air Force in 1945. This machine is depicted in the transitional period, where the RAF roundels have been overpainted with the Yugoslav stars and the fin flashes have the star added in the white section

All comments made about the standard Mk IIC apply here also.

Revell: Mk IIB

This kit was released in late 1998, and is a totally new tooling produced in Poland.

This first offering came with the following two colour options:

- Mk IIB No. 601 Squadron, RAF
- Mk IIB No. 402 Squadron, RAF

This kit has been tooled to make a number of variants, and the Mk IIB is the first one to be offered. The wings come with the twelve-gun fitment, although many Mk IIB's had the outer ones removed. The tooling suggests the kit will be released in a number of other variants and this has been confirmed with the announcement of the Sea Hurricane Mk IIC in 1999 (and the Mk IIC?).

Going by the plans published in a number of sources this kit is bang on in length and about 1.5mm short in span. The upper decking aft of the cockpit does not come forward far enough, resulting in a gap behind the pilot's seat

Revell 1/72nd scale
Mk IIB

where there should be decking. Both ejector and 'fish-tail' exhaust stacks are included and the Rotol propeller, although correct in diameter, does not have sufficent pitch on the blades.

The Hurricane in 1/48th Scale

Monogram: Mk IIC, IID and Mk IV

This kit was originally released in 1964 and has been reissued under the Monogram label in 1968-9, 1970-1977 and in 1988 was released in a boxed set with the Bf 109E in the 'Air Combat' series. It has also been issued by Necomisa in the early 1980's and by Bandai in 1976-8. It is not currently available in the Monogram range

The original kit was offered with the following five options (although they were all unidentified in the instructions):

- Mk IIC of the Battle of Britain Memorial Flight (PZ865)
- Mk IIC (Trop) of No. 213 Squadron, El Gamil
- Mk IID of No. 6 Squadron, Shandur
- Mk IV (Trop) of No. 6 Squadron, Grottaglie, Italy
- Mk IV of No. 6 Squadron, Grottaglie, Italy

It should be noted that the overall accuracy of this kit is good, being accurate in span and almost correct in length. The tailplane is correct in size, but the elevators are incorrect in shape. The fuselage centre-section is 3mm too wide, but the nose profile looks good and the exhaust pipes are parallel. Although it is only slightly noticeable in this scale, the vertical fin does not show the bias to port that was a feature of the real aircraft. Because the nose lower contour is too deep, leading to a central fuselage section that is too deep, the wing section is also 2mm too deep. All of this adds up to the model looking too 'thick' at the centre section, and none of this can be corrected without major surgery. The original issue had retractable undercarriage so it is a bit toy-like in overall detail.

There is nothing at all inside the cockpit bar the pilot figure and the retracting undercarriage has resulted in there being no wheel wells either. The panel lines (raised) on the wings only show the eight gun 0.303in machine gun armament, so the Mk IIC, Mk IID and Mk IV cannot be built from it without correction work.

The kit does come with a mass of ordnance, namely four 20mm Hispano cannons (Mk II), eight 60lb 3in. rocket projectiles, two underwing bomb racks with 250lb GP bombs (although their overall shape is very suspect), two 40mm Vickers 'S' cannons and two 44 gallon underwing fuel tanks. There are also the standard and Mk IV armoured radiators included (although they are both a little (2mm) too short), a Vokes tropical filter (also inaccurate) and a choice of the early and late ('Fishtail') exhaust stacks.

Verdict

This kit is showing its age, and is not one that can be recommended as there are better ones available now. The extra armament and accessories are very welcome, and can be used on other kits e.g. Airfix or Hobbycraft. One for the enthusiasts only.

Airfix: Mk I

This kit was issued in late 1979 and has since been issued in 1983 and 1987 and is currently available. This kit was also announced by USAirfix in 1987, but never happened.

The kit currently offers the following two colour options:

- Mk I, VY•G of No. 85 (F) Squadron, RAF with the AASF based at Lille/Seclin, France in April 1940
- Mk I, SD•X, V6799 of No. 501 (City of Gloucester) Squadron, RAuxAF based at RAF Kenley in October 1940

Airfix 1/48th scale Mk I

This is an accurate rendition of the Mk I, the only apparent problem area being behind the cockpit, where the upper decking tapers into the rest of the fuselage too quickly. This can be overcome with some plasticard and filler, but is annoying. The wheel well is offered as a 'box' on top of which is the cockpit 'floor'. This is incorrect, as the Hurricane's interior is tubular and therefore has no 'floor' as such. Both de Havilland (thin) and Rotol (blunt) spinners are included, along with the slim metal (D.H.) and Jablo (Rotol) propeller blades for each.

The vertical fin is correctly biased to port. The wing trailing edge is a bit thick and you must use tape to ensure that you do not get zero dihedral.

Verdict

Hobbycraft 1/48th scale Mk II

This was the best basis for a Mk I, and still is until the new Hasegawa example arrives? The spartan interior, especially when compared with the aforementioned Hasegawa examples, lets the model down a bit, but for a 19 year old tooling, it's not bad. This is certainly a good basis for all the early variants, and when cross-kitted with the Hobbycraft example, can also help with the Mk II's as well.

Hobbycraft: Mk II

The Mk IIB/C/D was released in 1988 and bears a passing similarity to the Airfix kit. The model has since been released with etched-brass parts in the 'Elite' series as a Night Raider in 1990 and has also been reboxed as a Russian Mk IIB, and a 'Desert Rat' RAF Mk IID.

The 'Russian' Mk IIB included decals for the following machines:

- Mk IIB, BM959, '60', Russia 1942. This machine was shot down near Tilksjärvi, Finland in 1942
- Mk IIB, HC465 of the Finnish A.F. in 1944

The kit is 1mm short in span, but correct in length. The fuselage and tail shape are correct, as are the wing and tail in plan view. The fin is not offset to port. As already said, this kit looks very similar to the Airfix kit, and to that end Hobbycraft have included a few inaccuracies for this variant. The straight-legged style of tailwheel that is appropriate to the Mk I is included, and will need to be replaced by the white metal one from Aeroclub. The overall dimensions are good, although the same error with the decking as in the Airfix kit is apparent here too. The model does include the Vickers 'S' 40mm cannon, although the barrels in this scale are a little thick, plus the 44 gallon fuel tanks and the Vokes filter. Only the Rotol (blunt) spinner is included along with the Jablo propeller blades and these will need to be slightly reprofiled and the sink marks in the backs filled.

Verdict

This is a good kit, the only real error was with the initial issue which tried to be a Mk IIB (with only eight guns!), or a Mk IIC and a Mk IID all without any changes in the panel lines on the wings! To be fair the Mk IIB depicted in that kit was a preserved example without guns, so the error is understandable. That said, this is a sound basis for an inexpensive Mk II series airframe and with the Airfix Mk I will be the option many go for.

Hasegawa: Mk IIC

This kit was issued in 1998.

The kit offered colour schemes for the following two machines:

- Mk IIC, BD962, QO•Q of No. 3 Squadron, RAF
- Mk IIC, Z3894, QO•R of No. 3 Squadron, RAF
- Mk IIC, PZ865, 'Last of the Many' owned by Hawker Aircraft Limited (now operated by the BBMF)

When originally released it was apparent that Hasegawa were not just going to make the Mk II series airframes, as this kit had the entire forward fuselage separate. In late 1998/early 1999 this was confirmed with the announcement of the planned release of the Mk I (and Mk IIB). In regard to accuracy this kit cannot be faulted with the correct span and length. The fuselage cross-section is very good and the tailplanes are the correct shape in plan. The decking aft of the canopy slopes correctly to the vertical fin, which is offset to port. The wing is suitable for the C and D versions, with the clever addition of the Hispano feed bulges on the upper surfaces as separate parts. There is no provision for a twelve-gun wing, although this will come with the Mk I, which will have the eight-gun wing suitable, with the addition of the outer guns, for the Mk IIB. It will be interesting to see how Hasegawa deal with this, either the outer gun access panels will be included on the Mk I wing, whereby the modeller has to fill them for that variant, or (more unlikely), the modeller will have to scribe them in for the Mk IIB.

Cockpit interior is excellent, with a framework of tubes being made up to take the head armour, seat, rudder pedals, kick-plates and instrument panel. Very little extra has to be added to

Hasegawa 1/48th scale Mk IIC

this, although it is all lost as the kit only includes a single piece canopy. Provision of a two-part canopy in the kit would have lead to the need to inaccurately depict the rear upper decking, as the injected sliding portion would not have fitted over the correctly shaped spine. This is a gold star for Hasegawa, and modellers will just have to buy a thin, vac-formed version if they wish to depict the canopy open. The only real criticism that has been levelled at this kit is the fabric effect on the rear fuselage. This is over-accentuated (as in their 1/72nd scale version), but with some primer and a light rub-down, the effect is still acceptable. The reasoning behind this I am sure is to give longevity to the tooling, which, with time, will wear and if this effect was 'accurately' portrayed at the start, would be non-existent ten or fifteen years later.

Verdict

Currently the kit to have. This will make up straight from the box as a stunning Mk IIC. Nearly as cheap as the Airfix and Hobbycraft examples, without your having to mess about correcting things, so for my money it's the only show in town.

Hasegawa: Mk IID

This kit was also released in 1998 and is a revision to the Mk IIC version described previously.

The kit offers the following two schemes:

• Mk IID, BP188, JV•Z of No. 6 Squadron, RAF
• Mk IID, HV663, 'U' of No. 6 Squadron, RAF
 N.B. Both of these machines were operated
 in the Western Desert

This kit is based on the Mk IIC and utilises all the main components. The revision comes in the wing leading edges, the Vokes tropical filter and, of course, the Vickers 'S' 40mm cannon. The leading edge area around the wing guns in the Mk IIC is an insert, to allow the fitment of the fairings for the Hispano cannon. In this kit it is a blanking plate with one .303in. Browning machine gun (used for bore-sighting the cannon). The Vokes filter is a simple add-on item, that goes in the area under the chin which is supplied separately in the Mk IIC kit. The 'S' cannon are depicted in the kit with a 'ball' end to them, and this is only correct for those aircraft being flown to the front, as this is a protective sleeve. The box artwork shows the guns with a normal end, but the real aircraft had a slight 'collar' on the extreme muzzle of the cannon! Only the Rotol 'blunt' spinner and Jablo propellers are supplied, although the anti-dazzle panels for a night intruder Mk IIC and the Mk IIC cannon fairings are still included on the sprues.

Verdict

Once again this is truly the only game in town at the moment. The model builds well, has excellent detail, and the only down side is that fabric effect on the rear fuselage.

The Hurricane in 1/32nd Scale

Revell: Mk I

This kit was originally issued in 1969 and has since been reissued in 1973 (PR Mk I), 1977 and 1986. It is not currently

Hasegawa 1/48th scale Mk IID

available. The kit has been issued with a number of colour options as follows:

 1969 – Mk I, DT•A of No. 257 Squadron flown by Wg Cdr
  R.R.S. Tuck DSO DFC*
 1973 – PR Mk I of No. 208 Squadron, Heliopolis.
 1977 – Both of the above options
 1986 – Both of the above options

This kit, and its Mk IIC incarnation, are the only Hurricanes that have been produced in this scale. Accuracy-wise the kit is correct in length and about 0.5mm short in span. The vertical fin is correctly offset, but the overall profile of the fuselage looks wrong around the nose and tail. The first problem is due to the top of the cowling being too flat, while the lower cowling does not curve in the correct manner. The latter point is due to the usual lack of the sharp taper to the last section of the fuselage and rudder. The flat on the upper decking just aft of the canopy is there, but it is too subtle in this scale and therefore does not look right.

As far as the detail parts go, the exhaust pipes are not accurate, looking more like the type fitted to a Tempest than the Rolls-Royce ejector type fitted to the Hurricane. The spinner and propeller are a real disappointment. The spinner is (I think) supposed to be the Rotol type, but is too long and pointed for this type (maybe it represents the type fitted to a Canadian Mk XII?). To make things worse the propeller blades are too thick and don't represent the metal or Jablo version fitted to any variant. Being a product of the 60s, this kit did have an operative canopy. This has led to the rails being heavily produced and accentuated, and the canopy being thick and clumsy. A very basic Merlin engine is included, but this looks underscale and is, as said, very 'basic'. Another spartan area is the cockpit interior, which only received rudimentary details, and therefore will benefit from extra detailing. The undercarriage is good, but the undercarriage bays are completely the wrong shape. The wheels however are totally incorrect, with a five-spoke hub unlike the three or four-spoke versions fitted to the Hurricane. The shape of the door on the radius rod is also very inaccurate in overall shape. The tailwheel is devoid of any hub detail, and the tailwheel yoke does not really depict the correct Dowty oil-spring unit. The 1977 version of this kit included a Vokes filter, although this was the wrong shape at the front and lappears too short in overall length.

Finally, the surface detail is a mass of heavy rivet and raised lines on the metal airframe components, and fabric effect with heavy stitching on the rear fuselage etc.

Verdict

This is the only Mk I in this scale you can get, and I doubt if another will ever be made (please prove me wrong someone!). This kit can offer the basis of a good Hurricane in this scale, but it needs work, a lot of work (especially considering my comments on the 'revised' Mk IIC).

Revell: Mk IIC

This kit first arrived in the 'Smithsonian Museum Collection' series in 1987, by Revell Germany in 1989 and by Revell-Monogram in 1998. It is currently available.

The kit has been offered with a number of colour options, but the current (1998) version offers the following options:

• Mk IIC, BP349 of No. 73 Squadron, based in the Western Desert in 1942
• Mk IIC (Night Intruder), HL864, LK•? of No. 87 Squadron, based at RAF Charmy Down in 1942

This model is in fact just the previous Mk I version with the addition of the 20mm Hispano cannon fitted to the wings! All of the comments about accuracy mentioned in the report on the Mk I also apply here, but more so. The tooling has been modified, but in such a manner that is totally inaccurate. The bulges for each Hispano cannon have been added to the upper wing surface, but these have been done over the existing gun-bay detail for the eight-gun wing of the Mk I. Anyone who has

Revell 1/32nd scale Mk IIC

reached this stage in this title will appreciate that the Mk I cannot be made into a Mk IIC without a number of changes, none of which have been made to this kit.

Therefore apart from all the points mentioned in the Mk I report, this example now has the wrong tailwheel unit fitted (being the early Dowty Oil-spring type), the wing now features all the access panels for the wing (eight) machine gun armament, but has two 20mm Hispano cannon installed! Revisions to the nose contours have not been undertaken, and the oil deflector ring is omitted completely. Once again the exhaust pipes are totally wrong, not representing the 'fish-tail' type fitted to the Mk II series. Finally the Hispano cannon do not represent the Mk I or Mk II version fitted to this type, as the external springs on the kit parts are supplemented with some rings around the main barrel which are totally inaccurate.

As a final note, the colour option offered for the No. 87 Squadron machine is inaccurate. The serial number should be in Medium Sea Grey characters just 4in high and underneath the leading edge of the tailplanes. Also, if this kit is supposed to depict a 'night intruder', then the 44 gallon fuel tanks are also missing.

Verdict

Oh dear, what can I say except that a Mk IIC cannot be made from this kit really. Use the kit parts to make the Mk I (or convert it to any other Mk I series airframe), but for a Mk II you would need to undertake a lot of additional work.

The Hurricane in 1/24th Scale

Airfix: Mk I

This kit was originally issued in 1973 and has since been reissued in 1976 (to 1979), 1983, 1990 and 1995 and is currently available.

The kit currently comes with the following options:

- 1. LK•A (serial unknown) of No. 87 Squadron flown by Ian Gleed
- 2. P3854, VY•Q of No. 85 Squadron flown by Peter Townsend

Airfix 1/24th scale Mk I

This kit is the only one we are ever likely to see in this big scale, and even though it has been around for over 25 years now, the current issue is standing up well to the passage of time.

Accuracy-wise the kit is 2mm over in span and 1mm short in length. Looking at the kit in side and plan view, the profiles of the wings, tail and fuselage look good. The upper nose cowling tapers too slowly, resulting in the cross-section of the nose at the rear of the spinner being 2mm too big. The flat section aft of the cockpit is once again not accentuated, with

the entire area being slightly curved if you look closely at it. The canopy rails are incorrect, being straight, and are a little heavy (for the 'opening' canopy). The canopy itself looks good in profile and is the correct length, but the operating requirements have made it a little wide in cross-section.

Detail-wise the kit includes both a Merlin engine and each machine gun bay in the wings. Both of these, although basic, will give the basis for as much detail as you want to add. Unfortunately Airfix modelled these items to scale; however the limitations of injection moulding coupled with the thickness of the plastic used means that the surround structure is overly thick. This may not sound a problem, but it means that Airfix seem to have dealt with this by 'modifying' the wing and cowling profile. This is probably why the upper engine cowling is too shallow, and why the wings look too thick.

All the fabric areas are well defined, all the rivets are raised, but all remaining panel lines are engraved, and that is from a kit that was created a quarter of a century ago. The cockpit interior is fully detailed, with the whole area being built up as a framework just like the real aircraft. A pilot figure is included if you want to add him, and the instrument panel even has the instruments as a clear insert in the back of the panel. The tail wheel correctly depicts the Dowty oil-spring version of this mark and the vertical fin is correctly offset. The undercarriage features rubber mainwheels (as does the tailwheel) and the units can be posed in the up or down position. All of the access panels around the engine, the knock-out panel in the cockpit and the wing gun bay panels are included separately to encourage the modeller to show off the detail offered in this kit, although their fit is not good so it would be best to leave them off anyway.

For those who would like their model to 'fly' a large stand is also included. Those who can recall this kit's release will remember that this was where the batteries were held to power the little motor built into the kit's engine to spin its propeller!

Verdict

It may be that there are a number of problems with this kit, but it is the only one you are ever likely to see in this scale. Overlooking the accuracy queries, this big scale has something for everyone. For the beginner it offers an excellent and impressive model straight from the box, the intermediate will be able to refine a few areas and get more from the kit's parts, while the expert will probably spend months building one, correcting the detail inaccuracies and adding all the detail and pipework. If you have never experienced a 1/24th scale model before, have a go at this one, you will love it!

The above tells you what is currently available (or not!) in 1/144th, 1/72nd, 1/48th, 1/32nd and 1/24th scales.

Now that we have a starting point it is time to get a better understanding of the actual aircraft, so read on...

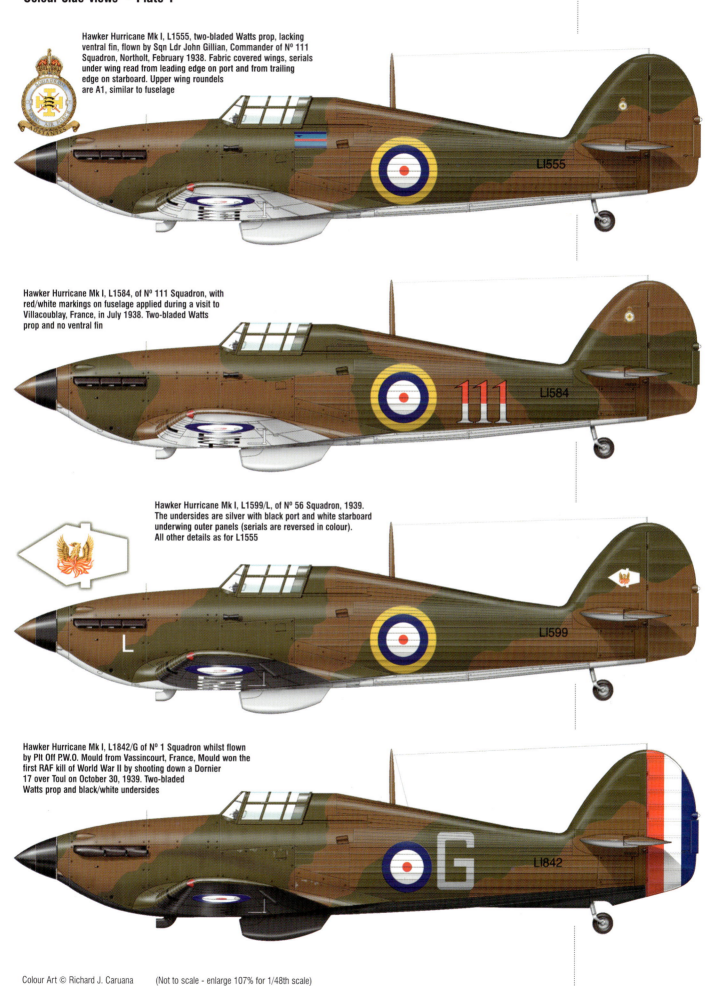

Hawker Hurricane Mk I, L1555, two-bladed Watts prop, lacking ventral fin, flown by Sqn Ldr John Gillian, Commander of Nº 111 Squadron, Northolt, February 1938. Fabric covered wings, serials under wing read from leading edge on port and from trailing edge on starboard. Upper wing roundels are A1, similar to fuselage

Hawker Hurricane Mk I, L1584, of Nº 111 Squadron, with red/white markings on fuselage applied during a visit to Villacoublay, France, in July 1938. Two-bladed Watts prop and no ventral fin

Hawker Hurricane Mk I, L1599/L, of Nº 56 Squadron, 1939. The undersides are silver with black port and white starboard underwing outer panels (serials are reversed in colour). All other details as for L1555

Hawker Hurricane Mk I, L1842/G of Nº 1 Squadron whilst flown by Plt Off P.W.O. Mould from Vassincourt, France, Mould won the first RAF kill of World War II by shooting down a Dornier 17 over Toul on October 30, 1939. Two-bladed Watts prop and black/white undersides

Colour Art © Richard J. Caruana   (Not to scale - enlarge 107% for 1/48th scale)

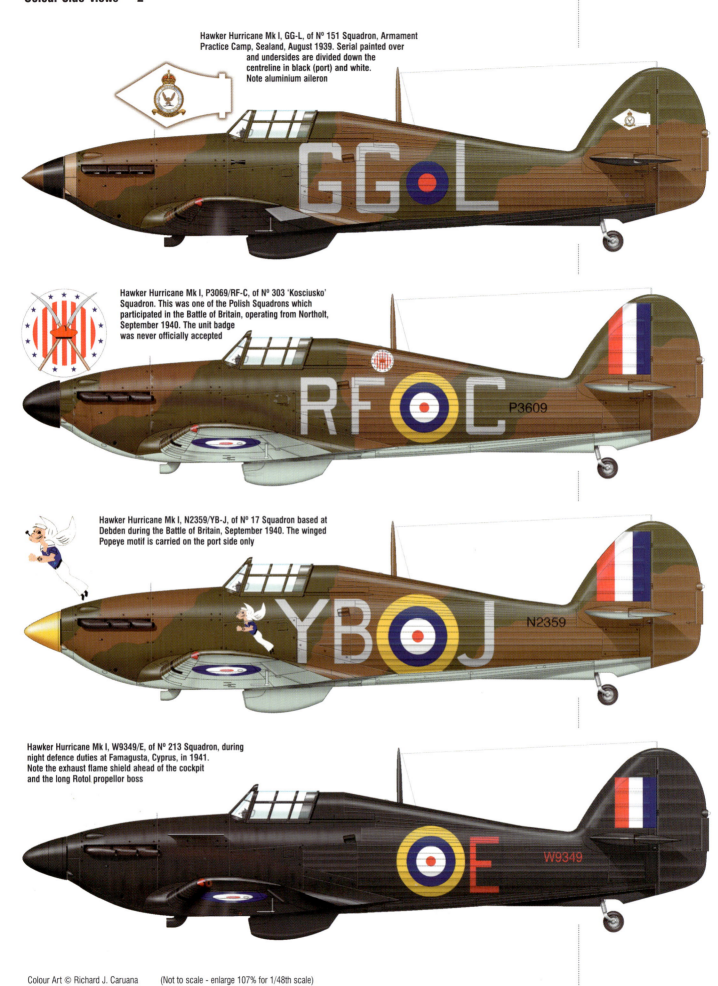

Hawker Hurricane Mk I, GG-L, of Nº 151 Squadron, Armament Practice Camp, Sealand, August 1939. Serial painted over and undersides are divided down the centreline in black (port) and white. Note aluminium aileron

Hawker Hurricane Mk I, P3069/RF-C, of Nº 303 'Kosciusko' Squadron. This was one of the Polish Squadrons which participated in the Battle of Britain, operating from Northolt, September 1940. The unit badge was never officially accepted

Hawker Hurricane Mk I, N2359/YB-J, of Nº 17 Squadron based at Debden during the Battle of Britain, September 1940. The winged Popeye motif is carried on the port side only

Hawker Hurricane Mk I, W9349/E, of Nº 213 Squadron, during night defence duties at Famagusta, Cyprus, in 1941. Note the exhaust flame shield ahead of the cockpit and the long Rotol propellor boss

Colour Art © Richard J. Caruana   (Not to scale - enlarge 107% for 1/48th scale)

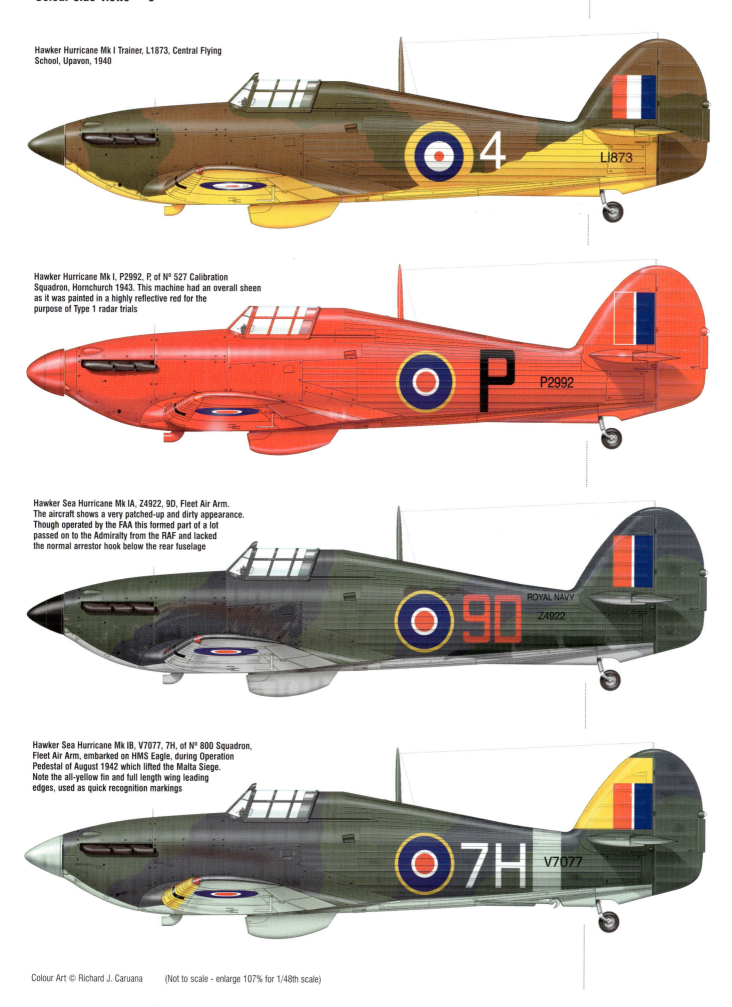

Hawker Hurricane Mk I Trainer, L1873, Central Flying
School, Upavon, 1940

Hawker Hurricane Mk I, P2992, P, of N° 527 Calibration
Squadron, Hornchurch 1943. This machine had an overall sheen
as it was painted in a highly reflective red for the
purpose of Type 1 radar trials

Hawker Sea Hurricane Mk IA, Z4922, 9D, Fleet Air Arm.
The aircraft shows a very patched-up and dirty appearance.
Though operated by the FAA this formed part of a lot
passed on to the Admiralty from the RAF and lacked
the normal arrestor hook below the rear fuselage

Hawker Sea Hurricane Mk IB, V7077, 7H, of N° 800 Squadron,
Fleet Air Arm, embarked on HMS Eagle, during Operation
Pedestal of August 1942 which lifted the Malta Siege.
Note the all-yellow fin and full length wing leading
edges, used as quick recognition markings

Colour Art © Richard J. Caruana   (Not to scale - enlarge 107% for 1/48th scale)

Hawker Hurricane Mk I, V7474, A, of Nº 261 Squadron operating
from Luqa, Malta early in 1941. This aircraft was ferried to Malta
from HMS Argus by Flt Lt JAF MacLachlan on November 17,
1940. MacLachlan (DFC+) was to become one of
Malta's aces with eight victories

Hawker Hurricane Mk I, V7101 of Nº 69 Squadron, Luqa,
Malta 1941. This Hurricane was a stripped-down
unarmed recce machine; note fin and rudder appear
to have been cannibalised from another aircraft

Hawker Hurricane PR Mk I, P2638, of Nº 208 (Army Co-operation)
Squadron, Burg-el-Arab, Egypt, 1942. This unarmed recce
aircraft was shot down by Bf 109Fs on July 24, 1942

Canadiar Foundry-built Hurricane Mk XIIA (Sea Hurricane I)
of Nº 126 Squadron, Royal Canadian Air Force.
Note 'Royal Navy' on rear fuselage
overpainted in Dark Green

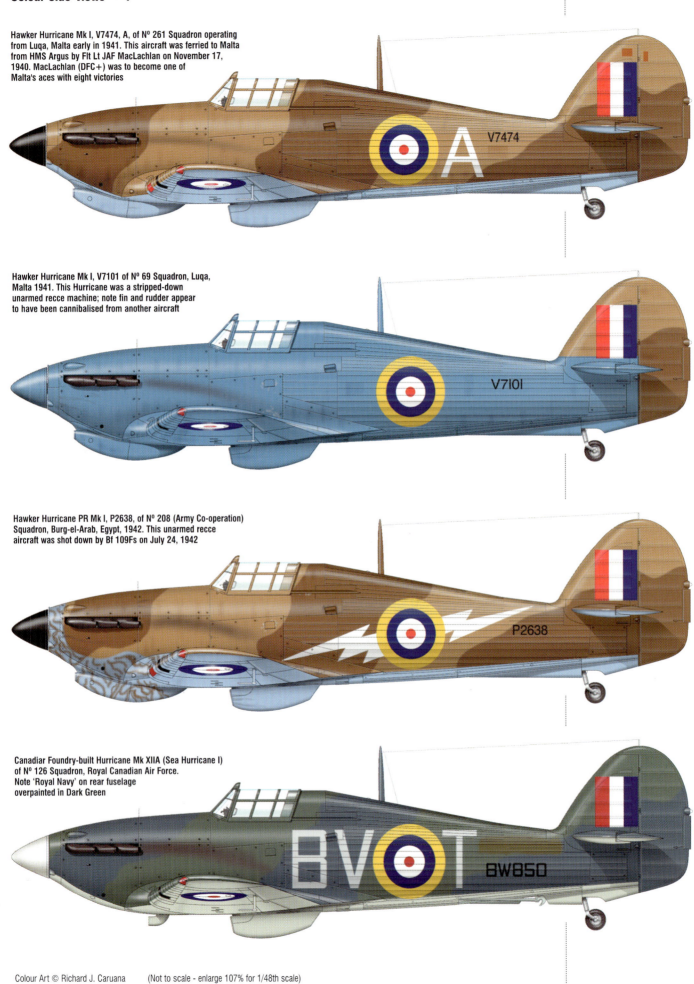

Colour Art © Richard J. Caruana   (Not to scale - enlarge 107% for 1/48th scale)

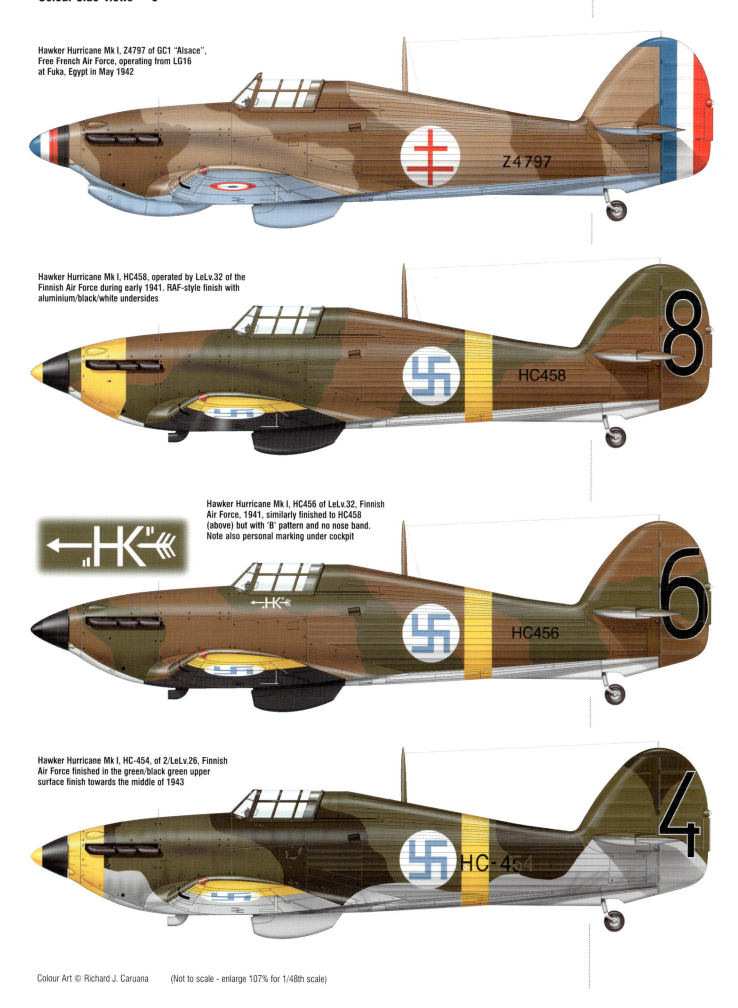

Hawker Hurricane Mk I, Z4797 of GC1 "Alsace",
Free French Air Force, operating from LG16
at Fuka, Egypt in May 1942

Hawker Hurricane Mk I, HC458, operated by LeLv.32 of the
Finnish Air Force during early 1941. RAF-style finish with
aluminium/black/white undersides

Hawker Hurricane Mk I, HC456 of LeLv.32, Finnish
Air Force, 1941, similarly finished to HC458
(above) but with 'B' pattern and no nose band.
Note also personal marking under cockpit

Hawker Hurricane Mk I, HC-454, of 2/LeLv.26, Finnish
Air Force finished in the green/black green upper
surface finish towards the middle of 1943

Colour Art © Richard J. Caruana   (Not to scale - enlarge 107% for 1/48th scale)

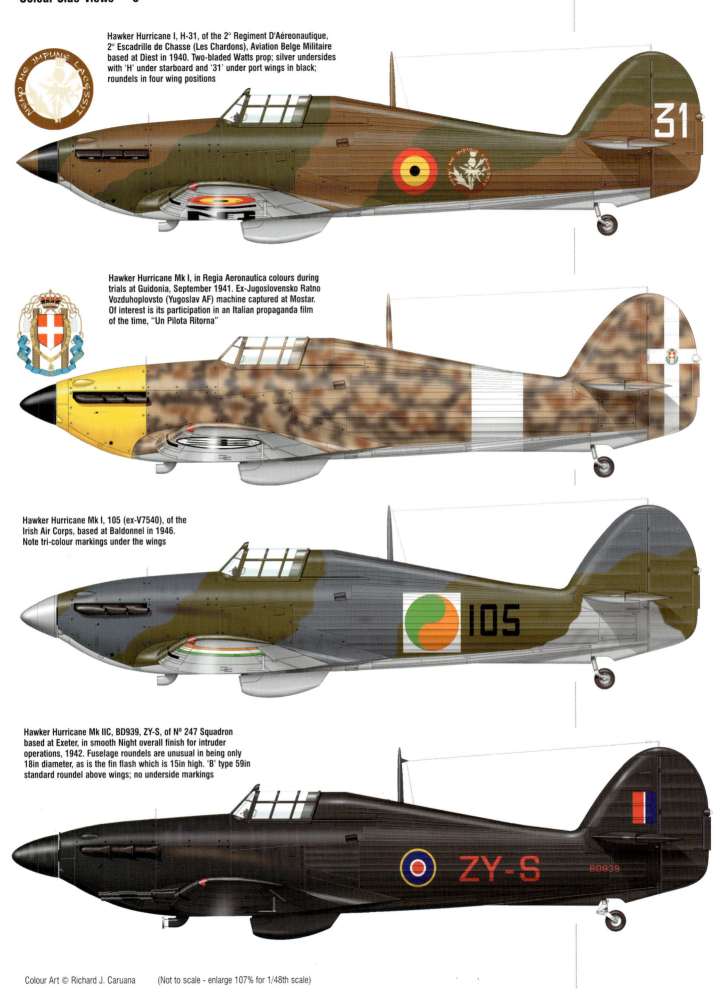

Hawker Hurricane I, H-31, of the 2° Regiment D'Aéreonautique, 2° Escadrille de Chasse (Les Chardons), Aviation Belge Militaire based at Diest in 1940. Two-bladed Watts prop; silver undersides with 'H' under starboard and '31' under port wings in black; roundels in four wing positions

Hawker Hurricane Mk I, in Regia Aeronautica colours during trials at Guidonia, September 1941. Ex-Jugoslovensko Ratno Vozduhoplovsto (Yugoslav AF) machine captured at Mostar. Of interest is its participation in an Italian propaganda film of the time, "Un Pilota Ritorna"

Hawker Hurricane Mk I, 105 (ex-V7540), of the Irish Air Corps, based at Baldonnel in 1946. Note tri-colour markings under the wings

Hawker Hurricane Mk IIC, BD939, ZY-S, of Nº 247 Squadron based at Exeter, in smooth Night overall finish for intruder operations, 1942. Fuselage roundels are unusual in being only 18in diameter, as is the fin flash which is 15in high. 'B' type 59in standard roundel above wings; no underside markings

Colour Art © Richard J. Caruana   (Not to scale - enlarge 107% for 1/48th scale)

Hawker Hurricane Mk IIC, BD946, JX-H, of Nº 1 Squadron
operating from Redhill during summer, 1942, until relinquishing
the type for the Typhoon in September of the same year. Mixed
Grey and Dark Green uppersurfaces with Medium Sea Grey
undersides and yellow wing leading edge markings

Hawker Hurricane Mk IIB, Z5227, FE-53, of Nº 81 Squadron
during operations from Vaenga, Russia, which
commenced in September 1941

Hawker Hurricane Mk IIB, BD776, WG-F, of Nº 128 Squadron
which operated from Hastings, Sierra Leone, West Africa,
toward the end of 1942. Unusual for the two-tone brown
scheme are the grey codes; some sources claim
they could be yellow but this is unconfirmed

Hawker Hurricane Mk IIC, BE402, LE-S, of Nº 242 Squadron
which arrived at Malta for operations from the Island on October
4, 1941. This aircraft was slightly damaged on landing after its
ferry flight from HMS Argus (Operation Perpetual) but was
repaired and went back into service

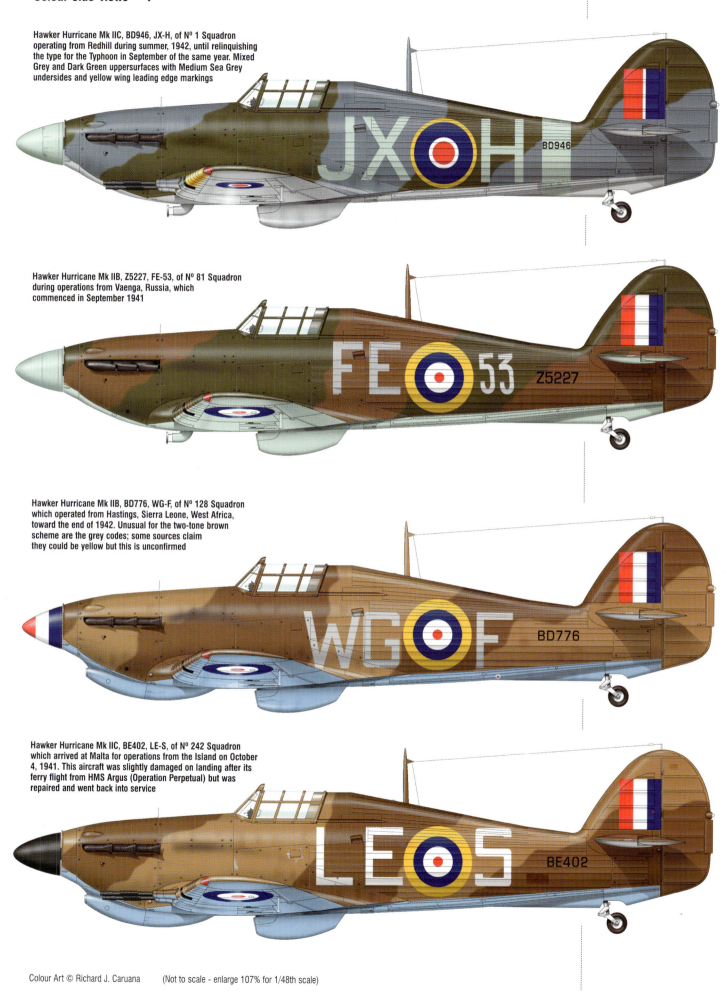

Colour Art © Richard J. Caruana   (Not to scale - enlarge 107% for 1/48th scale)

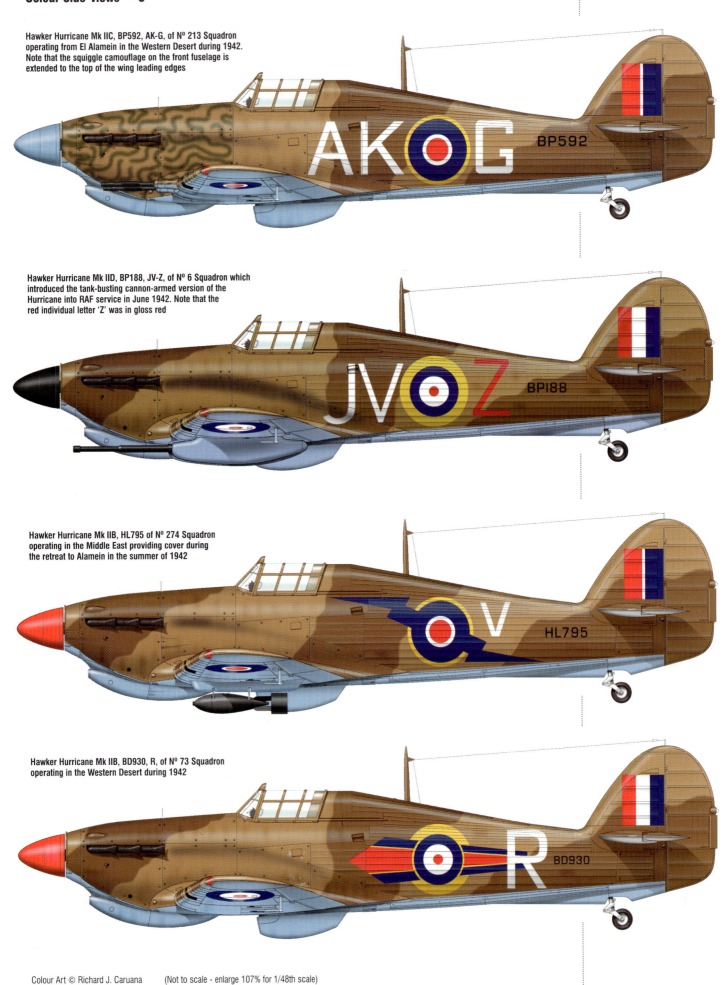

Hawker Hurricane Mk IIC, BP592, AK-G, of Nº 213 Squadron operating from El Alamein in the Western Desert during 1942. Note that the squiggle camouflage on the front fuselage is extended to the top of the wing leading edges

Hawker Hurricane Mk IID, BP188, JV-Z, of Nº 6 Squadron which introduced the tank-busting cannon-armed version of the Hurricane into RAF service in June 1942. Note that the red individual letter 'Z' was in gloss red

Hawker Hurricane Mk IIB, HL795 of Nº 274 Squadron operating in the Middle East providing cover during the retreat to Alamein in the summer of 1942

Hawker Hurricane Mk IIB, BD930, R, of Nº 73 Squadron operating in the Western Desert during 1942

Colour Art © Richard J. Caruana   (Not to scale - enlarge 107% for 1/48th scale)

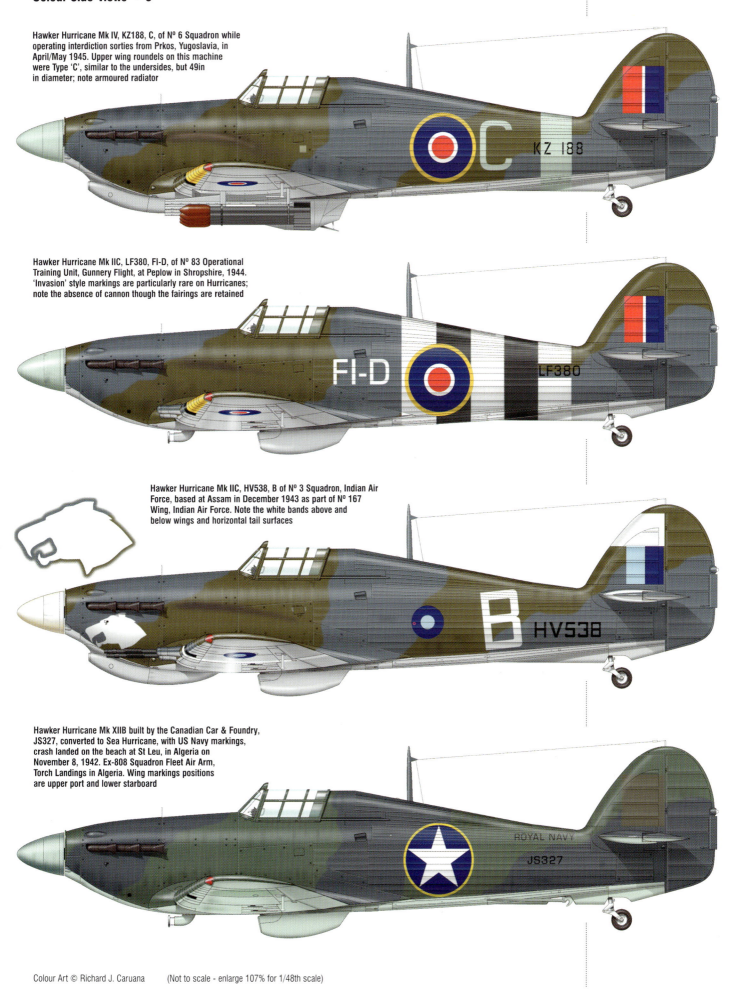

Hawker Hurricane Mk IV, KZ188, C, of Nº 6 Squadron while operating interdiction sorties from Prkos, Yugoslavia, in April/May 1945. Upper wing roundels on this machine were Type 'C', similar to the undersides, but 49in in diameter; note armoured radiator

Hawker Hurricane Mk IIC, LF380, FI-D, of Nº 83 Operational Training Unit, Gunnery Flight, at Peplow in Shropshire, 1944. 'Invasion' style markings are particularly rare on Hurricanes; note the absence of cannon though the fairings are retained

Hawker Hurricane Mk IIC, HV538, B of Nº 3 Squadron, Indian Air Force, based at Assam in December 1943 as part of Nº 167 Wing, Indian Air Force. Note the white bands above and below wings and horizontal tail surfaces

Hawker Hurricane Mk XIIB built by the Canadian Car & Foundry, JS327, converted to Sea Hurricane, with US Navy markings, crash landed on the beach at St Leu, in Algeria on November 8, 1942. Ex-808 Squadron Fleet Air Arm, Torch Landings in Algeria. Wing markings positions are upper port and lower starboard

Colour Art © Richard J. Caruana   (Not to scale - enlarge 107% for 1/48th scale)

Hawker Hurricane Mk IIB, BN779, 18, of the Soviet Air
Force operational on the Karelian Front in 1942

Hawker Hurricane Mk IIC, HL988, one of a number supplied
to Turkey during 1942 from RAF Maintenance Units in
the Middle East

Hawker Hurricane Mk IIC, 582 of the XV Esquadrilha, Portugese
Air Force, operating from Espinho Airport in 1948 within the
Grupo Independente de Aviaçao de Caça. Upper wing roundels
on white background like undersides

Hawker Hurricane Mk IIC, 2-13, of the Advanced Group, Flying
Training School, Iranian Air Force which flew this type from
Doshan Teppeh in 1947, together with a number of two-seat
Hurricanes. Note that the wing cannon have been removed
though the fairings are retained

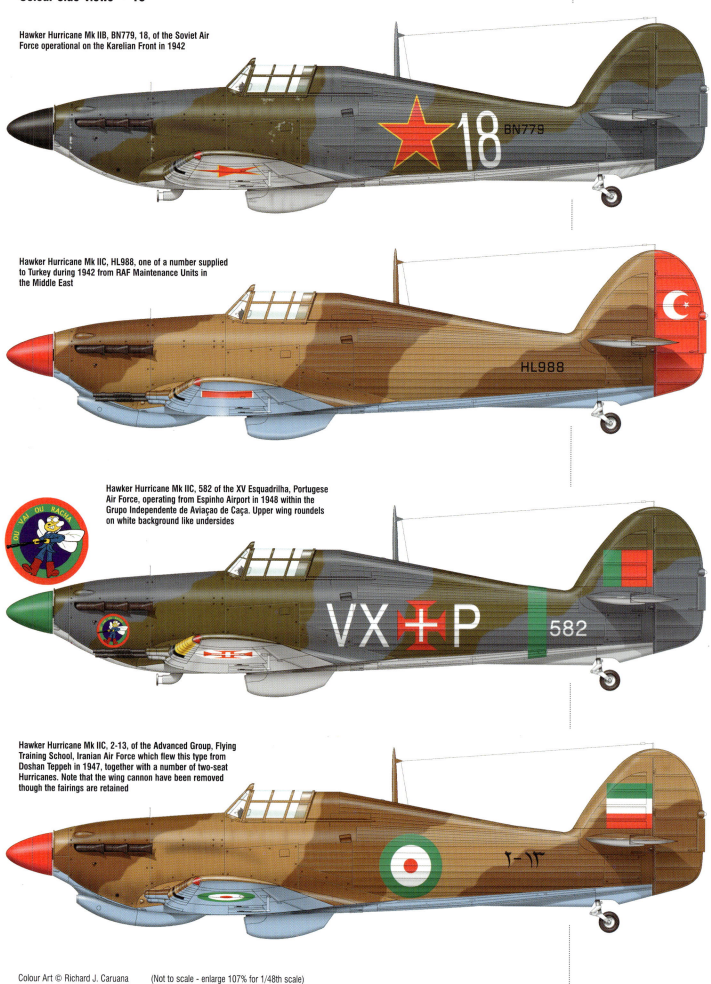

Colour Art © Richard J. Caruana   (Not to scale - enlarge 107% for 1/48th scale)

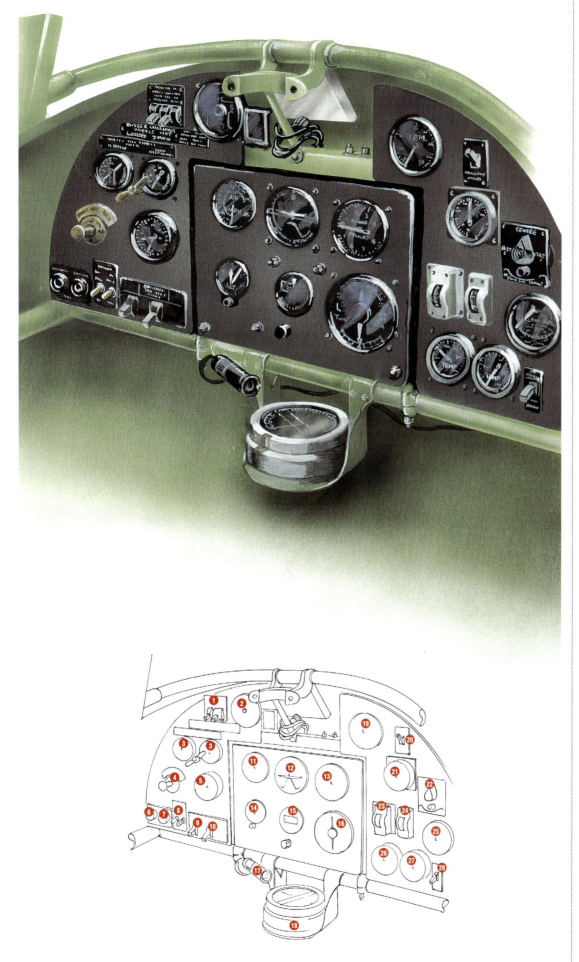

Instrument panel of the Mk I

Key to illustration

- 1 Undercarriage Indicator Lamp Switch
- 2 Undercarriage Indicator Lamp
- 3 Oxygen Regulator
- 4 Automatic Boost Emergency Cut-out
- 5 Clock
- 6 Engine Starter Push Button
- 7 Booster Coil Push Button (if fitted)
- 8 Main Magneto Switches
- 9 & 10 Navigation Lamp Switches
- 11 Air Speed Indicator
- 12 Artificial Horizon
- 13 Rate of Climb Indicator
- 14 Altimeter
- 15 Direction Indicator
- 16 Turn & Bank Indicator
- 17 Cockpit Light
- 18 Compass
- 19 Indicator R.P.M.
- 20 Reflector Gun Sight Lamp Switch
- 21 Boost Pressure Gauge
- 22 Fuel Contents Gauge Selector Switch & Push Button
- 23 Oil Pressure Gauge
- 24 Fuel Pressure Gauge
- 25 Fuel Contents Gauge (Reserve & Main)
- 26 Oil Temperature Gauge
- 27 Radiator Temperature Gauge
- 28 Starting Magneto Switch

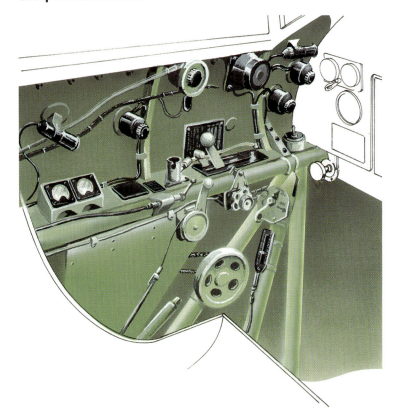

Port sidewall of the Mk I

Key to illustration
- 1 Cockpit Light
- 2 Cockpit Light Dimmer Switch
- 3 Undercarriage Warning Buzzer
- 4 Landing Lamp Switch
- 5 Throttle Control Lever
- 6 Mixture Control Lever
- 7 R/T Remote Controller
- 8 Engine Data Plate
- 9 Oxygen Supply Bayonet Socket
- 10 Generator Charge Regulating Switch
- 11 Ammeter
- 12 Voltmeter
- 13 Landing Lamps Control Lever
- 14 Hood Catch Lever
- 15 Throttle Lever Friction Adjuster
- 16 Mixture Lever Friction Adjuster
- 17 Fuel Control Cock
- 18 Radiator Flap Indicator
- 19 Elevator Trimming Tabs Control Wheel
- 20 Radiator Flap Control Lever

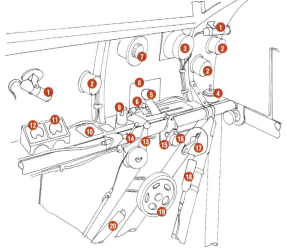

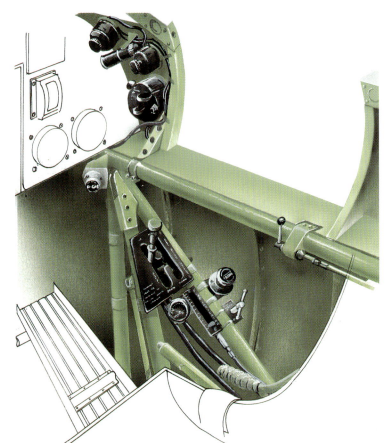

Starboard sidewall of the Mk I

Key to illustration
- 1 Dimmer Switch for Reflector Gun Sight
- 2 Dimmer Switch for Cockpit Light
- 3 Cockpit Light
- 4 Identification Lamp Switchbox
- 5 Cylinder Priming Pump
- 6. Hydraulic Selector Lever (Undercarriage & Flaps)
- 7 Flap Indicator
- 8 Windscreen De-icer Pump
- 9 Parachute Flares Release Lever
- 10. Hydraulic Hand Pump Lever
- 11. Seat Adjustment Lever
- 12. Sutton Harness Release

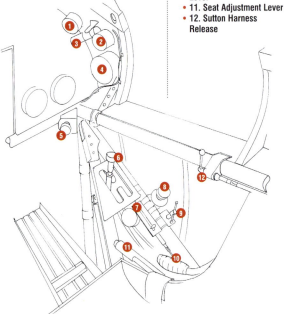

Colour Art © Anthony Oliver

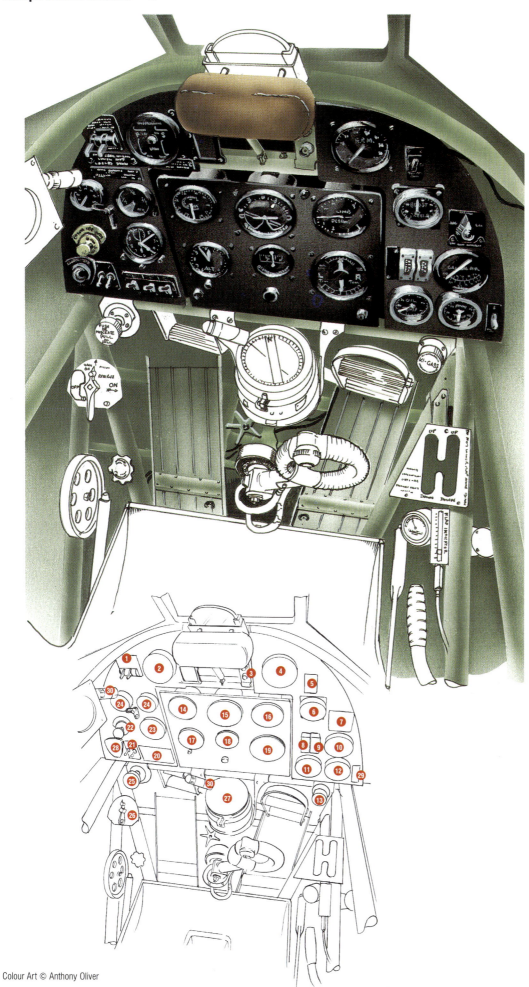

Colour Art © Anthony Oliver

Instrument panel of the Mk I (Late) & Mk IIA Series 1

Key to illustration
- 1 Undercarriage On-Off & Change-Over Switches
- 2 Undercarriage Indicator Lamp
- 3 Reflector Gunsight Spare Bulbs (x3)
- 4 Indicator R.P.M.
- 5 Reflector Gunsight Switch
- 6 Boost Gauge
- 7 Fuel Contents Gauge Selector Switch & Push-Button
- 8 Oil Pressure Gauge
- 9 Fuel Pressure Warning Light
- 10 Fuel Contents Gauge
- 11 Oil Temperature Gauge
- 12 Radiator Temperature Gauge
- 13 Cylinder Priming Pump
- 14 Air Speed Indicator
- 15 Artificial Horizon
- 16 Indicator, Climb & Descent
- 17 Altimeter
- 18 Direction Indicator
- 19 Turn & Slip Indicator
- 20 Navigation Light Switch
- 21 Main Magneto Switches
- 22 Boost Control Cut-out
- 23 Clock
- 24 Oxygen Regulator
- 25 Supercharger Control
- 26 Fuel Cock
- 27 Compass
- 28 Electric Starter Push-Button
- 29 Starting Magneto Switch
- 30 Cockpit Light

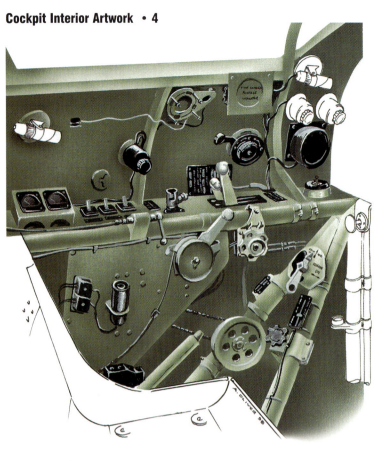

Port sidewall of the Mk I (Late) & Mk IIA Series 1

Key to illustration

- 1 Cockpit Light
- 2 Voltmeter
- 3 Ammeter
- 4, 5 & 6 Radio Contactor Master Switch & Generator Switches
- 7 Dimmer Switch for Cockpit Light
- 8 Oxygen Supply Bayonet Socket
- 9 Bracket for R/T Remote Controller
- 10 Hood Catch Lever
- 11 Mixture Control Lever
- 12 Throttle Control Lever
- 13 Propeller Speed Control
- 14 Undercarriage Warning Buzzer
- 15 Landing Lamp Switch
- 16 Engine Data Plate
- 17 Throttle Lever Friction Adjuster

- 18 Mixture Control Friction Lever
- 19 Landing Lamp Control Lever
- 20 Fuel Cock Control
- 21 Radiator Flap Indicator
- 22 Rudder Trimming Tab Control
- 23 Elevator Trimming Tab Control Wheel
- 24 Microphone/Telephone Socket
- 25 Radiator Flap Control Lever
- 26 Wedge Plate for Camera Gun Footage Indicator (if fitted)

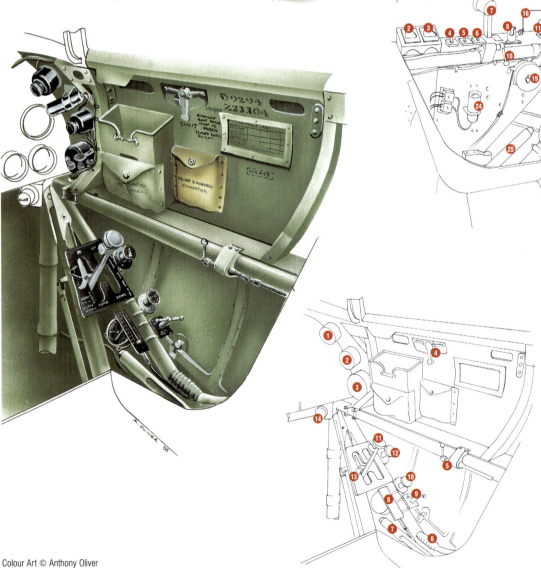

Starboard sidewall of the Mk I (Late) & Mk IIA Series 1

Key to illustration

- 1 Dimmer Switch for Reflector Gunsight
- 2 Cockpit Light Dimmer Switch
- 3 Signalling Switchbox
- 4 Emergency Exit Panel Jettison Lever
- 5 Sutton Harness Release
- 6 Hydraulic Hand Pump
- 7 Seat Adjustment Lever
- 8 Flap Indicator
- 9 Parachute Flare Release Control
- 10 Cockpit De-icer Hand Pump
- 11 Undercarriage & Flap Selector Lever
- 12 Slow Running Cut-out
- 13 Undercarriage Selector Safety Catch
- 14 Cylinder Priming Pump

Colour Art © Anthony Oliver

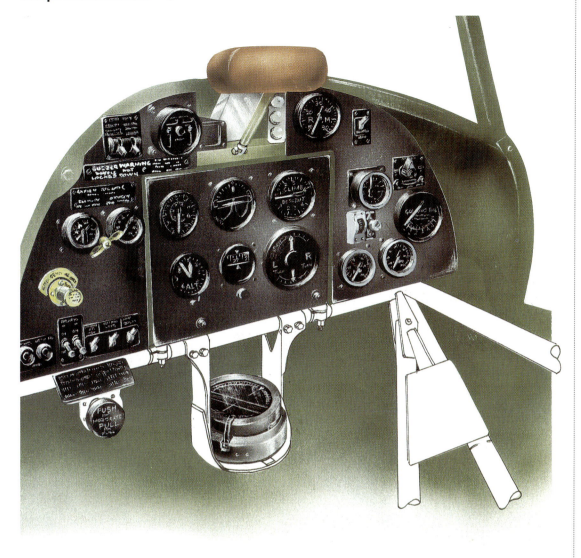

Colour Art © Anthony Oliver

Instrument panel of the Mk IIA Series II, Mk IIB, Mk IIC, Mk IID & Mk IV series

Key to illustration
- 1 Undercarriage On-Off & Change-Over Switches
- 2 Undercarriage Indicator
- 3 Indicator, R.P.M.
- 4 Reflector Gunsight Switch
- 5 Boost Gauge
- 6 Fuel Contents Gauge Selector Switch
- 7 Oil Pressure Gauge
- 8 Fuel Pressure Warning Light
- 9 Fuel Contents Gauge
- 10 Oil Temperature Gauge
- 11 Radiator Temperature Gauge
- 12 Air Seed Indicator
- 13 Artificial Horizon
- 14 Indicator, Climb & Descent
- 15 Altimeter
- 16 Direction Indicator
- 17 Turn & Bank Indicator
- 18 Compass
- 19 Oxygen regulator
- 20 Boost Control Cut-out
- 21 Engine Starter Push Button
- 22 Booster Coil Push Button
- 23 Ignition Switches
- 24 Pressure Head Heater Switch
- 25 Navigation Light Switch
- 26 Camera Gun Switch
- 27 Supercharger Control

Note: This illustration is applicable to all late production and modified Mk IIA & B airframes (inc Sea Hurricanes)

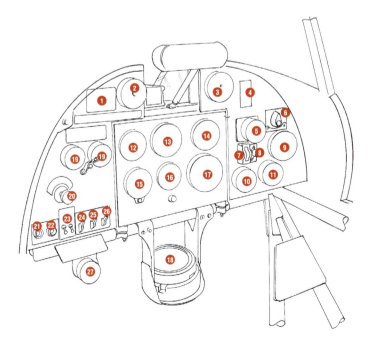

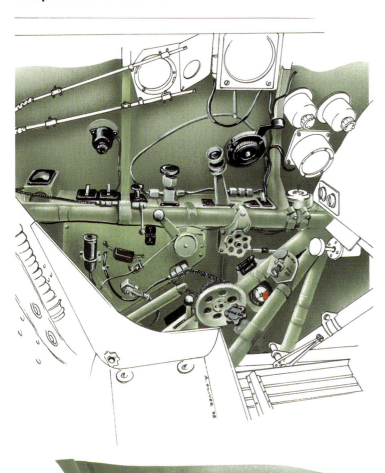

Port sidewall of the Mk II & Mk IV series

Key to illustration
- 1 Voltmeter
- 2 Radio Control Master Switch
- 3 Generator Switch
- 4 Cockpit Light Dimmer Switch
- 5 Oil Dilution Push Button
- 6 Landing Lamp Control Lever
- 7 Oxygen Supply Cock
- 8 Throttle Control Lever
- 9 Propeller Speed Control
- 10 Compass Light Dimmer Switch
- 11 Cockpit Light Dimmer Switch
- 12 Landing Lamp Switch
- 13 Microphone/Telephone Socket
- 14 Cannon Cocking Lever (Mk IIC)
- 15 Heated Clothing Socket
- 16 Radiator Flap Control Lever
- 17 Recognition Device Selector Lever
- 18 Elevator Trimming Tab Control
- 19 T.R. 9D Contactor Switch (when fitted)
- 20 Friction Adjuster
- 21 Fuel Cock Control
- 22 Radio Contactor
- 23 Rudder Trimming Tab Control
- 24 Hood Catch
- 25 Supercharger Control
- 26 Undercarriage Warning Buzzer

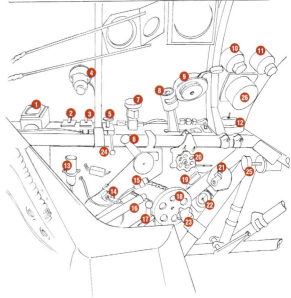

Starboard sidewall of the Mk II & Mk IV series

Key to illustration
- 1 Cockpit Light Dimmer Switch
- 2 Signalling Switchbox
- 3 Container Jettison Push Button
- 4 Undercarriage Selector Safety Catch
- 5 Undercarriage & Flap Selector Lever
- 6 Windscreen De-icing Pump
- 7 Drop Tank Jettison Lever
- 8 Drop Tank Fuel Cock Control
- 9 Seat Adjustment Lever
- 10 Hydraulic Hand Pump
- 11 Bomb Fusing & Selector Switches
- 12 Sutton Harness Release
- 13 Emergency Exit Panel Jettison Lever
- 14 IFF Push Button
- 15 IFF Master Switch

Note: These illustrations are applicable to all late production and modified Mk IIA & B airframes (inc Sea Hurricanes)

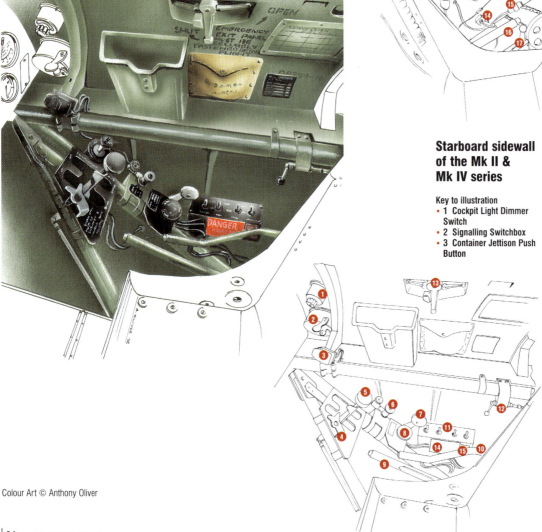

Colour Art © Anthony Oliver

Understanding the Subject

In this chapter we will take a detailed look at all the marks of the Hurricane, as well as giving details of how to model them in 1/72nd, 1/48th, 1/32nd and 1/24th scale. The following review has been based on a detailed study of over 7,000 photographs and close reference to all the official publications for each type. This has been backed up with the information carried in a great number of the titles listed in Appendix X of this book, along with many a pleasant hour in and around preserved examples here in the UK.

We appreciate that there are many areas of the Hurricane which we may highlight in a different manner to that which has been accepted so far, and we also know that we will still miss things, so if anyone reading this has points they would like to raise and has evidence to back them up, we would love to hear from you. Any reprinted examples of this title in the future can therefore incorporate any new information that may be brought to light.

Note: All items shown are to 1/72nd scale, 1/48th scale in brackets ( ), 1/32nd [ ] and 1/24th { }. 'K' denotes use of kit part, 'M' use of modified part, and 'S' scratch-build necessary.

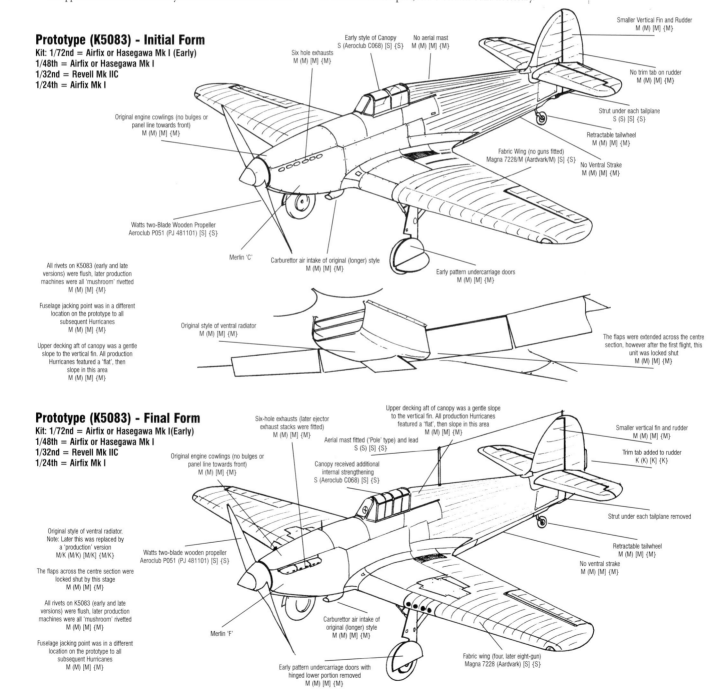

Prototype (K5083) - Initial Form
Kit: 1/72nd = Airfix or Hasegawa Mk I (Early)
1/48th = Airfix or Hasegawa Mk I
1/32nd = Revell Mk IIC
1/24th = Airfix Mk I

Smaller Vertical Fin and Rudder
M (M) [M] {M}

Early style of Canopy
S (Aeroclub C068) [S] {S}

No aerial mast
M (M) [M] {M}

Six hole exhausts
M (M) [M] {M}

No trim tab on rudder
M (M) [M] {M}

Strut under each tailplane
S (S) [S] {S}

Original engine cowlings (no bulges or panel line towards front)
M (M) [M] {M}

Retractable tailwheel
M (M) [M] {M}

Fabric Wing (no guns fitted)
Magna 7228/M (Aardvark/M) [S] {S}

No Ventral Strake
M (M) [M] {M}

Watts two-Blade Wooden Propeller
Aeroclub P051 (PJ 481101) [S] {S}

Merlin 'C'

Carburettor air intake of original (longer) style
M (M) [M] {M}

Early pattern undercarriage doors
M (M) [M] {M}

All rivets on K5083 (early and late versions) were flush, later production machines were all 'mushroom' rivetted
M (M) [M] {M}

Fuselage jacking point was in a different location on the prototype to all subsequent Hurricanes
M (M) [M] {M}

Upper decking aft of canopy was a gentle slope to the vertical fin. All production Hurricanes featured a 'flat', then slope in this area
M (M) [M] {M}

Original style of ventral radiator
M (M) [M] {M}

The flaps were extended across the centre section, however after the first flight, this unit was locked shut
M (M) [M] {M}

Prototype (K5083) - Final Form
Kit: 1/72nd = Airfix or Hasegawa Mk I(Early)
1/48th = Airfix or Hasegawa Mk I
1/32nd = Revell Mk IIC
1/24th = Airfix Mk I

Six-hole exhausts (later ejector exhaust stacks were fitted)
M (M) [M] {M}

Upper decking aft of canopy was a gentle slope to the vertical fin. All production Hurricanes featured a 'flat', then slope in this area
M (M) [M] {M}

Aerial mast fitted ('Pole' type) and lead
S (S) [S] {S}

Smaller vertical fin and rudder
M (M) [M] {M}

Original engine cowlings (no bulges or panel line towards front)
M (M) [M] {M}

Canopy received additional internal strengthening
S (Aeroclub C068) [S] {S}

Trim tab added to rudder
K (K) [K] {K}

Strut under each tailplane removed

Original style of ventral radiator.
Note: Later this was replaced by a 'production' version
M/K (M/K) [M/K] {M/K}

Retractable tailwheel
M (M) [M] {M}

The flaps across the centre section were locked shut by this stage
M (M) [M] {M}

No ventral strake
M (M) [M] {M}

All rivets on K5083 (early and late versions) were flush, later production machines were all 'mushroom' rivetted
M (M) [M] {M}

Watts two-blade wooden propeller
Aeroclub P051 (PJ 481101) [S] {S}

Fuselage jacking point was in a different location on the prototype to all subsequent Hurricanes
M (M) [M] {M}

Merlin 'F'

Carburettor air intake of original (longer) style
M (M) [M] {M}

Fabric wing (four, later eight-gun)
Magna 7228 (Aardvark) [S] {S}

Early pattern undercarriage doors with hinged lower portion removed
M (M) [M] {M}

Fighter & Fighter-bomber Mk I (Early)

Kit: 1/72nd = Airfix Mk I or Hasegawa Mk I (Early)
1/48th = Airfix or Hasegawa Mk I
1/32nd = Revell Mk IIC
1/24th = Airfix Mk I

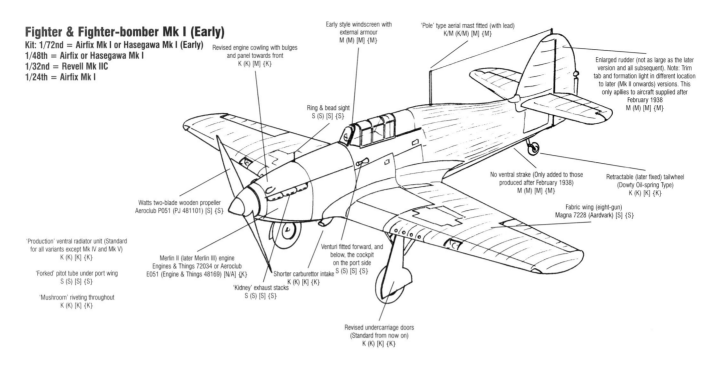

Early style windscreen with external armour
M (M) [M] {M}

'Pole' type aerial mast fitted (with lead)
K/M (K/M) [M] {M}

Enlarged rudder (not as large as the later version and all subsequent). Note: Trim tab and formation light in different location to later (Mk II onwards) versions. This only applies to aircraft supplied after February 1938
M (M) [M] {M}

Ring & bead sight
S (S) [S] {S}

Revised engine cowling with bulges and panel towards front
K (K) [M] {K}

Watts two-blade wooden propeller
Aeroclub P051 (PJ 481101) [S] {S}

No ventral strake (Only added to those produced after February 1938)
M (M) [M] {M}

Retractable (later fixed) tailwheel (Dowty Oil-spring Type)
K (K) [K] {K}

'Production' ventral radiator unit (Standard for all variants except Mk IV and Mk V)
K (K) [K] {K}

Fabric wing (eight-gun)
Magna 7228 (Aardvark) [S] {S}

'Forked' pitot tube under port wing
S (S) [S] {S}

Merlin II (later Merlin III) engine
Engines & Things 72034 or Aeroclub
E051 (Engine & Things 48169) [N/A] {K}

Venturi fitted forward, and below, the cockpit on the port side
S (S) [S] {S}

'Mushroom' riveting throughout
K (K) [K] {K}

Shorter carburettor intake
K (K) [K] {K}

'Kidney' exhaust stacks
S (S) [S] {S}

Revised undercarriage doors (Standard from now on)
K (K) [K] {K}

Mk I (Late)

Kit: 1/72nd = Airfix Mk I or Hasegawa Mk I (Late)
1/48th = Airfix or Hasegawa Mk I
1/32nd = Revell Mk IIC
1/24th = Airfix Mk I

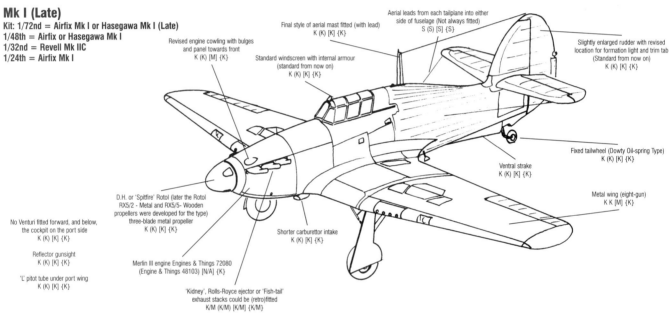

Aerial leads from each tailplane into either side of fuselage (Not always fitted)
S (S) [S] {S}

Final style of aerial mast fitted (with lead)
K (K) [K] {K}

Revised engine cowling with bulges and panel towards front
K (K) [M] {K}

Standard windscreen with internal armour (standard from now on)
K (K) [K] {K}

Slightly enlarged rudder with revised location for formation light and trim tab (Standard from now on)
K (K) [K] {K}

No Venturi fitted forward, and below, the cockpit on the port side
K (K) [K] {K}

Reflector gunsight
K (K) [K] {K}

'L' pitot tube under port wing
K (K) [K] {K}

D.H. or 'Spitfire' Rotol (later the Rotol RX5/2 - Metal and RX5/5- Wooden propellers were developed for the type) three-blade metal propeller
K (K) [K] {K}

Shorter carburettor intake
K (K) [K] {K}

Fixed tailwheel (Dowty Oil-spring Type)
K (K) [K] {K}

Ventral strake
K (K) [K] {K}

Metal wing (eight-gun)
K K [M] {K}

Merlin III engine Engines & Things 72080 (Engine & Things 48103) [N/A] {K}

'Kidney', Rolls-Royce ejector or 'Fish-tail' exhaust stacks could be (retro)fitted
K/M (K/M) [K/M] {K/M}

Mk I (Canadian)

See Mk X (Canadian)

Mk I (Two Cannon): L1750

Kit: 1/72nd = Airfix Mk I or Hasegawa Mk I (Late)
1/48th = Airfix or Hasegawa Mk I
1/32nd = Revell Mk IIC
1/24th = Airfix Mk I

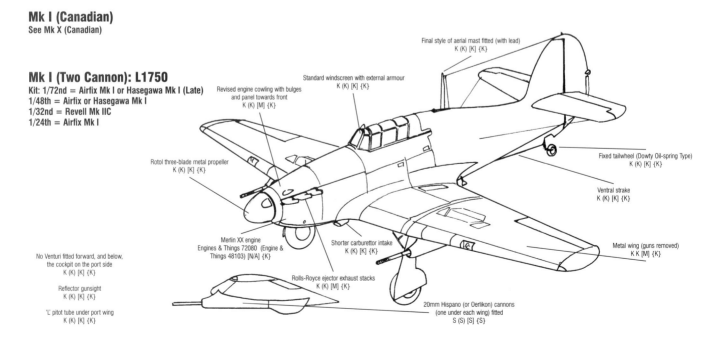

Final style of aerial mast fitted (with lead)
K (K) [K] {K}

Standard windscreen with external armour
K (K) [K] {K}

Revised engine cowling with bulges and panel towards front
K (K) [M] {K}

Rotol three-blade metal propeller
K (K) [K] {K}

Fixed tailwheel (Dowty Oil-spring Type)
K (K) [K] {K}

Ventral strake
K (K) [K] {K}

Merlin XX engine
Engines & Things 72080 (Engine & Things 48103) [N/A] {K}

Shorter carburettor intake
K (K) [K] {K}

Metal wing (guns removed)
K K [K] {K}

No Venturi fitted forward, and below, the cockpit on the port side
K (K) [K] {K}

Reflector gunsight
K (K) [K] {K}

'L' pitot tube under port wing
K (K) [K] {K}

Rolls-Royce ejector exhaust stacks
K (K) [M] {K}

20mm Hispano (or Oerlikon) cannons (one under each wing) fitted
S (S) [S] {S}

Mk I (Four Cannon): V7360

Kit: 1/72nd = Airfix Mk I or Hasegawa Mk I (Early)
1/48th = Airfix or Hasegawa Mk I
1/32nd = Revell Mk II
1/24th = Airfix Mk I

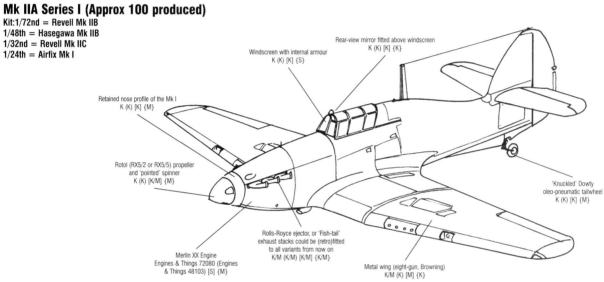

Enlarged rudder (not as large as the later version and all subsequent
*See 'Mk I (Early)'
M (M) [M] {M}

'Pole' type aerial mast fitted (with lead)
M (M) [M] {M}

Windscreen with internal armour
K (M) [M] {M}

Revised engine cowling with bulges and panel towards front
K (K) [M] {K}

Fixed tailwheel (Dowty Oil-spring Type)
K (K) [K] {K}

No ventral strake
M (M) [M] {M}

Metal wing (modified internal structure to take two 20mm Hispano cannon each)
K/M (K/M) [K/M] {K/M}

Venturi not fitted
K (K) [K] {K}

Reflector gunsight fitted
K (K) [K] {K}

'Forked' pitot tube under port wing
S (S) [S] {S}

Rotol 'Spitfire' three-blade metal propeller
K K [K] {K}

Shorter carburettor intake
K (K) [K] {K}

Merlin III engine
Engines & Things 72034 or Aeroclub E051 (Engine & Things 48169) [N/A] {K}

'Kidney' exhaust stacks
S (S) [S] {S}

No bulges on upper wing surfaces, as early cannon were belt-feed
K/M (K/M) [K/M] {K/M}

Mk IIA Series I (Approx 100 produced)

Kit: 1/72nd = Revell Mk IIB
1/48th = Hasegawa Mk IIB
1/32nd = Revell Mk IIC
1/24th = Airfix Mk I

Rear-view mirror fitted above windscreen
K (K) [K] {K}

Windscreen with internal armour
K (K) [K] {S}

Retained nose profile of the Mk I
K (K) [K] {M}

Rotol (RX5/2 or RX5/5) propeller and 'pointed' spinner
K (K) [K/M] {M}

'Knuckled' Dowty oleo-pneumatic tailwheel
K (K) [K] {M}

Rolls-Royce ejector, or 'Fish-tail' exhaust stacks could be (retro)fitted to all variants from now on
K/M (K/M) [K/M] {K/M}

Merlin XX Engine
Engines & Things 72080 (Engines & Things 48103) [S] {M}

Metal wing (eight-gun, Browning)
K/M (K) [M] {K}

Mk IIA Series II

Kit: 1/72nd = Revell Mk IIB
1/48th = Hasegawa Mk IIB
1/32nd = Revell Mk IIC
1/24th = Airfix Mk I

Rear-view mirror fitted above windscreen
K (K) [K] {K}

Oil deflector ring on extreme nose cowling
K (K) [K] {M}

Rotol (RX5/2 or RX5/5) propeller
K/M (K/M) [K/M] {M}

Merlin XX Engine
Engines & Things 72080 (Engines & Things 48103) [S] {M}

Rolls-Royce ejector, or 'Fish-tail' exhaust stacks could be (retro)fitted
K/M (K/M) [K/M] {K/M}

'Knuckled' Dowty oleo-pneumatic tailwheel
K (K) [K] {M}

Metal wing (eight-gun, with provision for twelve-gun, Browning)
K/M (K) [M] {K}

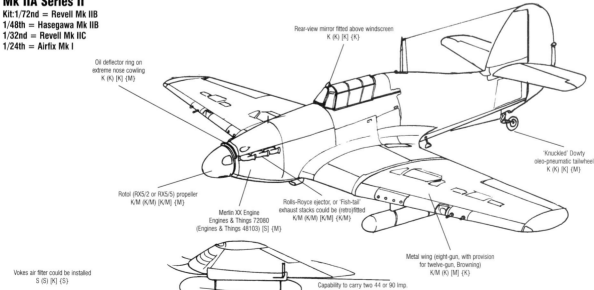

Vokes air filter could be installed
S (S) [K] {S}

Enlarged coolant capacity (some a/c only). No external differences

Capability to carry two 44 or 90 Imp. gallon fuel tanks under the wings
S (S) [S] {S}

Mk IIB (Fighter)

Kit: 1/72nd = Revell Mk IIB
1/48th = Hasegawa Mk IIB
1/32nd = Revell Mk IIC
1/24th = Airfix Mk I

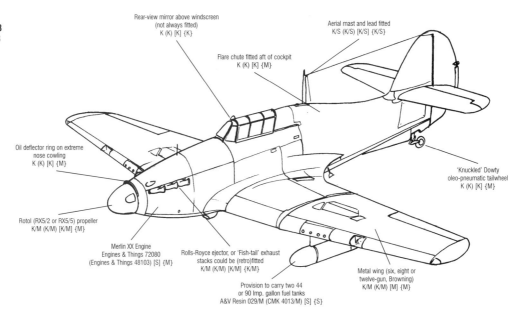

Rear-view mirror above windscreen
(not always fitted)
K (K) [K] {K}

Aerial mast and lead fitted
K/S (K/S) [K/S] {K/S}

Flare chute fitted aft of cockpit
K (K) [K] {M}

Oil deflector ring on extreme
nose cowling
K (K) [K] {M}

'Knuckled' Dowty
oleo-pneumatic tailwheel
K (K) [K] {M}

Rotol (RX5/2 or RX5/5) propeller
K/M (K/M) [K/M] {M}

Merlin XX Engine
Engines & Things 72080
(Engines & Things 48103) [S] {M}

Rolls-Royce ejector, or 'Fish-tail' exhaust
stacks could be (retro)fitted
K/M (K/M) [K/M] {K/M}

Metal wing (six, eight or
twelve-gun, Browning)
K/M (K/M) [M] {M}

Vokes air filter could be installed
(Airpart AP031) (S) [K] {S}

Provision to carry two 44
or 90 Imp. gallon fuel tanks
A&V Resin 029/M (CMK 4013/M) [S] {S}

Mk IIB (Fighter-bomber)

Kit: 1/72nd = Revell Mk IIB
1/48th = Hasegawa Mk IIB
1/32nd = Revell Mk IIC
1/24th = Airfix Mk I

Rear-view mirror above windscreen
(not always fitted)
K (K) [K] {K}

Oil deflector ring on
extreme nose cowling
K (K) [K] {M}

Rotol propeller
K (K) [K/M] {M}

'Knuckled' oleo-pneumatic tailwheel
K (K) [K] {M}

Merlin XX Engine
Engines & Things 72080 (Engines &
Things 48103) [S] {M}

Rolls-Royce ejector, or 'Fish-tail'
exhaust stacks could be (retro)fitted
K/M (K/M) [K/M] {K/M}

Capacity to carry two
44 or 90 Imp. gallon fuel tanks
A&V Resin 029/M (CMK 4013/M) [S] {S}

Vokes air filter could be installed
(Airpart AP031) (S) [K] {S}

Capability to carry two 250lb (later 500lb)
bombs under the wings
K (K) [S] {S}

Metal wing (six, eight or twelve-gun,
Browning) N.B. Only eight fitted
when 500lb bombs carried
K/M (K/M) [M] {M}

Mk IIC

Kit:1/72nd = Hasegawa Mk IIC
1/48th = Hasegawa Mk IIC
1/32nd = Revell Mk IIC
1/24th = Airfix Mk I

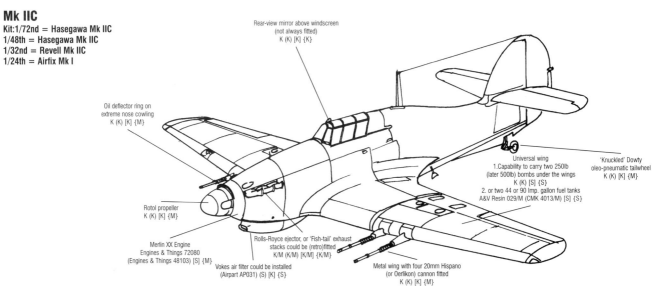

Rear-view mirror above windscreen
(not always fitted)
K (K) [K] {K}

Oil deflector ring on
extreme nose cowling
K (K) [K] {M}

Rotol propeller
K (K) [K] {M}

Merlin XX Engine
Engines & Things 72080
(Engines & Things 48103) [S] {M}

Rolls-Royce ejector, or 'Fish-tail' exhaust
stacks could be (retro)fitted
K/M (K/M) [K/M] {K/M}

Vokes air filter could be installed
(Airpart AP031) (S) [K] {S}

Universal wing
1.Capability to carry two 250lb
(later 500lb) bombs under the wings
K (K) [S] {S}
2. or two 44 or 90 Imp. gallon fuel tanks
A&V Resin 029/M (CMK 4013/M) [S] {S}

'Knuckled' Dowty
oleo-pneumatic tailwheel
K (K) [K] {M}

Metal wing with four 20mm Hispano
(or Oerlikon) cannon fitted
K (K) [K] {M}

Mk IIC 'Night Intruder'

Kit:1/72nd = Hasegawa Mk IIC
1/48th = Hasegawa Mk IIC
1/32nd = Revell Mk IIC
1/24th = Airfix Mk I

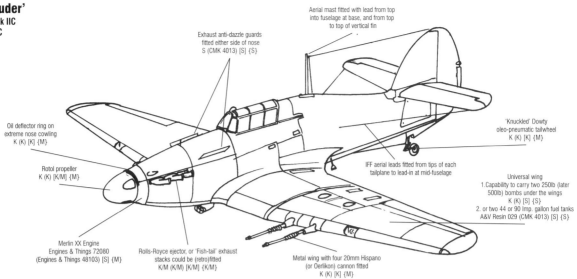

Aerial mast fitted with lead from top
into fuselage at base, and from top
to top of vertical fin

Exhaust anti-dazzle guards
fitted either side of nose
S (CMK 4013) [S] {S}

Oil deflector ring on
extreme nose cowling
K (K) [K] {M}

Rotol propeller
K (K) [K/M] {M}

'Knuckled' Dowty
oleo-pneumatic tailwheel
K (K) [K] {M}

IFF aerial leads fitted from tips of each
tailplane to lead-in at mid-fuselage

Universal wing
1.Capability to carry two 250lb (later
500lb) bombs under the wings
K (K) [S] {S}
2. or two 44 or 90 Imp. gallon fuel tanks
A&V Resin 029 (CMK 4013) [S] {S}

Merlin XX Engine
Engines & Things 72080
(Engines & Things 48103) [S] {M}

Rolls-Royce ejector, or 'Fish-tail' exhaust
stacks could be (retro)fitted
K/M (K/M) [K/M] {K/M}

Metal wing with four 20mm Hispano
(or Oerlikon) cannon fitted
K (K) [K] {M}

Mk IID

Kit:1/72nd = Hasegawa Mk IID
1/48th = Hasegawa Mk IID
1/32nd = Revell Mk IIC
1/24th = Airfix Mk I

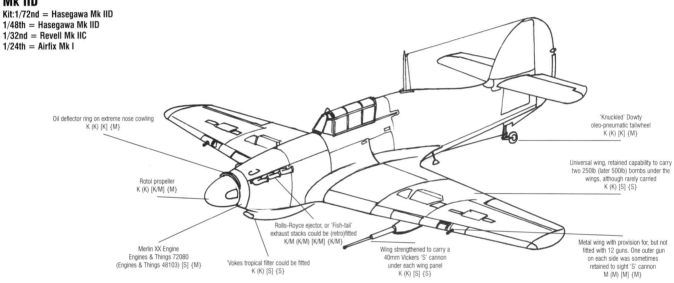

Oil deflector ring on extreme nose cowling
K (K) [K] {M}

'Knuckled' Dowty
oleo-pneumatic tailwheel
K (K) [K] {M}

Rotol propeller
K (K) [K/M] {M}

Universal wing, retained capability to carry
two 250lb (later 500lb) bombs under the
wings, although rarely carried
K (K) [S] {S}

Rolls-Royce ejector, or 'Fish-tail'
exhaust stacks could be (retro)fitted
K/M (K/M) [K/M] {K/M}

Merlin XX Engine
Engines & Things 72080
(Engines & Things 48103) [S] {M}

'Vokes tropical filter could be fitted
K (K) [S] {S}

Wing strengthened to carry a
40mm Vickers 'S' cannon
under each wing panel
K (K) [S] {S}

Metal wing with provision for, but not
fitted with 12 guns. One outer gun
on each side was sometimes
retained to sight 'S' cannon
M (M) [M] {M}

Mk IIE (*See Mk IV) - 2 Only built

Kit:1/72nd = Hasegawa Mk IIC
1/48th = Hasegawa Mk IIC
1/32nd = Revell Mk IIC
1/24th = Airfix Mk I

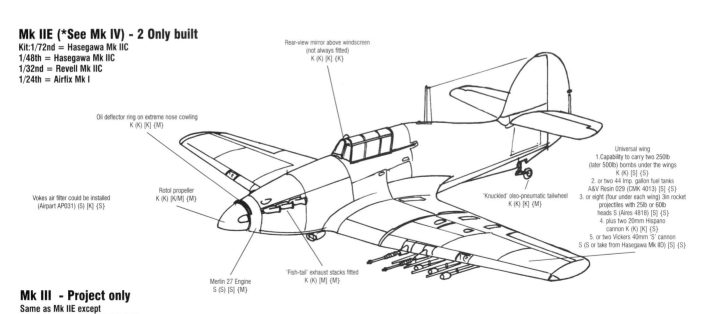

Rear-view mirror above windscreen
(not always fitted)
K (K) [K] {K}

Oil deflector ring on extreme nose cowling
K (K) [K] {M}

Vokes air filter could be installed
(Airpart AP031) (S) [K] {S}

Rotol propeller
K (K) [K/M] {M}

'Knuckled' oleo-pneumatic tailwheel
K (K) [K] {M}

Universal wing
1.Capability to carry two 250lb
(later 500lb) bombs under the wings
K (K) [S] {S}
2. or two 44 Imp. gallon fuel tanks
A&V Resin 029 (CMK 4013) [S] {S}
3. or eight (four under each wing) 3in rocket
projectiles with 25lb or 60lb
heads S (Aires 4818) [S] {S}
4. plus two 20mm Hispano
cannon K (K) [K] {S}
5. or two Vickers 40mm 'S' cannon
S (S or take from Hasegawa Mk IID) [S] {S}

Merlin 27 Engine
S (S) [S] {M}

'Fish-tail' exhaust stacks fitted
K (K) [M] {M}

Mk III - Project only

Same as Mk IIE except

Projected use of Packard-build R.R. Merlin 28
(no external differences). British propeller shaft
also meant that a standard Rotol propeller
could also be fitted

Mk IV

Kit:1/72nd = Hasegawa Mk IIC
1/48th = Hasegawa Mk IIC
1/32nd = Revell Mk IIC
1/24th = Airfix Mk I

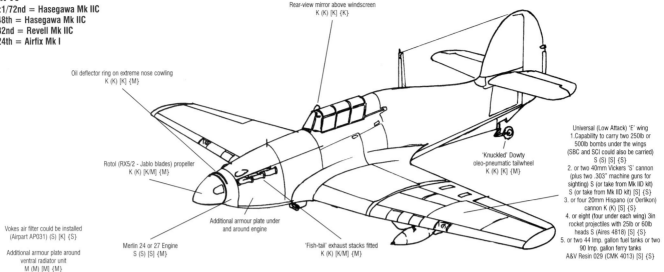

Rear-view mirror above windscreen
K (K) [K] {K}

Oil deflector ring on extreme nose cowling
K (K) [K] {M}

Rotol (RX5/2 - Jablo blades) propeller
K (K) [K/M] {M}

Vokes air filter could be installed
(Airpart AP031) (S) [K] {S}

Additional armour plate around
ventral radiator unit
M (M) [M] {M}

Additional armour plate under
and around engine

Merlin 24 or 27 Engine
S (S) [S] {M}

'Fish-tail' exhaust stacks fitted
K (K) [K/M] {M}

'Knuckled' Dowty
oleo-pneumatic tailwheel
K (K) [K] {M}

Universal (Low Attack) 'E' wing
1.Capability to carry two 250lb or
500lb bombs under the wings
(SBC and SCI could also be carried)
S (S) [S] {S}
2. or two 40mm Vickers 'S' cannon
(plus two .303" machine guns for
sighting) S (or take from Mk IID kit)
S (or take from Mk IID kit) [S] {S}
3. or four 20mm Hispano (or Oerlikon)
cannon K (K) [S] {S}
4. or eight (four under each wing) 3in
rocket projectiles with 25lb or 60lb
heads S (Aires 4818) [S] {S}
5. or two 44 Imp. gallon fuel tanks or two
90 Imp. gallon ferry tanks
A&V Resin 029 (CMK 4013) [S] {S}

Mk V - Three built, all converted from Mk IV's

Kit:1/72nd = Hasegawa Mk IIC or D
1/48th = Hasegawa Mk IIC or D
1/32nd = Revell Mk IIC
1/24th = Airfix Mk I

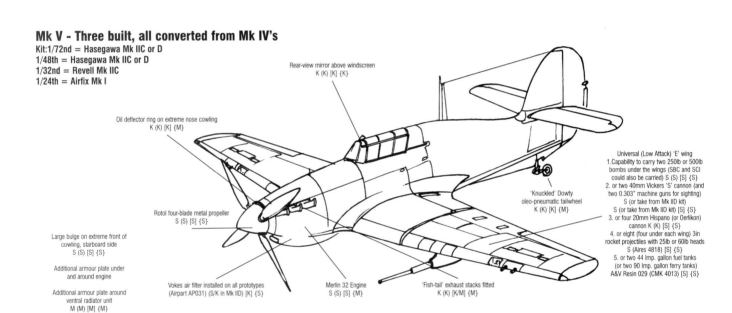

Rear-view mirror above windscreen
K (K) [K] {K}

Oil deflector ring on extreme nose cowling
K (K) [K] {M}

Large bulge on extreme front of
cowling, starboard side
S (S) [S] {S}

Additional armour plate under
and around engine

Additional armour plate around
ventral radiator unit
M (M) [M] {M}

Rotol four-blade metal propeller
S (S) [S] {S}

Vokes air filter installed on all prototypes
(Airpart AP031) (S/K in Mk IID) [K] {S}

Merlin 32 Engine
S (S) [S] {M}

'Fish-tail' exhaust stacks fitted
K (K) [K/M] {M}

'Knuckled' Dowty
oleo-pneumatic tailwheel
K (K) [K] {M}

Universal (Low Attack) 'E' wing
1.Capability to carry two 250lb or 500lb
bombs under the wings (SBC and SCI
could also be carried) S (S) [S] {S}
2. or two 40mm Vickers 'S' cannon (and
two 0.303" machine guns for sighting)
S (or take from Mk IID kit)
S (or take from Mk IID kit) [S] {S}
3. or four 20mm Hispano (or Oerlikon)
cannon K (K) [S] {S}
4. or eight (four under each wing) 3in
rocket projectiles with 25lb or 60lb heads
S (Aires 4818) [S] {S}
5. or two 44 Imp. gallon fuel tanks
(or two 90 Imp. gallon ferry tanks)
A&V Resin 029 (CMK 4013) [S] {S}

Mk X (Canadian)

Kit:1/72nd = Hasegawa Mk I (Late)
1/48th = Hasegawa Mk I or Airfix Mk I
1/32nd = Revell Mk IIC
1/24th = Airfix Mk I

Same as the Mk I (Late) except:

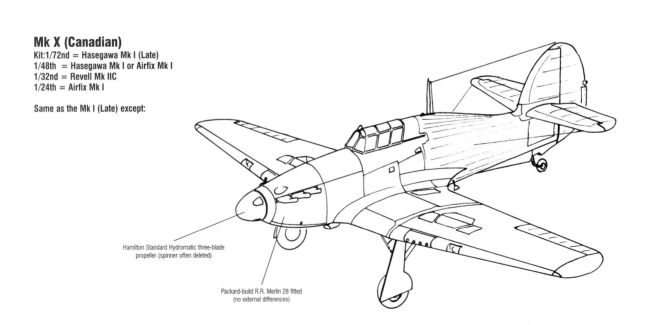

Hamilton Standard Hydromatic three-blade
propeller (spinner often deleted)

Packard-build R.R. Merlin 28 fitted
(no external differences)

Mk XI (Canadian)

Kit:1/72nd = Hasegawa Mk I (Late)
1/48th = Hasegawa Mk I or Airfix Mk I
1/32nd = Revell Mk IIC
1/24th = Airfix Mk I

Same as the Mk X except:

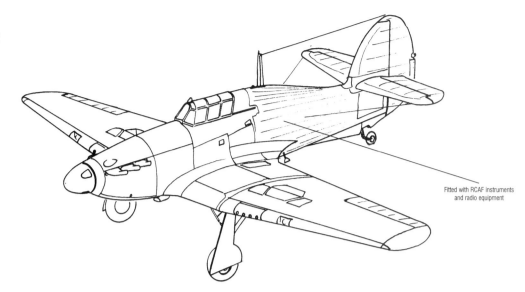

Fitted with RCAF instruments
and radio equipment

Featured 'pull-to-open' throttle system
(not used on British aircraft)

Some later passed to FAA and fitted
with twelve-gun wings and arrester
hooks as Sea Hurricane Mk XIB's
*See 'Sea Hurricanes'

Mk XII (Canadian)

Kit:1/72nd = Revell Mk IIB
1/48th = Hasegawa Mk IIB
1/32nd = Revell Mk IIC
1/24th = Airfix Mk I

Same as Mk IIA except:

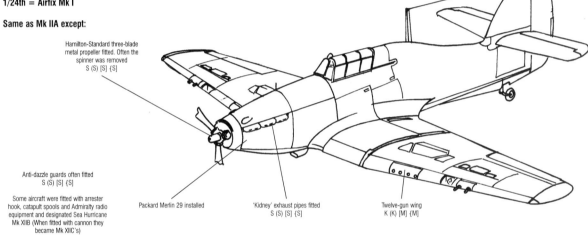

Hamilton-Standard three-blade
metal propeller fitted. Often the
spinner was removed
S (S) [S] {S}

Anti-dazzle guards often fitted
S (S) [S] {S}

Some aircraft were fitted with arrester
hook, catapult spools and Admiralty radio
equipment and designated Sea Hurricane
Mk XIIB (When fitted with cannon they
became Mk XIIC's)

Packard Merlin 29 installed

'Kidney' exhaust pipes fitted
S (S) [S] {S}

Twelve-gun wing
K (K) [M] {M}

Tactical-Reconnaissance (Tac R)

Tac R Mk I - Possibly 8 converted
Kit:1/72nd = Hasegawa Mk I (Late)
1/48th = Airfix Mk I
1/32nd = Revell Mk IIC
1/24th = Airfix Mk I

Same as a Mk I (Late) except:

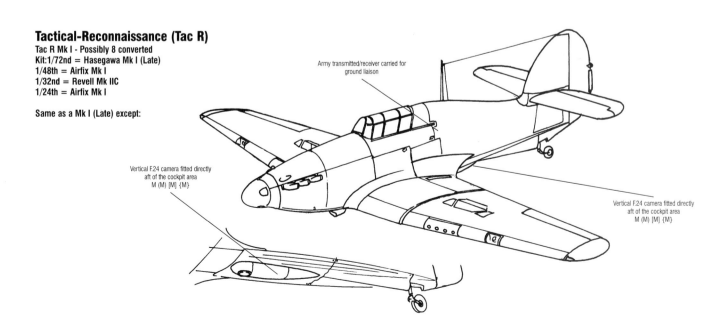

Army transmitted/receiver carried for
ground liaison

Vertical F.24 camera fitted directly
aft of the cockpit area
M (M) [M] {M}

Vertical F.24 camera fitted directly
aft of the cockpit area
M (M) [M] {M}

Tac R Mk IIB

Kit:1/72nd = Revell Mk IIB
1/48th = Hasegawa Mk IIB
1/32nd = Revell Mk IIC
1/24th = Airfix Mk I

Same as Mk IIB except:

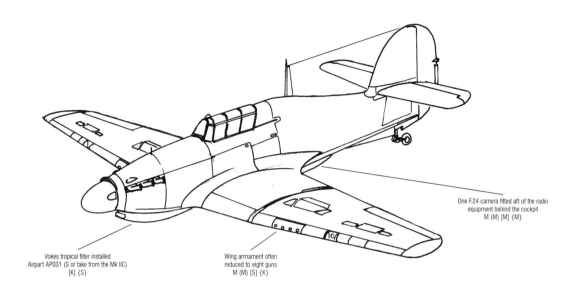

One F.24 camera fitted aft of the radio
equipment behind the cockpit
M (M) [M] {M}

Vokes tropical filter installed
Airpart AP031 (S or take from the Mk IIC)
[K] {S}

Wing armament often
reduced to eight guns
M (M) [S] {K}

Tac R Mk IIC

Kit:1/72nd = Hasegawa Mk IIC
1/48th = Hasegawa Mk IIC
1/32nd = Revell Mk IIC
1/24th = Airfix Mk I

Same as Mk IIC except:

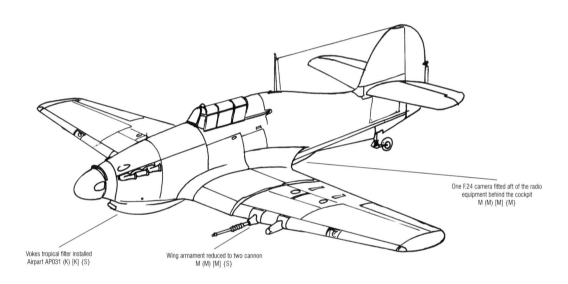

One F.24 camera fitted aft of the radio
equipment behind the cockpit
M (M) [M] {M}

Vokes tropical filter installed
Airpart AP031 (K) [K] {S}

Wing armament reduced to two cannon
M (M) [M] {S}

Photo-Reconnaissance (PR)

PR Mk I
Kit:1/72nd = Hasegawa Mk I (Late)
1/48th = Airfix Mk I
1/32nd = Revell Mk IIC
1/24th = Airifx Mk I

Same as a Mk I (Late) except:

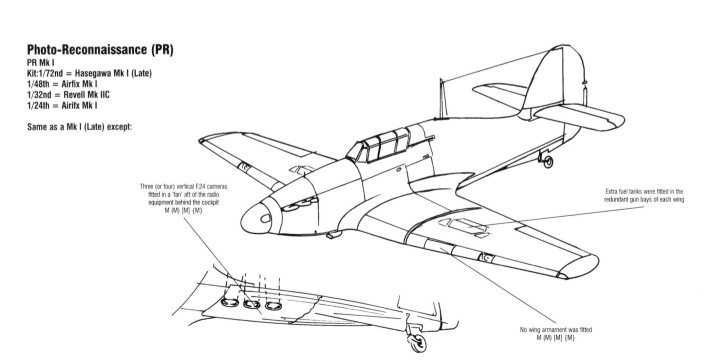

Three (or four) vertical F.24 cameras
fitted in a 'fan' aft of the radio
equipment behind the cockpit
M (M) [M] {M}

Extra fuel tanks were fitted in the
redundant gun bays of each wing

No wing armament was fitted
M (M) [M] {M}

PR Mk IIB

Kit:1/72nd = Revell Mk IIB
1/48th = Hasegawa Mk IIB
1/32nd = Revell Mk IIC
1/24th = Airfix Mk I

Same as Mk IIB except:

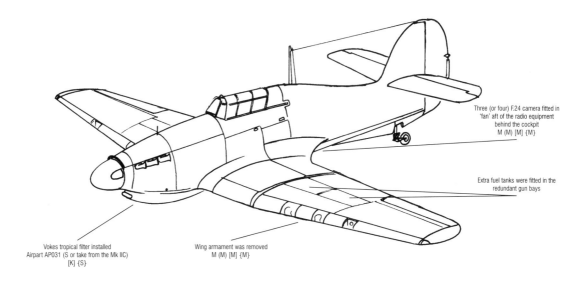

Three (or four) F.24 camera fitted in
'fan' aft of the radio equipment
behind the cockpit
M (M) [M] {M}

Extra fuel tanks were fitted in the
redundant gun bays

Vokes tropical filter installed
Airpart AP031 (S or take from the Mk IIC)
[K] {S}

Wing armament was removed
M (M) [M] {M}

PR Mk IIC

Kit:1/72nd = Hasegawa Mk IIC
1/48th = Hasegawa Mk IIC
1/32nd = Revell Mk IIC
1/24th = Airfix Mk I

Same as Mk IIC except:

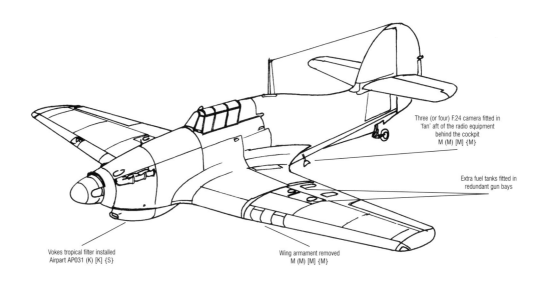

Three (or four) F.24 camera fitted in
'fan' aft of the radio equipment
behind the cockpit
M (M) [M] {M}

Extra fuel tanks fitted in
redundant gun bays

Vokes tropical filter installed
Airpart AP031 (K) [K] {S}

Wing armament removed
M (M) [M] {M}

Meteorological Flights (Met)

Met Mk I
Converted from Mk I
Kit: 1/72nd = Airfix Mk I or Hasegawa Mk I (Late)
1/48th = Airfix or Hasegawa Mk I
1/32nd = Revell Mk II
1/24th = Airfix Mk I

Same as the Mk I (Late) except:

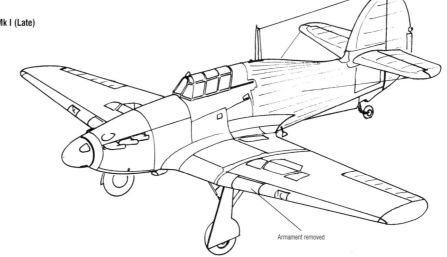

Vokes tropical filter fitted
Airpart AP031 (S or take from
the Hasegawa Mk IID) [K] {S}

Meteorological equipment mounted
above the starboard wing
S (S) [S] {S}

Armament removed

Met Mk IIC

Same as Mk IIC except
Kit:1/72nd = Hasegawa Mk IIC
1/48th = Hasegawa Mk IIC
1/32nd = Revell Mk IIC
1/24th = Airfix Mk I

Same as Mk IIC except:

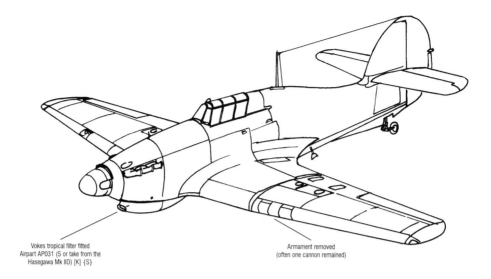

Meteorological equipment mounted
above the starboard wing
S (S) [S] {S}

Vokes tropical filter fitted
Airpart AP031 (S or take from the
Hasegawa Mk IID) [K] {S}

Armament removed
(often one cannon remained)

Night Fighters

NF Mk IIB
Kit: 1/72nd = Revell
1/48th = Hasegawa
1/32nd = Revell
1/24th = Airfix

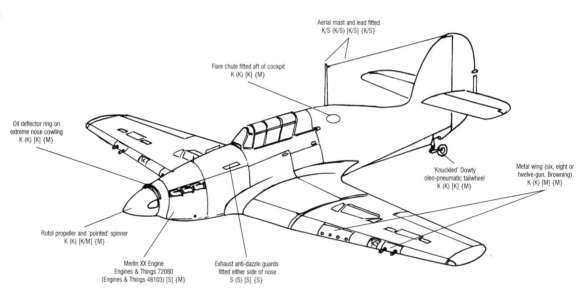

Aerial mast and lead fitted
K/S (K/S) [K/S] {K/S}

Flare chute fitted aft of cockpit
K (K) [K] {M}

Oil deflector ring on
extreme nose cowling
K (K) [K] {M}

'Knuckled' Dowty
oleo-pneumatic tailwheel
K (K) [K] {M}

Metal wing (six, eight or
twelve-gun, Browning)
K (K) [M] {M}

Rotol propeller and 'pointed' spinner
K (K) [K/M] {M}

Merlin XX Engine
Engines & Things 72080
(Engines & Things 48103) [S] {M}

Exhaust anti-dazzle guards
fitted either side of nose
S (S) [S] {S}

NF Mk IIC

Kit:1/72nd = Hasegawa Mk IIC
1/48th = Hasegawa Mk IIC
1/32nd = Revell Mk IIC
1/24th = Airfix Mk I

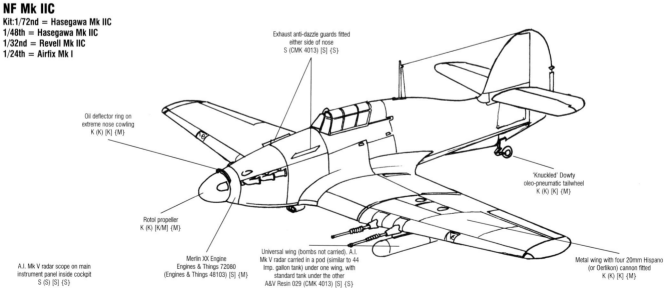

Exhaust anti-dazzle guards fitted
either side of nose
S (CMK 4013) [S] {S}

Oil deflector ring on
extreme nose cowling
K (K) [K] {M}

'Knuckled' Dowty
oleo-pneumatic tailwheel
K (K) [K] {M}

Rotol propeller
K (K) [K/M] {M}

A.I. Mk V radar scope on main
instrument panel inside cockpit
S (S) [S] {S}

Merlin XX Engine
Engines & Things 72080
(Engines & Things 48103) [S] {M}

Universal wing (bombs not carried). A.I.
Mk V radar carried in a pod (similar to 44
Imp. gallon tank) under one wing, with
standard tank under the other
A&V Resin 029 (CMK 4013) [S] {S}

Metal wing with four 20mm Hispano
(or Oerlikon) cannon fitted
K (K) [K] {M}

SEA HURRICANE

Sea Hurricane Mk IA

Kit: 1/72nd = Airfix Mk I or Hasegawa Mk I (Late)
1/48th = Airfix or Hasegawa Mk I
1/32nd = Revell Mk IIC
1/24th = Airfix Mk I

Same as standard Mk I (Late) except:

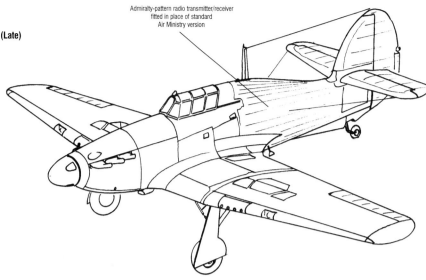

Admiralty-pattern radio transmitter/receiver
fitted in place of standard
Air Ministry version

Catapult spools fitted either side
of ventral radiator
S (S) [S] {S}

Pick-ups for the CAM launch platform
fitted under wings and fuselage
S (S) [S] {S}

Sea Hurricane Mk IB

Kit:1/72nd = Hasegawa Mk I (Late)
1/48th = Hasegawa Mk I or Airfix Mk I
1/32nd = Revell Mk IIC
1/24th = Airfix Mk I

Same as Mk I (Late) except:

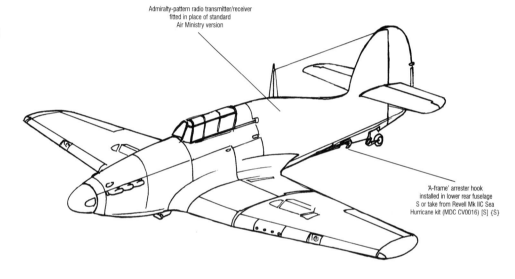

Admiralty-pattern radio transmitter/receiver
fitted in place of standard
Air Ministry version

'A-frame' arrester hook
installed in lower rear fuselage
S or take from Revell Mk IIC Sea
Hurricane kit (MDC CV0016) [S] {S}

Catapult spools fitted either side
of ventral radiator
S (S) [S] {S}

Note: Some Mk IIA Series 2 machines
were also converted in the above
manner, and were also refered
to as Sea Hurricane Mk IB's!

Sea Hurricane Mk IC

Kit:1/72nd = Hasegawa Mk I (Late)
1/48th = Hasegawa Mk I or Airfix Mk I
1/32nd = Revell Mk IIC
1/24th = Airfix Mk I

Same as Mk I (Late) except:

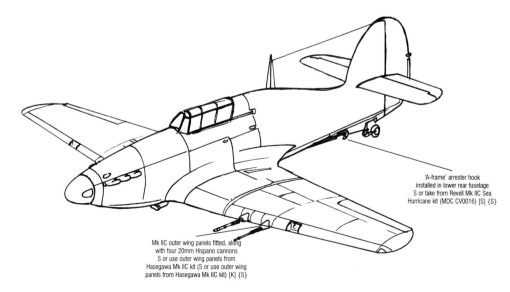

'A-frame' arrester hook
installed in lower rear fuselage
S or take from Revell Mk IIC Sea
Hurricane kit (MDC CV0016) [S] {S}

Catapult spools fitted either side
of ventral radiator
S (S) [S] {S}

Admiralty pattern radio transmitter/receiver
fitted in place of standard Air
Ministry version

Mk IIC outer wing panels fitted, along
with four 20mm Hispano cannons
S or use outer wing panels from
Hasegawa Mk IIC kit (S or use outer wing
panels from Hasegawa Mk IIC kit) [K] {S}

Sea Hurricane Mk IIC

Kit:1/72nd = Hasegawa Mk IIC
1/48th = Hasegawa Mk IIC
1/32nd = Revell Mk IIC
1/24th = Airfix Mk I

Same as Mk IIC except:

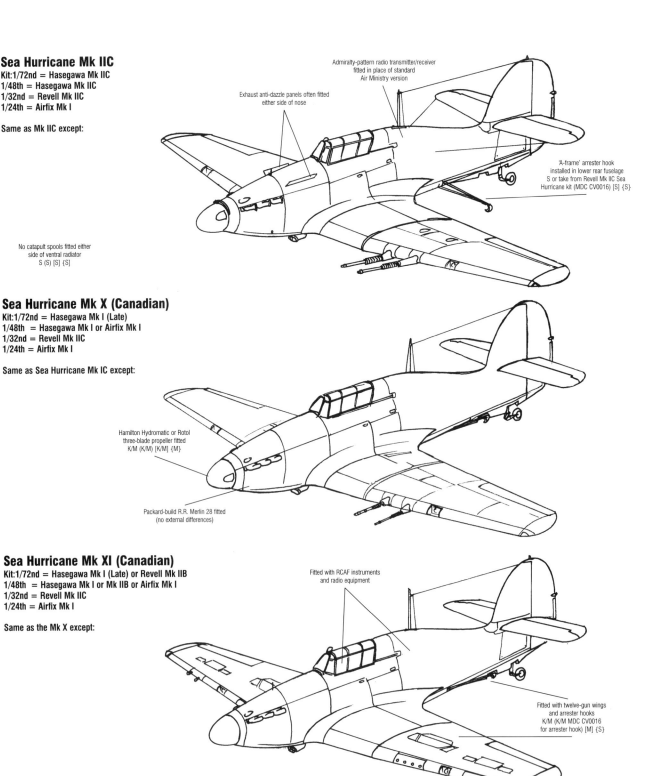

Admiralty-pattern radio transmitter/receiver
fitted in place of standard
Air Ministry version

Exhaust anti-dazzle panels often fitted
either side of nose

'A-frame' arrester hook
installed in lower rear fuselage
S or take from Revell Mk IIC Sea
Hurricane kit (MDC CV0016) [S] {S}

No catapult spools fitted either
side of ventral radiator
S (S) [S] {S}

Sea Hurricane Mk X (Canadian)

Kit:1/72nd = Hasegawa Mk I (Late)
1/48th = Hasegawa Mk I or Airfix Mk I
1/32nd = Revell Mk IIC
1/24th = Airfix Mk I

Same as Sea Hurricane Mk IC except:

Hamilton Hydromatic or Rotol
three-blade propeller fitted
K/M (K/M) [K/M] {M}

Packard-build R.R. Merlin 28 fitted
(no external differences)

Sea Hurricane Mk XI (Canadian)

Kit:1/72nd = Hasegawa Mk I (Late) or Revell Mk IIB
1/48th = Hasegawa Mk I or Mk IIB or Airfix Mk I
1/32nd = Revell Mk IIC
1/24th = Airfix Mk I

Same as the Mk X except:

Fitted with RCAF instruments
and radio equipment

Fitted with twelve-gun wings
and arrester hooks
K/M (K/M MDC CV0016
for arrester hook) [M] {S}

Sea Hurricane Mk XIIA (Canadian)

Kit:1/72nd = Hasegawa Mk I (Late) or Revell Mk IIB
1/48th = Hasegawa Mk I/Mk IIB or Airfix Mk I
1/32nd = Revell Mk IIC
1/24th = Airfix Mk I

Same as Mk IIA except:

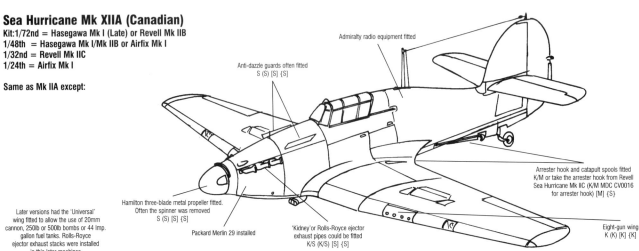

Admiralty radio equipment fitted

Anti-dazzle guards often fitted
S (S) [S] {S}

Later versions had the 'Universal'
wing fitted to allow the use of 20mm
cannon, 250lb or 500lb bombs or 44 Imp.
gallon fuel tanks. Rolls-Royce
ejector exhaust stacks were installed
in this later machines

Hamilton three-blade metal propeller fitted.
Often the spinner was removed
S (S) [S] {S}

Packard Merlin 29 installed

'Kidney' or Rolls-Royce ejector
exhaust pipes could be fitted
K/S (K/S) [S] {S}

Arrester hook and catapult spools fitted
K/M or take the arrester hook from Revell
Sea Hurricane Mk IIC (K/M MDC CV0016
for arrester hook) [M] {S}

Eight-gun wing
K (K) [K] {K}

Sea Hurricane Mk XIIB (Canadian)

Kit: 1/72nd = Revell Mk IIB
1/48th = Hasegawa Mk IIB
1/32nd = Revell Mk IIC
1/24th = Airfix Mk I

Same as the Mk IIB except:

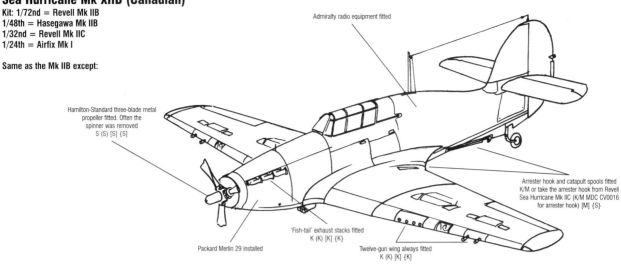

Admiralty radio equipment fitted

Hamilton-Standard three-blade metal propeller fitted. Often the spinner was removed
S (S) [S] {S}

Arrester hook and catapult spools fitted K/M or take the arrester hook from Revell Sea Hurricane Mk IIC (K/M MDC CV0016 for arrester hook) [M] {S}

'Fish-tail' exhaust stacks fitted
K (K) [K] {K}

Packard Merlin 29 installed

Twelve-gun wing always fitted
K (K) [K] {K}

Sea Hurricane Mk XIIC (Canadian)

Kit: 1/72nd = Revell Mk IIC
1/48th = Hasegawa Mk IIC
1/32nd = Revell Mk IIC
1/24th = Airfix Mk I

Same as the Mk IIC except:

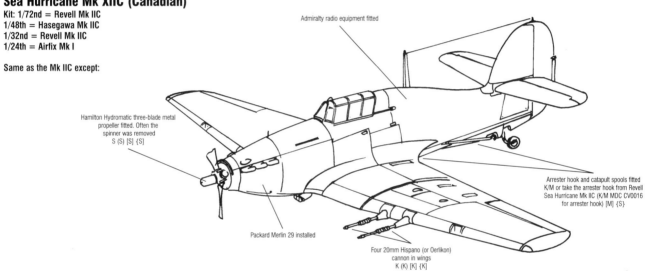

Admiralty radio equipment fitted

Hamilton Hydromatic three-blade metal propeller fitted. Often the spinner was removed
S (S) [S] {S}

Arrester hook and catapult spools fitted K/M or take the arrester hook from Revell Sea Hurricane Mk IIC (K/M MDC CV0016 for arrester hook) [M] {S}

Packard Merlin 29 installed

Four 20mm Hispano (or Oerlikon) cannon in wings
K (K) [K] {K}

TRAINERS
Persian Two-seat Trainer (Mk IIC) - Initial version

Kit:1/72nd = Hasegawa Mk IIC
1/48th = Hasegawa Mk IIC
1/32nd = Revell Mk IIC
1/24th Airfix Mk I

Same as Mk IIC except:

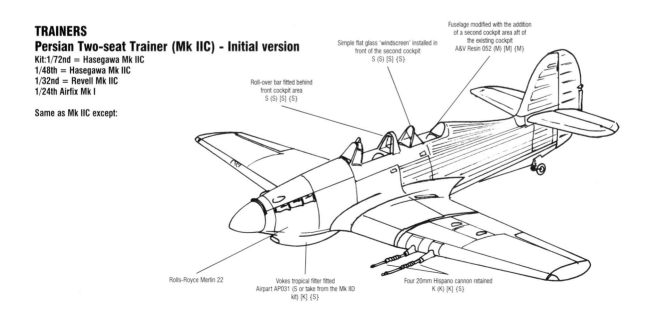

Fuselage modified with the addition of a second cockpit area aft of the existing cockpit
A&V Resin 052 (M) [M] {M}

Simple flat glass 'windscreen' installed in front of the second cockpit
S (S) [S] {S}

Roll-over bar fitted behind front cockpit area
S (S) [S] {S}

Rolls-Royce Merlin 22

Vokes tropical filter fitted Airpart AP031 (S or take from the Mk IID kit) [K] {S}

Four 20mm Hispano cannon retained
K (K) [K] {S}

Persian Two-seat Trainer (Mk IIC) - Later version

Kit:1/72nd = Hasegawa Mk IIC
1/48th = Hasegawa Mk IIC
1/32nd = Revell Mk IIC
1/24th Airfix Mk I

Same as Mk IIC except:

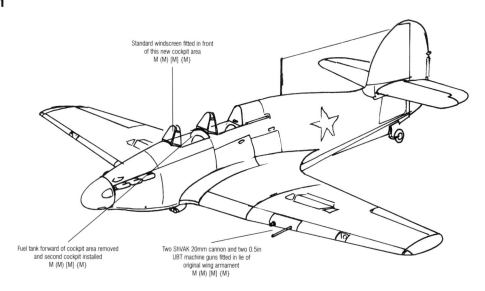

Modified Tempest canopy installed
over the rear cockpit
Falcon Clear-Vax Set 2 (Aeroclub C076)
[N/A] {N/A}

Fuselage modified with the addition
of a second cockpit area aft of
the existing cockpit
A&V Resin 052 (M) [M] {M}

Roll-over bar fitted behind
front cockpit area
S (S) [S] {S}

Vokes tropical filter fitted
Airpart AP031 (S or take from the Mk IID
kit) [K] {S}

The four 20mm cannon were deleted and
the outlets covered over
M (M) [M] {S}

Russian Conversion #1

Kit:1/72nd = Revell Mk IIB
1/48th = Hasegawa Mk IIB
1/32nd = Revell Mk IIC
1/24th = Airfix Mk I

Same as Mk IIB except:

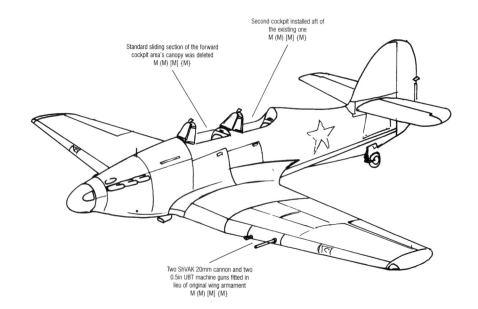

Standard windscreen fitted in front
of this new cockpit area
M (M) [M] {M}

Fuel tank forward of cockpit area removed
and second cockpit installed
M (M) [M] {M}

Two ShVAK 20mm cannon and two 0.5in
UBT machine guns fitted in lie of
original wing armament
M (M) [M] {M}

Russian Conversion #2

Kit:1/72nd = Revell Mk IIB
1/48th = Hasegawa Mk IIB
1/32nd = Revell Mk IIC
1/24th = Airfix Mk I

Same as Mk IIB except:

Second cockpit installed aft of
the existing one
M (M) [M] {M}

Standard sliding section of the forward
cockpit area's canopy was deleted
M (M) [M] {M}

Two ShVAK 20mm cannon and two
0.5in UBT machine guns fitted in
lieu of original wing armament
M (M) [M] {M}

EXPERIMENTS, PROJECTS & RESEARCH
Mk I with skis (Canadian)

Kit: 1/72nd = Hasegawa Mk I (Late)
1/48th = Hasegawa Mk I or Airfix Mk I
1/32nd = Revell Mk IIC
1/24th = Airfix Mk I

Same as the Mk I (Late) except:

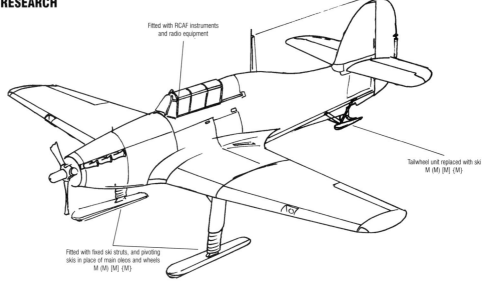

Fitted with RCAF instruments
and radio equipment

Tailwheel unit replaced with ski
M (M) [M] {M}

Note: Photographic evidence does not
seem to support the view that the
undercarriage units in these conversions
were skinned over. It is therefore believed
that the oleo and wheel was removed
from the bay, and the undercarriage doors
fixed in the 'up' position

Fitted with fixed ski struts, and pivoting
skis in place of main oleos and wheels
M (M) [M] {M}

Mk X with skis (Canadian)

Kit: 1/72nd = Hasegawa Mk I (Late)
1/48th = Hasegawa Mk I or Airfix Mk I
1/32nd = Revell Mk IIC
1/24th = Airfix Mk I

Same as the Mk X except:

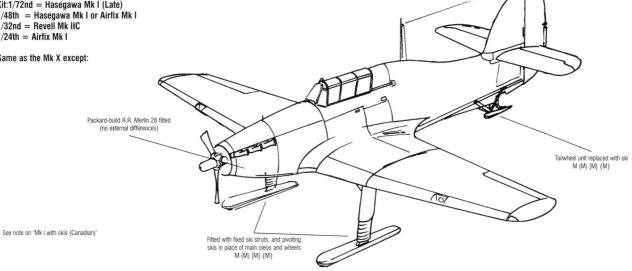

Packard-build R.R. Merlin 28 fitted
(no external differences)

Tailwheel unit replaced with ski
M (M) [M] {M}

See note on 'Mk I with skis (Canadian)'

Fitted with fixed ski struts, and pivoting
skis in place of main oleos and wheels
M (M) [M] {M}

Mk XII with skis (Canadian)

Kit: 1/72nd = Revell Mk IIB
1/48th = Hasegawa Mk IIB
1/32nd = Revell Mk IIC
1/24th = Airfix Mk I

Same as Mk XIIB except:

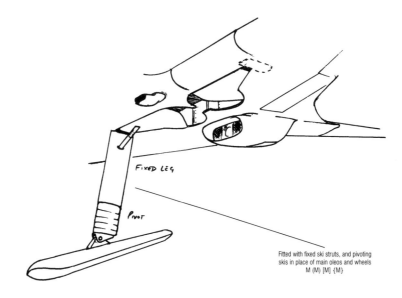

FIXED LEG

PIVOT

Tailwheel unit replaced with ski
M (M) [M] {M}

See note on 'Mk I with skis (Canadian)'

Fitted with fixed ski struts, and pivoting
skis in place of main oleos and wheels
M (M) [M] {M}

'Slip-wing' F.H. 40 (Mk I)

Kit: 1/72nd = Airfix Mk I or Hasegawa Mk I (Late)
1/48th = Airfix or Hasegawa Mk I
1/32nd = Revell Mk II
1/24th = Airfix Mk I

Same as Mk I (Late) except:

Dorsal aerial mast deleted
M (M) [M] {M}

Ventral 'pole' antenna mast installed with
aerial lead going into small pole
mast just forward of tailwheel
M (M) [M] {M}

Note:
In his 'Constant-Scale' column within RAF
Flying Review, August 1963, Philip Burden
stated that the "hinge lines of the elevators
should be altered because the elevators of
the 'Slip Wing' Hurricane were increased
in area by some ten percent". Detailed
studies of the photographs of the F.H.40
do not support this view, and the well-
known underside photograph of this
machine shows that the hinge lines of the
elevators are in exactly the same position
as that of all other Hurricanes, and it is
therefore this author's view that the
F.H.40's modifications did not include any
increase in the size of the elevators

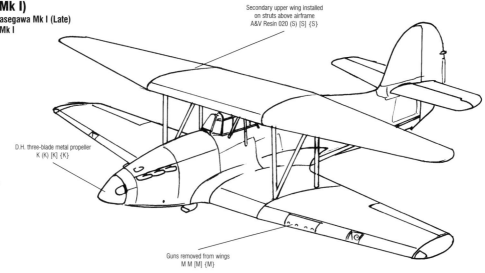

Secondary upper wing installed
on struts above airframe
A&V Resin 020 (S) [S] {S}

D.H. three-blade metal propeller
K (K) [K] {K}

Guns removed from wings
M M [M] {M}

Laminar-flow Wing (Mk IIB)

Kit: 1/72nd = Revell Mk IIB
1/48th = Hasegawa Mk IIB
1/32nd = Revell Mk IIC
1/24th = Airfix Mk I

Same as Mk IIB except:

IFF antenna added on centreline,
aft of ventral radiator
S (S) [S] {S}

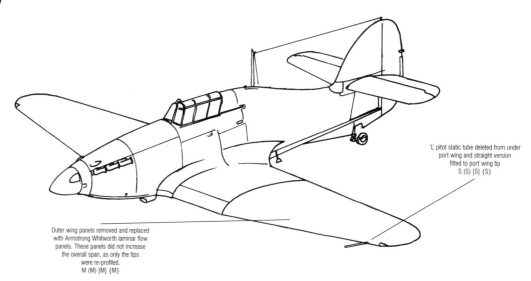

'L' pitot static tube deleted from under
port wing and straight version
fitted to port wing tip
S (S) [S] {S}

Outer wing panels removed and replaced
with Armstrong Whitworth laminar flow
panels. These panels did not increase
the overall span, as only the tips
were re-profiled.
M (M) [M] {M}

'Long Tom' rocket (Mk IV)

Kit: 1/72nd = Hasegawa Mk IIC
1/48th = Hasegawa Mk IIC
1/32nd = Revell Mk IIC
1/24th = Airfix Mk I

Same as Mk IV except:

IFF antenna added on centreline,
aft of ventral radiator
S (S) [S] {S}

Note:
There seems to be some confusion in
regard to this weapon, as Francis K.
Mason recently stated that this weapon
was also tested under a D.H. Mosquito
(NT220). However that machine was
involved in the trials of 'Uncle Tom'
rockets at A&AEE. The 'Long Tom' is
listed as being a 500lb (227kg) weapon
powered by five 3' solid fuel motors, while
'Uncle Tom' was an 11" rocket, powered
by four solid fuel motors, and two were
test fired from under NT220.
Either 'Long Tom' is being confused with
'Uncle Tom', or NT220 was not involved
with the trials of this weapon

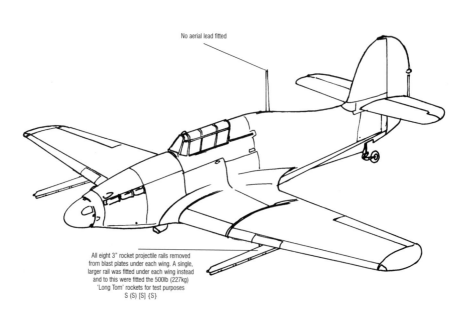

No aerial lead fitted

All eight 3" rocket projectile rails removed
from blast plates under each wing. A single,
larger rail was fitted under each wing instead
and to this were fitted the 500lb (227kg)
'Long Tom' rockets for test purposes
S (S) [S] {S}

Detailing

O ne of the most complex areas to deal with in any modelling project is that of interior (and exterior) detail. What precisely is in the cockpit? What do the interior of the wheel wells look like? etc are all questions which modellers make. It can be a time-consuming process gathering all the information you need to attempt to detail any subject, so what we are offering in this chapter is a concise (ish!) section dealing with all those areas of the subject that you will be wanting to know about.

Cockpit Interior • 1

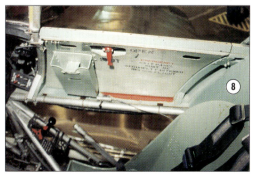

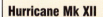

See also the Interior Cockpit artwork on pages 59 to 64.

Hurricane Mk XII
(The Fighter Collection, Duxford)

• 1 This view at the bulkhead behind the seat on the Mk XII shows the locker access panel fitted in this example. Originally this area was armour plate. The blue nylon straps are also a modern addition to this machine (© R.A. Franks)

• 2 A look down into the seat pan. Apart from the straps (which are modern to allow this machine to be flown), the area is very similar to a wartime configuration example (© R.A. Franks)

• 3 The port cockpit side of the Mk XII (© R.A. Franks)

• 4 A look towards the back of the port cockpit side (© R.A. Franks)

• 5 The starboard cockpit side of the Mk XII (© R.A. Franks)

• 6 Overall look at the instrument panel in the Mk XII. Very few of the instruments have been replaced, even though this machine is currently airworthy (© R.A. Franks)

• 7 The mounting bar for the gun sight above the instrument panel (© R.A. Franks)

• 8 The 'knock-out' door on the starboard cockpit side (© R.A. Franks)

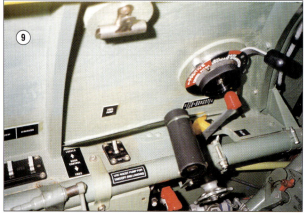

Hurricane Mk XII
(Museum of Flying, Santa Monica, USA)

•**9** Detail look at the port side of the cockpit. The throttle lever can be seen in the middle of the photo, with the propeller pitch control above, and in front of it. The 'bulldog' clip above the throttle is not a 'standard' fitment! (© J. Roeder)

•**10** A look down at the starboard side of the cockpit. The lever is for the adjustment of the seat. The undercarriage selection lever can be seen on the right and the gauge between the rudder 'kick-plates' is for brake pressure (© J. Roeder)

•**11** The instrument panel. Note the P series compass on the lower, centre, edge and the blind flying panel in the middle of the main panel (© J. Roeder)

•**12** The upper port cockpit side, showing the fuel tank selector switch (lower, middle), the fire extinguisher switch and the undercarriage position indicator (top right) (© J. Roeder)

•**13** The P series compass under the centre of the main instrument panel (© J. Roeder)

•**14** The upper corner of the starboard side of the main instrument panel. The RPM indicator (top left), boost gauge, Oil pressure gauge, fuel contents gauge, oil temperature indicator and the radiator temperature gauge can all be seen (© J. Roeder)

•**15** Close-up of the rudder pedal fitted to the Mk XII (© J. Roeder)

•**16** The brake pressure gauge that is situated between the 'kick-plates' for the rudder pedals (© J. Roeder)

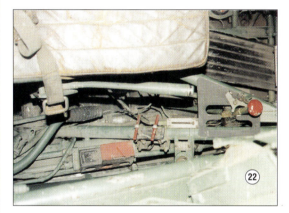

Hurricane Mk I

(Royal Air Force Museum, Hendon)

• **17** The port sidewall of the Mk I (© R.A. Franks)

• **18** The main instrument panel of the Mk I (© R.A. Franks)

• **19** The Mk II reflector gunsight fitted to the Mk I (© R.A. Franks)

• **20** The area behind the pilot's head, including the seat harness attachment point (© R.A. Franks)

• **21** An overall view of the pilot's seat (© R.A. Franks)

• **22** The seat adjustment lever (middle), undercarriage selector (right) and twin 'T' handles for the landing flares can all be seen here (© R.A. Franks)

Hurricane Mk IIA Series 2 (or Mk XII?)

(USAF Museum, USA)

• **23** An overall view of the cockpit forward section (© F.W. Coffman)

• **24** The main instrument panel and control column (© F.W. Coffman)

• **25** The port sidewall and seat of the Mk IIA. It is likely that this is a Canadian-built Mk XII, as the aluminium seat is certainly not the usual sort seen in British produced examples (© F.W. Coffman)

• **27** The 'knock-out' escape door fitted to all Hurricanes. The only thing missing from this genuine example is the conversion chart on the far right

• **28** This example of the charts on the 'knock-out' door on the Hurricane illustrate those missing on the previous example

Hurricane Mk XII

(Museum of Flying, Santa Monica, USA)

•1 The battery access panel and upper hand hold
(© J. Roeder)

•2 The foot step on the lower edge of the port fuselage side
(© J. Roeder)

•3 Close-up of the anti-dazzle guard on the nose. Note also the square style of rear-view mirror above the windscreen
(© J. Roeder)

Hurricane Mk XII

(Canadian Warplane Heritage)

•4 The starboard side of the Mk XII with all the access panels removed *(© F.W. Coffman)*

•5 The port fuselage side with all the access panels removed *(© F.W. Coffman)*

•6 Another view of the exposed starboard side
(© F.W. Coffman)

Hurricane Mk XII

(The Fighter Collection, Duxford)

•7 This is the support tubes at the lower rear edge of either side of the fuselage
(© R.A. Franks)

•8 With the lower decking removed from the fuselage, this is what the support tube looks like *(© R.A. Franks)*

•9 A very unusual look up into the upper rear decking of the fuselage *(© R.A. Franks)*

•10 Although not original, this shot gives some impression of how the radio 'crate' was installed *(© R.A. Franks)*

•11 Part of the radio equipment forward of the 'crate' on the starboard fuselage side *(© R.A. Franks)*

•12 Looking further forward on the starboard side, you can see much of the hydraulic pipework as well as the heating pipe coming from the ventral radiator *(© R.A. Franks)*

•13 The exposed port fuselage side showing all the electrical distribution connections *(© R.A. Franks)*

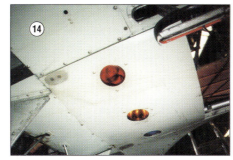

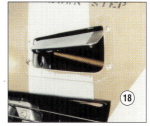

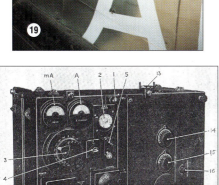

Hurricane Mk XII

•**14** The three downward identification lights aft of the ventral radiator *(© R.A. Franks)*

•**15** This is what the interior of the ventral fuselage looks like, with the three identification lamps visible *(© R.A. Franks)*

•**16** A look up into the foot step housing *(© R.A. Franks)*

•**17** The area directly aft of the battery housing on the port fuselage side *(© R.A. Franks)*

•**18** The hand hold on port side. The line inside operates the foot step *(© R.A. Franks)*

Hurricane Mk I
(Royal Air Force Museum, Hendon)

•**19** A view of the battery access panel on the port fuselage side *(© R.A. Franks)*

•**20** A different style of foot step fitted to this early mark *(© R.A. Franks)*

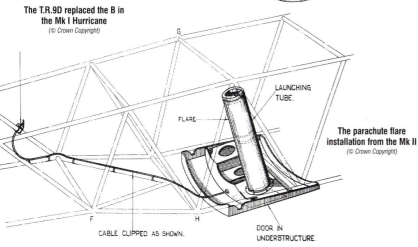

The T.R.9D replaced the B in the Mk I Hurricane
(© Crown Copyright)

The parachute flare chute
(© Crown Copyright)

Pilot's seat from the Mk I
(© Crown Copyright)

LAUNCHING TUBE.

FLARE

The parachute flare installation from the Mk II
(© Crown Copyright)

CABLE CLIPPED AS SHOWN.

DOOR IN UNDERSTRUCTURE.

The original T.R. 9B used in the early Hurricane
(© Crown Copyright)

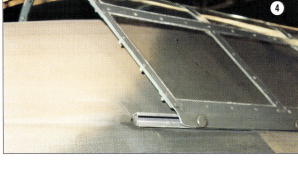

Hurricane Mk XII
(Museum of Flying, Santa Monica, USA)

•1 This shot gives you some idea of the placement and style of the rails for the canopy
(© J. Roeder)

Hurricane Mk II
(National Aviation Museum, Ottawa, Canada)

•2 An overall view of the canopy (© F.W. Coffman)

Hurricane Mk XII
(Canadian Warplane Heritage)

•3 Overall view of the cockpit area (© F.W. Coffman)

Hurricane Mk XII
(The Fighter Collection, Duxford)

•4 A good view of the canopy rail with the canopy fully back
(© R.A. Franks)

•5 A nice shot of the windscreen fitted to this machine (© R.A. Franks)

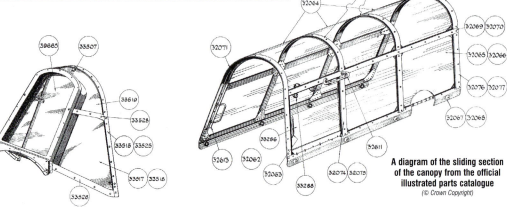

A diagram of the sliding section of the canopy from the official illustrated parts catalogue
(© Crown Copyright)

Official diagram of the windscreen fitted with external armour
(© Crown Copyright)

The early style of canopy (Mk I) with the addition of external armour plate
(© Crown Copyright)

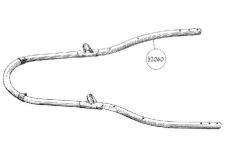

The demisting tube fitted inside the windscreen of the Hurricane
(© Crown Copyright)

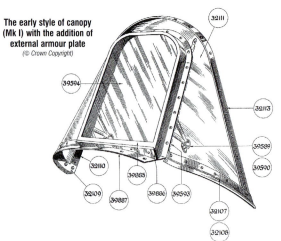

Radiator • 1

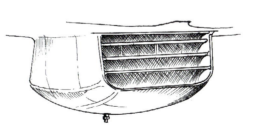

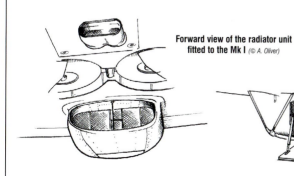

The original radiator unit fitted to
the prototype *(© A. Oliver)*

Forward view of the radiator unit
fitted to the Mk I *(© A. Oliver)*

Two view of the radiator fitted
to the Mk II *(© A. Oliver)*

Hurricane Mk XII
(The Fighter Collection,
Duxford)

• **1** A view of the stencil
applied to both side of the
ventral radiator unit
(© R.A. Franks)

• **2** A view into the back of the
radiator unit *(© R.A. Franks)*

• **3** View of the ventral radiator
shows the support struts
inside the lip of the unit, and
the actuating rod *(© R.A. Franks)*

• **4** A close-up into the rear of
the radiator, here can be seen
the support strut (foreground)
and the actuating rod
(background) *(© R.A. Franks)*

Hurricane Mk XII
(Museum of Flying, Santa
Monica, USA)

• **5** A clear view into the back
of the radiator unit in this
machine. Note the central
(round) oil cooler within the
main glycol engine coolant
matrix *(© J. Roeder)*

Hurricane Mk XII
(Canadian Warplane Heritage)

• **6** The radiator unit in this
machine has either flattened
tubes, or flight wires installed
as the rear support struts. The
actuating rods remain the
same style though *(© D. Frowen)*

Hurricane Mk I
(Royal Air Force Museum,
Hendon)

• **7** A clear front view of the
radiator unit installed in the
Mk I *(© R.A. Franks)*

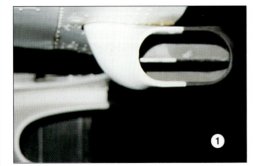

Hurricane Mk I

(Royal Air Force Museum, Hendon)

• **1** The carburettor intake under the centre-section
(© R.A. Franks)

• **2** The port side of the nose on the Mk I. Note the access panel on the main engine panel and the air scoop on the wing leading edge (© R.A. Franks)

• **3** On the starboard side of the engine on the Mk I is this hole. inside you can see the pick-up dog and chain for the engine started handle
(© R.A. Franks)

• **4** Clear view of the Rolls-Royce ejector exhaust stacks on the Mk I (© R.A. Franks)

• **5** On the port engine cowling, below the exhaust are these two outlets from the engine generator (© R.A. Franks)

• **6** The small gap between the propeller and engine cowling on the Mk I (© R.A. Franks)

Hurricane Mk XII

(Museum of Flying, Santa Monica, USA)

• **7** The exhaust stacks fitted to this Canadian-built machine. Note the cover fitted to the outlets below the exhaust
(© J. Roeder)

• **8** The revised nose profile of all versions after the Mk I series (© J. Roeder)

• **9** Close-up of the revised forward ring of the cowl. Note the oil anti-drip flange fitted around the top edge of the upper cowl (© J. Roeder)

• **10** Rear view of the exhaust stacks fitted to this version
(© J. Roeder)

• **11** An overall view of the starboard nose on the Mk XII
(© J. Roeder)

• **12** A close-up of the main propeller blade on this machine. the upper yellow band is for alignment purposes when the propeller is fitted
(© J. Roeder)

Hurricane Mk XII

(Canadian Warplane Heritage)

• **13** A nice view of the Packard Merlin fitted to this machine (© F.W. Coffman)

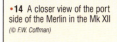

•14 A closer view of the port side of the Merlin in the Mk XII (© F.W. Coffman)

•14 A closer view of the port side of the Merlin in the Mk XII
(© F.W. Coffman)

•15 The starboard side of the Merlin installation in the Mk XII
(© F.W. Coffman)

•16 Another view of the Mk XII's Merlin (© F.W. Coffman)

•17 The mass of pipework behind the engine is clearly shown in this view of the port fuselage side on the Mk XII
(© F.W. Coffman)

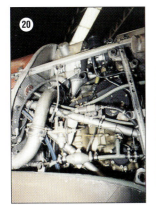

•18 This shot of the port side of the nose shows the revised single outlet port for the generator, differing from the Mk I and Mk XII shown elsewhere (© D. Frowen)

Hurricane Mk XII
(The Fighter Collection, Duxford)

•19 CH11-125. The rear area of the starboard side of the nose with the engine cowls removed (© R.A. Franks)

•20 CH11-126. Close-up of the starboard side rear area of the Packard Merlin
(© R.A. Franks)

•21 Lower area of the starboard side of the engine showing the sump and engine bearer (© R.A. Franks)

•22 The exhaust stacks
(© R.A. Franks)

•23 A view of the extreme nose, and propeller without spinner (© R.A. Franks)

•24 The port side of the Packard Merlin. Note that the gold colour for this engine is not original, and is just the colour applied by a certain engine restorer (© R.A. Franks)

•25 The lower area of the port side of the engine
(© R.A. Franks)

•26 The back section of the engine bay on the port side
(© R.A. Franks)

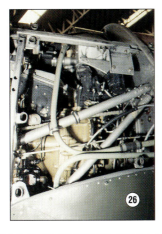

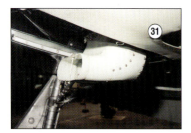

Hurricane Mk XII
(The Fighter Collection, Duxford)

•**27** A overall view of the port side of the engine (© *R.A. Franks*)

•**28** The pipework below the fuselage fuel tank
(© *R.A. Franks*)

•**29** A view from the cockpit with the fuel cell dominating
(© *R.A. Franks*)

•**30** An interesting item on all versions after the Mk II are the two bulges either side of the nose, just forward of the wing leading edge. Here you can see that these bulges cover the lower engine bearer pick-up points which are exposed here after the removal over the covers. The lower engine cowling has also been removed (© *R.A. Franks*)

•**31** A view from the port side of the carburettor air intake
(© *R.A. Franks*)

•**32** A view from the front of the carburettor intake with the lower engine cowl removed
(© *R.A. Franks*)

•**33** CH11-139. A look up directly up underneath the nose with the lower cowling removed (© *R.A. Franks*)

•**34** This larger view of the lower engine area with the cowling removed shows the tubular and wires in that area
(© *R.A. Franks*)

•**35** A close-up of the exhaust stacks (© *R.A. Franks*)

•**36** A close-up look into the front edge of the engine, looking into the area revised on all Mk II and later versions
(© *R.A. Franks*)

•**37** Note the gap between the spinner backplate and the engine cowling
(© *R.A. Franks*)

•**38** A close-up of the exposed Hamilton Standard Hydromatic propeller
(© *R.A. Franks*)

•**39** The 'paddle' propeller blade fitted to this Mk XII
(© *R.A. Franks*)

Tail & Rudder • 1

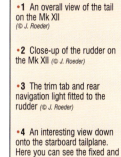

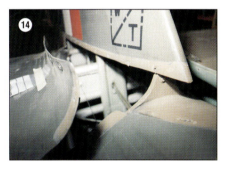

Hurricane Mk XII
(Museum of Flying, Santa Monica, USA)

•1 An overall view of the tail on the Mk XII
(© J. Roeder)

•2 Close-up of the rudder on the Mk XII (© J. Roeder)

•3 The trim tab and rear navigation light fitted to the rudder (© J. Roeder)

•4 An interesting view down onto the starboard tailplane. Here you can see the fixed and movable trim tabs (© J. Roeder)

•5 The prominent gap between tailplane and elevator (© J. Roeder)

•6 Note the rudder actuating cables coming out of the rear fuselage below the tailplane (© J. Roeder)

•7 Another close-up of the trim tab and light on the rudder (© J. Roeder)

Hurricane Mk XII
(Canadian Warplane Heritage)

•8 An overall view of the entire tail on this machine (© F.W. Coffman)

Hurricane Mk I
(Royal Air Force Museum, Hendon)

•9 Visible between the rudder and tailplane on this machine is the linkage for the elevators (© R.A. Franks)

Hurricane Mk XII
(The Fighter Collection, Duxford)

•10 The rather heavy linkage of the elevator trim tab (© R.A. Franks)

•11 This is the style of balance horn seen on the trim tabs of all Canadian-built Hurricanes (© R.A. Franks)

•12 The fairing seen fitted here over the elevator linkage was not installed on the RAF Museum Mk I (© R.A. Franks)

•13 The outer linkage on the elevator (© R.A. Franks)

•14 With the fillets removed, this is the structure below the vertical fin on a Hurricane (© R.A. Franks)

•15 The rudder control cables that exit the fuselage under the tailplanes (© R.A. Franks)

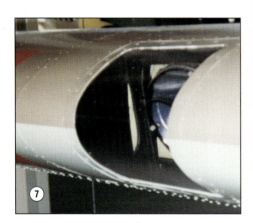

Hurricane Mk XI
(Museum of Flying, Santa Monica, USA)

• **1** The aileron on the port mainplane, note the total lack of any trim tabs (© J. Roeder)

• **2** The starboard mainplane (© J. Roeder)

• **3** A good view of the port wing tip light and the profile of the Hurricanes wing near the tip (© J. Roeder)

• **4** A view under the port wing tip light. Note that the bulb inside is red, not the entire glazing (© J. Roeder)

• **5** A good view of the starboard wing tip light. Note that the unit is sealed with doped linen (© J. Roeder)

• **6** An odd item fitted to this machine is this aerodynamic cover and outlet to the side of the radiator on the undersurface of the port mainplane. I suspect it is an emergency fuel dump for this airworthy example (© J. Roeder)

• **7** The landing light in the port mainplane leading edge (© J. Roeder)

Hurricane Mk I
(Science Museum, London)

• **8** With this example suspended from the roof it allows you to get this clear view of the centre section (© D. Frowen)

Hurricane Mk XII
(The Fighter Collection, Duxford)

• **9** Adjustment for the flight control cables in the mainplane is achieved via this access panel on the upper surface of the wing (© R.A. Franks)

• **10** This is the oil tank filler point in the inner leading edge of the port wing (© R.A. Franks)

Hurricane Mk XII
(The Fighter Collection, Duxford)

•**1** The pitot static head under the port mainplane. Note all the access panels are loose or removed for servicing
(© R.A. Franks)

•**2** The fillet between the fuselage and wing. Note the cover over the ground power socket (marked '24v')
(© R.A. Franks)

•**3** The deep fillet on the leading edge of the mainplane to fuselage join *(© R.A. Franks)*

•**4** The landing light in the wing leading edge. Note that this lamp is different from the usual sort, which features a 'swirl' of framing over the light lens *(© R.A. Franks)*

•**5** The port wing tip viewed from the rear *(© R.A. Franks)*

•**6** The extreme inner section of the flap under the starboard wing *(© R.A. Franks)*

•**7** The join between the inner and outer sections of the port flap. Note that the pipe is not standard, as this machine has additional wing tanks and this pipe is an emergency dump outlet *(© R.A. Franks)*

•**8** Clear shot of the inner section of the port wing
(© R.A. Franks)

•**9** The outer section of the port flap *(© R.A. Franks)*

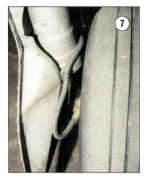

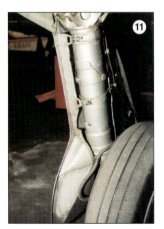

Hurricane Mk XII
(The Fighter Collection, Duxford)

•**1** This is the area behind the carburettor air intake which is usually covered with an aerodynamic cover. This shot shows how that cover is attached (via the frame in the foreground) *(© R.A. Franks)*

•**2** Up above where the aerodynamic faring should be is this oxygen bottle and duct *(© R.A. Franks)*

•**3** This is the first linkage and framework inside the starboard wheel well, looking outboard *(© R.A. Franks)*

•**4** This overall view outboard in the port wheel well gives an overall idea of the location of each component *(© R.A. Franks)*

•**5** The upper linkage of the starboard undercarriage leg, viewed from the front *(© R.A. Franks)*

•**6** On the second frame inside the wheel well is this 'rest' for the oleo leg which is made of a profile in wood *(© R.A. Franks)*

•**7** The route taken by the brake pipe once it moved in behind the wheel *(© R.A. Franks)*

•**8** The route of the hydraulic brake pie down the port undercarriage door *(© R.A. Franks)*

•**9** The retraction hydraulic unit outboard of the framework in the starboard wheel well *(© R.A. Franks)*

•**10** The section for the wheel in the undercarriage bay looking aft. The clear viewing panel (middle, top) ensured the pilot knew that the undercarriage was retracted (or extended) and the hole on the rear bulkhead below it is for the started handle stowage *(© R.A. Franks)*

•**11** The style of the undercarriage door, viewed from the rear *(© R.A. Franks)*

•**12** The three-spoke hub and plain tread fitted to this machine. The ant-creep marking is in red on the hub and wheel and the item in the centre of the hub is to facilitate towing *(© R.A. Franks)*

•**13** The complex upper linkage of the port oleo *(© R.A. Franks)*

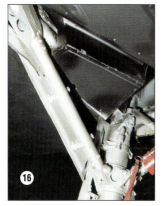

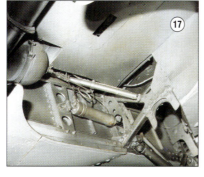

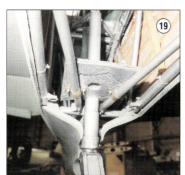

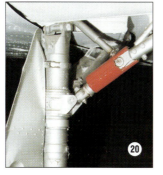

•**14** The undercarriage bay above the oleo leg itself is quite clear with the exception of the brake pipe that can be seen here (© *R.A. Franks*)

Huricane Mk I
(Royal Air Force, Museum)

•**15** Viewed from the outside, this is the secondary door fitted to the main leg of the Mk I (© *R.A. Franks*)

•**16** This is the overall view of the linkage at the back of the main oleo (© *R.A. Franks*)

•**17** The starboard section of the main wheel well, viewed from the back looking forward (© *R.A. Franks*)

•**18** The four-spoke hub and 6.00 - 10¼ tyre fitted to this machine (© *R.A. Franks*)

•**20** The starboard oleo leg and door. Note that this machine does not have the prominent brake pipe fitted and the red item is an undercarriage lock (© *R.A. Franks*)

•**21** An overall view of the oxygen bottle and duct in the wheel well, viewed from the back looking forward. The black and white wheel wells seem a little unlikely though! (© *R.A. Franks*)

•**22** A period shot of the centre section of a Hurricane being assembled at Langley in 1944 (© *Hawker-Siddeley*)

Mk XII
(Canadian Warplane Heritage)

•**19** With the ventral fairing removed on this Mk XII you can see the tubular structure for the tailwheel unit. The plate is a lead weight (© *R.A. Franks*)

•**23** An overall view of the port side wheel well (© *F.W. Coffman*)

•**24** An access panel on the port side of the fuselage below the tailplane (© *R.A. Franks*)

•**25** A view of the port side wheel well, looking outboard (© *D. Frowen*)

•**26** The Dowty Oleo-pneumatic tailwheel unit, often referred to as the 'knuckled' tailwheel (© *R.A. Franks*)

Armament • 1

Hurricane Mk IIB

(National Aviation Museum, Ottawa)

• **1** The port wing shows the correct location of the outer two wings, with the protruding Browning machine guns
(© F.W. Coffman)

Hurricane Mk XII

(The Fighter Collection, Duxford)

• **2** The inner four machine guns ports covered with red doped linen *(© R.A. Franks)*

• **3** The outer two gun ports. These would usually have the machine guns projecting from them, and therefore could not be covered as shown here. However, some bomb carrying Mk IIB's removed the outer guns, so I suspect the resulting holes were covered in this manner *(© R.A. Franks)*

• **4** Mk IIC, 'Cawnpore I' (LK•A, BE500) of No. 87 Squadron being rearmed
(© C.E. Brown)

• **5** Re-arming a Mk I of No. 601 Squadron at Tangmere in 1940
(© C.E. Brown/RAF Museum 5884-8)

Sea Hurricane • 1

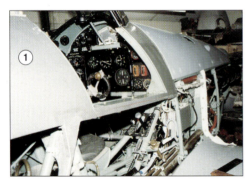

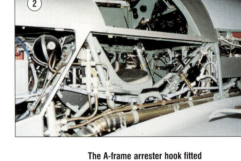

The A-frame arrester hook fitted to the Sea Hurricane
(© Crown Copyright)

This is the arrester hook in the stowed position
(© Crown Copyright)

Sea Hurricane Mk IB

(Shuttleworth Trust, operated at Duxford)

• **1** A nice view into the cockpit area with all the side access panel removed
(© D. Frowen)

• **2** A look at the starboard side of the cockpit area with the access panels removed and the 'knock-out' door removed *(© D. Frowen)*

• **3** The Merlin III engine installed in the Sea Hurricane Mk IB. Note the 'Fish-tail' exhaust stacks *(© D. Frowen)*

Cockpit Interior • 4

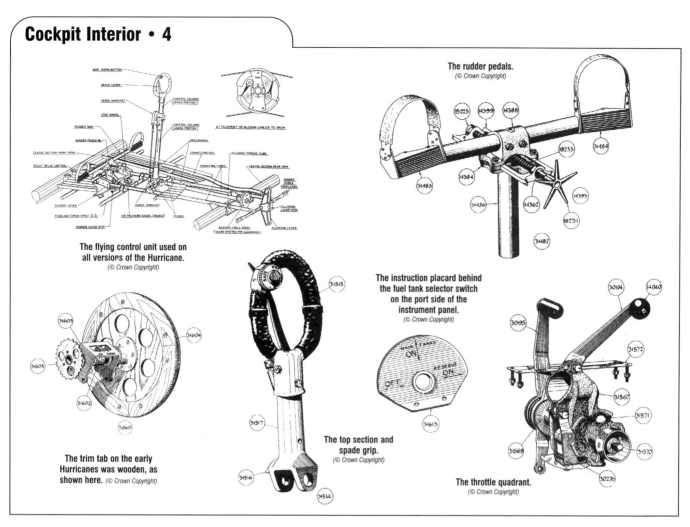

The flying control unit used on all versions of the Hurricane.
(© Crown Copyright)

The trim tab on the early Hurricanes was wooden, as shown here. *(© Crown Copyright)*

The top section and spade grip.
(© Crown Copyright)

The rudder pedals.
(© Crown Copyright)

The instruction placard behind the fuel tank selector switch on the port side of the instrument panel.
(© Crown Copyright)

The throttle quadrant.
(© Crown Copyright)

Fuselage • 3

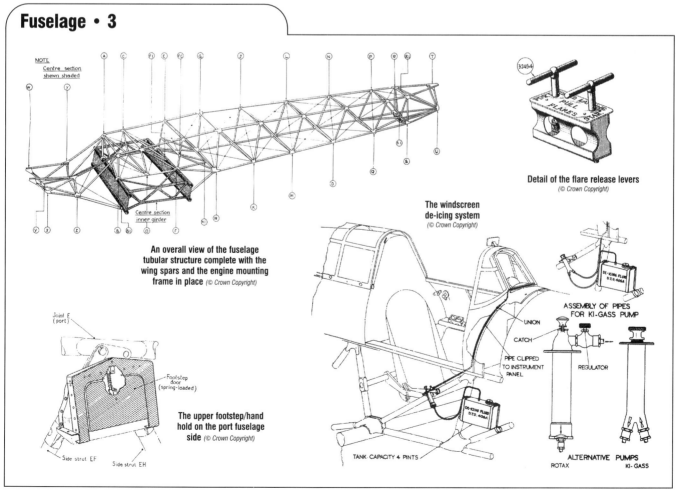

NOTE
Centre section shewn shaded

Centre section inner girder

An overall view of the fuselage tubular structure complete with the wing spars and the engine mounting frame in place *(© Crown Copyright)*

Joint E (port)

Footstep door (spring-loaded)

Side strut EF

Side strut EH

The upper footstep/hand hold on the port fuselage side *(© Crown Copyright)*

Detail of the flare release levers
(© Crown Copyright)

The windscreen de-icing system
(© Crown Copyright)

ASSEMBLY OF PIPES FOR KI-GASS PUMP

UNION

CATCH

PIPE CLIPPED TO INSTRUMENT PANEL

REGULATOR

TANK CAPACITY 4 PINTS

ALTERNATIVE PUMPS
ROTAX   KI-GASS

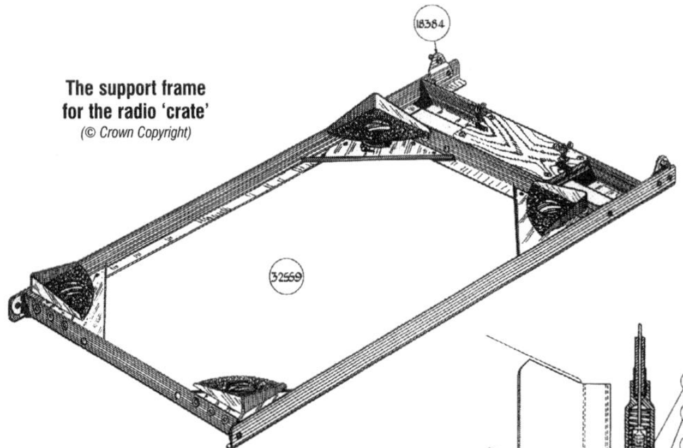

18384
32569

The support frame for the radio 'crate'
(© Crown Copyright)

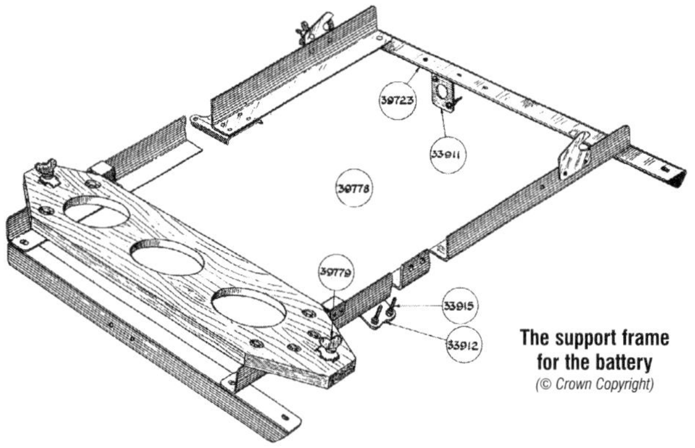

39723
33911
39778
39779
33915
33912

The support frame for the battery
(© Crown Copyright)

A
B
C
D
E
F

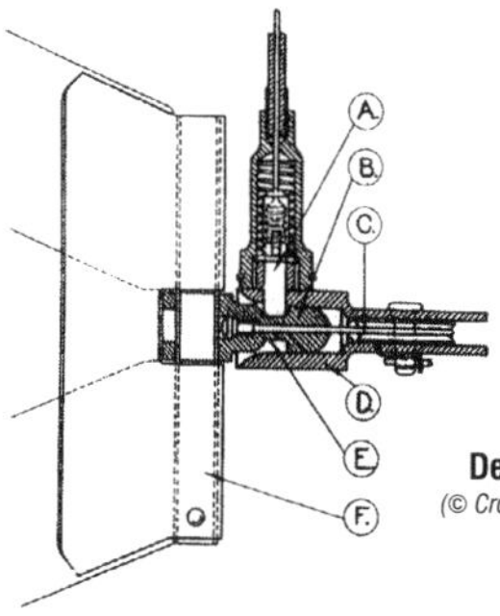

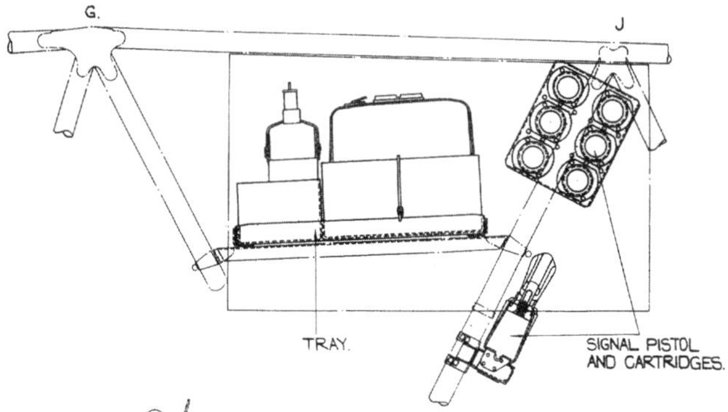

Detail at X
(© Crown Copyright)

The desert equipment items fitted to all 'tropical' Hurricanes
(© Crown Copyright)

G.
J
TRAY.
SIGNAL PISTOL AND CARTRIDGES.

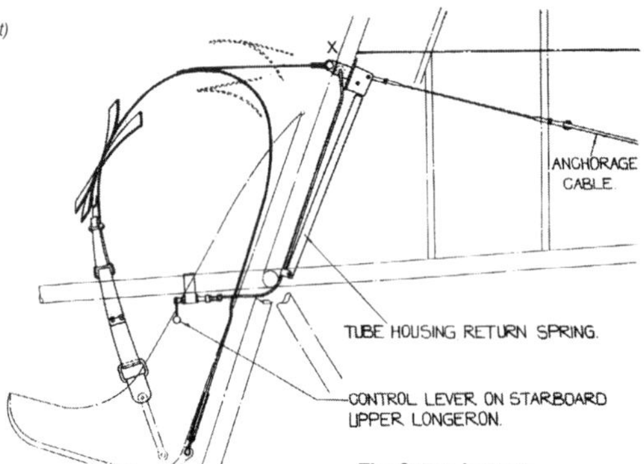

X
ANCHORAGE CABLE.
TUBE HOUSING RETURN SPRING.
CONTROL LEVER ON STARBOARD UPPER LONGERON.

The Sutton harness release control
(© Crown Copyright)

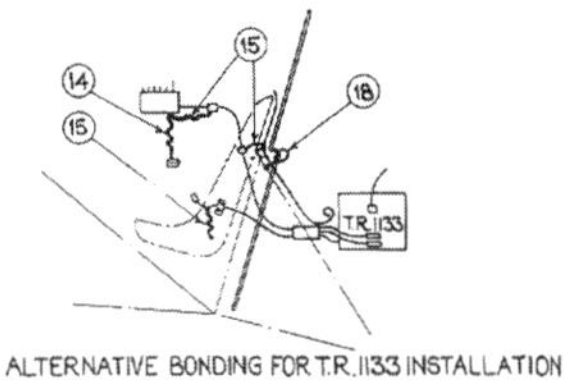

14
15
15
18
T.R.1133
ALTERNATIVE BONDING FOR T.R.1133 INSTALLATION

The alternative bonding diagram for the T.R.1133 installation
(© Crown Copyright)

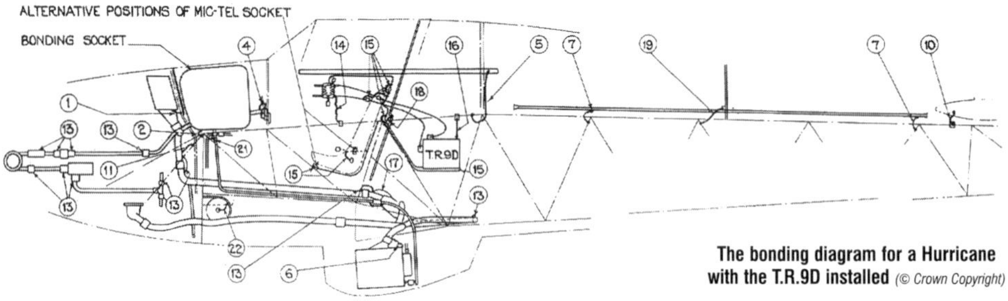

ALTERNATIVE POSITIONS OF MIC-TEL SOCKET
BONDING SOCKET
TR9D

The bonding diagram for a Hurricane with the T.R.9D installed *(© Crown Copyright)*

Handhole door
FORWARD
RETRACTABLE FOOTSTEP

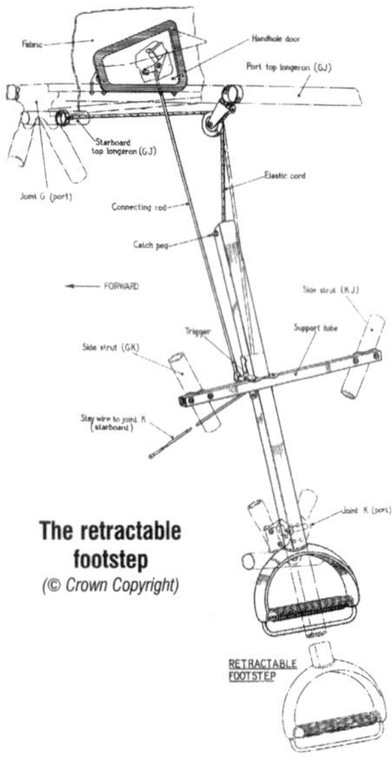

The retractable footstep
(© Crown Copyright)

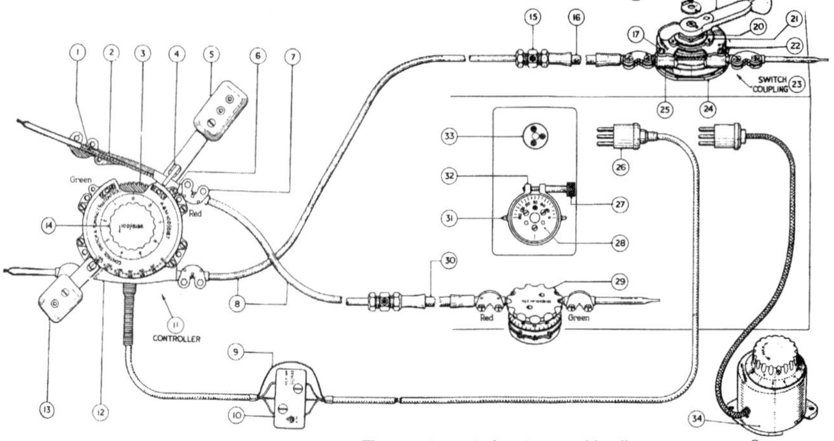

SWITCH COUPLING
Green
Red
CONTROLLER
Red
Green

The remote control system used in all T.R.9D installations *(© Crown Copyright)*

Radiator • 2

The flap fitted to the rear
of the radiator unit
(© Crown Copyright)

32025

32024

The official diagram of the
overall radiator unit
(© Crown Copyright)

A clear diagram of the
cooling system of the
type fitted to the Mk I

Filler cap

Relief valve

Vent pipe

Fireproof
bulkhead

Header tank
2 gall. Coolant
2 gall. air space

From starboard
cylinder block

From port
cylinder block

Thermometer
pipe line

Coolant temperature
gauge

Thermostat

Vent pipe outlet –
rubber connection
flush with cowling

Vent plug

Bonding wire

Inlet to engine

Bonding
wire

Vent plug

By-pass

Glands in centre section
spar webs

Oil cooler

Retaining
plate

Hose
clip

Rubber
connection

Thermostat

Typical section through
thermostat connections

Oil cooler inlet and outlet unions

Corrugated bonding strip

Rubber hose   Hose clips
Section of typical joint

Meteorological • 1

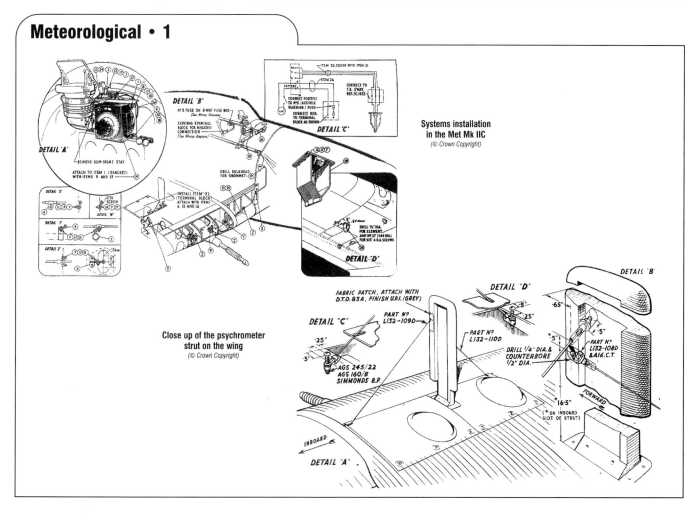

Systems installation
in the Met Mk IIC
(© Crown Copyright)

Close up of the psychrometer
strut on the wing
(© Crown Copyright)

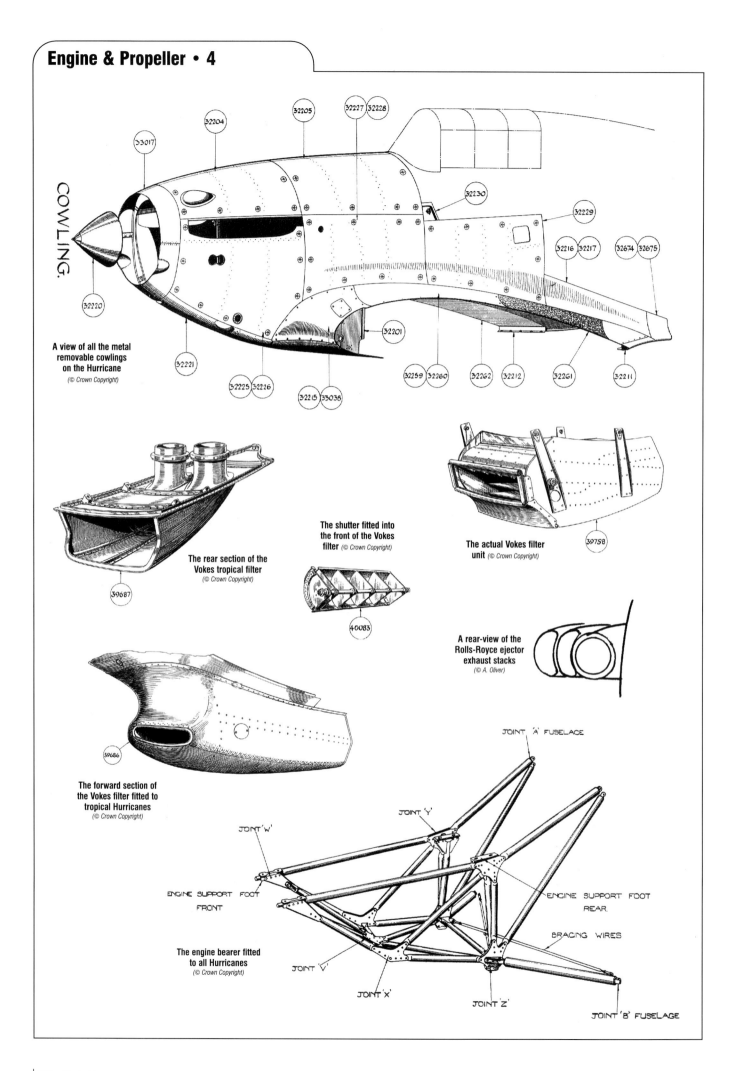

COWLING.

32220

33017

32204

32205

32227 32228

32230

32229

32216 32217

32674 32675

32201

32221

32225 32226

32215 33038

32259 32260

32262

32212

32261

32211

A view of all the metal removable cowlings on the Hurricane
(© Crown Copyright)

39687

The rear section of the Vokes tropical filter
(© Crown Copyright)

40083

The shutter fitted into the front of the Vokes filter *(© Crown Copyright)*

39758

The actual Vokes filter unit *(© Crown Copyright)*

A rear-view of the Rolls-Royce ejector exhaust stacks
(© A. Oliver)

39686

The forward section of the Vokes filter fitted to tropical Hurricanes
(© Crown Copyright)

JOINT 'A' FUSELAGE

JOINT 'Y'

JOINT 'W'

ENGINE SUPPORT FOOT
FRONT

ENGINE SUPPORT FOOT
REAR.

BRACING WIRES

JOINT 'V'

JOINT 'X'

JOINT 'Z'

JOINT 'B' FUSELAGE

The engine bearer fitted to all Hurricanes
(© Crown Copyright)

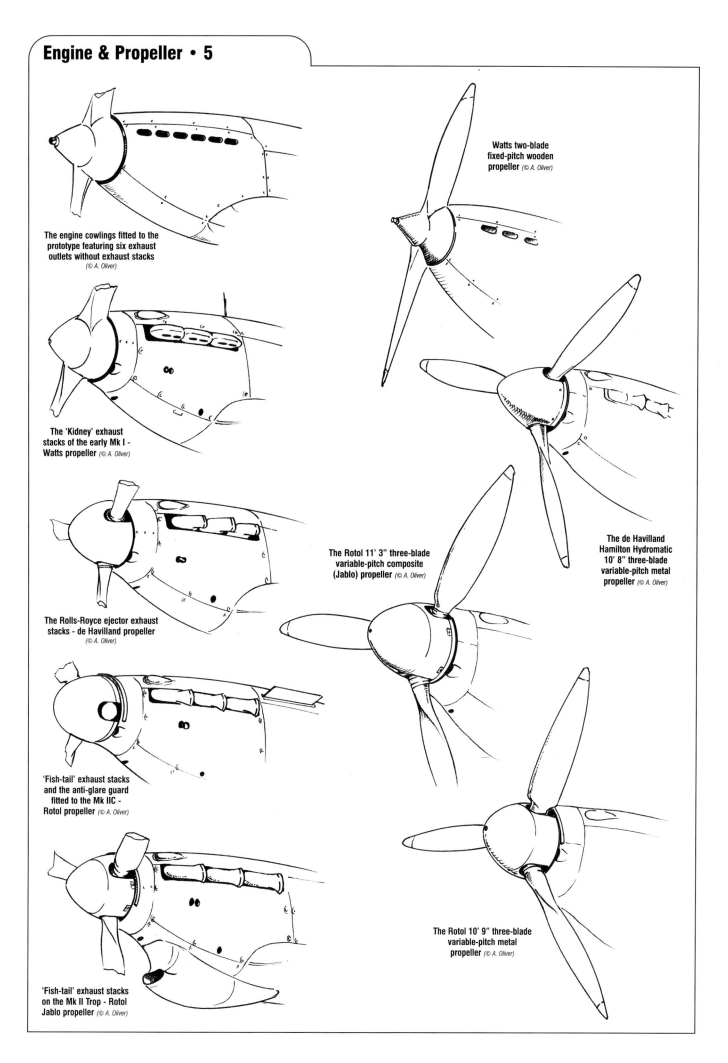

The engine cowlings fitted to the prototype featuring six exhaust outlets without exhaust stacks
(© A. Oliver)

The 'Kidney' exhaust stacks of the early Mk I - Watts propeller (© A. Oliver)

The Rolls-Royce ejector exhaust stacks - de Havilland propeller
(© A. Oliver)

'Fish-tail' exhaust stacks and the anti-glare guard fitted to the Mk IIC - Rotol propeller (© A. Oliver)

'Fish-tail' exhaust stacks on the Mk II Trop - Rotol Jablo propeller (© A. Oliver)

Watts two-blade fixed-pitch wooden propeller (© A. Oliver)

The Rotol 11' 3" three-blade variable-pitch composite (Jablo) propeller (© A. Oliver)

The de Havilland Hamilton Hydromatic 10' 8" three-blade variable-pitch metal propeller (© A. Oliver)

The Rotol 10' 9" three-blade variable-pitch metal propeller (© A. Oliver)

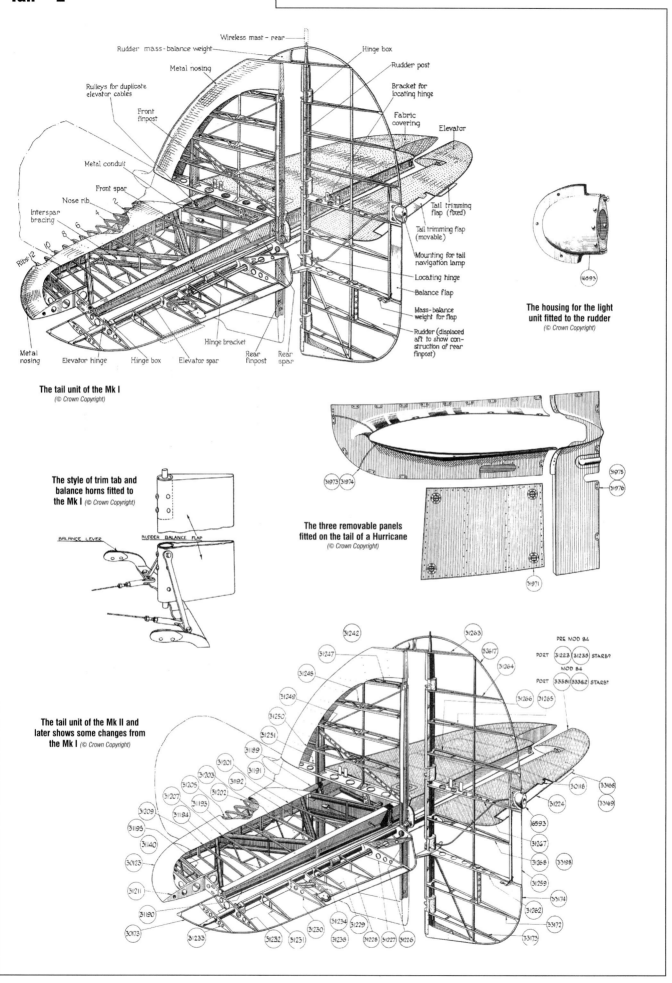

Wireless mast – rear

Rudder mass-balance weight

Metal nosing

Pulleys for duplicate elevator cables

Front finpost

Metal conduit

Front spar

Nose rib

Interspar bracing

Ribs 12

Metal nosing

Elevator hinge

Hinge box

Elevator spar

Rear finpost

Rear spar

Hinge box

Rudder post

Bracket for locating hinge

Fabric covering

Elevator

Tail trimming flap (fixed)

Tail trimming flap (movable)

Mounting for tail navigation lamp

Locating hinge

Balance flap

Mass-balance weight for flap

Rudder (displaced aft to show construction of rear finpost)

The tail unit of the Mk I
(© Crown Copyright)

16593

The housing for the light unit fitted to the rudder
(© Crown Copyright)

The style of trim tab and balance horns fitted to the Mk I *(© Crown Copyright)*

BALANCE LEVER

RUDDER BALANCE FLAP

The three removable panels fitted on the tail of a Hurricane
(© Crown Copyright)

31973 31974

31975

31976

31971

The tail unit of the Mk II and later shows some changes from the Mk I *(© Crown Copyright)*

31242
31247
31246
31249
31250
31251
31189
31201
31203
31205
31202
31207
31192
31209
31193
31194
31195
31140
30123
31211
31190
30173
31233
31232
31231
31230
31238
31234
31229
31228
31227
31226

31263
32617
31264
31266
31265

PRE MOD 84
PORT 31223 31235 STARB?
MOD 84
PORT 33381 33382 STARB?

30118
33168
31224
33169
16593
31267
31268
33198
31259
33174
31282
33172
33173

Wings • 3

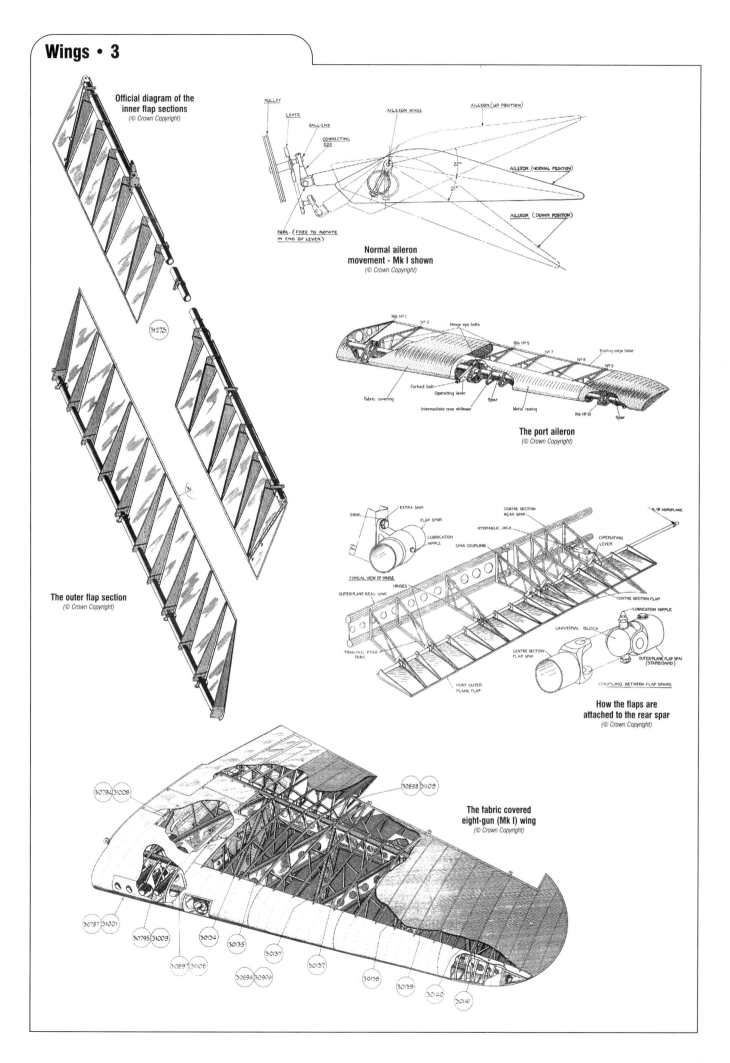

Official diagram of the inner flap sections
(© Crown Copyright)

POLLEY

LEVER

BALL-END

CONNECTING ROD

AILERON HINGE

AILERON. (UP POSITION)

22°

21°

AILERON. (NORMAL POSITION)

AILERON. (DOWN POSITION)

FORK. (FREE TO ROTATE IN END OF LEVER)

Normal aileron movement - Mk I shown
(© Crown Copyright)

31273

31.

The outer flap section
(© Crown Copyright)

Rib Nº 1.

Nº 2

Hinge eye bolts

Rib Nº 5

Nº 7

Trailing edge tube

Nº 8

Nº 9

Fabric covering

Forked bolt

Operating lever

Spar

Intermediate nose stiffener

Metal nosing

Rib Nº 10

Spar

The port aileron
(© Crown Copyright)

SHIM

EXTRA SHIM

FLAP SPAR

LUBRICATION NIPPLE

CENTRE SECTION REAR SPAR

HYDRAULIC JACK

SPAR COUPLING

OPERATING LEVER

₵ OF AEROPLANE

TYPICAL VIEW OF HINGE

HINGES

OUTER PLANE REAR SPAR

CENTRE SECTION FLAP

LUBRICATION NIPPLE

UNIVERSAL BLOCK

OUTER PLANE FLAP SPAR (STARBOARD)

TRAILING EDGE RIBS

CENTRE SECTION FLAP SPAR

COUPLING BETWEEN FLAP SPARS

PORT OUTER PLANE FLAP

How the flaps are attached to the rear spar
(© Crown Copyright)

30794 31008

30898 31109

The fabric covered eight-gun (Mk I) wing
(© Crown Copyright)

30787 31001

30795 31009

30134

30135

30137

30897 31108

30137

30694 30906

30138

30139

30140

30141

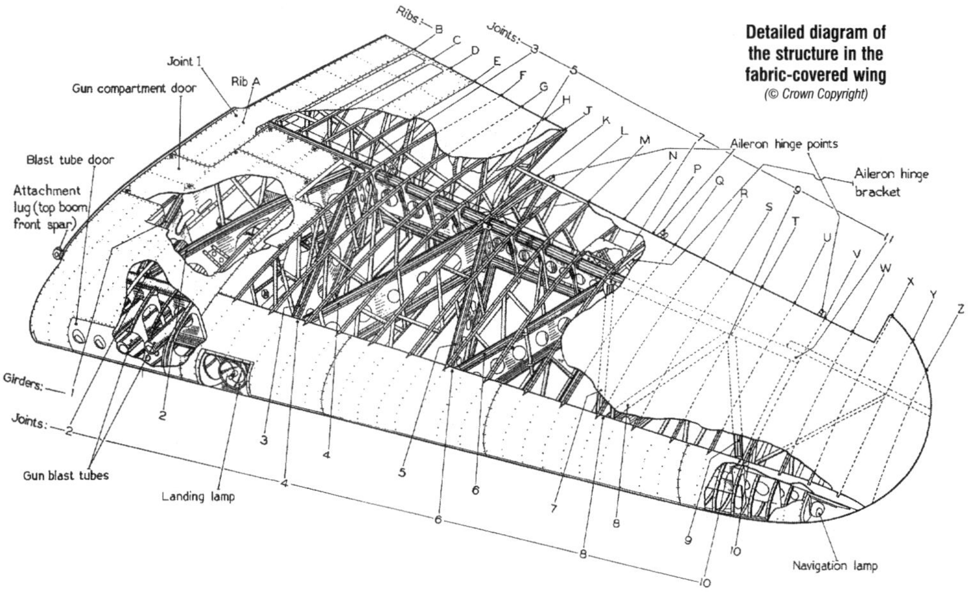

Detailed diagram of the structure in the fabric-covered wing
(© Crown Copyright)

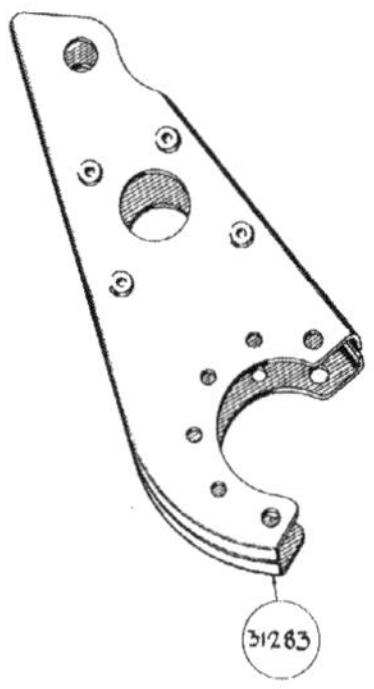

Ribs:- B
Joints:- 3
Joint 1
Rib A
Gun compartment door
C D E F G H J K L M N P Q R S T U V W X Y Z
Blast tube door
Aileron hinge points
Attachment lug (top boom front spar)
Aileron hinge bracket
Girders:- 1
Joints:- 2
Gun blast tubes
Landing lamp
Navigation lamp

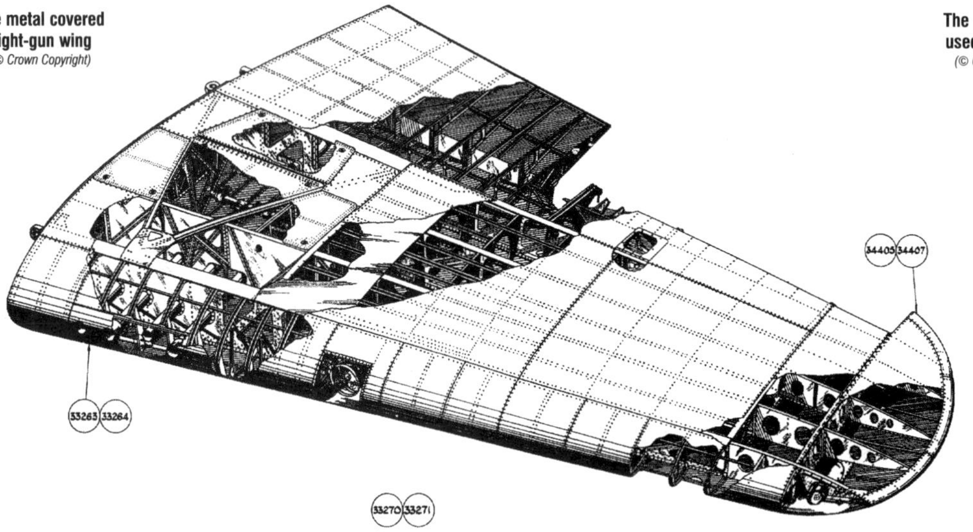

The metal covered eight-gun wing
(© Crown Copyright)

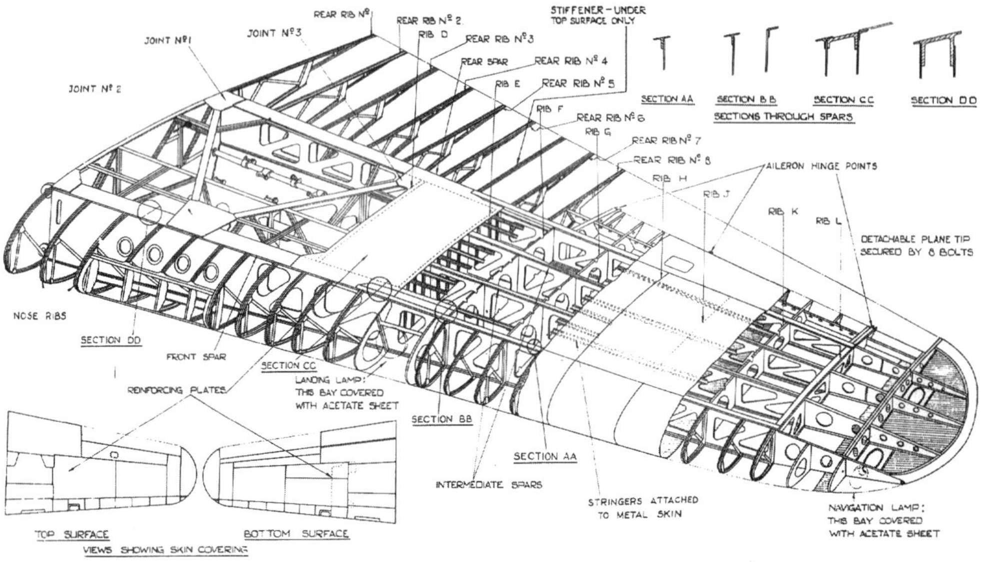

34405 34407
33263 33264
33270 33271

The style of hinge used on the flaps
(© Crown Copyright)

34283

Detailed structural diagram of the eight-gun metal wing
(© Crown Copyright)

REAR RIB Nº 1
REAR RIB Nº 2
RIB D
REAR RIB Nº 3
JOINT Nº 1
JOINT Nº 3
REAR SPAR
REAR RIB Nº 4
RIB E
REAR RIB Nº 5
JOINT Nº 2
RIB F
STIFFENER – UNDER TOP SURFACE ONLY
REAR RIB Nº 6
RIB G
REAR RIB Nº 7
REAR RIB Nº 8
RIB H
AILERON HINGE POINTS
RIB J
RIB K
RIB L
SECTION AA
SECTION BB
SECTION CC
SECTION DD
SECTIONS THROUGH SPARS
DETACHABLE PLANE TIP SECURED BY 6 BOLTS
NOSE RIBS
SECTION DD
FRONT SPAR
SECTION CC
REINFORCING PLATES
LANDING LAMP; THIS BAY COVERED WITH ACETATE SHEET
SECTION BB
SECTION AA
TOP SURFACE
BOTTOM SURFACE
VIEWS SHOWING SKIN COVERING
INTERMEDIATE SPARS
STRINGERS ATTACHED TO METAL SKIN
NAVIGATION LAMP; THIS BAY COVERED WITH ACETATE SHEET

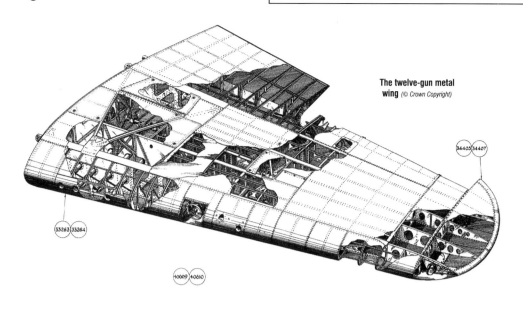

The twelve-gun metal
wing *(© Crown Copyright)*

33263 33264
40009 40610
34405 34407

**The bays for the 20mm
cannons in the Mk IIC wing**
(© Crown Copyright)

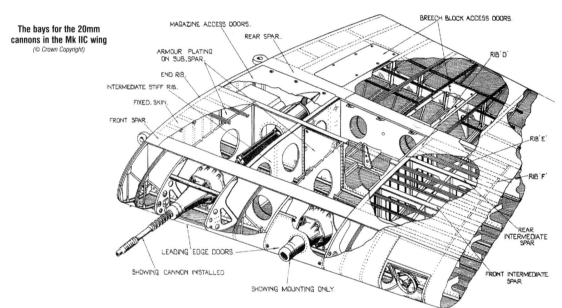

MAGAZINE ACCESS DOORS.
REAR SPAR.
BREECH BLOCK ACCESS DOORS.
ARMOUR PLATING ON SUB.SPAR.
END RIB.
INTERMEDIATE STIFF RIB.
FIXED. SKIN.
FRONT SPAR.
RIB 'D'
RIB 'E'
RIB 'F'
REAR INTERMEDIATE SPAR
FRONT INTERMEDIATE SPAR
LEADING EDGE DOORS
SHOWING CANNON INSTALLED
SHOWING MOUNTING ONLY

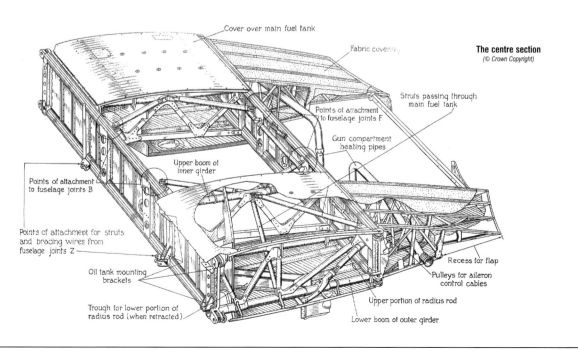

Cover over main fuel tank
Fabric covering
The centre section
(© Crown Copyright)
Struts passing through main fuel tank
Points of attachment to fuselage joints F
Gun compartment heating pipes
Upper boom of inner girder
Points of attachment to fuselage joints B
Points of attachment for struts and bracing wires from fuselage joints Z
Recess for flap
Oil tank mounting brackets
Pulleys for aileron control cables
Upper portion of radius rod
Trough for lower portion of radius rod (when retracted)
Lower boom of outer girder

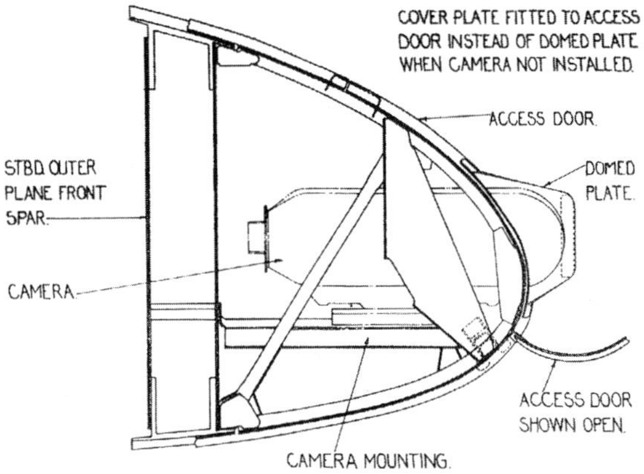

COVER PLATE FITTED TO ACCESS DOOR INSTEAD OF DOMED PLATE WHEN CAMERA NOT INSTALLED.

ACCESS DOOR.

DOMED PLATE.

STBD. OUTER PLANE FRONT SPAR.

CAMERA.

ACCESS DOOR SHOWN OPEN.

CAMERA MOUNTING.

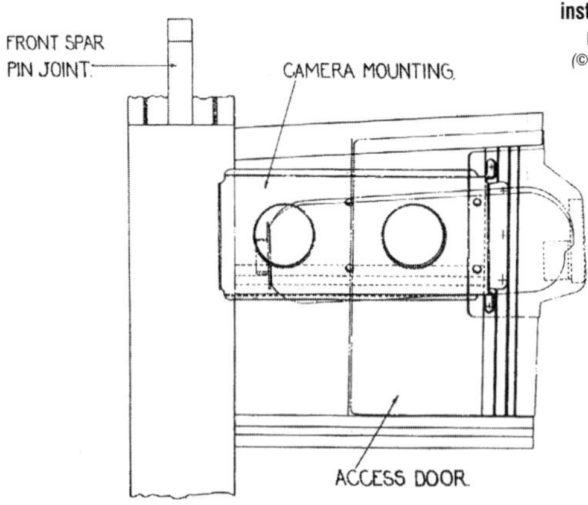

The ciné camera installation in the metal wing
(© Crown Copyright)

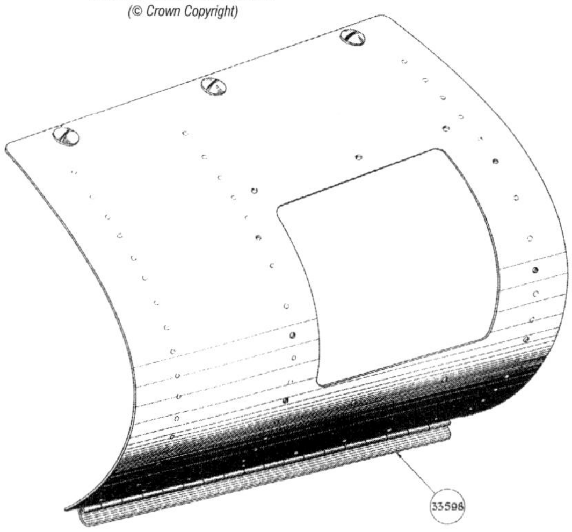

The wing panel for the ciné camera installation
(© Crown Copyright)

33598

FRONT SPAR PIN JOINT.

CAMERA MOUNTING.

ACCESS DOOR.

33592

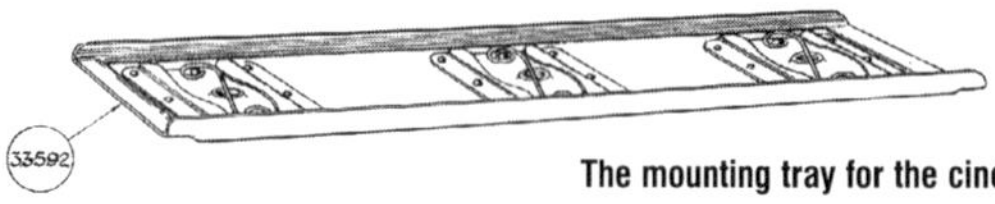

The mounting tray for the ciné camera *(© Crown Copyright)*

33621

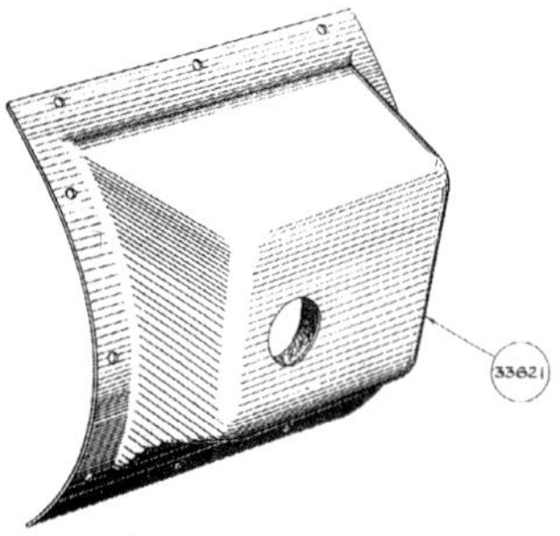

The inner domed plate for the ciné camera
(© Crown Copyright)

34403 34418

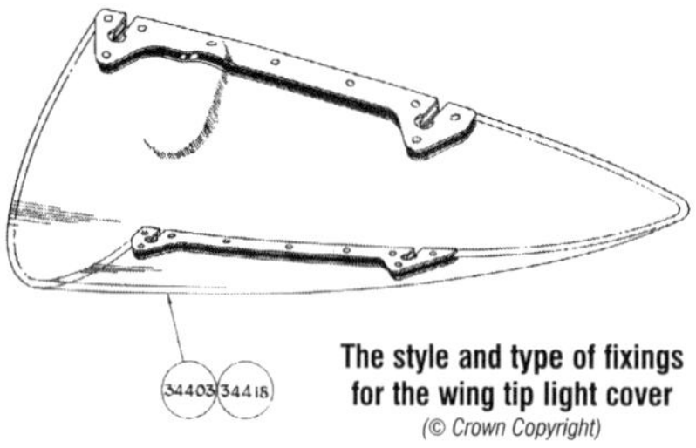

The style and type of fixings for the wing tip light cover
(© Crown Copyright)

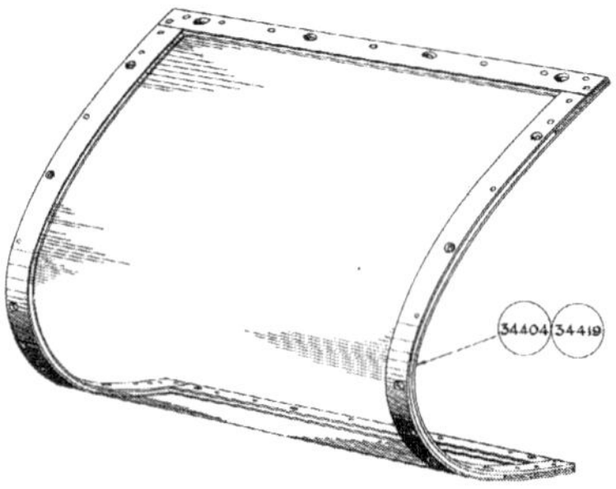

34404 34419

The leading edge landing light lens *(© Crown Copyright)*

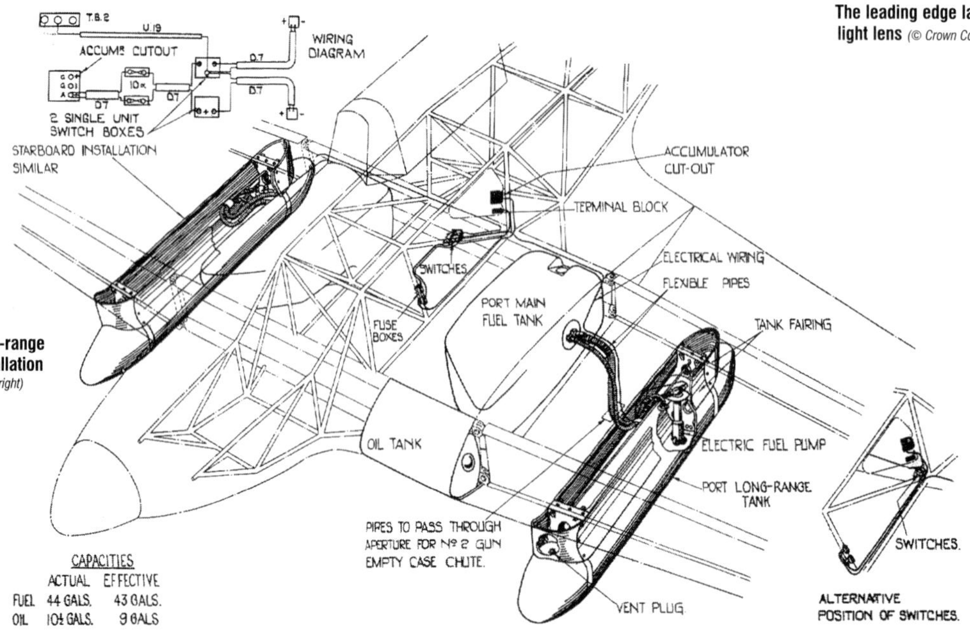

T.B.2

U.19

ACCUM.RS CUTOUT

WIRING DIAGRAM

2 SINGLE UNIT SWITCH BOXES
STARBOARD INSTALLATION SIMILAR.

ACCUMULATOR CUT-OUT

TERMINAL BLOCK

ELECTRICAL WIRING

FLEXIBLE PIPES

SWITCHES.

FUSE BOXES

PORT MAIN FUEL TANK

TANK FAIRING

The fixed long-range fuel tank installation
(© Crown Copyright)

OIL TANK

ELECTRIC FUEL PUMP

PORT LONG-RANGE TANK

SWITCHES.

PIPES TO PASS THROUGH APERTURE FOR Nº 2 GUN EMPTY CASE CHUTE.

VENT PLUG

ALTERNATIVE POSITION OF SWITCHES.

CAPACITIES

	ACTUAL	EFFECTIVE
FUEL	44 GALS.	43 GALS.
OIL	10½ GALS.	9 GALS

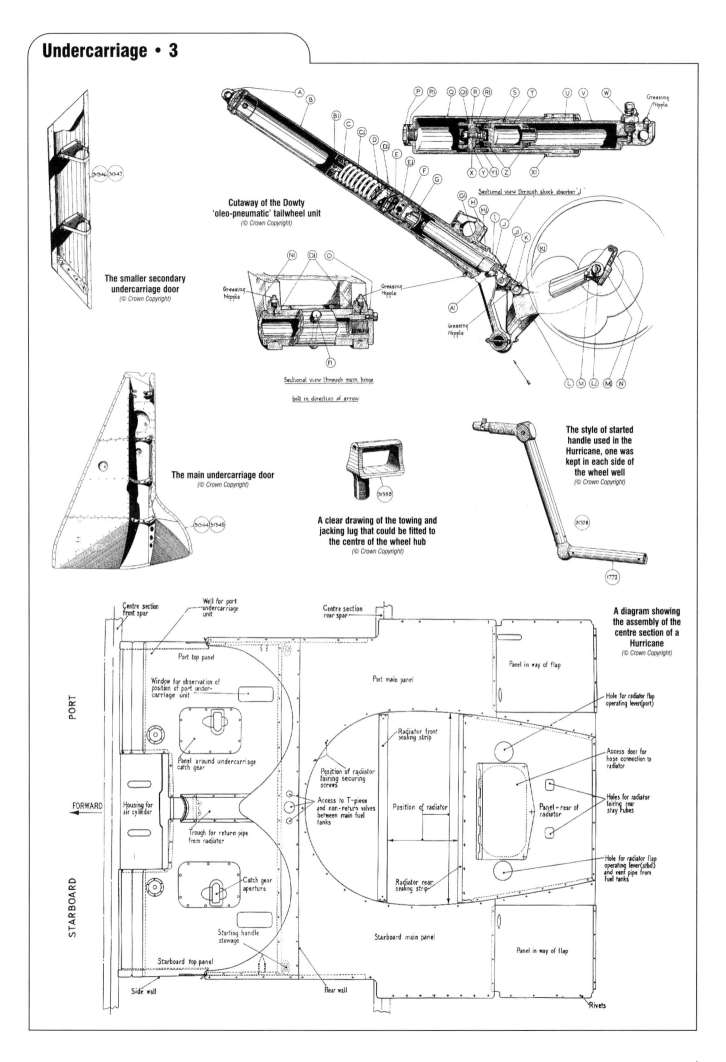

The smaller secondary
undercarriage door
(© Crown Copyright)

Cutaway of the Dowty
'oleo-pneumatic' tailwheel unit
(© Crown Copyright)

Sectional view through shock absorber J

Greasing Nipple

Greasing Nipple

Greasing Nipple

Sectional view through main hinge

bolt in direction of arrow.

The main undercarriage door
(© Crown Copyright)

A clear drawing of the towing and
jacking lug that could be fitted to
the centre of the wheel hub
(© Crown Copyright)

The style of started
handle used in the
Hurricane, one was
kept in each side of
the wheel well
(© Crown Copyright)

A diagram showing
the assembly of the
centre section of a
Hurricane
(© Crown Copyright)

PORT

FORWARD

STARBOARD

Centre section front spar

Well for port undercarriage unit

Centre section rear spar

Port top panel

Panel in way of flap

Window for observation of position of port under-carriage unit

Port main panel

Hole for radiator flap operating lever(port)

Panel around undercarriage catch gear

Radiator front sealing strip

Access door for hose connection to radiator

Housing for air cylinder

Position of radiator fairing securing screws

Access to T-piece and non-return valves between main fuel tanks

Position of radiator

Holes for radiator fairing rear stay tubes

Trough for return pipe from radiator

Panel - rear of radiator

Catch gear aperture

Hole for radiator flap operating lever(stbd.) and vent pipe from fuel tanks

Starting handle stowage

Radiator rear sealing strip

Starboard main panel

Starboard top panel

Panel in way of flap

Side wall

Rear wall

Rivets

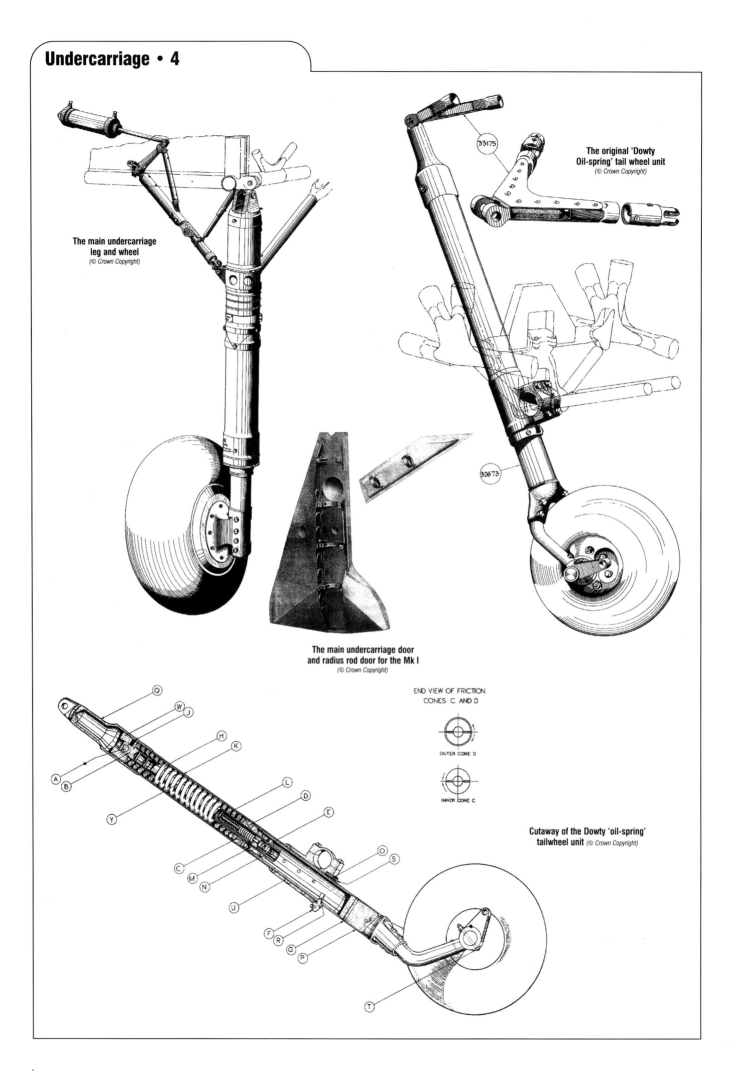

The main undercarriage
leg and wheel
(© Crown Copyright)

The original 'Dowty
Oil-spring' tail wheel unit
(© Crown Copyright)

33175

32673

The main undercarriage door
and radius rod door for the Mk I
(© Crown Copyright)

END VIEW OF FRICTION
CONES C AND D

OUTER CONE D

INNER CONE C

Cutaway of the Dowty 'oil-spring'
tailwheel unit *(© Crown Copyright)*

Armament • 2

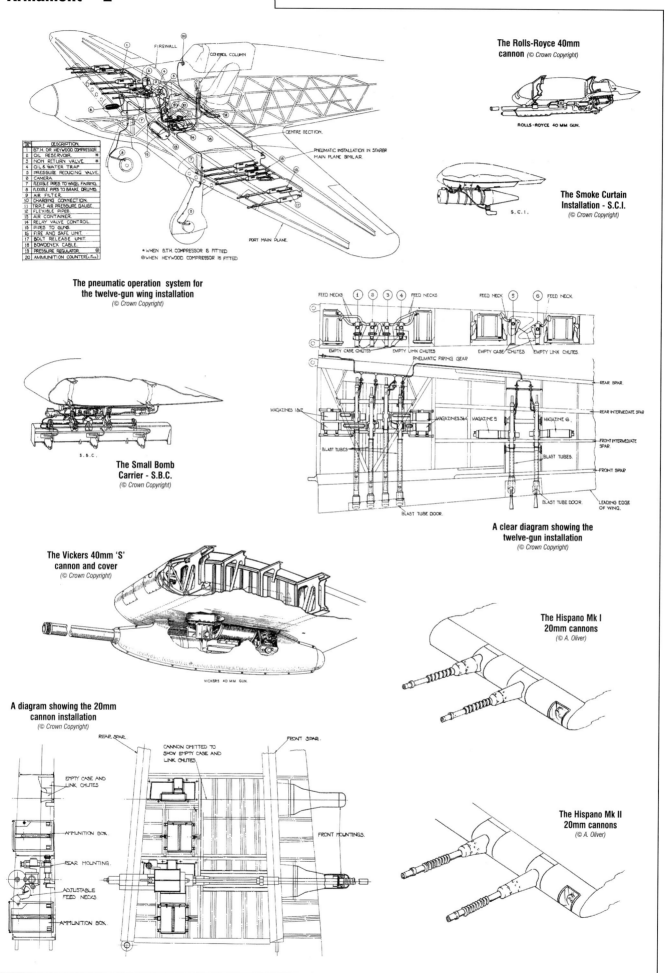

REF	DESCRIPTION.
1	B.T.H. OR HEYWOOD COMPRESSOR.
2	OIL RESERVOIR. ✻
3	NON RETURN VALVE. ✻
4	OIL & WATER TRAP.
5	PRESSURE REDUCING VALVE.
6	CAMERA.
7	FLEXIBLE PIPES TO WHEEL FAIRING.
8	FLEXIBLE PIPES TO BRAKE DRUMS.
9	AIR FILTER.
10	CHARGING CONNECTION.
11	TRIPLE AIR PRESSURE GAUGE.
12	FLEXIBLE PIPES.
13	AIR CONTAINER.
14	RELAY VALVE CONTROL.
15	PIPES TO GUNS.
16	FIRE AND SAFE UNIT.
17	BOLT RELEASE UNIT.
18	BOWDENEX CABLE.
19	PRESSURE REGULATOR. ⊗
20	AMMUNITION COUNTER (1 flea)

* WHEN B.T.H. COMPRESSOR IS FITTED
⊗ WHEN HEYWOOD COMPRESSOR IS FITTED

The pneumatic operation system for the twelve-gun wing installation
(© Crown Copyright)

The Small Bomb Carrier - S.B.C.
(© Crown Copyright)

The Vickers 40mm 'S' cannon and cover
(© Crown Copyright)

VICKERS 40 MM GUN.

A diagram showing the 20mm cannon installation
(© Crown Copyright)

The Rolls-Royce 40mm cannon *(© Crown Copyright)*

ROLLS-ROYCE 40 MM GUN.

The Smoke Curtain Installation - S.C.I.
(© Crown Copyright)

S.C.I.

A clear diagram showing the twelve-gun installation
(© Crown Copyright)

The Hispano Mk I 20mm cannons
(© A. Oliver)

The Hispano Mk II 20mm cannons
(© A. Oliver)

The installation of the Vickers 40mm 'S' cannon *(© Crown Copyright)*

REAR SPAR

REAR MOUNTING.

REAR MOUNTING.

2°

MAGAZINE FOR 40mm GUN.

MAGAZINE FOR 303" BROWNING GUN.

VICKERS 'TYPE 'S' 40mm GUN.

RIB 'D'

FRONT MOUNTING

BROWNING GUN.

FRONT SPAR

SUB-SPAR

FRONT MOUNTING

AEROFOIL DATUM

THE 40mm GUNS ARE TO BE SET TO POINT STRAIGHT AHEAD.

303" GUNS ALIGNED TO CONVERGE ON TARGET 500 YDS. AHEAD ON ℄ OF AIRCRAFT.

26" INBOARD

2° DOWN

SECTIONAL VIEW SHOWING 'S' GUN. FAIRINGS OMITTED FOR CLEARNESS.

SECTIONAL VIEW SHOWING 303" BROWNING GUN.

The Mk I fabric wing *(© A. Oliver)*

The Mk I metal wing - eight gun *(© A. Oliver)*

The Mk IIB metal wing - twelve gun *(© A. Oliver)*

REAR SPAR

REAR MOUNTING.

SUB SPAR

ROLLS ROYCE TYPE B-H 40 MM GUN

FRONT MOUNTING

SUB SPAR

FRONT SPAR

THE GUNS ARE SET TO POINT STRAIGHT AHEAD. ADJUSTMENT IS PROVIDED TO ENABLE THE GUNS TO BE CONVERGED ON TO A POINT 200 YDS. AHEAD ON THE ℄ OF THE MACHINE. VERTICAL ADJUSTMENT IS 10' UP & DOWN AT THE FRONT MOUNTING. THE MEAN POSITION BEING 2" BELOW WING DATUM (I.E. PARALLEL TO THRUST LINE).

FOR BROWNING INSTALLATION SEE FIG. 2

SECTIONAL VIEW

The Rolls-Royce 40mm (B.H.) installation *(© Crown Copyright)*

Alternative weapon installations available on the 'Universal Wing' of the Mk IID and Mk IV *(© Crown Copyright)*

VICKERS GUN INSTALLATION Mk. IId. & IV

ROLLS-ROYCE GUN INSTALLATION Mk. IID. & EARLY IV's only.

JETTISONABLE TANKS INSTALLATION Mk. IIb. & IV

BOMBS, SBC. OR SCI. INSTALLATION Mk. IV.

TRAILING EDGE

ACCESS DOORS TOP C.I21637 & BOTTOM BJ2841-2 Mk.IID.& EARLY IV'S ONLY.

ACCESS DOOR TOP C.I21638-9. DOORS C.I21637 & BJ2841-2 ARE NOT FITTED.

ACCESS DOORS TOP C.I21637 BOTTOM BJ2841-2 Mk.IID. & EARLY IV's ONLY.

ACCESS DOOR TOP C.I21637, BOTTOM BJ2841-2 EARLY IV's. ONLY.

REAR MOUNTINGS FOR BOMB RACKS.

REAR SPAR

REAR MOUNTING FOR VICKERS GUN.

JETTISONABLE TANK HOOK & INBOARD STABILISING PAD STOWED.

REAR MOUNTING FOR ROLLS-ROYCE GUN.

COVER PLATES Mk.IID & IV. INBOARD BJ8139-40. OUTBOARD BJ8141-42.

REAR JETTISONABLE TANK HOOK & STABILISING PAD.

BOLTS ETC FOR VICKERS GUN STOWED. BOLTS FOR ROLLS-ROYCE GUN REMAIN ASSEMBLED TO GUN. PLUG PART Nº A.J22537 FITTED & LOCKED WITH WIRE.

TORSION SUB-SPAR.

FRONT MOUNTING FOR VICKERS GUN. PLUG PART Nº A.J22537 STOWED.

FRONT MOUNTING FOR ROLLS-ROYCE GUN.

GUN MOUNTING SWUNG AFT AS SHOWN & RE-SECURED WITH EXISTING FIXINGS.

INTERMEDIATE MOUNTINGS FOR BOMB RACKS.

FRONT SPAR

INBOARD STABILISING PAD SWUNG AFT AS SHOWN & RE-SECURED WITH EXISTING FIXINGS

FRONT JETTISONABLE TANK HOOKS & STABILISING PAD.

FRONT MOUNTINGS FOR BOMB RACKS.

LEADING EDGE

NOTE :-
PARTS SHOWN IN DARK FULL LINES ARE THOSE USED FOR THE PARTICULAR INSTALLATION.
PARTS SHOWN IN LIGHT FULL LINES ARE THOSE FITTED BUT NOT USED.
PARTS SHOWN IN DOTTED ARE THOSE NOT FITTED BUT STOWED IN THE 303" GUN BAY.

The Mk IIC metal wing with 20mm Mk I Hispano cannons *(© A. Oliver)*

The Mk IID metal wing with a single 'sighting' machine gun and the Vickers 40mm cannon *(© A. Oliver)*

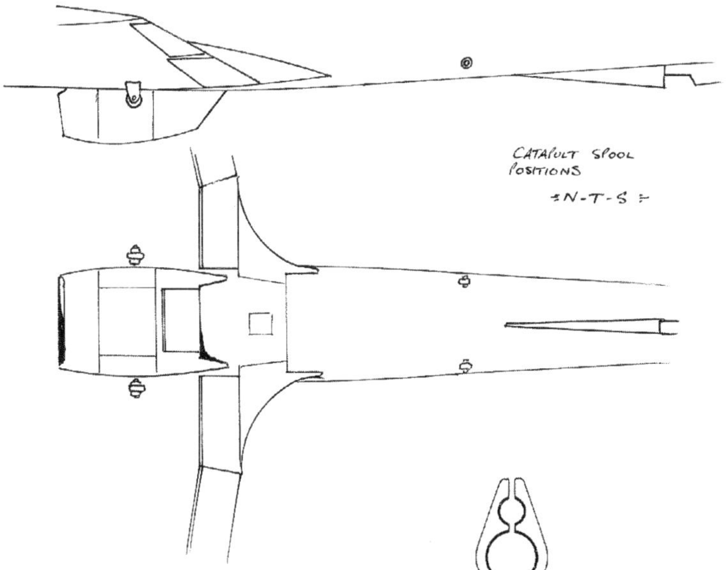

Sea Hurricane • 2

This diagram shows the location of the catapult spools (front and rear) on the Sea Hurricane - Not to Scale *(© A. Oliver)*

CATAPULT SPOOL POSITIONS

N-T-S-

Details of the sliding stop on the hook in both engaged and not engaged positions
(© Crown Copyright)

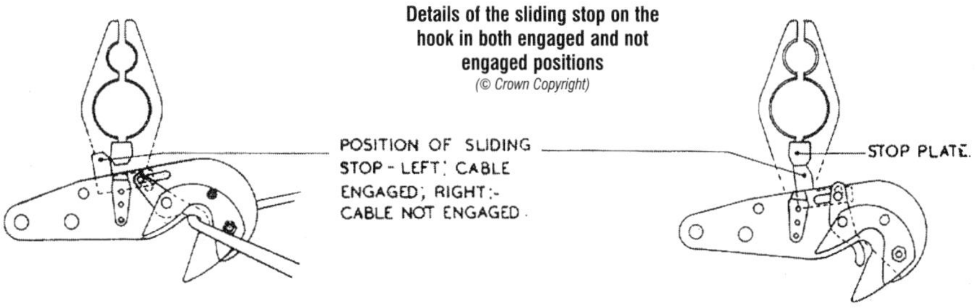

POSITION OF SLIDING STOP - LEFT: CABLE ENGAGED; RIGHT:- CABLE NOT ENGAGED.

STOP PLATE.

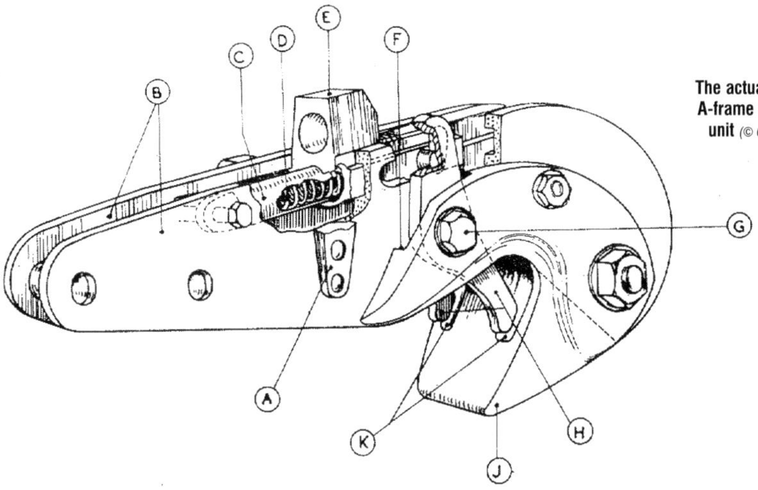

The actual hook on the A-frame arrester hook unit *(© Crown Copyright)*

The snap gear for the arrester hook
(© Crown Copyright)

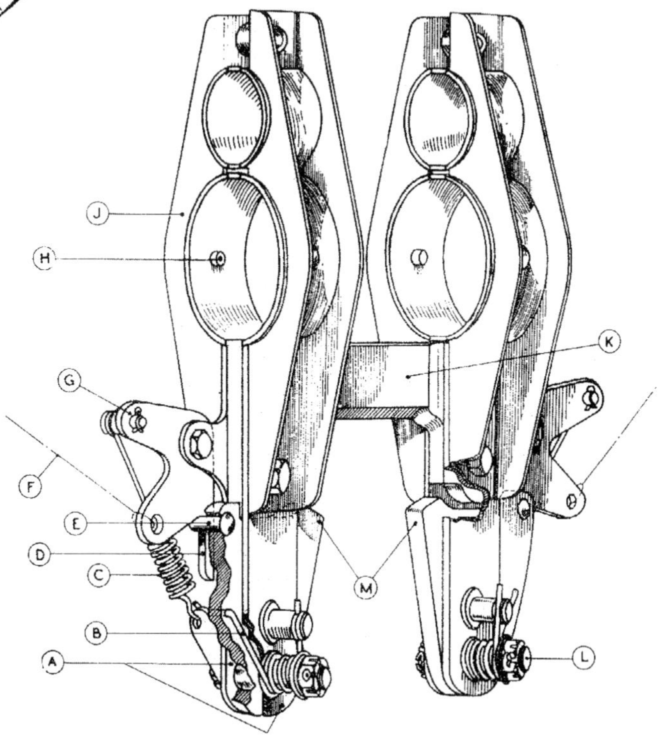

The type of catapult spool fitted on either side of the radiator unit of a Sea Hurricane *(© A. Oliver)*

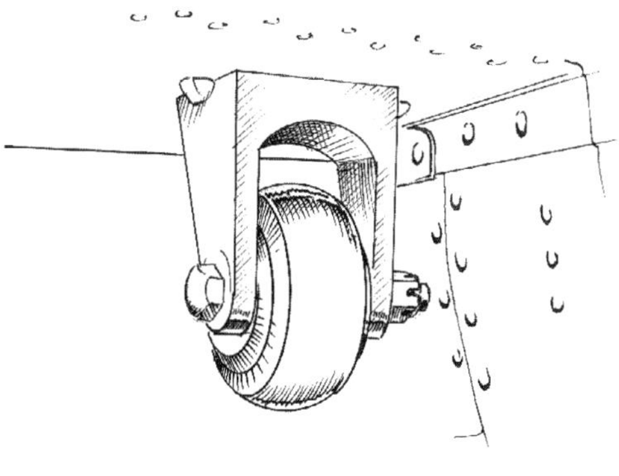

Sea Hurricane • 3

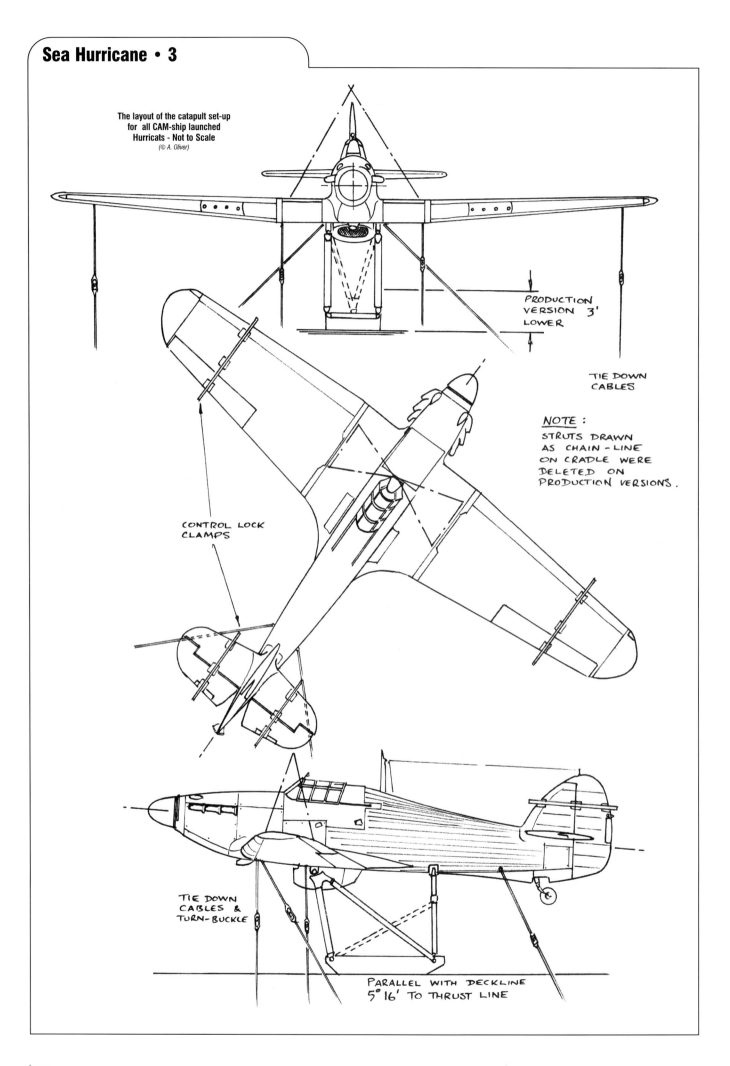

The layout of the catapult set-up
for all CAM-ship launched
Hurricats - Not to Scale
(© A. Oliver)

PRODUCTION
VERSION 3'
LOWER

TIE DOWN
CABLES

NOTE:
STRUTS DRAWN
AS CHAIN-LINE
ON CRADLE WERE
DELETED ON
PRODUCTION VERSIONS.

CONTROL LOCK
CLAMPS

TIE DOWN
CABLES &
TURN-BUCKLE

PARALLEL WITH DECKLINE
5° 16' TO THRUST LINE

Building the Hurricane

W ith our first title in the Modellers Datafile series (De Havilland Mosquito) I built a number of models in 1/48th scale to illustrate this chapter. However, with this second title we have decided to change the format, as there were a lot of comments about the 'bias' towards 1/48th scale. Therefore, what follows is a selection of builds on all available (and a couple of unavailable) kits in 1/72nd and 1/48th scale, as well as 1/32nd. Those covered here therefore are as follows:

- 1 Airfix 1/72nd Scale Mk IIB
- 2 SMER 1/72nd Scale Mk IIC
- 3 Revell 1/72nd Scale Mk I
- 4 Academy 1/72nd Scale Mk IIC
- 5 Matchbox 1/72nd Scale Mk IIC/IID
- 6 Airfix 1/48th Scale Mk I
- 7 Hobbycraft 1/48th Scale Mk IIB 'Russian'
- 8 Hasegawa 1/48th Scale Mk IIC
- 9 Hasegawa 1/48th Scale Mk IID
- 10 Revell-Monogram 1/32nd Scale Mk IIC

• 1 Airfix 1/72nd Scale Mk I/IIB
Constructive Comments by Steve Benstead

This kit claims to offer the Mk I, IIB, IID and Mk IV, and although 3in rocket projectiles are provided with two rails, the kit lacks the larger armoured radiator and Vokes intake filter that characterised the Mk IV aircraft; no Vickers 'S' cannon are included for the Mk IID. The mass of raised detail and the heavily rivetted wing and nose areas highlight the kit's older origins. The nose section is too flat on top and is 2mm too narrow. The overall shape of the nose is good though and the radiator appears to be dimensionally correct (except for the Mk IV). The flat top section to the fuselage top decking is missing and the tail is not tall enough, being approximately 2mm short. The rear fuselage is a little narrow in cross section where it joins the tail. The wings are of insufficient span but the narrow wing-tips offset the problem, allowing the kit to retain a fairly accurate interpretation of the Hurricane wing shape. The tailplanes also appear to be slightly too narrow at the outside and trailing edge. Interior detail is limited to a cockpit floor and a seat attached to a rear bulkhead. When the fuselage halves were joined together, the fit, being mediocre, left a prominent step between them. The top was aligned as well as possible and then lots of sanding and filler applied to the undersurfaces, especially around the underside fuselage to lower-wing joint. The bottom wing was glued into position first, then the upper wings added. Where the upper-wing inner sections (parts 18 and 19) butt up against the fuselage, they are too deep and require sanding down by approximately 0.5mm. You may also need to sand down some of the upper-wing inboard section between the landing lights and the fuselage join because the wing appears a little too thick here as well. The locating lugs on the lower-wing section are more of a nuisance than a help and were quickly cut away, the

upper sections being joined up against the fuselage to ensure as tight a fit as possible. Part of the join line was visible but this was not too worrying as the Hurricane has quite a prominent panel line in this area. The top join of the fuselage halves was sanded back and some filler was required around the lower nose section and the wing/fuselage underside join and this area is difficult to clean up due to the heavy fabric effect. Part of the join line was left in, as it did not look too obvious with all the fabric lines around it. The whole aircraft surface was sanded

Airfix 1/72nd Scale Mk I by Steve Benstead

to tone down the heavy rivet detail. Airfix are famous for their rivets and the Hurricane is no exception. With the model primed the panel lines and rivets appeared much more in scale. The aircraft undersurface was sprayed with AeroMaster RAF Sky and, as no colour is specified in the instructions, AeroMaster RAF Interior Green was painted into the wheel wells. Although some early Hurricanes had interior-green wheel wells, these were changed to a silver finish later in the war. The undersurfaces were RAF Dark Earth and RAF Dark Green.

Despite the Mk I, Mk IIB, Mk IID and Mk IV options presented on the sprues, the decals only give two options. P3069, RF•C, a Mk I of No. 303 (Polish) Sqn. based at RAF Northolt in 1940 and BE417, AE•K. a Mk IIB from No. 402 Sqn., RAF Warmwell in 1941. The No. 303 Sqn. aircraft carries the Dark Earth/Dark Green scheme with Sky undersurface whilst the No. 402 Sqn. aircraft is Ocean Grey/Dark Green over Medium Sea Grey and has a Sky identification band around the rear fuselage. The decals adhered well to the glossy surface, assisted by liberal amounts of Micro Sol, and silvering was minimal. The Airfix decals seemed to have poor colour density as many of the colours underneath each image showed through and the register was poor on several as well. The red showed through the blue quite prominently on the roundels and the inner red circle on the underwing roundels broke up slightly when applied. The decal colour was also out of register with the outline of the carrier film and this caused difficulties in alignment. I was impressed by the inclusion of the gas sensitive patch that adorned many RAF aircraft wings during the early part of the war. The undercarriage is very poorly detailed and very fragile. Great care should be taken when cutting the legs from the sprue. The instructions are rather vague as to the sequence for installing these parts but I would recommend placing the undercarriage doors in position first, then gluing the legs to

**Revell 1/72nd scale Mk I
by Steve Benstead**

the inside of the door as this affords them better protection against snapping or bending. This had to be done on this kit as a broken undercarriage leg refused to mend properly and was considerably weakened. Simply cut about 3mm off the top of the leg (the locating pin and a little bit of the leg itself) and then it should position nicely into the undercarriage door using the original locating point in line with the wheel hub. The broad Rotol propeller is nicely shaped and the rather squat spinner is well modelled, but is too big in diameter.

This kit offers plenty of scope due to the wide range of underwing stores supplied on the sprues. Although the Mk I was devoid of stores, you do get a pair of 250lb bombs, eight rocket projectiles and their launcher rails, a pair of 44 Imp gal fuel tanks and a set of Vickers 'S' 40mm cannon for a tank-busting Mk IID.

**SMER 1/72nd scale Mk IIC
by Steve Benstead**

•2 SMER 1/72nd Scale Mk IIC
Constructive Comments by Steve Benstead

This kit is a re-boxed version of the Heller one and is suitable as an assessment of both kits except for the decal sheet which, under the SMER label, is produced by Propagteam. The kit parts are moulded in a light grey plastic with delicately raised panel lines and features. The top decking of the fuselage, just behind the canopy, is not flat enough and this gives the aircraft a slightly humped appearance. The nose looks about 2mm too long from the forward bulkhead firewall and this results in the cockpit being pushed back slightly, relative to the nose. The underside of the nose cowling is too deep by 2mm from the point where it meets

the start of the wing-root fillet. The upper profile of the nose is fine but the oil collector ring is much too thick, being very overscale. It would be better to remove it and replace it with a plasticard version. The tail profile is good but the fabric effect is crude and incorrect and although the tailplanes are nicely detailed, the span is incorrect. This results in the outer profile being wrong, the shape of the curve is incorrect and the trailing edge is too sharply angled. The wings are of reasonable accuracy in span but the outer section is too broad. Because of this, the wing-tip edge is rather too flat in profile to keep the correct wingspan. The landing light is too far inboard and the cannon are slightly too far outboard, so it all looks rather squashed together. Interior detail is minimal, you get a seat (of sorts), a rather chunky control column and the pedals are integral with the cockpit floor. The fuselage halves fit together well with just some filler required along the top of the nose and on the top of the fuselage behind the canopy. The original Heller kit was based on a nightfighter version and the instruction sheet still makes reference to the anti-glare plates either side of the nose. I have not been able to confirm that either of the options in the SMER kit used these plates, so I did not use them (they are not mentioned or featured in the decal instructions or artwork). The general assembly of the kit was very straightforward with only a small amount of filler required along the main join lines and seams. The most difficult area was the underside seam between the nose and the bottom of the wing. The kit has some nice touches like the gunsight and rear-view mirror being included as plastic parts.

The decals are very nice and very straightforward to apply. Adhesion is excellent and the clarity and colour register is generally very good. I did use Micro Sol on some of the decals, such as those on the fuselage. There are two options provided. The first is Z3094, QO•R of No. 3 Squadron, described as 'late 1941'. This would mean an aircraft based at RAF Hunsdon or one of the detachments at Manston and Shoreham. During this period, the squadron was engaged in nightfighter operations with some daylight sweeps and intruder patrols. The second option is for BP592 from No. 213 Squadron operating in North Africa late in '41 through 1942, although the instruction sheet and decal instructions do not tell you anything at all about this aircraft. This option is for one of the 'Italian' type schemes with the disruptive camouflage around the nose and along the leading edge of the wings.

Overall an excellent kit. There are certainly some dimensional problems, but until the new Hasegawa example came along this was the best show in town. Even if you cannot afford the Hasegawa examples, the Heller or SMER examples will still form the basis for a reasonable Mk IIC; all you need to spend is a little more effort.

•3 Revell 1/72nd Scale Mk I
Constructive Comments by Steve Benstead

This is the oldest of all the 1/72nd scale kits currently available, and the Revell Hurricane is definitely beginning to show its age. The sprues are very messy with lots of flash and distortion evident and the gates which join the parts to the sprue are, in many instances, very large and awkward to cut around. The overall length is good but the profile is very wrong. The underside of the nose is too sharply angled when sloping aft of the prop. The kit has the right amount of height to the top of the canopy but the distinctive flattened fuselage fairing behind the canopy is not represented, giving the kit a pronounced humpback look. The radiator is far too big, looking almost 1/48th scale. It is too acutely angled, giving it the appearance of the armoured radiator fitted to the ground attack Mk IV variant. Moving further aft, the ventral fin beneath the tail is only half the size it should be and the tail is completely the wrong shape. It is too rounded, lacking any sort of angle to the leading edge. The wings are slightly too small in span and the wing tip is too broad. This makes the trailing edge too shallow and gives the kit a very short and fat wing shape. With regard to colour schemes, two options are provided; P3975, RF•U of No. 303 (Polish) Sqn., RAF. and P3369, JX•B of No.1 Sqn. The kit has absolutely no interior detail with only a rather diminutive, deformed pilot to occupy the inside of the aircraft. The fuselage halves had quite a step when joined together so the top was aligned as well as possible and then lots of sanding and filling applied to the undersurfaces, especially around the nose underside and lower wing joint. The join between the wings and the fuselage is very poor, so the bottom wing was glued into position first, then the upper wing panels were added. The radiator is an integral part of the lower wing and has no internal structure so you can look straight through it. Lots of filler is required around the upper wing panel join. The sanding was extended to the whole aircraft surface in order to tone down the heavy rivet detail and this certainly improved the overall appearance of the kit. The undersurface was sprayed with Halfords White Primer and then the starboard undersurface was carefully masked. The port lower surface was then sprayed with Halfords Flat Black. Reference sources show the gear doors and wheel wells to be the same colour as the undersurface colour so AeroMaster black and white were added to the relevant wheel wells. The undersurface was then completely masked and AeroMaster RAF Dark Earth sprayed across the entire upper surface. Once dry, the Dark Earth areas were masked off and AeroMaster RAF Dark Green was sprayed over the top. The masking tape was removed and several layers of AeroMaster Gloss were sprayed to give a smooth surface prior to decal application.

Revell decals are very thick with a severe matt carrier film. With the raised detail and fabric effect on the aircraft the decals could provide some problems. Having achieved a smooth, gloss finish, Micro Sol was painted onto the approximate decal position and then the decal applied. More Micro Sol was added. The decals, somewhat surprisingly, adhered well and conformed to the shape very nicely. Excess carrier film was trimmed off a number of decals, including the code letters and the aircraft serial numbers. To ease application, the code letters were cut into individual letters, rather than a single decal of three letters and the roundel. Only the wing roundels showed any evidence of silvering. Two red fabric gun-covers were added from sections of Xtradecal red decal stripes. With the decals in position the aircraft was sprayed with several coats of AeroMaster Flat. The undercarriage is very poorly detailed and the wheels themselves bear no relation to any wheel unit that I have seen on Hurricanes. The instructions state that the complete undercarriage and door assembly should be constructed and then positioned. To ensure more accuracy when aligning, the undercarriage doors were glued in position first. The undercarriage legs were then located onto the doors, having first test fitted and trimmed about 1mm from the upper section. The centre pins (part number 7) that secure the wheels to the undercarriage legs are just dreadful. The ones on the sprue were completely deformed and unusable and the wheels were therefore attached to the undercarriage legs with a gap filling superglue. The tail wheel was very badly deformed and probably warranted replacing completely, but I just cut away the lower section of the tail wheel and then filled it with Milliput to restore the shape. The rather crude exhaust stacks were painted with a combination of Tamiya Copper, Flat Black and Metallic Grey. The De Havilland propeller is very well modelled, although the

propeller and spinner are one piece. The kit does not include the antennae mast, one being made from stretched sprue.

Overall a very basic and old kit, and one I would not recommend to anyone. To be completely fair Revell have removed this item from their range, replacing it with the much newer Mk IIB version reviewed elsewhere. So, if you have one of these in your kit collection, keep it in the box, as that is where it's at its best!

•4 Academy 1/72nd Scale Mk IIC
Constructive Comments by Steve Benstead

The kit has very crisp engraved panel details and has the best interior detail of all the 1/72nd scale Hurricanes available (with the exception of the upgraded SMER Hurricane Mk IV). The wing is very accurate compared with scale plans, having the right dimensions and shape to the tip and trailing edge. The nose is a little bit too long although the profile is good. The flat fairing is well defined but the tail is a bit short. The kit's main shortcoming is the narrowness of the fuselage. This can be solved by inserting a 20 thou strip of plasticard to bulk out the fuselage and

Academy 1/72nd scale Mk IIC by Steve Benstead

using a vac-form canopy instead of the one supplied with the kit. The interior is very nice with a separate cockpit floor/rear bulkhead, rudders, control column, side consoles and a seat. Everything was painted AeroMaster RAF Interior Green and then the detail picked out with some gentle dry brushing in flat white. The instrument panel was painted AeroMaster Flat Black. The fuselage halves were joined together and filler was not needed at all. The cockpit tub was glued onto the lower wing section and then the whole unit was joined to the fuselage. With the lower wing section in place, the upper wings were added. A small amount of sanding was required around the wing tips and leading edges but that was all. The tailplanes slotted in beautifully. The canopy was carefully masked and then the kit was sprayed with Halfords Grey Primer overall. Next the undersurfaces were sprayed flat black and masked off. AeroMaster Ocean Grey was sprayed across the entire top surface before being carefully masked. Several layers of Aeromaster RAF Dark Green was then applied. Finally, masking tape strips were positioned along the wing leading edge and AeroMaster trainer yellow was sprayed on for the leading edge ID markings. Several layers of AeroMaster Gloss were sprayed across the kit before the decals were added.

The decals are very thin and very glossy. Adhesion is excellent and the clarity and colour register is generally very good. The tail decals did have a white line where the base colour was slightly out of register but this was the only problem encountered. Micro Sol was used to facilitate the decal adhesion onto the fabric-covered fuselage sides with good results. Once matted down with AeroMaster Flat a small amount of silvering was apparent on the port serial number and on the starboard aircraft codes. The canopy masking was removed and then the landing lights added. These may well need to be trimmed slightly to fit. The cannon stubs were fitted by cutting off the locating pin and shaping the rear section to correspond with the wing leading edge. The undercarriage is superb and just slots straight in to the locating points in the wheel well (which is very well detailed). The undercarriage doors have a locating recess that attaches to the leg, simple but effective. The spinner and props were sprayed with Halfords Flat Black and then attached with PVA glue. The aerial wire was made from GoldZack.

A very straightforward and simple kit to make.

•5 Matchbox 1/72nd Scale Mk IIC/IID
Constructive Comments by Steve Benstead

The Matchbox Hurricane has a very nice plan shape but is rather let down, like the Revell kit, by its profile. The wing shape is very good with the 20mm Hispano cannon being in the correct position relative to the join for wing centre-section/outboard section. The main failings are that the landing lights are too far outboard and that the panel lines are a little too deeply engraved, giving the appearance that nothing actually fits together. Viewed from the side, the canopy and rear fuselage upper decking are too low, giving a rather squashed-down appearance. In fact, it looks more like a 'Speed Hurricane' version than a standard aircraft. This problem is accentuated by the canopy being too long by 1.5 mm. The flat upper fuselage fairing has been well represented and the nose is the correct length although it isn't quite the right shape. The tail has a nice profile but the rudder post is only 26mm high. Scale plans show it to be 28mm. The ventral strake is well proportioned but the radiator is a little on the narrow side. The kit offers options for two aircraft; a No. 87 Sqn. nightfighting Hurricane Mk IIC, BE500, LK•A based at Warmwell in 1941 or a No. 6 Sqn. Mk IID aircraft at LG.89 during the North African campaign in July, 1942. The kit is mid-way between the Revell and Airfix examples for interior detail, in other words you get a seat to put the pilot on and all other detail is deemed unnecessary. For a kit of this simplicity and price the fuselage sections join together very well. No filler was necessary, just a gentle sanding down of the join line. The tailplanes fitted on with no fuss and the wings went together equally well. The radiator has a top section in order to remove a centre seam line and this works well, the shape formed

Matchbox 1/72nd scale Mk IIC by Steve Benstead

being easily filled and sanded. The wings slot into the fuselage well, although you do get a rather large 'engraved' line on the underside of the wing which will need filling.

Matchbox decals do not look very good, with thick carrier film and lots of it. The decals for the codes were cut into separate pieces and applied with lots of Micro Sol as this gets the decals pulled right down onto the paint. It is advisable to trim off as much excess carrier film as possible, especially when doing the black nightfighter scheme. Even carrier film between the code letters 'K' and 'A' was removed. The undercarriage is very simple, and the actual undercarriage leg is part of the undercarriage door (parts 19 and 22) which makes alignment easier and improves the strength of the units, which slot easily into the wheel wells. Finally, the 20mm cannon were added and the instructions require you to drill out the holes and locate the cannon prior to gluing the wing sections together. Instead the wings were completed and the locating points for the cannon cut away with a sprue cutter. The back of the cannon stub was shaped to fit onto the wing leading edge and then superglued in place. Alignment is easy as the cannon port attachment plates are engraved onto the wing, simply glue each cannon stub into the middle of the square.

Overall this is a basic, but easy-to-build model. The panel lines are a little too deep at times, but as a 'buildable' kit I don't think you have much to complain about with this one.

•6 Airfix 1/48th Scale Mk I
Constructive Comments by Richard A. Franks

The whole assembly task for this Airfix kit is quite straightforward and the age of the kit is now showing just in how simple it is. The first task is to choose which colour option you are making, as each requires a different style of spinner and propeller. The No. 85 Sqn. machine has a De Havilland propeller and (pointed) spinner, while the No. 501 Sqn. machine has the Rotol (blunt) spinner and propeller. I was going for the early machine, so I built up the DH unit and then turned my attention to the cockpit. With this kit interior detail is adequate, although basic, and the cockpit 'floor' also forms part of the undercarriage bay roof. I say 'floor' as the Hurricane did not have such a thing in reality, as the whole cockpit area is made up of tubes. Returning to the the kit I actually deviated from the assembly sequence prescribed in the instructions, as I wanted to make up the wings and fuselage as two units, then just join them together. Therefore I added the wheel well (14) to the lower wing (18) and then fitted the control column (17), rear bulkhead (15) and seat (16) to it. Remember that the rear bulkhead is not at 90 degrees to the floor, so you will need to have the fuselage together and then place the wing assembly up underneath, so that you can position the bulkhead at the correct angle. The instrument panel (22) is added to the fuselage halves and then I added the upper wing panels (25 & 26), radiator (46 & 47) and carburettor intake (48) to make up the whole unit. At this point I also added the machine gun port inserts (49 & 50) - horrible idea! The fit of these latter items, you may have guessed, was appalling and a lot of filler was required. The tailplanes are made up of four parts and I am afraid to say that in my example one lower half (28) was missing a large area at the trailing edge caused by a 'short-shot' during the injection process. The same was true of the other side (30), but thankfully this was far less so. In the end, because of the timescale, I added filler to build up the missing areas, but if you encounter such a problems I would recommend writing to Airfix for replacement parts.

At this stage I did some filling and sanding, as well as preparing the small undercarriage and detail parts, and then I joined the completed fuselage to the wing. Filler is once again required at the wing joint, and the raised detail of this kit will suffer as a result of the sanding required on all the filler. Once all of the filling and sanding was complete the model was primed, re-sanded and then sprayed with the chosen colour scheme. In the example I had there were the following colour options:

•1. No. 85 (Fighter) Squadron, RAF Advanced Air Striking Force, Lille/Seclin, France, April 1940. This machine is Dark Earth and Dark Green over a 50/50 split of white and black;

•2. No. 5091 (County of Gloucester) Sqn., RAuxAF. RAF Kenley, October 1940. This machine is also Dark Earth and Dark Green, but this time it is over Sky (not 'Duck Egg Blue' as stated on the instructions).

I went for the first option and used colours from the AeroMaster and Xtracolor enamel ranges. The decals supplied in the current release of this kit are matt, with noticeable areas of carrier film around each image. I trimmed most of these areas off the decals before application, although the paint scheme was nice and glossy and this may have made this stage easier. Once all the decals were applied, including the small number of stencils, the model was sprayed with Humbrol Matt Cote and the undercarriage, pitot, aerial mast and canopy were added. Overall this is a simple and effective kit, and one which makes up into a pleasant Mk I, although for the more adventurous of you there is a big need to upgrade the detail throughout the kit, and especially that cockpit interior.

•7 Hobbycraft 1/48th Scale Mk IIB 'Russian'
Constructive Comments by Richard A. Franks

Now having made the Airfix Mk I, opening this kit gave me a very real sense of having been here before! The kit is so reminiscent of the Airfix kit that I am sure we have all heard the stories about this being an upgrade (or copy) of the Airfix kit, whatever is the case this kit builds up in a very similar manner to the Airfix Mk I. The first job is the propeller, and here you have a problem as Hobbycraft have not even given you any lugs to secure each blade to the backplate. This does make getting everything lined up a real trial, but the end result is acceptable (the profile of the spinner is another matter though). As with the Airfix kit, this one also includes the wheel well as part of the floor of the cockpit, and other interior details just comprise the seat, control column and rear bulkhead. I mixed up the assembly stages again, adding the upper-wing panels now instead of later, so that I could have the wings and fuselage as two separate assemblies. The radiator unit (34 & 9) and the carburettor air intake (33) were also added to the lower wing and the instructions note on this example that the bulges on the upper wing must be removed, as you are making the Mk IIB. Alas the wing's access panels depict a Mk IIC, and even with the bulges removed, the panels are all wrong for an eight-gun version. The kit would also have you add the 44 gallon drop tanks to the Russian and Finnish versions offered in it, but to my knowledge neither of these countries operated the Hurricane with these tanks fitted, so leave them off. Detail parts such as the exhaust stacks, undercarriage and canopy were all left off until after the model was painted.

This example of the tooling offers the following two options:

•1. Mk IIB, BM959 on the Russian Front. This machine is

listed as being Dark Green and Ocean Grey over Medium Sea Grey and has Russian stars in six locations and a large white wolf on the vertical fin. Watch out for the confusion between the box artwork and the painting guide, as the latter shows the leading edges without a yellow strip,

Airfix 1/48th scale Mk I by Richard A. Franks

while the box art has one;

•2. Mk II, HC-465 of the Finnish Air Force. This machine is listed as being black and RLM 71 over RLM 76 with the bands around the nose and fuselage and under each outer wing panel in yellow. Because of the international law in relation to the swastika, the blue Finnish crosses are offered in two parts only.

The decals included in the kit are not bad, although the Russian example can be obtained on the AeroMaster sheet. No stencilling is included at all. I went for the Finnish example, using the prescribed colours from the AeroMaster range and then a coat of gloss varnish was applied to accept the decals. The decals themselves were of a

Hobbycraft 1/48th scale Mk IIB 'Russian' by Richard A. Franks

good quality, as they were glossy and reacted well to Micro Set solution.

Overall this is a neat kit; like the old Monogram example it comes with a mass of very useful extra parts, such as the drop tanks, a tropical filter and two Vickers 40mm 'S' cannon. However, with the arrival of a dedicated Mk II series from Hasegawa this kit can only hope to offer the 'cheaper alternative', and as far as a Mk IIB goes, it cannot hope to be one. The comments about detail apply to this kit as well, but just remember to replace that inaccurate tailwheel with the Aeroclub version and see if you can use the Airfix Rotol propeller instead of the kit-supplied example.

•8 Hasegawa 1/48th Scale Mk IIC

Constructive Comments by Richard A. Franks

When this kit was first released I for one was glad to see that the Hurricane had not been forgotten in Japan and my only concern was whether Hasegawa were going to consider the earlier versions seeing as they started with the Mk IIC (I am glad to say it now seems they will!).

The breakdown of the kit hinted at a Mk I series airframe, as the entire nose is separate. The cockpit interior is made up of a very realistic tubular structure, and once painted looks very effective. The most criticism levelled at this kit has been the fabric effect on the rear fuselage. This is far too heavy, with a more 'scalloped' effect than the subtle curves of the real machine. To be fair to Hasegawa, the tooling is designed to last a considerable time, and during the injection process over the coming years this effect will become less and less dramatic. If the manufacturers had been completely accurate in reproducing this area, in ten years time the whole fuselage would have been devoid of any detail! In the end just remember to spray a good primer over the fuselage and then gently sand it back. the primer will 'fill' the recesses of the fabric, while the sanding will remove it from the ridges, thereby reducing the fabric effect overall. The whole cockpit and rear fuselage can be assembled, and then the nose can be added. This has the double benefit of easing the handling difficulties involved with manipulating five items, as well as allowing you to adjust the fit of the nose to ensure you don't need any filler at its joint. Because this kit is generic, in the sense that it will offer both Mk I and Mk II series machines, the wings have to have the magazine bulges for the 20mm Hispano cannon added, although this is clearly noted in the instructions. Later, two inserts will allow the cannon barrels to be fitted, although the fit of these leaves a lot to be desired. The lower engine cowling (B2) is a separate part, and this is simply because the Mk IID features a Vokes filter at this point. The undercarriage is excellent, with the main legs and radius rods as separate parts and, unlike the previous two examples, the undercarriage bay does not feature the cockpit floor on its back. The two-part carburettor air intake (J21 & J22) does feature the FOD guard (J14), but this is a little overscale and is best replaced with a suitable etched-brass screen. The radiator features interior matrix front and back and the actuating rods for the flap at the rear of the unit are also included. Attention to detail is obviously Hasegawa's watchword here, as both Mk I and Mk II Hispano cannon are included. If you are making PZ865 take heed of the note about painting out the starboard landing light (G6) (guess who didn't!)

There are three options offered in the kit and they are:

- 1. BD962, QD•Q of No. 3 Sqn., RAF;
- 2. Z3894, QD•R of No. 3 Sqn., RAF;
- 3. PZ865, 'Last of the Many' owned by Hawker-Siddeley Aviation Ltd.

The first two options are listed as being in a 'Mixed Grey and Dark Green over Medium Sea Grey scheme, while PZ865 is Ocean Grey and Dark Green over Medium Sea Grey. The instructions note that the No. 3 Sqn machines featured a 'mixed grey' that was basically Medium Sea Grey (70%) and black (30%) and that this colour was specified by the 1941 Soviet Army standards for use in place of Ocean Grey, which was in short supply. I opted for PZ865, and applied the appropriate colours from the Xtracolor range of enamel paints. Once dry the decals were applied and these are of excellent quality and register. I had no real problems with any of them, although the smaller ones did not like too much Micro Sol decal solvent being used. Once all of this was dry I sprayed the model with Humbrol Satin Cote, as PZ865 never saw service and was always kept very clean by Hawker-Siddeley. Overall this is certainly a state-of-the-art kit and one that can be highly recommended to all. The attention to detail is nice to see and the fact that the basic moulds will offer both Mk I and Mk II series machines means that we should all soon be able to make each version of the Hurricane we like, and to a very high standard.

Hasegawa 1/48th scale Mk IIC by Richard A. Franks

Hasegawa 1/48th scale Mk IID by Richard A. Franks

•9 Hasegawa 1/48th Scale Mk IID

Constructive Comments by Richard A. Franks

As you may guess, this kit is just a revision of the Mk IIC, and all the points I raised about that kit also apply here. The first change arrives as you assemble the wings. Here you have to open up the holes in the lower section (F1) to later take the lugs for the 'S' cannon. The standard lower chin cowling is replaced with a Vokes tropical filter, and unlike the one in the Hobbycraft kit, this one definitely looks the part. The undercarriage is approached in the same manner as that in the Mk IIC but when you have added the wings you will have to put the blanks (A9 & A10) into the machine gun/cannon port area of the leading edge and fit the Vickers 40mm 'S' cannon gondolas. The barrels of these cannon feature a pronounced bulge at the tip, and although this probably reproduces the fabric covers fitted to these machines in transit, it is unlikely that this is applicable to any operational Mk IID. By this stage it is time to consider the colour scheme of your model.

The kit currently includes the following two options:
1. BP188, JV•Z of No. 6 Sqn., Western Desert;
2. HV663, 'U' of No. 6 Sqn., Western Desert.

Each of these options is Dark Earth and Middle Stone over Azure Blue with a red spinner. Fading of these colours would be pronounced in a desert environment, and although I have yet to 'fade' the colours on my model I would suggest that you do this once the decals are applied (they have to be faded also). The decals are of the highest quality. They are in perfect register and the lighter colours do not show darker shades below. A number of small stencils are included and I had no trouble with any of the markings, as they settled down nicely on the gloss surface of the colour scheme. Once all the decals had set the model was sprayed with an overall coat of Humbrol Matt Cote, and once this was dry all the detail parts such as the undercarriage and canopy were added.

As with the Mk IIC, this kit is a great leap forward from both the Monogram and Hobbycraft Mk II series kits and all we can hope for now is that Hasegawa will do the Mk IV before too much longer (with the correct radiator), as well as the fabric wing Mk I.

•10 Revell-Monogram 1/32nd Scale Mk IIC
Constructive Comments by Richard A. Franks

Let me start this report by shaking my head and saying "oh dear, oh dear, oh dear!". This kit is a classic example of accountants at work in the model industry. Someone with no idea of what a Hurricane is, decided that a bit more life could be wrung out of the previous Mk I mould, by modifying it to a Mk II. Fine you may think, but not when you appreciate that the 'modification' consists of adding some bulges to the upper wings and some cannon barrels! This kit is not a Mk II, it is a Mk I and that is all you will ever be able to make from it without considerable modification.

Having said all that let's now get on with the assembly. The first stage is to make up the Merlin engine. This six-part unit is basic, and could do with extra time being spent on it. The cockpit interior is not much better, consisting of a floor, side consoles and rear bulkhead. These look all right from a distance, but in this scale they would have to be replaced. The tailwheel assembly has to be made up before the cockpit 'tub' can be trapped into the fuselage and here again you come across the Mk I origins of the mould, as the unit in this kit is the original oil-spring type fitted to the Mk I series, and totally inaccurate for the Mk IIC. The wheel in the tail yoke isn't much better, being no more than a plastic button! Once the interior is sprayed the wings and fuselage are joined together and the tailpanes added. All of the major joints in this kit will need filler and the removal of any excess will result in large areas of the raised detail being removed. The radiator unit includes the matrix effect in the front only and the tropical filter unit included for the desert option is a very odd shape. Final details added before I moved on to the painting stage were the upper engine cowling (to cover that engine) and the cannon. It is good to see that the instruction illustrator knew what the Hispano cannon looked like, and if you look at the instructions, then at the kit parts, you will find these bear no resemblance to each other. The instructions show the barrels, with external springs and base farings being installed directly into the wing. The kit however features the farings on the wings and the barrels for the Hispano cannon separate. To say that these components are reproductions of no part of a Hurricane is probably true and if they are supposed to look like a Hispano, they fail.

The current issue of this kit comes with the following two colour options:
•1. Mk IIC, BP349 of No. 73 Sqn., RAF, Western Desert, 1942. This machine is Dark Earth and Middle Stone over Azure Blue;
•2. Mk IIC Intruder, HL864, LK•? of No. 87 Sqn., RAF Charmy Down, 1942. This machine is listed as being Medium Sea Grey and Dark Green over black.

Now you have already probably noted the first error, as HL864 should be Ocean Grey and Dark Green, not Medium Sea Grey and Dark Green. The situation gets worse though, as the serial for HL864 is in a computer font, is way too big and is black, when it should be Medium Sea Grey. The decals themselves are quite well printed, have good colour density and registration, but the errors make that a little superficial really. I went for HL864 simply because I already had the Hasegawa Mk IID in a desert scheme. The initial colours were all from the AeroMaster range and the entire model was then sprayed with Humbrol Gloss Cote prior to the application of the decals. I found the decals went on very well, and did not need much decal solvent, even though the entire model is covered in raised rivets. Once these were all dry a coat of Matt Cote was applied to finish the model off and the undercarriage, aerial mast, landing lights, canopy and tip lights were all added. Note that the canopy is horrible, being too thick and having rails that originally were designed to allow the canopy to open.

What can I say... This kit is not what it says it is and the modifications made by Revell–Monogram to it have reduced it to a mish-mash of versions all rolled into one. All you can make from this kit is a Mk I, as serious modifications and scratch building will be required to make this into a Mk IIC. It is a great shame that this kit is the only one ever produced in this scale and I only hope that some manufacturer considering 1/32nd scale products will take a hard look at this aircraft. For now though, you have really got your work cut out with this kit.

Well, there you have it, a brief overview of some of the Hurricane models in a number of the popular scales. For those of you wanting to create other variants, I would direct your attention to Chapter 10, which lists all the modifications and accessories you will need to build any of the Hurricane variants.

Revell-Monogram 1/32nd Scale Mk IIC by Richard A. Franks

Colour and Marking Notes

As you will see this subject is by no means a simple one and what we will try to do in this chapter is give you a baseline from which to work. There is no way we can cover all areas and eventualities, as the subject of colour and markings is a hotly debated one and we could easily fill this entire book with it. What follows is a basic guide that has been created from the official RAF regulations, coupled with the study of a number of articles and features on the subject over the past thirty years and a detailed study of a huge number of photographs.

The Prototype

K5083 was always to remain in an aluminium dope and bare (polished) metal scheme. Initially only white-outlined black serials, a 25in dia fuselage roundel and 50in diamater wing roundels were applied. During service trials at Martlesham Heath however the fuselage roundel was increased in size. At no time during its flying career did K5083 ever carry a fin flash. The two-blade Watts wooden propeller featured a polished aluminium spinner, while the rest of the propeller and blades were fabric-covered and painted light grey on the forward faces of the blades, and matt black on the rear. A brass leading-edge cover was nailed to each blade, and the extreme root of each remained as varnished wood.

RAF Operations

The early Hurricanes in RAF service were finished in a disruptive camouflage pattern of Dark Earth and Dark Green over doped aluminium. Type A roundels of 45in diameter were carried under the wings, positioned with their centres 57in from the wing tip. The roundel was positioned in such a way that at no time did any portion of it touch the ailerons. The serial number was carried under each mainplane in 30in black characters, with the starboard wing being read from the trailing edge, and the port wing being read from the leading edge. Fuselage roundels were 35in diameter Type A1 style, while the upper wing ones were 49in diameter. The fuselage serial number was applied in black 6in high figures and during the early days no fin flash was applied, but the squadron's badge was often carried on either side of the vertical fin. The extreme tip of the Watts propeller spinner was often picked out in Dark Earth.

The first Tactical recognition markings were applied to the Hurricane soon after reaching service, where the starboard outer wing panel lower surface was painted white, and the port black. The 30in serial numbers remained, but those on the black wing were applied in white. All other markings and roundels remained the same.

After the Munich Crisis in August 1938, all the roundels and serials were removed from underneath the Hurricane's wings. The outer wing panel colours (black and white) were extended inwards to meet at the centreline. The flaps and elevators were repainted in aluminium dope and the lower nose, rear fuselage

LF345, ZA•P was a Mk IIC supplied to Belgium post-war and it was lost in an accident on the 2nd July 1947
(© R. Binneman)

and underneath of each tailplane remained in aluminium. Variations in this scheme appear however, and it is not uncommon to see the entire aircraft under-surface split 50/50 in black and white (including fuselage and tail) with the ailerons on each wing picked out in the opposite wing's colour i.e. white wing = black aileron. Squadron codes were applied either side of the fuselage roundel in 38in high Medium Sea Grey letters. Type B roundels of 25in diameter with a 10in centre were applied to the fuselage, while 49in Type B roundels were applied to the upper wings. No roundels were carried under the wings, and those applied to the fuselage and upper wings were painted directly over the existing Type A1 examples.

During the September 1939 to May 1940 period, Nos. 60 and 67 Squadron machines carried a 50/50 split scheme of black and white on the entire under surface of their machines. The original 45in diameter Type A roundels returned and the elevators were painted in the same colour are the remainder of that wing. During this period it was common for the fin flashes to be applied on the entire rudder, in a manner not dissimilar to the French national tricolour. This was to aid international recognition of the aircraft by its allies. UK operated Hurricanes at this time were seen with Medium Sea Grey squadron codes approximately 27in. high. The 35in fuselage and upper wing roundels had been converted from the existing Type A1, with a 14in centre. The black serial numbers were often painted out in Dark Green on all aircraft that did (or could) operate over France at this stage in the war.

This Mk IIC, PZ769, ZA•M, has come to the end of its flying career and it later became an instructional airframe at a technical school
(© R. Binneman)

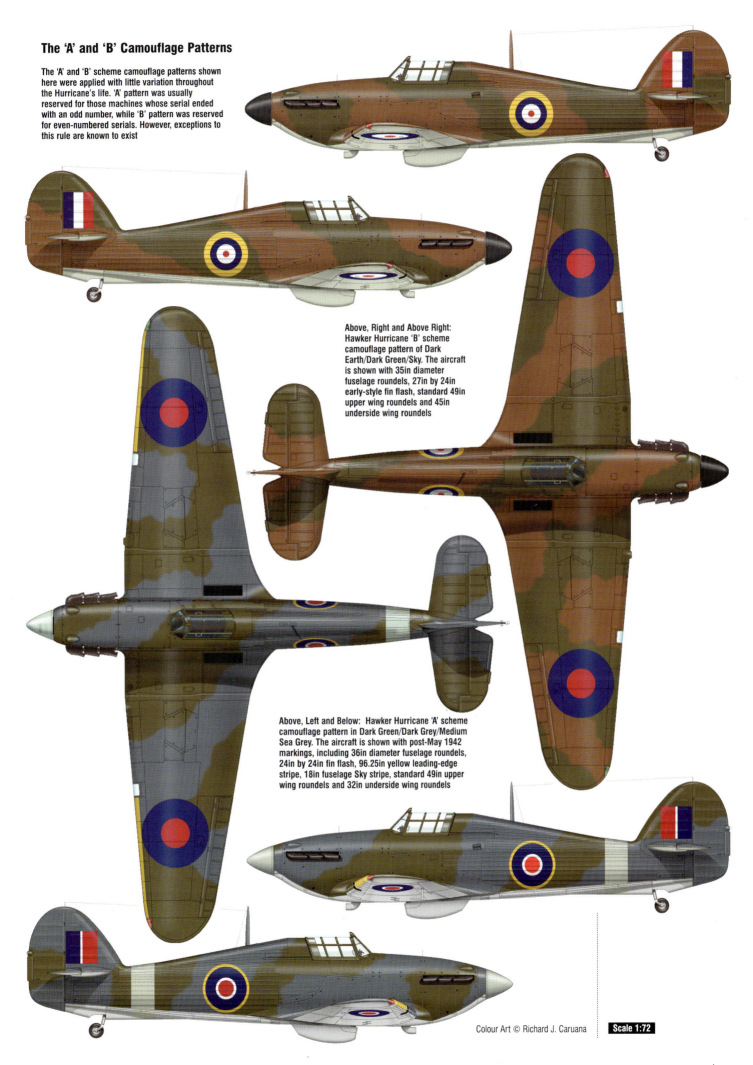

The 'A' and 'B' Camouflage Patterns

The 'A' and 'B' scheme camouflage patterns shown here were applied with little variation throughout the Hurricane's life. 'A' pattern was usually reserved for those machines whose serial ended with an odd number, while 'B' pattern was reserved for even-numbered serials. However, exceptions to this rule are known to exist

Above, Right and Above Right: Hawker Hurricane 'B' scheme camouflage pattern of Dark Earth/Dark Green/Sky. The aircraft is shown with 35in diameter fuselage roundels, 27in by 24in early-style fin flash, standard 49in upper wing roundels and 45in underside wing roundels

Above, Left and Below: Hawker Hurricane 'A' scheme camouflage pattern in Dark Green/Dark Grey/Medium Sea Grey. The aircraft is shown with post-May 1942 markings, including 36in diameter fuselage roundels, 24in by 24in fin flash, 96.25in yellow leading-edge stripe, 18in fuselage Sky stripe, standard 49in upper wing roundels and 32in underside wing roundels

Colour Art © Richard J. Caruana   **Scale 1:72**

Mk I, W9200, DX•? of
No. 245 Sqn, at Aldergrove
in 1941 (© RAF Museum P015414)

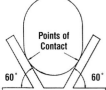

**Boundary Template for
Marking**

Points of
Contact

60°   60°

**Boundary template for colour
demarcation on the fuselage**

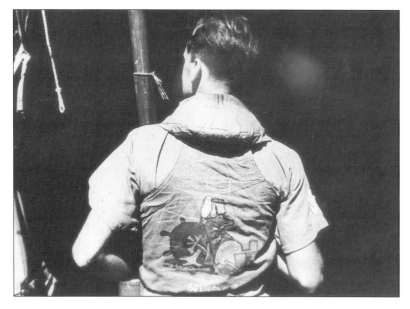

Not all artwork was confined
to the aircraft as can be seen
in this shot of Sgt R.
McInnes-Wilson of No. 260
Sqn, showing off the Donald
Duck artwork on the back of
his Mae West
(© RAF Museum P014389)

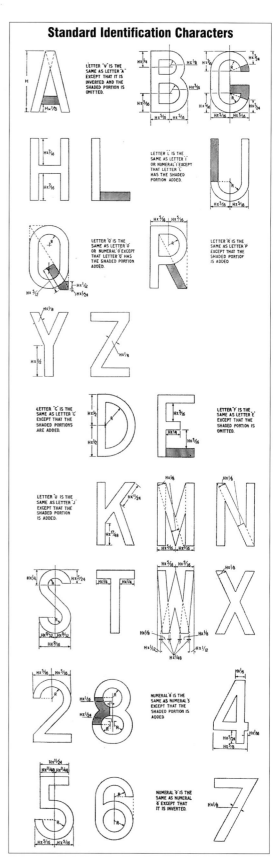

Standard Identification Characters

Mk I Hurricanes being painted in the black and white undersurface scheme during manufacture usually had a scheme similar to the one adopted right after the Munich Crisis. However the flaps and elevators were not aluminium, being either black or white and the demarcation between the wing and fuselage colours went straight across the back of the ventral radiator. No lower-surface roundels were carried.

On the 6th June 1940, the split black and white lower surface scheme was dropped, and a single application of Sky was made. Spinners were usually black at this stage and the squadron codes were applied in 30in high Medium Sea Grey characters. The black serial number on the rear fuselage was increased to 8in high characters. Roundels consisted of 35in Type A1 on the fuselage and 49in Type B on the upper wings. The fin flash was often applied to almost all of the vertical fin, with three bands (red, white, blue) 9in wide. At this stage no roundels were applied to the under surface of the wings. This all changed on the 1st August 1940, as the 50in. diameter Type A roundels were to be applied underneath each wing with their centres 80in. from the wing tip. This is by no way what happened, as one can imagine, as the Battle of Britain was reaching its height, so examples with a 30in diameter Type A roundel much closer to each wing tip is not uncommon for this period. At this time the

fin flash was also revised to a 24in width, therefore being made up of 8in stripes of red, white and blue. Variations to the fin flash include the type which covered the entire vertical fin, with the rear blue and white portions being 9in wide, with the red forward section covering the remainder of the fin.

On the 27th November 1940 the 'tactical' scheme made a return, with an instruction to apply black to the port lower wing, with its demarcation at the centreline and not extending past the leading and trailing edges of the wing in the middle of the aircraft. A 2in yellow border was added to the Type A roundel on

the black wing. On the 11th November 1940 Sky had also been specified for all spinners and for an 18in wide band around the rear fuselage. By the 22nd April 1941 the black port wing was eliminated and the under surface of the Hurricane once again returned to Sky overall. The fin flash also changed to a square 24in style with equal stripes of red, white and blue (8in). The fuselage roundel remained a 35in Type A1, with a 49in Type B on the upper wing surface. The lower wing roundel changed to a 45in Type A.

On the 15th August 1941 the overall scheme for the Hurricane

Evolution of Underside Colour Schemes

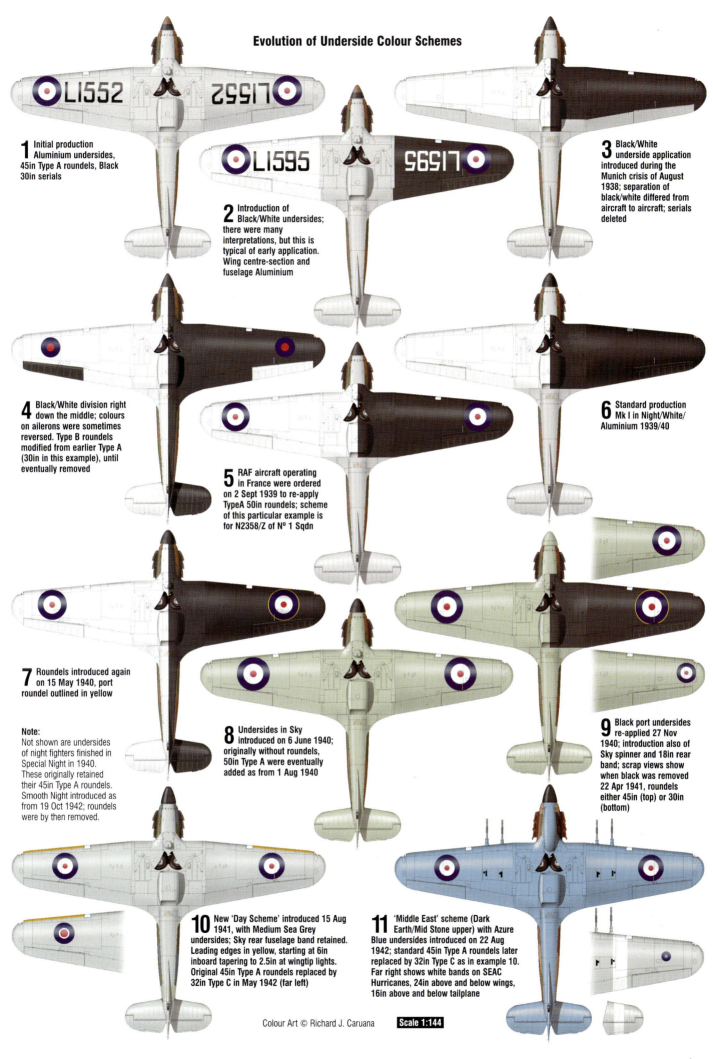

1 Initial production Aluminium undersides, 45in Type A roundels, Black 30in serials

2 Introduction of Black/White undersides; there were many interpretations, but this is typical of early application. Wing centre-section and fuselage Aluminium

3 Black/White underside application introduced during the Munich crisis of August 1938; separation of black/white differed from aircraft to aircraft; serials deleted

4 Black/White division right down the middle; colours on ailerons were sometimes reversed. Type B roundels modified from earlier Type A (30in in this example), until eventually removed

5 RAF aircraft operating in France were ordered on 2 Sept 1939 to re-apply TypeA 50in roundels; scheme of this particular example is for N2358/Z of Nº 1 Sqdn

6 Standard production Mk I in Night/White/Aluminium 1939/40

7 Roundels introduced again on 15 May 1940, port roundel outlined in yellow

Note:
Not shown are undersides of night fighters finished in Special Night in 1940. These originally retained their 45in Type A roundels. Smooth Night introduced as from 19 Oct 1942; roundels were by then removed.

8 Undersides in Sky introduced on 6 June 1940; originally without roundels, 50in Type A were eventually added as from 1 Aug 1940

9 Black port undersides re-applied 27 Nov 1940; introduction also of Sky spinner and 18in rear band; scrap views show when black was removed 22 Apr 1941, roundels either 45in (top) or 30in (bottom)

10 New 'Day Scheme' introduced 15 Aug 1941, with Medium Sea Grey undersides; Sky rear fuselage band retained. Leading edges in yellow, starting at 6in inboard tapering to 2.5in at wingtip lights. Original 45in Type A roundels replaced by 32in Type C in May 1942 (far left)

11 'Middle East' scheme (Dark Earth/Mid Stone upper) with Azure Blue undersides introduced on 22 Aug 1942; standard 45in Type A roundels later replaced by 32in Type C as in example 10. Far right shows white bands on SEAC Hurricanes, 24in above and below wings, 16in above and below tailplane

Colour Art © Richard J. Caruana   Scale 1:144

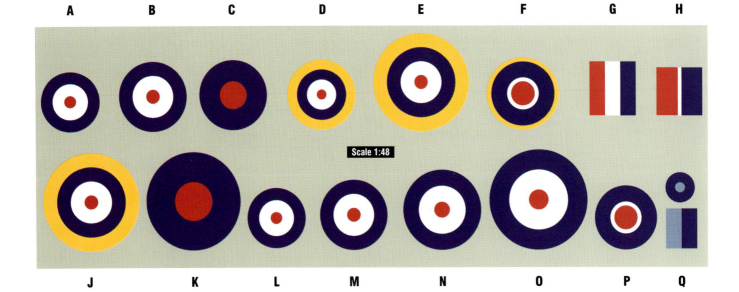

Scale 1:48

RAF Markings

Fuselage/Fin Markings
(Figures in parenthesis show dimensions, starting from outer to inner colours)

A 30in Type A
(30/18/6in)

B 35in Type A
(35/21/7in)

C 35in Type B (conv.of existing 35in) (35/14in)

D 35in Type A1
(35/25/15/5in)

E 49in Type A1
(49/35/21/7in)

F 36in C1
(36/32/16/12in)

G Early Fin Flash
(8/8/8x27in)

H 1942 Fin Flash
(11/2/11x24in)

Upper Wing Markings
J 49in Type A1
(49/35/21/7in)

K 49in Type B
(49/19/5in)

Lower Wing Markings
L 30in TypeA
(30/18/6in)

M 35in TypeA
(35/21/7in)

N 40in TypeA
(40/24/8in)

O 50in TypeA
(50/30/10in)

P 32in TypeC
(32/26/12in)

SEAC Markings
Q 15in dia. fuselage roundel (15/5in) and 16x21in fin flash

Colour Art © Richard J. Caruana

Early Style Fin Markings

Scale 1:48

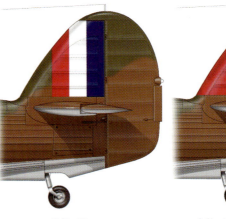

Narrowest known 3x5in wide; could also be 3x6in, 3x7in

3x9in stripes

2x9in stripes and forward portion of fin in Ident Red

Squadron Code Letters

Scale 1:48

Left to right: 27in MSG; 38in MSG; 30in MSG; 24in Sky; 24in Dull Red; 25in Black; note that the design style practically varied from squadron to squadron

Serial Numbers

Scale 1:48

L2001
MW339
HV608

ROYAL NAVY
NF 717

First three from top represent some of the different styles of 8in fuselage serials; 4in Royal Navy and serial

was totally revised and the introduction of the Dark Green and Ocean Grey disruptive camouflage over Medium Sea Grey was implemented. Note that until stocks of the new Ocean Grey paint arrived, a directive was issued that instructed a mix of seven parts Medium Sea Grey to one part Night to be applied over all the Dark Earth areas of the upper surface camouflage and this accounts for the various tonal variations in photographs of Hurricanes at this time. The fin flash at this stage was also sometimes seen as a 24in wide, 27in high version. A further tactical element added to this scheme was the application of a yellow band along the leading edge of each wing, outboard of the landing lamp. The bands were 6in wide at the light, tapering to just 2.5in wide at the tip. Type A roundels in 50in diameter remained in use on the lower wing surfaces.

In May 1942, the national insignia on the lower wings were changed to the 32in Type C and these were to remain in use throughout the rest of the war.

By the 1943 it was not uncommon to see Mk IID's with the Ocean Grey and Dark Green over Medium Sea Grey scheme, although the camouflage pattern (Type A) was reversed, with the Dark Green in place of the Ocean Grey and vice versa. Squadrons codes were applied in 24in high Sky characters and the roundels were 36in Type C1 (fuselage), 49in Type B (upper wing) and 32in Type C (lower wing). The fin flash was 24in square, but the proportions were changed to 11in for the red and blue, but only 2in for the central white stripe.

Guns

Remember that it was common practice to seal the gun ports in the wings of an eight-gun Hurricane with doped linen. Usually

Scale 1:48

1   2   3   4   5   6   7

8   9   10   11   12   13

The personal markings of Plt Off Bird-Wilson of No. 17 Squadron on the side of his Mk I *(© RAF Museum P010056)*

this was done with red dope, but any colour could be used and a colour not dissimilar to Sky has been seen. The outer guns of a twelve-gun wing could not be sealed in this manner (as they were proud of the wing leading-edge), so each muzzle was wrapped in linen and then sealed with red dope. The same applies to the Vickers 'S' cannon. The end of the barrel is just a little bigger in diameter than the rest of the barrel and the 'flared' or 'ball' end stated by many as being applied to this type is either linen doped on, or some form of transit cover applied during test flights and shipping.

Night Intruders & Night Fighters

In these roles the Hurricane gained black undersurfaces or an overall black scheme and in May 1940 the use of R.M.O.2 'Special Night' was specified for application on all night-operation Hurricanes. This paint was very sooty, with a very matt and rough texture. Initially the roundels remained on the lower wing surfaces, but these were soon overpainted. By 19th October 1942 the resistance offered by the 'Special Night' paint, along with its high rate of wear, lead to its replacement with 'Night DTD 308'.

Tropical Operations

The Hurricane in a desert environment was initially supplied in the Dark Earth and Dark Green over Sky scheme, however this was soon replaced. During the initial supply of Mk I's on the Takoradi to Cairo route, these machines had the rear upper decking, each tailplane and (sometimes) the upper section of the canopy painted white to aid rescue operations should they crash enroute.

The above scheme was replaced by the Dark Earth and Middlestone over Azure Blue scheme on the 22nd August 1942. Some Mk IIB's were seen in this scheme, but with the spinner in Dark Earth and the squadron codes applied in white outline

only of approx. 27in. height. Roundels were again 36in. Type C1 (fuselage), 49in Type B (upper wing) and 32in Type C (lower wing). The fin flash was 24in square, with equal stripes of red, white and blue. Most tank-busting Mk IID's flew in the Dark Earth/Middlestone and Azure Blue scheme, but it was not uncommon for the spinners to be painted red.

The Tac R conversions used in the desert were also in the above scheme, however it was not rare for the crews to have applied a 'sand and spinach' scheme to the lower engine cowl and wing leading edges. Many say this was for ground camouflage, but it was more likely to make Italian (and German) ground forces think that the approaching aircraft was one of theirs and therefore stay put!

The Free French-operated Mk IIs had the fuselage roundels reduced to a 25in white circle, onto which was applied the Free French Cross of Lorraine. The upper wing (49in) Type B, and lower wing (45in) Type A roundels were retained. The RAF fin flash was overpainted in dark green and the French style of tricolour was applied to the rudder, although the order was in the RAF style (i.e. red at the front).

Malta

Some sources list the Mk Is initially operated by No. 261 Squadron as being in Dark Earth and Light Earth over Sky, with the code letters in a non-standard size of Medium Sea Grey characters. The Mk I and II's operated on Malta were usually in a standard Dark Green/Ocean Grey and Medium Sea Grey scheme. Squadron codes were a mix (or combination) of Medium Sea Grey and Sky and were usually 27in high. The serial number was 8in high black characters and the roundels were 35in Type A1 (fuselage), 49in Type B (upper wing) and 45in Type A (lower wing). The fin flash was 24in wide by 27in high.

National Markings

(Dimensions are either for roundel diameters or flash sizes)
1   Persian 36in roundel
2   Portuguese wing marking, 36in white disc with 27in cross
3   Portuguese fuselage 27in cross
4   Egypt 36in roundel
5   Yugoslavia 36in roundel, modified from RAF Type C1; 24x24in fin flash
6   Operation Torch 40in roundel
7   Russian AF 40in star, fuselage and wing undersides; outline could also be white
8   Iranian 36in fuselage and wing roundel; 28x21in fin flash
9   Turkish 40x40in wingmarkings; rudder marking sizes varied
10   Finnish 32in roundel, all positions
11   Belgian 25in fuselage roundel; 38in wing roundels
12   Irish Air Corps 32x32in fuselage marking; 3x8in wing stripes
13   Free French 25in roundel

Colour Art © Richard J. Caruana

Mk I, P3878, YB•W of No. 17 Sqn. Note the wavy colour demarcation on the wing leading edge
(© RAF Museum P010065)

No. 504 Squadron's Bulldog mascot held by an an airman next to Plt Off Royce in the cockpit of his Mk I
(© RAF Museum P010550)

Cyprus

One of the last operational uses for the Hurricane was by No. 6 (F) Squadron in Nicosia in December 1946. These machines were aluminium overall with the older Dark Green applied as an anti-dazzle panel on the upper nose. The squadron codes were in 24in high black characters, and the serial was once again 8in high and in black. Roundels consisted of 36in Type C1 (fuselage), 50in Type C1 (upper wing) and 32in Type C1 (lower wing). These latter two markings were applied in a non-standard position just 27in (to centres) from the wing tips. The fin flash was 24in square, but was of the 11in, 2in, 11in variety.

South-East Asia Command

Operations in the 1943-4 period saw the widespread use of the Ocean Grey and Dark Green over Medium Sea Grey scheme. Squadron codes would usually be just 15in high and in white, while the individual aircraft letter was 24in high (white also). The 24in wide bands around the wing (inboard of the aileron cut-outs) did not always extend over the flaps on the lower wings. The 16in wide white band on the vertical fin was positioned above the 16in wide fin flash, and once again this did not always extend over the rudder. SEAC roundels (Dull Blue/Azure Blue) were of the 15in diameter style with a 5in centre and were carried in all six locations.

Mk IIB's operating in Burma in late 1945 still carried the Dark Earth and Dark Green over Sky scheme, but the camouflage pattern was usually in the B style. White 18in wide bands were applied around the vertical tail, rudder and tailplanes and 24in versions were applied around the wings just inboard of the aileron cut-outs. Serials remained in black (8in

Mk IIC, HL973, RZ•G of No. 241 Sqn
(© RAF Museum P007915)

high), with an individual squadron letter in white (24in high). All the roundels were Dull Blue/Azure Blue and were 15in diameter with 5in centres. The white rudder band meant that the tail flash was reduced to a mere 5in high by 16in wide.

At a later stage an overall coat of aluminium was applied to many Hurricanes. A single identifying letter was applied in black 27in high aft of the fuselage roundel and the serial number remained in 8in high black characters. The SEAC roundels were 15in diameter, with 5in centres and the fin flash was 16in (8in stripes) wide by 21in high. All of these national markings were Dull Blue and Azure Blue.

Sea Hurricanes

Initially the Hurricanes used for CAM work were in the standard RAF camouflage of the day. The Mk IB's evolved in the 'Pedestal' convoy to Malta in August 1942 were Dark Sea Grey and Dark Slate Grey over Sky with a Sky band around the rear fuselage, and for this operation the entire vertical fin was yellow, although

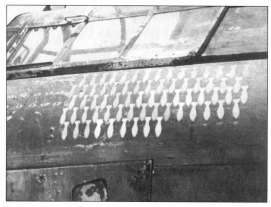

Close up of the bomb log on the cockpit side of HL973, RZ•G
(© RAF Museum P007916)

this did not cover the fin flash. By the time the Mk IIC Sea Hurricane came into service an Extra Dark Sea Grey and Dark Slate Grey over Sky scheme had been adopted. Fuselage squadron codes were dull red and 24in high. The serial number and 'Royal Navy' were 4in high black and the usual combination of 36in Type C1 (fuselage), 49in Type B (upper wing) and 32in Type C (lower wing) roundels were applied. The fin flash was 24in square, but was in the unequal split of two bands (red and blue) at 11in and the central white stripe at just 2in.

One of the most publicised Sea Hurricanes is 'Nicki' a Mk IIC operated by No. 805 Squadron on HMS Nairana. This machine had obviously started out in an Extra Dark Sea Grey and Dark Slate Grey over Sky scheme, but had been overpainted in white. Only the upper decking of the nose remained in the original upper-surface camouflage to act as an anti-dazzle panel. Remains of invasion stripes could be seen on the under surface of the wings only and the fuselage serial had been overpainted. Roundels consisted of 36in Type C1 (fuselage), 49in Type B (upper wing) and 32in Type C (lower wing), with the 24in square-style fin flash

Canadian-built Mk X, XI and XII machines that were retained in Canada for use were still to retain the FAA colour scheme. These aircraft were Extra Dark Sea Grey and Dark Slate Grey over Sky, with the spinner also usually in Sky. The squadron codes were 24in Sky and the serial was black and in 6in. characters. The 'Royal Navy' legend above the serial number was in 4in characters and this was usually painted out on all examples retained in Canada. Roundels consisted of 35in Type A1 (fuselage), 49in Type B (upper wing) and 45in Type A (lower wing). The fin flash was 24in square (equal stripes).

Photo-reconnaissance

As all of the reconnaissance versions of the Hurricane were conversions, the colour schemes applied were basically standard.

The PR Mk I operated by No. 208 Squadron were in a standard scheme of Dark Earth and Middlestone over Azure Blue with a C1 roundel on the fuselage, a Type B on the upper wing and Type A underneath. The squadron emblem of a lightning bolt was painted either side of the fuselage roundel in Sky and the fuselage serial was in 8in high black characters. As with some of the other aircraft operating in the desert, the forward lower engine cowling and each wing leading edge was painted with a shade of sand and blotches of dark green to simulate the 'sand and spinach' camouflage applied to Italian aircraft.

The PR Mk IIs operated by No. 208 Squadron at Kabrit were finished in a colour called Mediterranean Blue overall. Roundels were all Type B, and to the usual sizes, and the serial only was applied to each fuselage side in 8in high black characters. No fin flash was applied. The PR Mk IIA's of No. 3 PRU were painted in a dark blue that was made from a mix of Bosun Blue and Black. The roundels were again all Type B to the usual sizes, but they were each outlined (2in) in yellow and no fin flash was applied. No. 681 Squadrons PR Mk IIB's were in a mixed dark blue overall with the fuselage code letter in Medium Sea Grey and the serial once again in black (8in). No fuselage roundels were applied, but like the No. 3 PRU machines the wing roundels were Type B with a 2in yellow surround. A 24in by 27in fin flash was applied, although it too was outlined in yellow. A variation with this squadron seen at the same time was the application of a Type C1 roundel on the fuselage in place of the code letter. The fin flash was 24in square and was not outlined in yellow.

Foreign Production

Canada

All Canadian-produced machines were painted in the same schemes as those that applied to the British equivalents at the time. Roundels and markings were also standard depending on the time period. The paints are unlikely to have come from the UK so I am sure that there were great tonal variations in the actual colours applied to these machines.

Foreign Service

French

Apart from the Free French examples operated in WWII some Mk IICs were used by the French Air Force in Morocco in 1945-1946. These machines had all the bomb racks, cannon and gunsights removed and were repainted in Kaki (Khaki) over Gris Bleu Clair (Light Blue-Grey). Single aircraft serial letters were applied in white, 24in high letters on the fuselage sides and the serial number was reapplied (higher up the fuselage) in Gris Bleu Clair 8in high characters. The entire rudder carried the French tricolour and French roundels were applied in 16in. diameter on the fuselage and 24in under the wings. No upper wing roundels were applied.

Finnish Air Force

The Finnish Air Force received Mk Is and they operated with LeLv.32, LeLv.30 and LeLv.26 and LeLv.10. Initially these machines were usually still in their RAF camouflage of Dark Earth and Dark Green with the lower wing split 50/50 into white (starboard) and black (port) and the lower nose, rear fuselage and tailplanes being aluminium. The outer, lower portion of the wing tip (approximately 80in) was in yellow, with a narrow 16in yellow band around the fuselage just aft of the roundel. Roundels, 32in on fuselage and 40in diameter on the wings, were carried in six positions and the serial was applied in 8in high black letters on the rear fuselage. A large white-outlined black number (the last of the serial) was applied on the rudder (approx 50in high by 22in wide). After the 1st September 1941 the entire nose of these machines was also painted yellow. Some Finnish Hurricanes had the extreme tip of the spinner in yellow, while others were all black.

By 1943 most of the remaining machines had be refurbished and repainted. Now these machines featured a Green and Black Green upper surface camouflage with a Light Grey undersurface. The roundels, fuselage, nose and wing tip bands all remained the same as the previous scheme, but the serial number was repainted in 10in high characters. These characters were black where they hit the yellow fuselage band or Green camouflage, but where they crossed the Black Green camouflage they were applied in the camouflage Green. The demarcation of the upper and lower colours changed, as the fuselage sides and nose featured a wavy demarcation that rose to the datum line at the spinner and to the centre of the tailplanes. As with the Rumanian examples, the colour crossed under the tailplanes, then dropped slightly before reaching the edge of the rudder. The demarcation on the wing leading edges remained straight however.

Belgian Air Force

The Hurricanes supplied by Hawkers to Belgium came in the standard RAF scheme of Dark Earth and Dark Green over Aluminium. The Belgium roundel was applied in six positions,

Fitters and riggers of No. 260 Squadron in front and on top of a Hurricane at Skitten in December 1941, note the yellow spinner with the black spiral effect
(© RAF Museum P014379)

with each being outlined in black. The fuselage ones were of about 35in diameter, while those on the upper surface of the wings were approximately 50in, and those underneath 40in. The aircraft serial number was applied in white on the rudder and the complete code was applied across the under surface of the wings, between the roundels in 40in high black letters. Note that two Mk I RAF machines landed in error in Belgium during the 'Phoney War' and were operated by the Belgium Air Force. These machines featured three-blade D.H. propellers and retained their RAF Dark Earth and Dark Green over half-white, half-black lower surfaces. It is not known if Belgian insignia were applied to these machines, but if they were (most likely), then the sizes of each roundel would probably have corresponded to the existing RAF example.

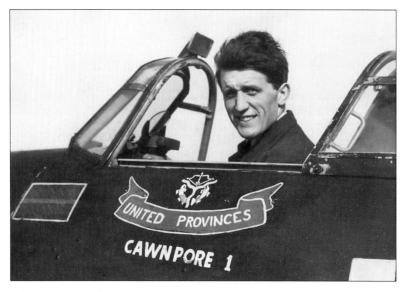

Mk IIC, LK•A, 'Cawnpore I' of No. 87 Squadron with the CO, Sqn Ldr D.G. Smallwood in the cockpit *(© C.E. Brown)*

Only two machines were completed under license by Fairey Avions in Gosselies before German occupation, so it is impossible to say whether these machines carried any variation in the RAF camouflage scheme.

Post, or late war, some Mk IIs were operated in Belgium and these were painted aluminium overall with the roundels in six positions. The upper wing roundel was 50in diameter, with the lower one being 32in The fuselage roundel had increased in size to 36in and I think it is a safe bet to assume that these dimensions were arrived at because they would have been those needed to cover any existing RAF roundels. The serial number was in 8in high black letters on the rear fuselage and the squadron code (?) was in black, forward of the fuselage roundel in 24in high characters. A Belgian fin flash of 24in square was applied to the vertical fin.

USAAF

The USAAF did not really ever operate the Hurricane, however some examples carried American insignia during 'Operation Torch', Algeria in November 1942. These machines were all Canadian-built Mk XIIs and they were all fitted out to Sea Hurricane standard. The usual FAA scheme of extra Dark Sea Grey and Dark Slate Grey over Sky was applied and the upper wing and fuselage roundels were replaced with larger American stars outlined in yellow. The lower wing roundel was completely painted out and the aircraft retained their 'Royal Navy' and serial numbers in 4in black characters. No other markings were applied and the spinners were Sky.

Yugoslavian Air Force

The Hurricanes that were supplied to the Yugolsavians prior to their own licensed production of the type were in a standard RAF scheme of Dark Earth and Dark Green over aluminium. This scheme is seen to have been modified with the addition of Light Earth on areas of the upper surface. National insignia of approximately 45in diameter were applied to the upper and lower wing surfaces only and no fin flash was applied. The lower surface roundels on some machines were positioned quite far outboard, resulting in their touching the leading edge at the front and the aileron hinge-line at the rear. A three figure serial was applied to the rear fuselage in 8in high black characters and the Watts propeller was black, with the tip painted in Dark Earth. Hurricane Mk Is produced at the Zmaj factory were painted in a brown and green over light grey scheme. The demarcation of the fuselage colours came up from the wing leading edge, in a wavy line, to the leading edge of the tailplanes. This demarcation then came out from behind the tailplane to slightly drop before reaching the back edge of the rudder. The camouflage pattern on the upper fuselage surface was lightly sprayed, with no hard demarcation between the colours and the pattern was very different to any applied to an RAF machine. Usually the lower engine cowls were left as bare metal. A white band was carried around the rear fuselage and Yugoslavian roundels were only carried above and below the wings. The fin stripe was carried high up, horizontally across the entire rudder, but only encroached slightly onto the vertical fin. Spinners were black.

Whilst the Hurricane was used by Yugoslavian squadrons in the RAF, they remained in the usual Dark Green/Ocean Grey over Medium Sea Grey scheme. The spinner and 18in wide fuselage band were in Sky and aircraft identification letters were also usually in Sky (24in high). The serial remained 8in high black characters and although the usual RAF roundels were applied, later these were converted to Yugoslavian national insignia by applying a red star in the middle of each roundel, and the fin flash. Therefore the fuselage 36in Type C1 roundel had the centre white section enlarged to 22in and a red star applied over it, the 49in Type B upper wing roundel just had the star added, as did the 36in type C1 lower wing roundel. On the 24in square fin flash a small star was added to the white section. Post-war many of these machines were refurbished and repainted, becoming silver-grey overall with the serial stencilled in 8in high black characters on the top of the vertical fin. The fuselage and wing roundels remained as they were, but the revised (horizontal) fin flash was applied across the rudder, just above the tailplane.

Russian Air Force (VVS)

The two-seat conversions seen in use within Russia during WWII were basically to retain their standard RAF Dark Earth/Dark Green and Sky scheme, however the areas around the cockpit where the conversion work had taken place were repainted in Russian Dark Olive. Spinners were black or a 50/50 split of Sky and black. Repair patches on the lower wings and

Modeller's Cross-reference Colour Chart

ROYAL AIR FORCE

COLOUR	FS 595A	BS or RAL	USE	AVAILABLE PAINTS
Dark Earth			Topside camouflage with Dark Green	AeroMaster Warbird Enamel: 9110 Dark Earth
				AeroMaster Warbird Acrylic: 1110 Dark Earth
	~0118			Floquil M189: Field Drab 30118
	~0118			Floquil 145: Dark Earth 30118
				Gunze Sangyo: H072 Dark Earth
				Humbrol Authentic: HU02, Dark Earth
				Humbrol Authentic: HF03, Terre Fonce
	~0118			Humbrol Authentic: HU18, Brown 30118
		450		Humbrol Super Enamel: No.29 Dark Earth
	~0118			Lifecolor UA0116 Dark Earth
				ModelMaster: 1702 Field Drab
	~0118			Pactra Acrylics: A24, Brown Drab FS 30118
	~0118			Poly-S 830: Field Drab
	~0118			Poly-S Acrylic 5252: British Dark Earth 30118
		450		Xtracolor: X2 Dark Earth BS450
	~0118			Xtracolor: X101 Earth 30118
Dark Green	~4079		Topside camouflage with Dark Earth	AeroMaster Warbird Enamel: 9111 Dark Green
	~4079			AeroMaster Warbird Acrylic: 1111 Dark Green
				Compucolor: CAC2, Forest Green
	~4079			Floquil M196, Dark Green 34079
	~4079			Floquil: 3143, British Dark Green (34079)
	~4079			Humbrol Authentic: HG02, Dark Green RLM71
	~4079			Humbrol Authentic: HU07, Green 34079
	~4079			Lifecolor UA001 Dark Green
	~4079			ModelMaster: 1710, Dark Green
	~4079			Mr Color: 309, Dark Green FS34079
				Pactra: M5
	~4079			Pactra Acrylics: A29, Jungle Green FS34079
				Poly-S: 835, Forest Green
				Poly-S: 814 Dark Green
	~4079			Poly-S Acrylic: Dark Green (34079)
	~4079			Poly-S Enamel: Dark Green 34079
				Tamiya: XF58, Olive Green
	~4079			Xtracolor: X110, Forest Green FS14079
		451		Xtracolor: X1 Dark Green (BS451)
Sky			Undersurface from 6/6/40 to 15/8/41	AeroMaster Warbird Enamel: 9114
				AeroMaster Warbird Acrylic: 1114
	~4424			Compucolor: CAS10, Light Grey Green
	~4424			Gunze Sangyo Acrylic: H074, Sky
		210		Humbrol Authentic: HB05, Sky Type S
	~4424			Lifecolor UA095 Sky
				Monogram-Promodeler Acrylic: 88-0038
	~4424			Poly Scale Acrylic: 505254
	~4424			Poly-S Acrylic: 500108
	~4454			Tamiya: XF21, Sky
		210		Xtracolor: X7, Sky
Medium Sea Grey			Early code letters, Under surface colour from 15/8/41	AeroMaster Warbird Enamel: 9113
	~6270			AeroMaster Warbird Acrylic: 1113
	~6270			Compucolor: CAC28, Neutral Grey
	~6270			Floquil: M206, Neutral Grey
				Floquil Enamel: 3151, Sea Grey, Medium
		640		Gunze Sangyo Acrylic: Medium Sea Grey
	~6270			Gunze Sangyo Acrylic: Grey
	~6270			Humbrol Authentic: HF04 Gris Bleu Clair
	~6440			Humbrol Authentic: HB06 Sea Grey Medium
	~6270			Humbrol Authentic: USN2, Medium Gray
		637		Humbrol Super Enamel: No.165
	~6270			Lifecolor UA094 Medium Sea Grey
				ModelMaster: 1725, Neutral Grey
	~6293			Poly Scale: 505258, Sea Grey, Medium
	~6293			Poly-S Acrylic: British Sea Grey, Medium
	~6270			Replicolor: Grey
	~6424			Tamiya: XF20 Medium Grey
	~6270			Xtracolor: X133, Neutral Gray (FS 16270)
		637		Xtracolor: X3, Medium Sea Grey
Ocean Grey			Upper surface camouflage with Dark Green from 8/41	AeroMaster Warbird Enamel: 9112, Ocean Grey
				AeroMaster Warbird Acrylic: 1112, Ocean Grey
	~6152			Floquil: 3149, Ocean Grey
	~6152			Humbrol: HN02 Dark Grey
				Humbrol Super Enamels: No.106 Ocean Grey
	~6187			Lifecolor UA093 Ocean Grey
	~6187			Poly-S: 823, Ocean Grey
	~5237			Poly-S: 5256, Ocean Grey
	~5237			Xtracolor: X6, Ocean Grey
Dark Slate Grey	~4096		Upper surface camouflage with Ocean Grey on Sea Hurricanes	AeroMaster Warbird Acrylic: 1119, Slate Grey
	~4091			Floquil Classic: 3159, Dark Slate Grey
	~4091			Gunze Sangyo Acrylic: H036, Dark Green
	~4096			Gunze Sangyo Acrylic: H052, Olive Drab
	~4096			Gunze Sangyo Acrylic: H320, Dark Green
	~4091			Humbrol Authentic: HB01, Dark Green
	~4096			Humbrol Authentic: HI03, Overall Green
	~4096			Humbrol Authentic: HG17, Dark Green
	~4127			Humbrol Authentic: HJ01, Green N1
	~4127			Humbrol Authentic: HI01, Mottle Green
				Humbrol Authentic: HM07, Khaki Drab
	~4127			Humbrol Super Enamel: No.102 Dark Slate Grey
	~4127			Humbrol Super Enamel: No.150 Forest Green
	~4096			Lifecolor UA006 Green
	~4127			Pactra: MG54, Sherwood Green
	~4096			Pactra Acrylic: A34, Artillery Olive
	~4127			Poly-S Acrylic: 5266, Dark Slate Grey
				Floquil: M200, Forest Green
	~4127			ModelMaster: 1714, Forest Green
				Xtracolor: X25, Dark Slate Grey
Extra Dark Sea Grey			Sea Hurricanes	AeroMaster Warbird Acrylic: 1118
	~6118			Compucolor: CAC16, Gunship Grey
	~6118			Floquil: M204, Sea Grey
	~6118			Floquil Classic: 3157, Extra Dark Sea Grey
	~6118			Gunze Sangyo Acrylic: H032, Field Grey
	~6118			Gunze Sangyo Acrylic: H072, Dark Sea Grey
	~6118			Gunze Sangyo Acrylic: H305, Grey
	~6118	638		Gunze Sangyo Acrylic: H331, Dark Sea Grey
	~6118			Humbrol Authentic: HF02, Gris Blue Fonce
	~6118			Humbrol Authentic: HM04, German Panzer Grey
	~6118			Humbrol Authentic: HU03, Neutral Grey
	~6118			Humbrol Authentic: HU22, Grey ANA 603
	~6118			Humbrol Authentic: USN1, Dark Grey
	~6118	638		Humbrol Super Enamel: No.123, Extra Dark Sea Grey
	~6118			Lifecolor UA0022 Dark Grey
	~6118			ModelMaster: 1723, Gunship Gray
	~6118			Mr Color: 305, Grey
	~6118			Poly-S, 822, Sea Grey
	~6118			Poly-S Acrylic: 5264, Extra Dark Sea Grey
	~6118			Xtracolor: X130, Gunship Grey
Night	~7038		Night fighters Under surfaces	AeroMaster Warbird Enamel: 9001, Black
	~7038			Floquil Classic: 3010, Black
	~7038			Gunze Sangyo Acrylic: H002, Black
	~7038			Gunze Sangyo Acrylic; H012, Flat Black
	~7038			Humbrol Authentic: HB1, Night Black
	~7038			Humbrol Authentic: HU12, Night Black
		624		Humbrol Super Enamels: No.33, Black
	~7038			Lifecolor LC02 Matt Black
	~7038			ModelMaster: 1747, Gloss Black
	~7038			ModelMaster: 1749, Flat Black
	~7038			Pactra: MG61, Ebony Black
	~7038			Pactra: A46, Black
	~7038			Poly-S: PF-10, Black
	~7038			Poly-S: 5214, Night Black
		RAL9005		Revell: 07, Black
		RAL9011		Revell: 08, Black
	~7038			Tamiya: X01, Black
	~7038			Tamiya: X18, Semigloss Black
	~7038			Tamiya: XF01, Flat Black
	~7038			Testors: 1749, Black
	~7038			Testors: 1747, Black
		624		Xtracolor: X12, Night Black
Identification Blue (Dull)	~5044		Roundels	Gunze Sangyo Acrylic: H326, Blue
	~5044			ModelMaster: 1719, Insignia Blue
	~5044			Mr Color: 326, Blue
	~5044			Tamiya: XF17, Sea Blue
	~5044			Xtracolor: X122, Insignia Blue
		110		Xtracolor: X30, RAF Roundel Blue
Identification Blue (Bright)	~5056		Post war Roundels	Compucolour: CIS7, Insignia Blue
Identification Red (Dull)	~0109		Roundel centre & codes	N/A
Identification White	~7875		Roundels Post war codes	AeroMaster Warbird Enamel: 9002, White
	~7875			Compucolor: CAC12, White
	~7875			Humbrol Super Enamel: No.22, White
	~7875			Humbrol Super Enamel: No.34, Matt White
	~7925			Lifecolor LC01 Matt White
	~7778			Gunze Sangyo Acrylic: H021, Off White
	~7875			Gunze Sangyo Acrylic: H001, White
	~7875			Gunze Sangyo Acrylic: H011, Flat White
	~7875			Humbrol Authentic: USN6, White
	~7875			ModelMaster: 1745, Insignia White
	~7875			ModelMaster: 1768, Flat White
	~7875			Mr Color: 316, White
	~7875			Pactra: MG52, Alpine White
	~7875			Pactra Acrylic: A47, White
	~7875			Poly-S: PG-10, White
	~7875			Poly-S: Il-33, White
	~7875			Poly-S: PF-11, White
	~7875			Tamiya: X02, White
	~7875			Tamiya: XF02, Flat White
	~7875			Testors: 1168, White
	~7875			Xtracolor: X141, White
Aluminium	~7178		Overall Post-war	Compucolor: CIS12, Aluminium
				Halford Acrylic: Aluminium
				Halford Acrylic: Nissan Silver (Met)
				Humbrol Super Enamel: No.11, Silver
				Humbrol Super Enamel: No.191, Chrome Silver
	~7178			Lifecolor LC24 Natural Metal
	~7178			ModelMaster: 1790, Chrome Silver
				ModelMaster Metalizer: 1401 Aluminium Plate
	~7178			Poly-S, IJ-17
	~7178			Tamiya: XF16, Flat Aluminium
	~7178			Testors: 1146 Aluminium
	~7178			Xtracolor: X142, Aluminium
Identification Yellow			Markings Wing Leading Edges etc.	AeroMaster Warbird Enamel: 9003, Yellow
	~3538			Gunze Sangyo Acrylic: H024, Orange Yellow
	~3538			Gunze Sangyo Acrylic: H329, Yellow
				Humbrol Super Enamel: No.24, Trainer Yellow
				Humbrol Super Enamel: No.154, Insignia Yellow
	~3538			Lifecolor UA140 RLM 04 yellow
	~3538			ModelMaster: 1707, Chrome Yellow
	~3538			ModelMaster: 1708, Insignia Yellow
	~3538			Pactra Acrylics: A27, Flat Yellow
	~3538			Poly-S, F-3, Yellow
	~3538			Poly-S: PF-40, Yellow
	~3538			Testors: 1169, Yellow
	~3538			Xtracolor: X11, Trainer Yellow
	~3538			Xtracolor: X106, Insignia Yellow

BELGIAN AIR FORCE

Hurricanes were delivered to this country in standard RAF schemes. Therefore see the entries for Dark Earth, Dark Green and Aluminium in the 'Royal Air Force' section.

COLOUR	FS 595A	BS or RAL	USE	AVAILABLE PAINTS
Red	~1105		Roundels	Gunze Sangyo Acrylic: H003, Red
	~1105			Gunze Sangyo Acrylic: H013, Flat Red
	~1105			Humbrol Authentic: HM09, Scarlet
				Humbrol Super Enamel: No.19, Bright Red
		RAL3000		Revell: No.31, Fiery Red
	~1105			Tamiya: X07, Red
				Testors: 1503, Red
Yellow			Roundels	Gunze Sangyo Acrylic: H004, Yellow
	~3655			Humbrol Authentic: HT06, Insignia Yellow
				Humbrol Super Enamel: No.69, Lemon Yellow
		RAL1026		Revell: Luminous Yellow
	~3655			Tamiya: XF08, Lemon Yellow
	~3655			Tamiya: XF03, Flat Yellow
				Testors: 1514, Yellow
	~3655			Xtracolor, Blue Angles Yellow
Black	~7038			See entry in 'Royal Air Force' section

CANADA

The machines supplied from this country were in the standard RAF scheme. Therefore see the entries for Dark Earth, Dark Green and Aluminium in the 'Royal Air Force' section. Note that the tonal value of these colours, which were made by Canadian sources, may have differed from the BS standard examples.

COLOUR	FS 595A	BS or RAL	USE	AVAILABLE PAINTS
Dark Green	~4096		Upper surface camouflage	See entry under 'Royal Air Force' section
Dark Earth	~0118		Upper surface camouflage	See entry under 'Royal Air Force' section
Sky	~4504		Under surface colour	See entry under 'Royal Air Force' section

Modeller's Cross-reference Colour Chart continued

COLOUR	FS 595A	BS or RAL	USE	AVAILABLE PAINTS
Ocean Grey	~6152		Upper surface camouflage	See entry under 'Royal Air Force' section
Dark Green	~4079		Upper surface camouflage	See entry under 'Royal Air Force' section
Medium Sea Grey	~6270		Under surface colour	See entry under 'Royal Air Force' section
Extra Dark Sea Grey	~4092		Upper surface camouflage	See entry under 'Royal Air Force' section
Dark Slate Grey	~4096		Upper surface camouflage	See entry under 'Royal Air Force' section

FREE-FRENCH AIR FORCE

COLOUR	FS 595A	BS or RAL	USE	AVAILABLE PAINTS
Kaki	~4052		Upper surface colour	AeroMaster Warbird Acrylic: 1102
	~4052			Lifecolor Acrylic: UA051 (RLM 70)
	~4096			Lifecolor Acrylic: UA142 French Kaki
	~4052			ModelMaster Enamel: 2106 Khaki
	~4052			ModelMaster Acrylic: 50113
	~4052			Poly Scale Acrylic: 505238
	~4052			Pactra Acrylic: A32
	~4052			Xtracolor: X384 French WWII Kaki
Gris Bleu Clair	~6473		Under surface colour & code letters	AeroMaster Warbird Acrylic: 1101
	~6473			Lifecolor Acrylic: UA141 French Blue-Grey
				ModelMaster Enamel: 2109
				Poly Scale Acrylic: 505242
				Xtracolor: X389 French WWII Gris Bleu Clair

FINNISH AIR FORCE
Initially the machines supplied to this country were in the standard RAF scheme. Therefore see the entries for Dark Earth, Dark Green and Aluminium in the 'Royal Air Force' section.

COLOUR	FS 595A	BS or RAL	USE	AVAILABLE PAINTS
Dark Olive Green	~4098		Upper surface camouflage	AeroMaster Warbird Acrylic: 1231 Olive Green
Black Green (RLM 70)	~4050		Upper surface camouflage	AeroMaster Warbird Acrylic: 1023 RLM 70
				Lifecolor Acrylic: UA111 Dark Olive 2
				ModelMaster Enamel: 2080 RLM 70
				Poly Scale Acrylic 505055 RLM 70
				Poly S Acrylic: 500086 RLM 70
				Tamiya Acrylic: XF27 Black Green
				Gunze Sangyo Acrylic: H65 RLM 70
				Monogram Promodeler Acrylic: 88-0043 RLM 70
				Niche Acrylic: 5909 RLM 70
				Xtracolor: X204 RLM 70
Light Blue	~5414		Undersurface colour	AeroMaster Warbird Acrylic: 1232 Light Blue
				Lifecolor Acrylic: UA062 RLM 78 Bright Blue
				ModelMaster Enamel: 2033
				Poly Scale Acrylic: 505318
				Tamiya Acrylic: XF23 Light Blue
Keltainen (Yellow)	~3655		Identification markings	AeroMaster Warbird Enamel: 9080 ID Yellow
				AeroMaster Warbird Acrylic: 1230 ID Yellow
				ModelMaster Enamel: 2023 Blue Angels Yellow
				Poly Scale Acrylic: 414236 Yellow
				Tamiya Acrylic: X8 Lemon Yellow
				Xtracolor Enamel: X108 Blue Angels Yellow

YUGOSLAVIAN AIR FORCE
Hurricanes were delivered to this country in the standard RAF scheme. Therefore see the entries for Dark Earth, Dark Green and Aluminium in the 'Royal Air Force' section.

COLOUR	FS 595A	BS or RAL	USE	AVAILABLE PAINTS

RUMANIAN AIR FORCE
Hurricanes were delivered to this country in the standard RAF scheme. Therefore see the entries for Dark Earth, Dark Green and Aluminium in the 'Royal Air Force' section.

IRISH AIR CORPS
Hurricanes were initially ex-RAF machines that had crash landed in Ireland. Therefore see the entries for Dark Earth, Dark Green and Aluminium in the 'Royal Air Force' section.

COLOUR	FS 595A	BS or RAL	USE	AVAILABLE PAINTS
Ocean Grey	~6152		Upper surface camouflage (Mk IIC)	See entry under 'Royal Air Force' section
Dark Green	~4079		Upper surface camouflage (Mk IIC)	See entry under 'Royal Air Force' section
Medium Sea Grey	~6270		Under surface colour (Mk IIC)	See entry under 'Royal Air Force' section
Insignia Green			National insignia	
Insignia Orange	~2300		National insignia	
Identification White	~7875		National insignia	See entry under 'Royal Air Force' section

RUSSIAN AIR FORCE (VVS)
The Hurricanes used by the VVS were all ex-RAF.

COLOUR	FS 595A	BS or RAL	USE	AVAILABLE PAINTS
Ocean Grey	~6152		Upper surface camouflage	See entry under 'Royal Air Force' section
Dark Green	~4079		Upper surface camouflage	See entry under 'Royal Air Force' section
Medium Sea Grey	~6270		Under surface colour	See entry under 'Royal Air Force' section
Insignia Red	~1302		National Insignia	
Insignia White	~7886		National Insignia	

PORTUGUESE AIR FORCE
Hurricanes were delivered to this country in the standard RAF scheme.

COLOUR	FS 595A	BS or RAL	USE	AVAILABLE PAINTS
Ocean Grey	~6152		Upper surface camouflage	See entry under 'Royal Air Force' section
Dark Green	~4079		Upper surface camouflage	See entry under 'Royal Air Force' section
Medium Sea Grey	~6270		Under surface colour	See entry under 'Royal Air Force' section
Verde Bronze	~4115		Spinner and fuselage band	Lifecolor Acrylic: UA055 RLM 25

PERSIAN AIR FORCE
Hurricanes were delivered to this country in the standard RAF scheme.

COLOUR	FS 595A	BS or RAL	USE	AVAILABLE PAINTS
Dark Earth	~0118		Upper surface camouflage	See entry under 'Royal Air Force' section
Middlestone	~0266		Upper surface camouflage	See entry under 'Royal Air Force' section
Azure Blue	~5231		Under surface colour	See entry under 'Royal Air Force' section
Identification Red	~0109		Spinner	See entry under 'Royal Air Force' section
Aluminium	~7178		Overall colour {Mk IIC (T)}	See entry under 'Royal Air Force' section

NOTE:
The above lists references to Federal Standard (FS 595A) numbers do not include the prefix number.
This just denotes the sheen of the colour e.g. 1 = Gloss, 2=Semi-gloss and 3 =Matt.
The above list has been compiled using manufacturers paint lists and in conjunction with the 'IPMS Color Cross-Reference Guide' by David Klaus. Although every care has been taken to offer modellers the broadest spectrum of appropriate colours, further research for each scheme is advisable.

---

flight controls were often repainted with Airframe Grey and Russian stars were carried either side of the fuselage and under the wings only. Normally a tactical number would be carried in Airframe Grey on the fuselage sides or on the vertical fin.

The fighter and fighter-bomber versions left behind by the RAF for VVS service also retained their standard RAF scheme. This was Dark Green, Ocean Grey and Medium Sea Grey. BM959 the famous 'wolf'-marked example shot down near Tiiksjärvi in 1942 featured this scheme with a light grey (Airframe Grey?) spinner. The fuselage stars featured yellow surrounds, while those under the wing were plain (no upper wing stars were applied). the tactical number ('60') was in white on each side of the fuselage and the RAF serial remained in 8in high black

characters. The usual RAF yellow wing leading edges were also retained. Some overall black ('Night') Mk IIBs were also used in Russian service and these retained this overall scheme, although all the British roundels and fin flashes were over-painted in green and replaced with red stars. The serial remained unchanged in Dull Red 8in characters either side of the rear fuselage.

Rumanian Air Force
Details of the colours applied to these machines are rare, as only a few saw service. Looking at the photographic material that is available it is best to assume that the aircraft were in an RAF scheme (or one very similar) of Dark Earth and Dark Green over a 50/50 split under surface of black (port wing) and white (starboard wing). National insignia was applied in all six locations and a single tactical number (stencil style) was applied in red on the vertical fin. The propeller and spinner remained black, but the entire forward section of the nose was bare metal, although some sources list the vertical fin and engine cowlings as being yellow. A small blue, yellow and red fin stripe was applied to the top of the rudder.

Irish Air Corps
Initially Eire acquired two aircraft that crash landed, and these were in the colour scheme of that era, namely Dark Earth and Dark Green over Aluminium. The aircraft were actually repainted in this scheme, with all RAF markings removed, but the demarcation on the lower surfaces stopped aft of the wing leading edge, as the entire rear fuselage featured a wrap-around camouflage. The lower surface colour is also believed to have been changed from aluminium to a 'mixed silver-grey' colour. The Irish roundel was carried on the upper wings and fuselage

Close-up of the artwork, 'Ou Vai Ou Racha' on the port side of the nose of a Mk IIC of XV Esquadrilha based at Espinho Airport in 1948
(© RAF Museum P002621)

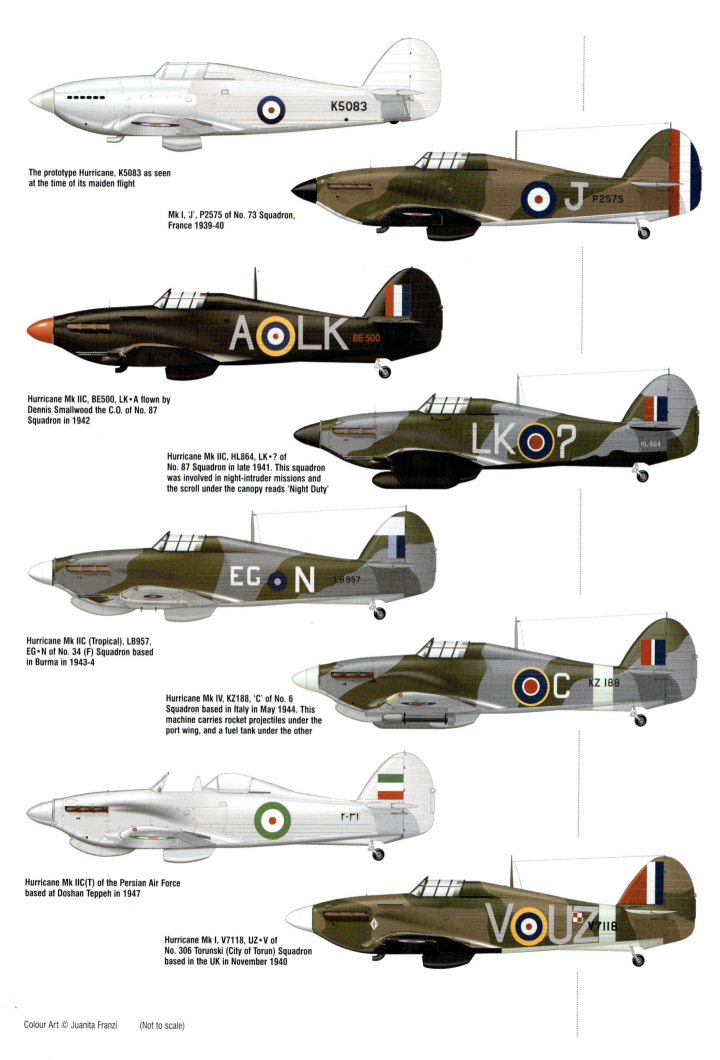

The prototype Hurricane, K5083 as seen at the time of its maiden flight

Mk I, 'J', P2575 of No. 73 Squadron, France 1939-40

Hurricane Mk IIC, BE500, LK•A flown by Dennis Smallwood the C.O. of No. 87 Squadron in 1942

Hurricane Mk IIC, HL864, LK•? of No. 87 Squadron in late 1941. This squadron was involved in night-intruder missions and the scroll under the canopy reads 'Night Duty'

Hurricane Mk IIC (Tropical), LB957, EG•N of No. 34 (F) Squadron based in Burma in 1943-4

Hurricane Mk IV, KZ188, 'C' of No. 6 Squadron based in Italy in May 1944. This machine carries rocket projectiles under the port wing, and a fuel tank under the other

Hurricane Mk IIC(T) of the Persian Air Force based at Doshan Teppeh in 1947

Hurricane Mk I, V7118, UZ•V of No. 306 Torunski (City of Torun) Squadron based in the UK in November 1940

Colour Art © Juanita Franzi   (Not to scale)

sides, the latter item being superimposed on a white square. The twin-colour bands were applied to each lower wing panel, and did extend over the ailerons, or at least on '93' which served with though. Other sources list an early Mk I operated by No. 1 Squadron in 1945 as having the lower surfaces in 'light blue-grey', approximating to Federal Standard 35622.

Later the Irish Air Corps was supplied six Mk IICs from the last production batch and these were supplied in Overall Medium Sea Grey with a disruptive camouflage of Dark Green on the upper surfaces. The fuselage roundel was applied over a white square, while the ones on the upper wings were not. The lower wings once again featured the two-colour bands and did not extend out over the ailerons. A three digit code number was applied in black aft of the fuselage roundel and also under each wing panel (viewed from the rear on the port wing and from the front on the starboard).

Portuguese Air Force

A number of Hurricanes were acquired by this nation both during and after WWII. Most were Mk IICs and were in RAF camouflage of Ocean Grey, Dark Green and Medium Sea Grey. Later in their life they were refurbished and we are sure that the camouflage was re-applied. It is not known if the colours used were similar to those originally applied by the RAF, but they look similar. Yellow leading edges were applied to all the Mk IICs at Espinho and the spinners were a light green colour. A similar green band (the same green as the national fin stripe), was carried around the aft fuselage. The serial number was carried in 14in high white characters aft of the fuselage band and the squadron codes were also white. Only the Portuguese cross was carried on either side of the fuselage, with the lower wing examples being mounted on a white disc. A 27in wide by 24in high fin flash was applied, with the green (forward) portion representing 1/3rd of the overall width of this marking.

South African Air Force

All the machines operated by this nation during WWII were to retain their RAF camouflage and markings. The Mk IICs of No. 11 OTU in 1946 were entirely Dark Earth on top and Sky underneath. The serials were applied (stencil style) in 27in high white characters aft of the fuselage roundels, and this serial was repeated in black on the under surface of each mainplane (read from the rear for the starboard wing, and from the front for the port). A Mk IIB of this unit in June 1945 was light and dark green over Azure Blue. There were wide yellow bands around each wing panel inboard of the roundels, plus a yellow band around the rear fuselage and under the forward section of each fuselage code. The aircraft serial was applied in 8in high black characters slightly under the leading edge of each tailplane, with a unit serial applied in 27in high black characters that were applied directly onto the yellow bands and patches already mentioned. The serial was repeated in black under each wing (on the yellow bands) and was read from the trailing edge on the starboard side, and from the leading edge on the port.

Captured Machines

Italian

A Mk I was captured by Italian forces at the Yugoslav Air Force Fighter School, Mostar on the 16th April 1941. This machine was repainted before it was inspected by Mussolini in an overall scheme of Sand and a mottle of Dark Olive Green over Light Blue Grey. The upper-surface colours wrapped around the leading edges of the wings, as was the case with all Italian fighters of the time, and a wide white band was applied around the rear

Fg Off C.I.R. Arthur of No. 242 Sqn, sitting on the wing of Douglas Bader's Mk I at Martlesham Heath
(© RAF Museum P012653)

fuselage. The entire nose was either left bare metal, or painted in yellow and the Italian national insignia was applied as black silhouette fasces only on the upper and lower wing surfaces.

Luftwaffe

There are at least two photographed examples of ex-RAF machines that were captured by the Luftwaffe. The first is a Mk I captured in the North Africa (V7670). This machine was later 'recaptured' by allied forces and by this time it was displaying Luftwaffe markings. A standard RAF scheme of Middlestone and Dark Earth over Azure Blue had been its original scheme, but by the time of its 'return' it had had all the roundels and fin flashes painted out in RLM 80 Grun (Green) on the upper surfaces and RLM 78 Hellblau (Bright Blue) on the under surface. Crosses had only been applied to either side of the fuselage and the original serial in 8in high black characters had been retained.

Another Mk I was later seen at Maddeburg test centre. This machine featured a three-blade D.H. propeller and had been totally repainted in Luftwaffe colours. It is likely that the scheme applied was RLM 74 Graugrun over RLM 04 Gelb (yellow) with a dense mottle of RLM 75 Grauviolett on the upper surfaces. A swastika had been applied to both sides of the vertical fin and national crosses had been applied in all six positions. A radio call-sign had been applied in black either side of the fuselage, although DF+ is all that can currently be determined from photographs. It is likely that this call-sign was repeated under the wings as well, with 'DF' on one wing panel and the remaining letters on the other.

Mk I, V7670 after recapture and still in Luftwaffe markings, Gambut, January 1943
(© RAF Museum P009602)

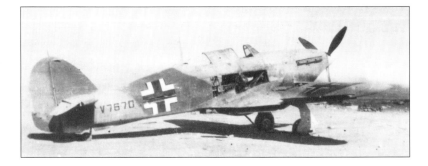

Hurricane Kit Listing

MANUFACTURER	SCALE	TYPE	SUBJECT	RELEASED	NOTES
Academy	1/72nd	IM	Mk IIC	1997	
Advent	1/72nd	IM	Mk II	1979-80	Ex-Revell
AHM	1/148th	IM	Mk IIC	1970's	Ex-Ikko
Airfix	1/72nd	IM	Mk IV (RP)	1956	
Airfix	1/72nd	IM	Mk I/IIB	1972	Conversion of the Mk IV (RP) mould
Airfix	1/72nd	IM	Mk I	1978	
Airfix	1/48th	IM	Mk I	1980	
Airfix	1/24th	IM	Mk I	1973	
Airfix Corporation	1/72nd	IM	Mk IV (RP)	1963	Ex-Airfix
Airfix Craftmaster	1/72nd	IM	Mk IV (RP)	1965	Ex-Airfix
AMT	1/72nd	IM	Mk II	1979	Ex-Matchbox
Aoshima	1/72nd	IM	Mk II	D	1964
Arii	1/148th	IM	Mk IIC	1983	Ex-Ikko
C.A. Atkins	1/72nd	Pewter	Prototype	1980's	
Bandai	1/48th	IM	Mk II	1976	Ex-Monogram
Bienengraber	1/72nd	IM	Mk IIC	1970's	Ex-Frog
Classic Aircraft Collections Ltd	N/A	IM	Mk IIC	1990's	Reproduction of WWII recognition model
Crown	1/148th	IM	Mk II	1976	Ex-Ikko
Eagle	1/97th	IM	Mk II	1960's	
Eko	1/150th	IM		1978	
Farmtex	1/72nd	IM	Mk IIC	1987	Ex-Lotnia
Farmtex	1/72nd	VF	Mk IIC	1987	
Frog	1/72nd	IM	Mk IIC	1967	Inc. Sea Hurricane parts
Frog Penguin	1/72nd	IM	Mk I	1939	
Hasegawa	1/72nd	IM	Mk I	1997	Finnish A.F decals
Hasegawa	1/72nd	IM	Mk I	1997	'Nightfighter'
Hasegawa	1/72nd	IM	Mk I	1997	Douglas Bader decals
Hasegawa	1/72nd	IM	Mk IB	1997	
Hasegawa	1/72nd	IM	Mk II	1997	Eagle Squadron decals
Hasegawa	1/72nd	IM	Mk IIB	1997	'Red Star'decals
Hasegawa	1/72nd	IM	Mk IIC	1997	
Hasegawa	1/72nd	IM	Mk IIC	1997	'Nightfighter'
Hasegawa	1/72nd	IM	Mk IIC	1997	Yugoslav Air Force decals
Hasegawa	1/72nd	IM	Mk IID	1997	
Hasegawa	1/48th	IM	Mk I	1999	
Hasegawa	1/48th	IM	Mk IIB	1999	
Hasegawa	1/48th	IM	Mk IIC	1998	
Hasegawa	1/48th	IM	Mk IIC	1998	SEAC decals
Hasegawa	1/48th	IM	Mk IIC	1998	Special issue 'Night Fighter'
Hasegawa	1/48th	IM	Mk IIC	1999	Sea Hurricane
Hasegawa	1/48th	IM	Mk IID	1998	
Hasegawa	1/48th	IM	Mk IID	1998	'Super Detail' with KMC resin update
Heller	1/72nd	IM	Mk I	1970's	
Heller	1/72nd	IM	Mk IIC	1970's	
Hema	1/72nd	IM	Mk IIC	1969	Ex-Frog
Hobbycraft	1/48th	IM	Mk IIB	1988	
Hobbycraft	1/48th	IM	Mk IIB/C/D	1988	
Hobbycraft	1/48th	IM	Mk IID	1988	
Hobbycraft	1/48th	IM	Mk IIC	1988	'Night Raider' Hi-tech issue
Humbrol	1/72nd	IM	Mk IIC	1973	Ex-Frog, in 'Make & Paint' series
Idea	1/48th	IM	Mk II	1980's	
Ikko	1/148th	IM	Mk IIC	1970's	Never issued by this firm, later issued by Arii and Academy
KeilKraft	1/72nd	IM	Mk IIC	1958	
Lotnia	1/72nd	IM	Mk IIC	1980's	
Matchbox	1/72nd	IM	Mk IIC	1974	
Matchbox	1/72nd	IM	Mk IIC/D	1978	
Mikro	1/134th	IM	Mk IIC	1976	
Milion Plamo	1/50th	IM	N/K	N/K	
Minicraft	1/72nd	IM	Mk IIC	1972	Ex-Frog
Minix	1/72nd	IM	Mk IIC	1968	Ex-Frog
Monogram	1/48th	IM	Mk II	1965	
MPC	1/72nd	IM	Mk II	1977	Ex-Airfix
MPC	1/24th	IM	Mk I	1974	Ex-Airfix
Necomisa	1/48th	IM	Mk II	1980's	Ex-Monogram
Novo	1/72nd	IM	Mk IIC	1979	Ex-Frog: Planned but not issued
NovoExport	1/72nd	IM	Mk IIC	1982	Ex-Frog
Plasty	1/72nd	IM	Mk IV	1950's	Ex-Airfix
Remus	1/72nd	IM	Mk IIC	1977	Ex-Frog
Revell	1/72nd	IM	Mk I	1963	
Revell	1/72nd	IM	Mk IIB	1998	
Revell	1/32nd	IM	Mk II	1971	
Roly Toys	1/72nd	IM	Mk IIC	1970's	Ex-Frog
Sankyo	1/150th	IM		1950's	
Sanwa/Tokyo Plamo	1/104th	IM	Mk II	1950's	
SMER	1/72nd	IM	Mk IIC	1985	Ex-Heller
SMER	1/72nd	IM	Mk IIC	1988	Ex-Heller 'Hi-Tech' issue
SMER	1/72nd	IM/R	Mk IV	1996	Ex-Heller, updated with resin parts
Storia	1/72nd	IM	Mk II	1973	Ex-Revell
Tashigrushka	1/72nd	IM	Mk IIC	1980's	Ex-Frog
Toltoys	1/72nd	IM	Mk I/II	1970's	Ex-Airfix
USAirfix	1/48th	IM	Mk I	1980	Ex-Airfix: Planned but never issued
Vulcan	1/97th	IM	Mk II	1950's	

KEY

IM = Injection Moulded Plastic
R = Resin
VF = Vac-form Plastic

Conversions & Accessories

MANUFACTURER	SCALE	TYPE	PRODUCT NO	ITEM	DESIGNED FOR/NOTES
Aardvark Avaition	1/48th	R	-	Conversion	Fabric Wing Mk I
A&V Resin	1/72nd	R	052	Conversion	2-seat trainer conversion for Heller kit
A&V Resin	1/72nd	R	027	Conversion	Mk IID Vickers 'S' pods
A&V Resin	1/72nd	R	029	Accessory	44 Gallon drop tanks
A&V Resin	1/72nd	R/M	020	Conversion	F.H.40 'Slip-Wing'
Aeroclub	1/72nd	M	E051	Merlin Mk II Engine	
Aeroclub	1/72nd	M	V025	4-slot Ballon Tyres	
Aeroclub	1/72nd	VF	C050	Canopy	Mk II
Aeroclub	1/72nd	M	P051	Watts Propeller	Mk I
Aeroclub	1/48th	VF	C068	Canopy	Prototype
Aeroclub	1/48th	VF	C069	Canopy	Mk II
Aeroclub	1/48th	WM	V146	Dowty tailwheel	Mk I
Aires	1/48th	R	4035	Control Surfaces	Hasegawa kits
Aires	1/48th	R	4850	Cockpit Update	Hasegawa kits
Airkit	1/72nd	A	C01	Instrument Panel	
Airpart	1/72nd	R	AP029	Conversion	Mk IIA
Airpart	1/72nd	R	AP031	Conversion	Mk II Tropical Filter
Airpart	1/72nd	R	AP030	Conversion	Mk IIB
Airwaves	1/48th	EB	48044	Detail Set	Airfix kit
Airwaves	1/72nd	EB	72065	Detail Set	
Airwaves	1/72nd	EB	72175	Detail Set	Hasegawa kit
Birdman	1/72nd	A	7203	Canopy Mask	Hasegawa kit
Birdman	1/48th	A	4809	Canopy Mask	Hasegawa kit
Blueprint	1/48th	R	4802	Conversion	Fabric Wing Mk I
Blueprint	1/48th	R	4802A	Detail Set	Cockpit Interior: Mk I
BMW	1/72nd	P	0272	Instrument Panel	
BMW	1/48th	P	1248	Instrument Panel	
BMW	1/32nd	P	2232	Instrument Panel	
Canovak	1/72nd	VF	CA016	Canopy	Mk I
CMK	1/48th	R/VF	4011	Interior Update	Hasegawa Mk II kits
CMK	1/48th	R	4012	Control Surfaces	Hasegawa kits
CMK	1/48th	R	4013	Conversion	'Night Intruder' Hasegawa Mk II kits
Delta Aviation	1/72nd	M	7206	Conversion	PR Mk II camera cover
Delta Bits	1/72nd	M	DB5006	Conversion	PR Mk II camera pack
Eduard	1/72nd	EB	72005	Detail Set	
Eduard	1/72nd	EB	72059	Detail Set	Heller/SMER kit
Eduard	1/72nd	EB	72207	Detail Set	Hasegawa Mk I kit
Eduard	1/72nd	EB	72217	Detail Set	Hasegawa Mk II kit
Eduard	1/72nd	EB	72264	Detail Set	Academy Mk IIC kit
Eduard	1/72nd	EB	72289	Detail Set	Revell Mk IIB kit
Eduard	1/48th	EB	48009	Detail Set	Hobbycraft kit
Eduard	1/48th	EB	48169	Detail Set	Airfix kit
Eduard	1/48th	EB	48232	Detail Set	Hasegawa Mk IIB kit
Engine 'n' Things	1/72nd	R	72-034	Merlin II/III Engine	
Engine 'n' Things	1/72nd	R	72-080	Merlin XX/21 Engine	
Engine 'n' Things	1/48th	R	48-035	Merlin II/III Engine	
Engine 'n' Things	1/48th	R	48-103	Merlin XX/21 Engine	
Falcon	1/72nd	VF	Set No. 02	Canopy	Mk I (Airfix) & Mk II (Heller)
Falcon	1/48th	VF	Set No. 03	Canopy	Mk
Falcon	1/48th	VF	Set No. 31	Canopy	Mk I (Airfix), Mk II (Hobbycraft)
Formatex	1/48th	R/EB	06	Detail Set	Hasegawa kits
Hi-Tech	1/72nd	R	72007	Detail Set	Heller/Hasegawa kit
Jaguar	1/72nd	R	67202	Detail Set	Hasegawa kit
KMC	1/72nd	R	72-7010	Interior & Control Surfaces	Hasegawa kit
KMC	1/48th	R	48-5018	Control Surfaces	Hasegawa kit
Magna Models	1/72nd	R	7228	Fabric Wing Conversion	Airfix kit
MDC	1/48th	R	CV0016	Conversion	Hasegawa Mk II kit to Sea Hurricane
Omega Models	1/72nd	R	PH 006	RS-82 & FAB 100 bombs	Mk IIB
PART	1/72nd	EB	S72-063	Detail Set	Hasegawa kit (Mk I)
PART	1/48th	EB	S48-035	Detail Set	Hasegawa kit (Mk IIC)
PART	1/48th	EB	S48-039	Detail Set	Hasegawa kit (Mk IID)
PJ Productions	1/48th	R	481101	Watts Propeller	
Squadron	1/72nd	VF	9109	Canopy	
Squadron	1/48th	VF	9509	Canopy	Airfix or Hobbycraft kits
True Detail	1/72nd	R	72041	Main Wheels	
True Details	1/48th	R	48027	Main Wheels	
True Details	1/48th	Vi	41046	Vinyl Pre-cut Canopy Mask	Hasegawa Mk IIC/D kits

KEY

EB = Etched Brass
VF = Vac-form Plastic
R = Resin
M = Metal or Pewter
P = Paper
A = Acetate
V = Vinyl

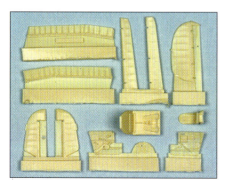

Kendall Model Company Inc. 1/72nd scale (72-7010) interior update & control surfaces set for the Hasegawa kit

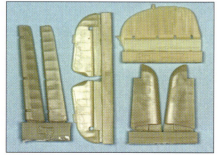

CMK 1/48th scale set of control surfaces for the Hasegawa Mk II kits

Magna Models 1/72nd scale (7228) fabric wing conversion for the Airfix kit

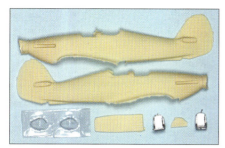

A&V Resin 1/72nd scale 2-seat trainer conversion for Heller kit

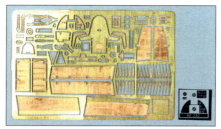

Eduard 1/48th scale detail set (48-232) for the Hasegawa Mk II kit

Delta Bits 1/72nd scale PR Mk II camera pack

CMK 1/48th scale interior update for the Hasegawa Mk II kits

Eduard 1/72nd scale detail set (72-217) for the Hasegawa Mk II kit

Eduard 1/72nd scale detail set (72-207) for the Hasegawa Mk I kit

True Details 1/72nd scale (72041) replacement main wheels

PJ Productions 1/48th scale (481101) Watts propeller

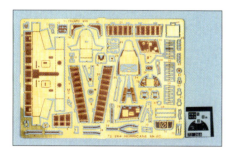

Eduard 1/72nd scale detail set (72-264) for the Academy Mk IIC kit

Omega Models 1/72nd scale (PH 006) set of RS-82 & FAB 100 bombs that are suitable for the Mk IIB

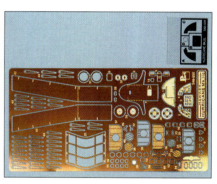

PART 1/48th scale (S48-035) detail set for the Hasegawa Mk IIC kit

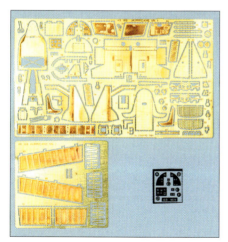

Eduard 1/48th scale detail set (48-169) for the Airfix kit

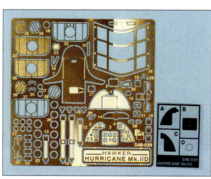

PART 1/48th scale (S48-039) detail set for the Hasegawa Mk IID kit

Aeroclub 1/48th scale Dowty oleo-pneumatic tailwheel (V146)

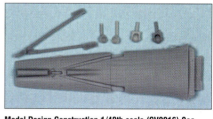

Model Design Construction 1/48th scale (CV0016) Sea Hurricane Mk IIC conversion for the Hasegawa Mk II kit

PART 1/72nd scale (S72-063) detail set for the Hasegawa Mk I kit

Kendall Model Company Inc. 1/48th scale (48-5018) control surfaces set for the Hasegawa kit

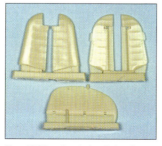

Aires 1/48th scale set of control surfaces for the Hasegawa kits

Engine 'n' Things 1/48th scale (48035) Merlin II/III Engine

CMK 1/48th scale 'Night Intruder' conversion for the Hasegawa Mk II kits

Hurricane Decals

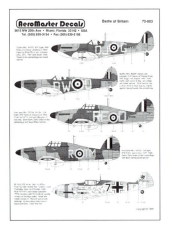

AeroMaster 72-003
'Battle of Britain Hurricanes'

AeroMaster 72-024
'Foreign Hurricanes'

AeroMaster 72-134
'Hurricanes at War Part 1'

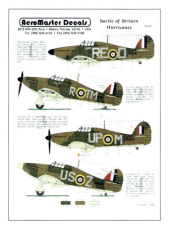

AeroMaster 72-137
'Battle of Britain Hurricanes'

MANUFACTURER	SCALE	SHEET NO.	TITLE	SUBJECTS	NOTE
AeroMaster	1/72nd	72003	Battle of Britain	Mk I, P3039, RE•D, 'Be Bé', No.229 Sqn, RAF Northolt	Plt Off V. Ortmans
				Mk I, V6702, TM•R, No.504 Sqn, RAF Filton	
AeroMaster	1/72nd	72024	Foreign Hurricanes	Mk IIB, BM959, '60', Red Air Force, Finland, 1942	
				Mk IIC, KZ352, A•A, No.1 (Fighter) Sqn, R.I.A.F., 1944	
				Mk I, HC-454, 2 LeLv.26, Finnish Air Force, 1943	
				Mk I, '3', Royal Rumanian Air Force, 1940	
				Mk I, '105', No.1 Fighter Sqd., Irish Air Force, 1945.	
				Mk IIB, BG707, Free French forces, North Africa, 1942	
				Mk IIC, LB886, 'O', No. 351 (Yugoslav) Sqn, Libya, 1944	
AeroMaster	1/72nd	72029	British Hurricane Aces	Mk I, P3039, RE•D, 'Be Bé', No.229 Sqn, RAF Northolt	Plt Off V. Ortmans
				Mk I, V6702, TM•R, No.504 Sqn, RAF Filton	
				Mk I, V6879, UP•M, No.605 Sqn, RAF Croydon	Sqn Ldr McKellar
				Mk I, R2869, US•Z, No.56 Sqn, RAF Northolt	
AeroMaster	1/72nd	72050	Spitfire/Hurricane Roundels (Late)		
AeroMaster	1/72nd	72051	Spitfire/Hurricane Roundels (Early)		
AeroMaster	1/72nd	72117	Hurricanes at War Part I		
AeroMaster	1/72nd	72118	Hurricanes at War Part II		
AeroMaster	1/72nd	72119	Hurricanes at War Part III		
AeroMaster	1/72nd	72134	Hurricanes at War Part IV	Mk I (Trop), P2638, No. 274 Sqn	
				Mk I, LK•A, P2798, No. 87 Sqn	Sqn Ldr I.R. Gleed
				Mk IIC, LK•A, LE500, No. 87 Sqn, RAF Charmy Down	Sqn Ldr I.R Gleed
				Sea Hurricane Mk IA, 8E•W, P3090, RNAS Lee-on-Solent	
				Sea Hurricane Mk IIC, 7•N, No. 835 Sqn, FAA	HMS Nairana
AeroMaster	1/72nd	72137	Battle of Britain Hurricanes	Mk I, P3039, 'Bébé', No. 229 Sqn, RAF Norholt, 1940	Plt Off. V. Ortmans
				Mk I, V6702, TM•R, V6072, No. 504 Sqn, RAF Filton	
				Mk I, UP•M, V6879, No. 605 Sqn, RAF Croydon	Sqn Ldr A.McKellar
				Mk I, US•Z, R2869, No. 56 Sqn, RAF North Weald	
				Mk I, RF•R, R4175, No. 303 Sqn, RAF Northolt	Sgt J. Frantisek
				Mk I, UZ•V, V7118, No. 306 (Polish) Sqn	
AeroMaster	1/72nd	SP7205	Battle of Britain Special	*Not released at time of publication*	
AeroMaster	1/48th	48005	Battle of Britiain	Mk I, DT•A, V6555, No.272 Sqn	Sqn Ldr Stanford Tuck
				Mk I, DT•A, V6864, No.272 Sqn	Sqn Ldr Stanford Tuck
				Mk I, UP•M, V6879, No.605 Sqn	Sqn Ldr A. McKellar
				Mk I, LE•A, P2691, No.242 Sqn	Plt Off W. McKnight
				Mk I, DX•L, W9145, No.245 Sqn	Sqn Ldr J. Simpson
AeroMaster	1/48th	48009	Red Stars in the Sky	Mk IIB, BM959, '60', Red Air Force, Finland, 1942	
AeroMaster	1/48th	48026	Spitfire/Hurricane Roundels (Early)		
AeroMaster	1/48th	48027	Spitfire/Hurricane Roundels (Late)		

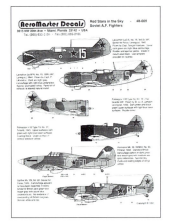

AeroMaster 48-009
'Red Stars in the Sky - Soviet A.F. fighters'

AeroMaster 48-045
'Foreign Hurricanes Part 2'

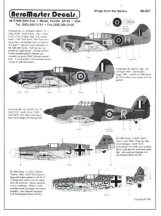

AeroMaster 48-057
'Wings over the Sahara'

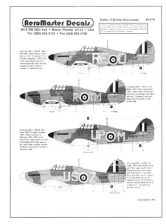

AeroMaster 48-079
'Battle of Britain Hurricanes'

AeroMaster 48-193
'Hurricanes at War Part 1'

AeroMaster 48-194
'Hurricanes at War Part II'

AeroMaster 48-363
'The Eagle Squadron Part 1'

17. InTech 1/72nd scale
'Polish Air Force Part 3'

MANUFACTURER	SCALE	SHEET NO.	TITLE	SUBJECTS	NOTE
AeroMaster	1/48th	48045	Foreign Hurricanes Part 2	Sea Hurricane Mk IIB, JS327, 1942 Mk IIB, BG707, Free French A.F Mk I, H-25, Eacadrille 2, Belgium Air Force, 1940. Mk IIC, 2013, Advanced Group, Persian Flying Training School, 1947	Operation Torch North Africa, 1942
AeroMaster	1/48th	48057	Wings over the Sahara	Inc. Mk IIB, BD930, 'R', No.73 Sqn, North Africa, 1942	
AeroMaster	1/48th	48079	Battle of Britain Hurricanes	Mk I, P3039, RE•D,'Bebé', No.229 Sqn, RAF Northolt Mk I, V6702, TM•R, No.504 Sqn, RAF Filton Mk I, V6879, UP•M, No.605 Sqn, RAF Croydon Mk I, R2869, US•Z, No.56 Sqn, RAF Northolt Mk I, R4175, RF•R, No. 303 Sqn, RAF Northolt Mk I, V7118, UZ•V, No. 306 (Polish) Sqn	Plt Off V. Ortmans Sqn Ldr McKellar Sgt F. Frantisek
AeroMaster	1/48th	48193	Hurricanes at War Part I	Mk I (Trop), P2638, No. 274 Sqn Mk I, LK•A, P2798, No. 87 Sqn Mk IIC, LK•A, LE500, No. 87 Sqn, RAF Charmy Down Sea Hurricane Mk IA, 8E•W, P3090, RNAS Lee-on-Solent Sea Hurricane Mk IIC, 7•N, No. 835 Sqn, FAA	Sqn Ldr I.R. Gleed Sqn Ldr I.R Gleed HMS Nairana
AeroMaster	1/48th	48194	Hurricanes at War Part II	Mk I, GG•K, L1766, No. 151 Sqn, RAF North Weald Mk IIB (Trop), 'V', HL795, No. 274 Sqn, North Africa Mk IIC, LK•?, HL664, No. 87 Sqn Mk IID, BN795, 'Our John'	
AeroMaster	1/48th	48195	Hurricanes at War Part III	'White 55', Russian A.F., 1942 Mk IIB, FH•41, Z4018, No. 81 Sqn, Russia 1941 Mk IIB, 'J', P3731, No. 262 Sqn, Malta Mk IIC, 5336, No. 11 OTU, SAAF Sea Hurricane W9219, No. 8880 Sqn, NAS, 1941	
AeroMaster	1/48th	48243	Spitfire/Hurricane Roundels (Early)		
AeroMaster	1/48th	48244	Spitfire/Hurricane/Typhoon Roundels (Late)		
AeroMaster	1/48th	48363	The Eagle Squadron Pt.I	Mk IA, V7608, XR•V, No. 71 Sqn, Summer 1941 Mk IA, XR•V, No. 71 Sqn, RAF Kirton-on-Lindsay Mk IA, P7308, XR•D, No. 71 Sqn, RAF Kirton-on-Lindsay	Chesley Petterson Wm.R Dunn
AeroMaster	1/48th	148011	Hurricane Stencils		
AeroMaster	1/48th	SP48-05	Battle of Britain Special	Mk I, DT•A, V6555, No. 257 Sqn Mk I, UP•M, V6879, No. 605 Sqn Mk I, LE•A, P2691, No. 242 Sqn Mk I, DX•L, W9145, No. 245 Sqn	Sqn Ldr R.S. Tuck Sqn Ldr A. McKellar Plt Off W. McKnight Sqn Ldr J. Simpson
Almark	1/72nd	C02	Battle of Britian	RF•U, No. 303 (Polish) Sqn Mk IIC, P2798, LK•A, No. 87 Sqn	Sqn Ldr I.R. Gleed
Almark	1/72nd	C05	North Africa	Mk IIB, No. 274 Sqn	
Almark	1/48th	A4826	RAF PRU Aircraft		
Aviation Usk	1/72nd	7118	Hurricane	Romania Air Force	
Aviation Usk	1/72nd	7119	Hurricane	HC-45, Finnish Air Force	
Dutch Decals	1/72nd	72035	RNeth Navy	Inc. Hurricane Mk IIA Hurricane Mk IIB Trop	
Eduard	1/72nd	72003	Czech Aces in the RAF	RF•U, No. 303 (Polish) Sqn DU•K	
InScale	1/72nd	1872	Mk I & II in Finnish Air Force service 1940-7	HC-460 HC-451 HC-452 HC-454 HC-455 HC-456 HC-465 OH-IPL (HC-460 on delivery flight)	
InScale	1/48th	2448	Mk I & IIB In Finnish Air Force Service 1940-44		
InTech	1/72nd	4	Polish Air Force Part 3	Inc. Mk I, V7118, UZ•V, No. 306 Sqn, November 1940	
Max	1/72nd	72-002	Irish Air Corps 1938-48	Mk I, '93' Irish Air Corps Training School, 1942 Mk IIC, '115', Irish Air Corps, 1945	
Max	1/48th	48-001	Irish Air Corps 1922-97	Inc. Mk IIC, '115', Irish Air Corps, 1945	
MSAP	1/48th	4827	Hurricane Mk IIc/d	Mk IID, BP188, JV•Z, No.6 Sqn MK IIC, HL795 'V', No.274 Sqn Mk IIC, BD930 'R', No.73 Sqn, North Africa, 1942 Mk IIC, BD389, GO•C, No.94 Sqn	
Propagteam	1/72nd	01372	Stencil Data		
Propagteam	1/72nd	72022	Hurricane Mk I	Mk I, V7467, LE•D, No.242 Sqn	Sqn Ldr D.Bader
Propagteam	1/72nd	72027	Hurricane Mk I	Mk I, V6864, DT•A, No.257 Sqn	Sqn Ldr R.S. Tuck

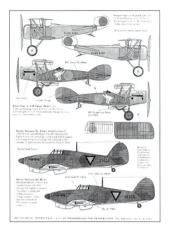

Dutch Decals 72035
'RNethNavy'

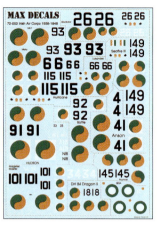

Max Decals 72-002
'Irish Air Corps 1938-1948'

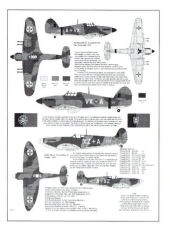

Tally Ho! 4206 (1/48th scale)
'Portugese Air Force'

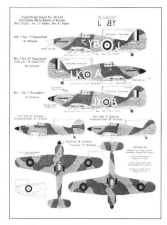

SuperScale 48-559
'Hurricane Mk I Battle of Britain'

MANUFACTURER	SCALE	SHEET NO.	TITLE	SUBJECTS	NOTE
Propagteam	1/48th	01248	Stencil Data		
Propagteam	1/48th	48004	Hurricane Mk I	Mk I, V7467, LE•D, No.242 Sqn	Sqn Ldr D.Bader
SuperScale	1/72nd	72055	British Empire Aces		
SuperScale	1/72nd	72140	Hurricane		
SuperScale	1/72nd	72294	Hurricane Aces		
SuperScale	1/72nd	72728	Battle of Britain	Mk I, N2359, YB•J, No. 17 Sqn	
				Mk I, P2798, LK•A, No. 87 Sqn	Sqn Ldr I.R. Gleed DFC
				Mk I, P3395, JX•B, No. 1 Sqn	
				Mk IIC, BE581, JX•E, No. 1 Sqn	Flt Lt K.M. Kuttlewascher
			Mk IIC, LD836, ZY-S, No. 247 Sqn		
				Sea Hurricane Mk IIC, 7•N, 835 Sqn, FAA	HMS Nairana
				Mk IIC, LK•?, No. 87 Sqn	
				MK IIB (Trop), HL795, 'V', No. 274 Sqn	
SuperScale	1/48th	48383	Hurricane	Mk I, V7467, LE•D, No. 242 Sqn	Sqn Ldr D.R.S. Bader
				Mk I, DT•A, No.257 Sqn	Sqn Ldr R.R.S. Tuck
				Mk I, P3059, SD•N, No.501 Sqn	Plt Off. K.N.T. Lee
SuperScale	1/48th	48559	Hurricane Mk I	Mk I, P2798, LK•A, No.87 Sqn	Sqn Ldr I.R. Gleed DFC
				Mk I, N2359, YB•J, No.17 Sqn	
				Mk I, P3395, JX•B, No. 1 Sqn	
SuperScale	1/48th	48560	Hurricane	Mk IIB (Trop), HL795 'V', No. 274 Sqn, North Africa	
				Mk IIC, BE581, JX•E, No. 1 Sqn	
				Mk IIB (Trop), LD936, ZY•S, No.247 Sqn	
				Sea Hurricane Mk IIC, 7•N, 835 Sqn, FAA	HMS Nairana
				Mk IIC, LK•?, No.87 Sqn	
SuperScale	1/32nd	32007	Battle of Britain	YB•J, N2359, No.17 Sqn	
				JX•B, P3395, No. 1 Sqn	
				LE•D, V7467, No.242 Sqn	Sqn Ldr. D. Bader
				DX•L, W9145, No. 245 Sqn	Sqn Ldr J. Simpson
Tally Ho!	1/72nd	7116	Irish Air Corps	Mk I, '105', No. 1 (Fighter) Sqn, Irish Air Corps	
Tally Ho!	1/72nd	7134	Portugese Air Force	Mk IIC, VX•A, '517', Portugese Air Force	
Tally Ho!	1/48th	4206	Portugese Air Force	Mk IIC, VX•A, '517', Portugese Air Force	
Techmod	1/72nd	72073	Hurricane	Mk IIC, LF363, WC•F, No.309 (Polish) Sqn	
				Mk IIC, BP588, RS•X, No.30 Sqn, 1942	
				Mk IIC, BP592, AK•G, No.213 Sqn, El Alamein 1942	
				Mk IIC, BE581, JX•E, No. 1 Sqn	
				Mk IIC, HV608, Turkish Air Force, 1943	

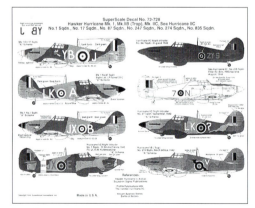

SuperScale 72-728
'Battle of Britain'

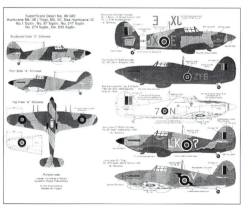

Superscale 48-560
(Various)

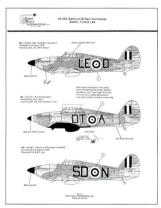

Superscale 48-383
'Battle of Britain'

Hurricane Powerplants

The Rolls-Royce Merlin
Hurricane Usage

Merlin 'C'

This 890hp engine was based on the 'B' and featured the supercharged, spur-geared, .477:1 compression ratio of that type. The type was first tested in April 1935 and the 11th engine was fitted to the Hurricane Prototype for its first flight. It failed the civil type-test and Rolls-Royce decided to redesign the coolant system to pure ethylene-glycol.

Fitted to: Prototype

Production: 4 Derby

Total Production: 4

Production Period: 1935-6

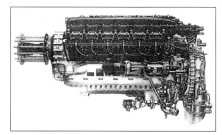

Rolls-Royce Merlin 'F' *(Rolls-Royce Ltd)*

Merlin 'F'

This engine was developed from the Merlin 'E' and featured a single-speed supercharger. The engine had a pure ethylene-glycol coolant system and had the redesigned cylinder head. Maximum power recorded from this engine was 1,212bhp at +10.21lb boost.

Fitted to: Prototype

Production: 25 Derby

Total Production: 25

Production Period: 1935-7

Rolls-Royce Merlin II *(Rolls-Royce Ltd)*

Merlin II

This engine was originally the 'G' type and it featured the one-piece flat head cylinder block. The type had 100% ethylene-glycol coolant, a maximum boost of +6.25lb and a propeller reduction of .477:1. Piston-ring flutter at maximum boost lead to their disintegration, swiftly followed by total engine failure. The development of the specialist material 4K6 by Wellworthy Ltd allowed Rolls-Royce to employ this for the rings and overcome this problem. Maximum power of 1,030bhp at +6.25lb boost at 16,500ft was achieved.

Fitted to: Hurricane Mk I & Sea Hurricane Mk I

Production: 1,283 Derby

Total Production: 1,283

Production Period: 1937-9

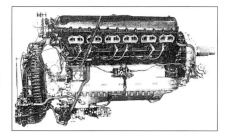

The Merlin III *(Rolls-Royce Ltd)*

Merlin III

This engine was similar to the Mk II, with a single-speed supercharger. Coolant, boost and propeller reduction were identical to the Mk II. The engine had a necked-down propeller shaft to protect the shaft threads and this was adopted as a universal shaft for all D.H. and Rotol propellers. The power rating of this engine was identical to the Merlin II.

Fitted to: Hurricane Mk I & Sea Hurricane Mk I

Production: 6,444 Derby, 2,012 Crewe

Total Production: 8,456

Production Period: 1938-41

Merlin XX

This two-speed supercharged engine was a modified version of the Mk X, for which it was the replacement. A 70-30% ethylene-glycol pressure cooling system was used and a propeller reduction gear of .42:1. Maximum boost was +12lb and 100 octane fuel was used. The maximum power output of this engine was 1,390hp.

Fitted to: Hurricane Mk IIA, IIB, IIC, IID, IV & Sea Hurricane Mk II

Production: 2,592 Derby, 3,391 Crewe, 9,500 Glasgow, 12,538 Ford

Total Production: 28,021

Production Period: 1940-44

Merlin 25

This was a two-speed single-stage supercharged engine, similar to a Merlin 24, but with reverse coolant-flow. The type featured an R.A.E anti-G carburettor and a two-peice block. Due to the double girdle pistons installed, the type could operate at +18lb boost. A maximum power output of 1,610hp was attained by this type.

Fitted to: Hurricane Mk XII (Canada)

Production: 542 Derby, 229 Crewe, 2,550 Glasgow, 10,400 Ford

Total Production: 13,721

Production Period: 1943-7

The Merlin 45 *(Rolls-Royce Ltd)*

Merlin 45

This engine was basically a modified Merlin III with a single-speed supercharger capable of 1,210hp at +3lb boost at 18,000ft.

Fitted to: Hurricane Mk I

Production: 2,000 Derby, 1,574 Crewe

Total Production: 3,574

Production Period: 1941-3

The Rolls-Royce Merlin
The American Connection

Packard Merlin 28

This was a two-speed single-stage supercharged engine and was fitted with a British propeller shaft and a two-piece Packard block (similar to the V-1650-1). The type was an interim one, while Rolls-Royce changed from the single piece, to the two-piece block. The type featured a Bendix carburettor and American magnetos, propeller gearing was .42:1. and a maximum power rating of 1,610hp was available.

Fitted to: Hurricane Mk X (Canada) - Projected use in Mk III

Packard Merlin 29

This 1.390hp two-speed single-stage supercharged engine never reached series production, as it was just a modification of existing Merlin 28s. The modification consisted of a U.S.-splined propeller shaft and propeller reduction was .477:1

Fitted to: Hurricane Mk XII (Canada)

No. 111 Squadrons Mk I being 'wound-up' prior to ground running, Northolt 1938 *(© RAF Museum P002637)*

Hurricane Variants

Designation: **Prototype (K5083)**
First Flight: November 1935
Span: 40ft (12.19m)
Length: 31ft 6in (9.60m)
Height: 13ft 6in (4.11m)
Engine: 1,025hp Rolls-Royce Merlin 'C'
Weight: 5,672lb (2,578kg) (Normal Loaded)
Max Speed: (clean at 15,000ft) 312mph (501km/h)
Stalling Speed: (wheels & flaps up at sea level) 70mph (112km/h)
Time to 20,000ft: (clean) 12 minutes
Operation Ceiling: 33,000ft (estimated)
Range: 500 miles
Armament: Eight 0.303" Browning machine guns

Designation: **Mk I (Early production)**
Span: 40ft (12.19m)
Length: 31ft 4in (9.33m)
Height: 13ft 2in (4.02m) (Watts propeller vertical)
Engine: 1,030hp Rolls-Royce Merlin 'G' (Mk II)
Weight: 6,447lb (Normal Loaded - Rotol), 6,499lb (Normal Loading - DH propeller)
Max Speed: (clean at 15,000ft) 317mph (509km/h)
Stalling Speed: (clean at sea level) 72-80mph (115km/h-128km/h)
Time to 20,000ft: (clean) 11 minutes
Operation Ceiling: 33,400ft
Range: 525 miles (at 15,000ft)
Armament: Eight 0.303in. Browning machine guns
Propeller: Watts two-blade right-hand wooden (Type Z38) 10ft 9in diameter

Designation: **Mk I (Late production)**
Type: Fighter
Span: 40ft (12.19m)
Length: 31ft 4in (9.55m)
Height: 12ft 11.5in (3.95m) (Rotol propeller, one blade vertical).
Engine: 1,029hp Rolls-Royce Merlin III
Fuel: 97 gallons
Weight: 6,218lb (Normal Loaded)
Max Speed: (clean at 15,000ft) 317mph (509km/h)
Stalling Speed: (clean at sea level) 72-80mph (115km/h-128km/h)
Cruising Speed: At 20,000ft 212mph (most economical)
Time to 20,000ft: (max weight) 9.7 minutes
Operation Ceiling: 32,500ft (Max. Weight), 33,500ft (Mean Weight), (32,100ft - Mk I Tropical)
Range: 585 miles (460 miles - Mk I Tropical)
Armament: Eight 0.303in. Browning machine guns with 334 rnds per gun
Propeller: D.H. Hamilton Hydromatic or Rotol (Type R.M.S. 7) three-blade, constant-speed, variable-pitch propeller of 10ft 9in diameter

Designation: **Mk I (Two Cannon)**
First Flight: L1750 converted
Type: Heavy Fighter
Span: 40ft (12.19m)
Length: 31ft 4in (9.55m)
Height: 12ft 11.5in (3.95m)
Engine: Rolls-Royce Merlin XX
Weight: 6,218lb (Normal Loaded)
Max Speed: At 13,000ft (3962m) 260mph (418km/h) (estimated)
Operation Ceiling: N/K
Range: N/K
Armament: Two Oerlikon 20mm cannon in gondolas under the outer wing panels
Propeller: Rotol three-blade variable-pitch propeller

Designation: **Mk I (Four Cannon)**
First Flight: V7360 converted and flew at Langley in July 1940
Type: Heavy Fighter
Span: 40ft (12.19m)
Length: 31ft 4in (9.55m)
Height: 12ft 11.5in (3.95m)
Engine: Rolls-Royce Merlin III
Weight: 6,610lb (2,998kg) (fully-armed)
Max Speed: 304mph (489km/h) at 17,600ft (5365m)
Operation Ceiling: N/K
Range: N/K
Armament: Four Hispano 20mm cannon in modified metal wings
Propeller: Rotol three-blade variable-pitch prop

Designation: **Mk IIA Series I**
First Flight: 11th June 1940 (P3269)
Span: 40ft (12.19m)
Length: 32ft 2.25in (9.83m)
Height: 13ft 1in (3.99m)
Engine: 1,260hp Rolls-Royce Merlin XX
Max Speed: 348mph (560km/h) at 17,400ft (5,304m)
Operation Ceiling: 36,300ft
Range: 468 miles (946 miles - 2x44 gallon fuel tanks, 1,090 miles - 2x90 galon fuel tanks)
Armament: Eight 0.303in. Browning machine guns

The Prototype, K5083, at Martlesham Heath in 1937 *(© C.E. Brown/RAF Museum 5684-6)*

Designation: **Mk IIA Series II**
First Flight: N/K
Type: Tropicalised fighter
Span: 40ft (12.19m)
Length: 32ft 2.25in (9.83m)
Height: 13ft 1in (3.99m) (One propeller blade vertical, tailwheel on the ground)
Weight: Maximum: 7,110lb (3,232kg) Mean: 6,760lb (3,072kg) Light: 6,100lb (2,773kg)
Engine: Rolls-Royce Merlin XX
Engine Rating: 1,260hp at 12,250ft 1,175hp at 20,500ft
Operation Ceiling: 37,000ft (max weight), 37,500ft (mean weight)
Maximum speed: 342mph (at 22,000ft), 322mph (at 13,500ft)
Cruising Speed: At 20,000ft 212mph
Time to 20,000ft: 8.2 minutes (max weight)
Range: 468 miles (946 miles - 2x44 gallon fuel tanks, 1,090 miles - 2x90 galon fuel tanks. Tropical: 440 miles (900 miles - 2x44 gallon fuel tanks, 1,015 miles 2x90 gallon fuel tanks)
Armament: Eight 0.303in. Browning machine guns (334 rnds per gun), although the type had provision for the 12-gun wing armament
Note: Some were fitted with an arrestor hook for Naval operations and were simply refered to as 'hooked' Mk IIA's

Designation: **Mk IIB (Fighter)**
Type: Fighter
Span: 40ft (12.19m)
Length: 32ft 2.25in (9.83m)
Height: 13ft 1in (3.99m) (One propeller blade vertical, tailwheel on the ground)
Fuel: 97 Gallons
Engine: Rolls-Royce Merlin XX
Engine Rating: 1,260 at 12,250ft, 1,175hp at 20,500ft
Weight: Maximum; 7,340lb (3,336kg) Mean; 6,990lb (3,177kg) Light; 6,240lb (2,836kg)
Max Speed: 322mph (at 13,500ft). 342mph (at 22,000ft)
Cruising Speed: At 20,000ft 212mph
Stalling Speed: (clean at sea level) 75-85mph (120km/h-137km/h)
Time to 20,000ft: 8.4 minutes
Operation Ceiling: 36,000ft (Tropical: 33,600ft)
Range: 465 miles (935 miles - 2x44 gallon fuel tanks, 1,080 miles - 2x90 gallon fuel tanks. Tropical: 436 miles (880 miles - 2x44 gallon fuel tanks, 1,010 miles - 2x90 gallon fuel tanks)
Armament: Six, eight or twelve 0.303in. Browning machine guns
Note: Some were fitted with an arrestor hook for Naval operations and refered to as a 'hooked' Mk IIB

Designation: **Mk IIB (Fighter-bomber)**
First Flight: N/K
Type: Fighter-bomber
Span: 40ft (12.19m)
Length: 32ft 2.25in (9.83m)
Height: 13ft 1in (3.99m) (One propeller blade vertical, tailwheel on the ground)
Engine: 1,260hp Rolls-Royce Merlin XX
Weight: 7,733lb (3,515kg) (Normal Loaded)
Max Speed: (clean at 15,000ft) 301mph (484km/h)
Stalling Speed: (clean at sea level) 75-85mph (120km/h-137km/h)
Time to 20,000ft: (clean) 12 minutes
Operation Ceiling: 36,000ft
Range: 460 miles (920 miles - 2x44 gallon fuel tanks, 1,086 miles - 2x90 gallon fuel tanks. Tropical: 426 miles (908 miles - 2x44 gallon fuel tanks, 1022 miles - 2x90 galon fuel tanks)
Armament: Six, eight or twelve 0.303in. Browning machine guns plus two 250lb bombs below the outer wing panels

Designation: **Mk IIC**
First Flight: 5th December 1940 (V7360)
Type: Fighter
Span: 40ft (12.19m)
Length: 32ft 2.25in (9.83m)
Fuel: 97 Gallons
Height: 13ft 1in (3.99m) (One propeller blade vertical, tailwheel on the ground)
Engine: Rolls-Royce Merlin XX
Engine Rating: 1,260hp at 12,250ft, 1,175hp at 20,500ft
Weight: Maximum 7,640lb (3,473kg) Mean 7, 290lb (3,314kg) Light 6,580lb (2,991kg) Normal Loaded 7,544lb (3,429kg) Normal Loaded (Tropical) 7,707lb (3,503kg)
Max Speed: 301mph (484km/h) (clean at 15,000ft), 336mph (540km/h) (at 16,600ft (5,060m)). When fitted with a Vokes filter the top speed was reduced to 320mph (515km/h) at 16,200ft (4,938m)
Cruising Speed: At 20,000ft, 212 mph
Stalling Speed: (clean at sea level) 75-85mph (120km/h-137km/h)
Time to 20,000ft: (clean) 9.1 minutes
Ceiling: 35,600ft (max weight), 35,900ft (mean weight), 33,200ft (Tropical)
Range: 460 miles (895 miles - 2x44 gallon fuel tanks, 1,020 miles - 2x90 gallon fuel tanks). Tropical: 404 miles (870 miles - 2x44 gallon fuel tanks, 995 miles, 2x90 gallon fuel tanks)
Armament: Four 20mm (Oerlikon or Hispano) cannon (90 rnds per gun) plus two 250lb (later able to carry 500lb) bombs or two 44 Imp. gallon (200 litre) fuel tanks below the outer wing panels

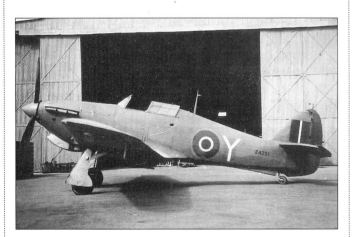

Mk I (Tropical), Z4251, 'Y' on the ground in North Africa *(© RAF Museum P015190)*

Designation: NF Mk IIC
Type:	Night fighter
Span:	40ft (12.19m)
Length:	32ft 2.25in (9.83m)
Height:	13ft 1in (3.99m) (One propeller blade vertical, tailwheel on the ground)
Engine:	1,260hp Rolls-Royce Merlin XX
Weight:	7,544lb (3,429kg) (Normal Loaded), 8,044lb (3,656kg) (Overload Combat Weight)
Max Speed:	301mph (484km/h) (clean at 15,000ft), 336mph (540km/h) (at 16,600ft (5,060m).
Stalling Speed:	75-85mph (120km/h-137km/h)
Armament:	Four 20mm (Oerlikon or Hispano) cannon plus two 250lb (later able to carry 500lb) bombs or two 44 Imp. gallon (200 litre) fuel tanks below the outer wing panels
Note:	This machine was fitted with A.I. Mk V radar in a container, similar to a 44 Imp. gallon fuel tank under one outer wing panel. A standard fuel tank was carried under the other wing and both were fixed

Designation: Mk IID
First Flight:	18th September 1941 (Z2326)
Type:	Anti-tank
Span:	40ft (12.19m)
Length:	32ft 2.25in (9.83m)
Height:	13ft 1in (3.99m) (One propeller blade vertical, tailwheel on the ground)
Engine:	1,260hp Rolls-Royce Merlin XX
Weight:	7,850lb (3,568kg) (Normal Loaded - Tropical)
Max Speed:	N/K
Stalling Speed:	(clean at sea level) 75-85mph (120km/h-137km/h)
Operation Ceiling:	Tropical: 29,100ft
Armament:	Two 40mm Vickers 'S' cannon and two 0.303" Browning machine guns. Provision to, but did not carry, bombs or fuel tanks

Designation: Mk IIE (see also Mk IV)
Type:	Ground-attack
Span:	40ft (12.19m)
Length:	32ft 2.25in (9.83m)
Height:	13ft 1in (3.99m) (One propeller blade vertical, tailwheel on the ground)
Engine:	Rolls-Royce Merlin 27
Weight:	8,462lb (3,846kg) (Normal Loaded)
Max Speed:	(clean at 15,000ft) 280mph (450km/h)
Stalling Speed:	(clean at sea level) 75-85mph (120km/h-137km/h)
Time to 20,000ft:	(clean) 12 minutes
Operation Ceiling:	29,100ft
Range:	450 miles
Armament:	'Universal' wing allowing the installation of four 20mm (Oerlikon or Hispano) cannon or two 40mm Vickers 'S' guns or eight 3in rocket projectiles or two 44 Imp. gallon (200 litre) fuel tanks

Designation: Mk III
First Flight:	N/A
Type:	Ground-attack
Span:	40ft (12.19m)
Length:	32ft 2.25in (9.83m)
Height:	13ft 1in (3.99m) (One propeller blade vertical, tailwheel on the ground)
Engine:	Packard Merlin 28
Weight:	N/K
Max Speed:	N/K
Operation Ceiling:	N/K
Range:	N/K
Armament:	'Universal' wing allowing the installation of four 20mm (Oerlikon or Hispano) cannon or two 40mm Vickers 'S' guns or eight 3in rocket projectiles or two 44 Imp. gallon (200 litre) fuel tanks
Note:	Proposed Langley-built version utilising the Packard Merlin 28 if the Merlin XX was in short supply. Never produced

Mk IIA, Z3451, March 1943 *(© Real Photographs)*

Designation: Mk IV
Type:	Ground-attack
Span:	40ft (12.19m)
Length:	32ft 2.25in (9.83m)
Height:	13ft 1in (3.99m)
Engine:	Rolls-Royce Merlin 27
Weight:	8,462lb (3,846kg) (Normal Loaded)
Max Speed:	(clean at 15,000ft) 280mph (450km/h)
Stalling Speed:	(clean at sea level) 75-85mph (120km/h-137km/h)
Time to 20,000ft:	(clean) 12 minutes
Operation Ceiling:	29,100ft
Range:	450 miles
Armament:	'Universal - Low Attack' wing allowing the installation (in asymmetric combination) of either four 20mm (Oerlikon or Hispano) cannon, two 40mm Vickers 'S' guns, eight 3in. rocket projectiles, two 44 Imp. gallon (200 litre) fuel tanks, two 250lb or 500lb bombs. The 90 Imp. gallon (400 litre) ferry tank could also be fitted, although not asymmetrically

Designation: Mk V
Type:	Ground-attack
Span:	40ft (12.19m)
Length:	32ft 2.25in (9.83m)
Height:	13ft 1in (3.99m)
Engine:	1,700hp (1275 kW) Rolls-Royce Merlin 32
Weight:	9,300lb (4,218kg)
Max Speed:	326mph (525km/h) at 500ft (152m)
Range:	N/K
Propeller:	Rotol four-blade variable-pitch propeller
Armament:	'Universal' wing allowing the installation (in asymmetric combination) of either four 20mm (Oerlikon or Hispano) cannon, two 40mm Vickers 'S' guns, eight 3in. rocket projectiles, two 44 Imp. gallon (200 litre) fuel tanks, two 250lb or 500lb bombs. The 90 Imp. gallon (400 litre) ferry tank could also be fitted, although not asymmetrically
Production:	Only three prototypes (NL255, KX405 & KZ193) built

Reconnaissance

Designation: Tac R Mk I
Type:	Tactical Reconnaissance
Span:	40ft (12.19m)
Length:	31ft 4in (9.55m)
Height:	12ft 11.5in (3.95m)
Engine:	Rolls-Royce Merlin III
Weight:	(Similar to Mk I)
Max Speed:	(Similar to Mk I)
Operation Ceiling:	N/K
Range:	N/K
Armament:	None
Propeller:	D.H. Hamilton Hydromatic or Rotol three-blade variable-pitch propeller.
Sqn Allocations:	No. 208 Squadron, Western Desert, November/December 1940.
Note:	Converted from standard Mk I's at No. 103 MU, Aboukir in October 1940. Beleived that eight such machines were converted with the addition of a vertical camera aft of the cockpit and the installation of an additional radio for liaison with the army

Designation: Tac R Mk IIB
Type:	Tactical Reconnaissance
Span:	40ft (12.19m)
Length:	32ft 2.25in (9.83m)
Height:	13ft 1in (3.99m)
Engine:	Rolls-Royce Merlin XX
Operation Ceiling:	N/K
Range:	N/K
Armament:	Some retained eight 0.303in. Browning machine guns
Propeller:	D.H. Hamilton Hydromatic or Rotol three-blade variable-pitch propeller.
Note:	Converted from repaired Mk IIB's at No. 103 MU, Aboukir in 1941. The type was converted with the addition of a vertical camera aft of the cockpit and the installation of an additional radio for liaison with the army

Designation: Tac R Mk IIC
Type:	Tactical Reconnaissance
Span:	40ft (12.19m)
Length:	32ft 2.25in (9.83m)
Height:	13ft 1in (3.99m)
Engine:	Rolls-Royce Merlin XX
Armament:	None
Propeller:	D.H. Hamilton Hydromatic or Rotol three-blade variable-pitch propeller
Note:	Converted from repaired Mk IIC's at No. 103 MU, Aboukir in 1941. The type was converted with the addition of a vertical camera aft of the cockpit and the installation of an additional radio for liaison with the army

Photo-Reconnaissance

Designation: PR Mk I
Type:	Photo-Reconnaissance
Span:	40ft (12.19m)
Length:	31ft 4in (9.55m)
Height:	12ft 11.5in (3.95m)
Engine:	Rolls-Royce Merlin III
Weight:	N/K
Operation Ceiling:	30,000ft (9,144m)
Armament:	None
Propeller:	D.H. Hamilton Hydromatic or Rotol three-blade variable-pitch propeller
Sqn Allocations:	Intelligence Photo Flight (IPF), Cairo and later with No. 2 PRU
Note:	Converted from standard Mk I's at Heliopolis in late 1940 with the addition of three F.24, 8in. (20cm) or four 14in. (36cm) camera arranged in a fan aft of the cockpit. Additional fuel was carried in the redundant wing armament bays

Mk IIB, BE485, AE•W of No. 402 Sqn in flight

Mk IIC (Night Intruder) 'Cawnpore I' (BE500, LK•A) of No. 87 Squadron in flight *(© C.E. Brown)*

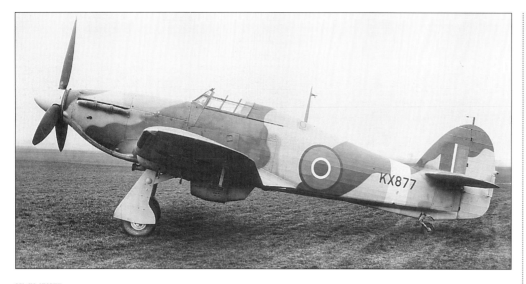

Mk IV, KX877 *(© Real Photographs)*

Designation:	Sea Hurricane Mk IIC
Type:	Naval Fighter (Fleet carrier)
Span:	40ft (12.19m)
Length:	32ft 2.25in (9.83m)
Height:	13ft 1in (3.99m) (One propeller blade vertical, tailwheel on the ground)
Engine:	1,260hp Rolls-Royce Merlin XX
Weight:	7,618lb (3,463kg) (Normal Loaded)
Max Speed:	301mph (484km/h) (clean at 15,000ft), 336mph (540km/h) (at 16,600ft (5,060m)).
Stalling Speed:	(clean at sea level) 75-85mph (120km/h-137km/h)
Time to 20,000ft:	(clean) 12 minutes
Operation Ceiling:	35,600ft
Range:	452 miles (908 miles - 2x44 gallon fuel tanks, 1,062 miles - 2x90 gallon fuel tanks). Tropical: 415 miles (895 miles - 2x44 gallon fuel tanks, 998 miles - 2x90 gallon fuel tanks)
Armament:	Four 20mm (Oerlikon or Hispano) cannon plus two 250lb (later able to carry 500lb) bombs or two 44 Imp. gallon (200 litre) fuel tanks below the outer wing panels
Note:	Differed from RAF Mk IIC by the installation of a Royal Naval radio set, an A-frame arrestor hook and catapult spools

Trainers

Designation:	Persian Two-seat trainer (Mk IIC)
First Flight:	1947 (S/No's. 2-31 & 2-32)
Type:	Two-seat Trainer
Span:	40ft (12.19m)
Length:	32ft 2.25in (9.83m)
Height:	13ft 1in (3.99m)
Engine:	1,435hp Rolls-Royce Merlin 22
Weight:	8,140lblb (3,700kg)
Max Speed:	320mph (518km/h) at 21,500ft (6,555m)
Time to 20,000ft:	10 minutes
Stalling Speed:	70mph (112km/h) (wheels & flaps down)
Operation Ceiling:	36,000ft
Range:	1,100 miles (2x44 gallon fuel tanks)
Armament:	Four 20mm (Oerlikon or Hispano) cannon, although these were later deleted
Propeller:	Rotol three-blade variable-pitch Type R.S.5/11

Sea Hurricane

Designation:	Sea Hurricane Mk IA
Type:	Catapult-launched convoy defence fighter ('Hurricat')
Span:	40ft (12.19m)
Length:	31ft 4in (9.55m)
Height:	12ft 11.5in (3.95m)
Engine:	Rolls-Royce Merlin III
Weight:	6,589lb (Normal Loaded)
Max Speed:	(clean at 15,000ft) 317mph (509km/h)
Stalling Speed:	(clean at sea level) 72-80mph (115km/h-128km/h)
Time to 20,000ft:	(clean) 11 minutes
Operation Ceiling:	34,200ft
Range:	505 miles
Armament:	Eight 0.303in. Browning machine guns
Propeller:	D.H. Hamilton Hydromatic or Rotol three-blade variable-pitch propeller
Note:	Differed only from RAF version by the inclusion of a Naval radio set and catapult spools (no arrestor hook)

Designation:	PR Mk IIB
Type:	Photo-Reconnaissance
Span:	40ft (12.19m)
Length:	32ft 2.25in (9.83m)
Height:	13ft 1in (3.99m)
Engine:	Rolls-Royce Merlin XX
Weight:	N/K
Operation Ceiling:	30,000ft (9,144m)
Armament:	None
Propeller:	D.H. Hamilton Hydromatic or Rotol three-blade variable-pitch propeller.
Sqn Allocations:	Intelligence Photo Flight (IPF), Cairo and later with No. 2 PRU
Note:	Converted from standard Mk IIB's at Heliopolis in 1941 with the addition of three F.24, 8in. (20cm) or four 14in. (36cm) camera arranged in a fan aft of the cockpit. Additional fuel was carried in the redundant wing armament bays

Designation:	PR Mk IIC
Type:	Photo-Reconnaissance
Span:	40ft (12.19m)
Length:	32ft 2.25in (9.83m)
Height:	13ft 1in (3.99m)
Engine:	Rolls-Royce Merlin XX
Weight:	N/K
Operation Ceiling:	30,000ft (9,144m)
Armament:	None
Propeller:	D.H. Hamilton Hydromatic or Rotol three-blade variable-pitch propeller
Sqn Allocations:	Intelligence Photo Flight (IPF), Cairo and later with No. 2 PRU
Note:	Converted from standard Mk IIC's at Heliopolis in 1941 with the addition of three F.24, 8in. (20cm) or four 14in. (36cm) camera arranged in a fan aft of the cockpit. Additional fuel was carried in the redundant wing armament bays

Sea Hurricane Mk IC, V6741 *(© Real Photographs)*

Designation:	Sea Hurricane Mk IB
Type:	Naval Fighter (Escort carrier)
Span:	40ft (12.19m)
Length:	31ft 4in (9.55m)
Height:	12ft 11.5in (3.95m)
Engine:	Rolls-Royce Merlin III
Weight:	7,410lb (Normal Loaded)
Max Speed:	(clean at 15,000ft) 317mph (509km/h)
Stalling Speed :	(clean at sea level) 72-80mph (115km/h-128km/h)
Time to 20,000ft:	(clean) 11 minutes
Operation Ceiling:	34,200ft
Range:	505 miles
Armament:	Eight 0.303in. Browning machine guns
Propeller:	D.H. Hamilton Hydromatic or Rotol three-blade variable-pitch propeller
Note:	Differed only from RAF version by the inclusion of a Naval radio set, an A-frame arrestor hook and catapult spools

Designation:	Sea Hurricane Mk IC
Type:	Naval Fighter (Fleet carrier)
Span:	40ft (12.19m)
Length:	31ft 4in (9.55m)
Height:	12ft 11.5in (3.95m)
Engine:	Rolls-Royce Merlin III
Weight:	7,605lb (Normal Loaded), 8,210lb (Normal Loaded - tropical)
Max Speed:	276mph (444km/h) at 17,400ft (5,304m)
Operation Ceiling:	34,200ft
Range:	505 miles
Armament:	Four 20mm (Oerlikon or Hispano) cannon plus two 250lb (later able to carry 500lb) bombs or two 44 Imp. gallon (200 litre) fuel tanks below the outer wing panels
Propeller:	D.H. Hamilton Hydromatic or Rotol three-blade variable-pitch propeller.
Note:	Differed from Sea Hurricane Mk IB version by the installation of the Mk IIC outer wing panels, a Royal Naval radio set, an A-frame arrestor hook and catapult spools

Designation:	Sea Hurricane Mk X (Canadain)
Type:	Naval Escort Fighter
Span:	40ft (12.19m)
Length:	32ft 2.25in (9.83m)
Height:	13ft 1in (3.99m)
Engine:	Packard Merlin 28
Weight:	N/K
Max Speed:	N/K
Operation Ceiling:	N/K
Range:	N/K
Armament:	Four Hispano 20mm cannon
Propeller:	Hamilton Hydromatic or Rotol three-blade variable-pitch propeller

Designation:	Sea Hurricane Mk XIIA (Canadain)*
Type:	Naval Fighter
Span:	40ft (12.19m)
Length:	32ft 2.25in (9.83m)
Height:	13ft 1in (3.99m)
Engine:	1,300hp (970kW) Packard Merlin 29
Weight:	N/K
Max Speed:	N/K
Operation Ceiling:	N/K
Range:	N/K
Armament:	Twelve 0.303in. Browning machine guns or four 20mm (Oerlikon or Hispano) cannon. Later production machines had the 'Universal' wing allowing it to carry two 250lb or 500lb bombs or two 44 Imp. gallon (200 litre) fuel tanks below the outer wing panels
Propeller:	Hamilton Hydromatic three-blade variable-pitch propeller (sometimes the spinner was omitted)
*Note:	See 'Sea Hurricane Mk XIIB & C'

Designation:	Sea Hurricane Mk XIIB & C (Canadian)
Type:	Royal Naval Fighter
Span:	40ft (12.19m)
Length:	32ft 2.25in (9.83m)
Height:	13ft 1in (3.99m)
Engine:	1,300hp (970kW) Packard Merlin 29
Weight:	N/K
Max Speed:	N/K
Operation Ceiling:	N/K
Range:	N/K
Armament:	Twelve 0.303in. Browning machine guns (Mk XIIB) or four 20mm (Oerlikon or Hispano) cannon (Mk XIIC)
Propeller:	Hamilton Hydromatic three-blade variable-pitch propeller (sometimes the spinner was omitted)
Note:	This type was only designated 'Mk XIIB' or 'Mk XIIC' by the Royal Navy, remaining the Sea Hurricane Mk XIIA in Canadian documentation

Rocket-armed Mk IV, BP173 in flight *(© RAF Museum P012036)*

Foreign Production – Canada

Designation: Mk I (often called 'Canadian Mk I's')
Type: Fighter
Span: 40ft (12.19m)
Length: 31ft 4in (9.56m)
Height: 12ft 11.5in (3.95m)
Engine: Rolls-Royce Merlin II or III
Weight: 6,218lb (Normal Loaded)
Max Speed: (clean at 15,000ft) 317mph (509km/h)
Stalling Speed: (clean at sea level) 72-80mph (115km/h-128km/h)
Time to 20,000ft: (clean) 11 minutes
Operation Ceiling: 34,200ft
Range: 505 miles
Armament: Eight 0.303in. Browning machine guns
Propeller: D.H. Hamilton Hydromatic or Rotol three-blade variable-pitch propeller
Note: As these machines were powered by Rolls-Royce engines, no separate mark was allocated to the type

Designation: Mk X
Type: Fighter
Span: 40ft (12.19m)
Length: 32ft 2.25in (9.83m)
Height: 13ft 1in (3.99m)
Engine: Packard Merlin 28
Weight: N/K
Max Speed: N/K
Operation Ceiling: N/K
Armament: Six, eight or twelve 0.303in. Browning machine guns
Propeller: Hamilton Hydromatic three-blade variable-pitch propeller (sometimes the spinner was omitted)

Designation: Mk XI
Type: Fighter
Span: 40ft (12.19m)
Length: 32ft 2.25in (9.83m)
Height: 13ft 1in (3.99m)
Engine: Packard Merlin 28
Weight: N/K
Max Speed: N/K
Operation Ceiling: N/K
Range: N/K
Armament: Six, eight or twelve 0.303in. Browning machine guns
Propeller: Hamilton Hydromatic three-blade variable-pitch propeller (sometimes the spinner was omitted)
Note: This mark allocated to the 5th and 6th Canadian production batches, which utilised a lot of RCAF equipment. Some were later converted to Sea Hurricane Mk XI's

Designation: Mk XII
Type: Fighter
Span: 40ft (12.19m)
Length: 32ft 2.25in (9.83m)
Height: 13ft 1in (3.99m)
Engine: 1,300hp (970kW) Packard Merlin 29
Weight: N/K
Max Speed: N/K
Operation Ceiling: N/K
Range: N/K
Armament: Twelve 0.303in. Browning machine guns or four 20mm (Oerlikon or Hispano) cannon. Later production machines had the 'Universal' wing allowing it to carry two 250lb or 500lb bombs or two 44 Imp. gallon (200 litre) fuel tanks below the outer wing panels
Propeller: Hamilton Hydromatic three-blade variable-pitch propeller (sometimes the spinner was omitted)

Designation: Mk I with skis
First Flight: 1942 (S/No. 1362)
Type: Ski-equipped Fighter
Span: 40ft (12.19m)
Length: 31ft 4in (9.55m)
Height: N/K
Engine: Rolls-Royce Merlin II or III
Weight: 6,218lb (Normal Loaded)
Max Speed: N/K
Operation Ceiling: N/K
Range: N/K
Armament: Four .0303" Browning machine guns
Propeller: Hamilton Hydromatic three-blade variable-pitch propeller

Designation: Mk XII with skis
First Flight: 1942 (S/No. 5624)
Type: Ski-equipped Fighter
Span: 40ft (12.19m)
Length: 32ft 2.25in (9.83m)
Height: 13ft 1in (3.99m)
Engine: 1,300hp (970kW) Packard Merlin 29
Weight: N/K
Max Speed: N/K
Operation Ceiling: N/K
Range: N/K
Armament: None
Propeller: Hamilton Hydromatic three-blade variable-pitch propeller without a spinner

Mk IIC (Dual Control) in the markings of the Iranian Air Force on a test flight (© Hawker-Siddeley)

Projects

Designation: Floatplane
First Flight: N/A
Type: Waterborne Fighter
Span: 40ft (12.19m)
Length: 31ft 4in (9.55m)
Height: N/K
Engine: Rolls-Royce Merlin III
Weight: N/K
Max Speed: N/K
Operation Ceiling: N/K
Range: N/K
Armament: Eight 0.303" Browning machine guns
Propeller: D.H. Hamilton Hydromatic or Rotol three-blade variable-pitch propeller
Note: Originally designed for use in Norway, which possessed few established airfields, therefore plans were drawn up to fit a set of floats off a Blackburn Roc to a standard Mk I. The floats arrived at Hawkers in June 1940, but the Norwegian campaign had ended by this time and therefore the project was dropped

Designation: 'Slip Wing' F.H.40
First Flight: 1944
Type: Experimental 'bi-mono'
Span: 40ft (12.19m)
Length: 31ft 4in (9.55m)
Height: N/K
Engine: Rolls-Royce Merlin III
Weight: N/K
Max Speed: N/K
Operation Ceiling: N/K
Range: N/K
Armament: None
Propeller: D.H. Hamilton Hydromatic three-blade variable-pitch propeller.

Designation: Laminar Flow Wing (Mk IIB)
First Flight: (Z3687)
Type: Laminar flow wing research airframe
Span: 40ft (12.19m)
Length: 32ft 2.25in (9.83m)
Height: 13ft 1in (3.99m)
Engines: Rolls-Royce Merlin XX
Weight: N/K
Max Speed: N/K
Operation Ceiling: N/K
Range: N/K
Armament: None
Note: Experimentally fitted with Armstrong Whitworth laminar flow outer wing panels for research undertaken at R.A.E. Farnborough

Designation: 'Long Tom' Rocket (Mk IV)
First Flight: 1944 (KZ706)
Type: Experimental installation
Span: 40ft (12.19m)
Length: 32ft 2.25in (9.83m)
Height: 13ft 1in (3.99m)
Engine: Rolls-Royce Merlin 27
Weight: N/K
Max Speed: N/K
Operation Ceiling: N/K
Range: N/K
Armament: The type's 'Universal' wing was used to install two (one under each outer wing panel) 500lb (227kg) 'Long Tom' rocket projectiles by R.A.E. Farnborough

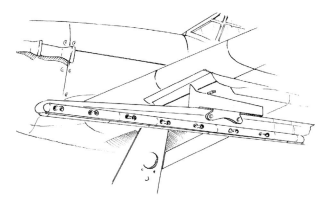

The rails fitted to the Mk IV (KZ706) for the 'Long Tom' trials (© A. Oliver)

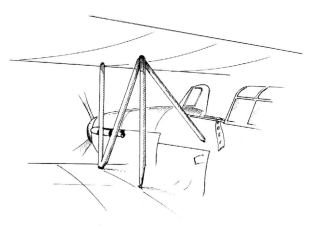

A detailed shot of the struts on the F.H. 40 'Slip-wing' Hurricane (© A. Oliver)

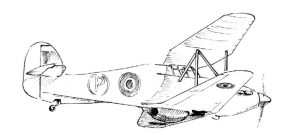

An overall view of the F.H. 40 'Slip-wing' Hurricane in flight (© A. Oliver)

Hurricane Genealogy

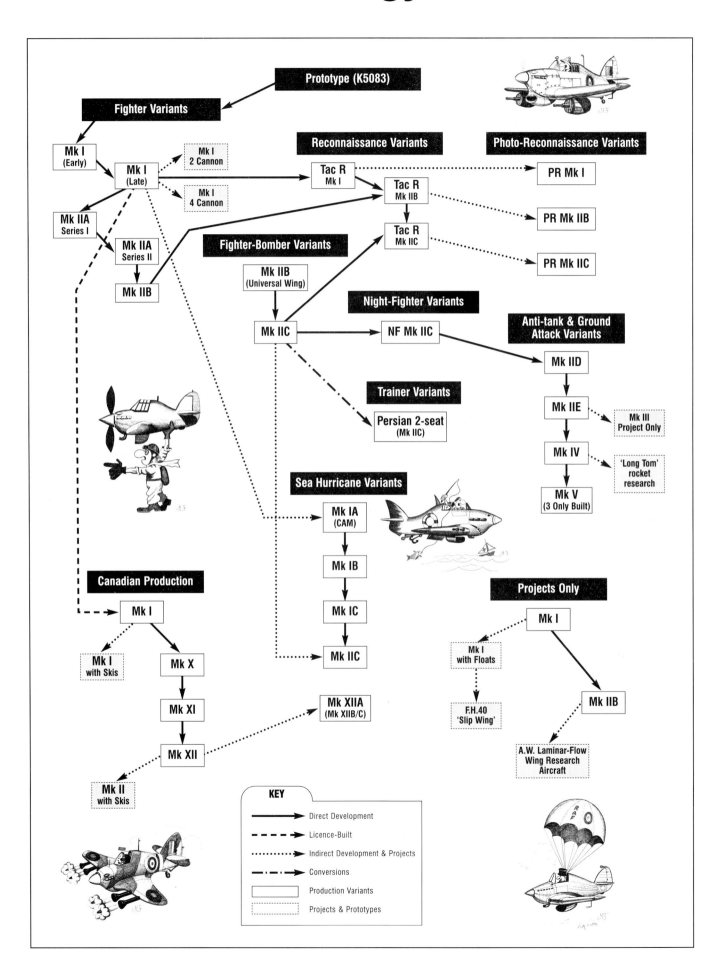

Prototype (K5083)

Fighter Variants

- Mk I (Early)
- Mk I (Late)
- Mk I 2 Cannon
- Mk I 4 Cannon
- Mk IIA Series I
- Mk IIA Series II
- Mk IIB

Reconnaissance Variants

- Tac R Mk I
- Tac R Mk IIB
- Tac R Mk IIC

Photo-Reconnaissance Variants

- PR Mk I
- PR Mk IIB
- PR Mk IIC

Fighter-Bomber Variants

- Mk IIB (Universal Wing)
- Mk IIC

Night-Fighter Variants

- NF Mk IIC

Anti-tank & Ground Attack Variants

- Mk IID
- Mk IIE
- Mk IV
- Mk V (3 Only Built)
- Mk III Project Only
- 'Long Tom' rocket research

Trainer Variants

- Persian 2-seat (Mk IIC)

Sea Hurricane Variants

- Mk IA (CAM)
- Mk IB
- Mk IC
- Mk IIC

Canadian Production

- Mk I
- Mk I with Skis
- Mk X
- Mk XI
- Mk XII
- Mk XIIA (Mk XIIB/C)
- Mk II with Skis

Projects Only

- Mk I
- Mk I with Floats
- F.H.40 'Slip Wing'
- Mk IIB
- A.W. Laminar-Flow Wing Research Aircraft

KEY

- Direct Development
- ----- Licence-Built
- ········· Indirect Development & Projects
- ·-·-·-· Conversions
- Production Variants
- Projects & Prototypes

Hurricane Squadrons

No.1 Squadron
Code: **NA** & **JX**
Started Hurricane Operations: Tangmere Oct 1938
UK Based: Tangmere 10/38-9/39, Northolt (detached to Hawkinge) 6/40, Tangmere 6/40-8/40, Northolt 8/40-9/40, Wittering 9/40-12/40, Norhtolt 12/40-1/41, Kenley 1/41-4/41, Croydon 4/41-5/41, redhill 5/41-6/41, Kenley 6/41, Redhill 6/41-7/41, Tangmere 7/41-7/43
Foreign Based: Octeville, Norrent Fontes, Vassicourt, Berry-au-Bac, Conde, Anglure, Chanteaudun, Boos, Angers & Nantes 9/39-5/40.
Reformed: N/A
Disbanded: N/A
Re-equipped: September 1942 (Typhoon Mk Ib)
Variants Operated: Mk I, Mk IIA, Mk IIB & Mk IIC

No.3 Squadron
Code: **OP** & **QO**
Started Hurricane Operations: Kenley May 1938
UK Based: Kenley 5/38-5/39, Biggin Hill 5/39-9/39, Croydon 9/39-12/39, Hawkinge 12/39-1/40, Kenley 1/40-5/40, Merville 5/40, Kenley 5/40, Wick 5/40-9/40, Castletown 9/40, Turnhouse 9/40-10/40, Castletown 10/40-1/41, Skeabrae 1/41-2/41, Castletown 2/41-4/41, Martlesham Heath 4/41-6/41, Stapleford Tawney 6/41-8/41, Hunsdon 8/41-5/43.
Foreign Based: N/A
Reformed: N/A
Disbanded: N/A
Re-equipped: February 1943 (Typhoon Mk Ib)
Variants Operated: Mk I, Mk IIB & Mk IIC

No.5 Squadron
Code: None
Started Hurricane Operations: Khangpur 6/43
UK Based: N/A
Foreign Based: Khangpur 6/43-12/43, Amarda Road 12/43, Sapam 12/43-3/44, Wangjing 3/44, Lanka 3/44-6/44, Dergaon 6/44, Vizagapatam 6/44-9/44, Yelhanka 9/44-10/44, Cholavarum 10/44, Kajamalai 10/44-12/44
Reformed: N/A
Disbanded: N/A
Re-equipped: October 1944 (Republic Thunderbolt Mk II)
Variants Operated: Mk IIC & Mk IID

No.6 Squadron
Code: **JV**
Started Hurricane Operations: Western Desert 3/41
UK Based: N/A
Foreign Based: Western Desert 3/41-5/42, Shandur (Palestine) 5/42-7/42, LG91 7/42, LG89 7/42-11/42, LG172 11/42-12/42, Edku 12/42-1/43, Sidi Bu Amund 1/43-3/43, Sorman 3/43, Senem 3/43-4/43, Sfax 4/43, Ben Goubrine 4/43-5/43, Ben Gardane 6/43-9/43, Fayid 9/43-2/44, Grottaglie 2/44-7/44, Foggia 7/44-8/44, Canne 8/44-3/45, Vis 3/45-4/45, Prkos 4/45-5/45, Campomarino 5/45, Canne 5/45-7/45, Megiddo 7/45-8/45, Petah Tiqva 8/45-6/46, Ramat David 6/46, Ein Shemer 6/46-9/46, Nicosia 9/46-7/47
Reformed: N/A
Disbanded: N/A
Re-equipped: January 1947
Variants Operated: Mk I, Mk IIC, Mk IID & Mk IV

No.11 Squadron
Code: None
Started Hurricane Operations: Ranchi 8/43
UK Based: N/A
Foreign Based: Ranchi 8/43, Yelahanka 8/43-9/43, St. Thomas Mount 9/43-10/43, Cholavurm 10/43-12/43, Lalmai 12/43-1/44, Lyons 1/44-3/44, Sapam 3/44, Tulihall 3/44-4/44, Lanka 4/44-7/44, Dunapur 7/44-10/44, Imphal 10/44-11/44, Tamu 11/44-1/45, Kau 1/45-2/45, Sinthe 2/45-5/45, Feni 5/45, Chettinad 5/45-8/45
Reformed: N/A
Disbanded: N/A
Re-equipped: August 1945 (Spitfire Mk XIV)
Variants Operated: Mk I, Mk IIC, Mk IID & Mk IV

No.17 Squadron
Code: **UV** & **YB**
Started Hurricane Operations: North Weald 6/39
UK Based: North Weald 6/39-9/39, Croydon 9/39, Debden 9/39-12/39, Debden & Martlesham Heath 12/39-5/40, Hawkinge 5/40, Debden 5/40-6/40, Debden 6/40-8/40, Tangmere 8/40-9/40, Debden 9/40-10/40, Martlesham Heath 10/40-2/41, Croydon 2/41-3/41, Martlesham Heath 3/41-4/41, Castletown 4/41-6/41, Elgin 6/41-8/41, Dyce 8/41-9/41, Elgin 8/41-9/41, Tain 9/41-10/41, Catterick 10/41-11/41
Foreign Based: Le Mans 6/40, Dinard 6/40, Jersey 6/40, en route to Far East 11/41-1/42, Mingaladon 1/42-2/42, Magwe 2/42-3/42, Lashio 3/42, Pankham Fort 3/42-4/42, Jessore 5/42-8/42, Alipore 8/42-3/43, Agartala 3/43-4/43, Alipore 4/43-5/43, Agartala 5/43-8/43, China Bay 8/43-1/44, Minneriya 1/44-6/44
Reformed: N/A
Disbanded: N/A
Re-equipped: June 1944 (Spitfire Mk VII)
Variants Operated: Mk I, Mk IIA, Mk IIB & Mk IIC

No.20 Squadron
Code: **HN**
Started Hurricane Operations: Charra 3/43
UK Based: N/A
Foreign Based: Charra 3/43-5/43, Kalyan 5/43-11/43,

Mk I, ???73, YB•E of No. 17 Sqn, with pilots of A Flight sitting on the nose and wings in 1940 (© RAF Museum P010059)

Nidania 11/43-2/44, Madhaibunia ("Hove") 2/44-5/44, Chiringa 5/44-7/44, Trichinopoly 7/44-9/44, St. Thomas Mount 9/44-12/44. Sapam 12-44-1/45, Thazi 1/45-2/45, Monywa 2/45-4/45, Thedaw 4/45, Tennant 4/45-5/45, Thedaw 5/45-6/45, Chettinad 5/45-6/45, St. Thomas Mount 6/45-7/45, Hathazarai 7/45-8/45, Amarda Road 8/45-9/45
Reformed: N/A
Disbanded: N/A
Re-equipped: September 1945 (Spitfire Mk VIII)
Variants Operated: Mk IIC, Mk IID & Mk IV (RP)

No.28 Squadron
Code: **BF**
Started Hurricane Operations: Ranchi Dec 1942
UK Based:N/A
Foreign Based: Ranchi 12/42-3/43, Imphal/Dalbumgarh/Tamu 3/43-1/45, Ye-U/Sadaung/Meiktila/Mingaladon 1/45-10/45
Reformed: N/A
Disbanded: N/A
Re-equipped: December 1945 (Spitfire Mk XI)
Variants Operated: Mk IIB & Mk IIC

No.30 Squadron
Code: **RS**
Started Hurricane Operations: Edku 6/41
UK Based:
Foreign Based: Edku 6/41-10/41, LG102 10/41-11/41, LG05 11/41-1/42, LG121, 1/42-2/42, Heliopolis 2/42, HMS Indomitable 2/42-3/42, Ratmalana 3/42-8/42, Dambulla 8/42-2/43, Colombo 2/43-8/43, Dambulla 8/43-1/44, Fazilpur 1/44-4/44, Comilla 4/44-5/44, Yelahanka 5/44-9/44,
Reformed: N/A
Disbanded: N/A
Re-equipped: September 1944 (Republic Thunderbolt II)
Variants Operated: Mk I, Mk IIB & Mk IIC

No.32 Squadron
Code: **GZ** & **KT**
Started Hurricane Operations: Biggin Hill 10/38
UK Based: Biggin Hill 10/38-1/40, Gravesend 1/40-3/40, Manston 3/40, Gravesend 3/40, Biggin Hill 3/40-5/40, Wittering 5/40-6/40, Biggin Hill 6/40-8/40, Acklington 8/40-12/40, Middle Wallop 12/40-2/41, Ibsley 2/41-4/41, Pembrey 4/41-6/41, Angle 6/41-11/41, Manston 11/41-5/42, West Malling 5/42-6/42, Friston 6/42-7/42, West Malling 7/42-9/42, Honiley 9/42-10/42, Baginton 10/42-11/42
Foreign Based: Phillippeville 12/42-1/43, Maison Blanche 1/43-5/43, Tingley 5/43-8/43
Reformed: N/A
Disbanded: N/A
Re-equipped: August 1943 (Spitfire Mk V)
Variants Operated: Mk I, Mk IIB & Mk IIC

No.33 Squadron
Code: **NW** & **RS**
Started Hurricane Operations: Fuka Satellite 9/40
UK Based: N/A
Foreign Based: Fuka Satellite 9/40-1/41, Amriya 1/41-2/41, Eleusis 2/41-3/41, Larissa 3/41-4/41, Eleusis 4/41, Maleme 4/41-5/41, Amriya 6/41-9/41, Sidi Haneish North 9/41, Gerawla 9/41-10/41, Giarabub 11/41, LG125 11/41-1/42, Msus 1/42, Antelat 1/42, , Msus 1/42, Meclule 1/42, Gazala 1/42-2/42, Gambut 2/42, Sidi Haneish 2/42-3/42, Gambut 3/42-6/42, Sidi Assiz 6/42, LG075 Satellite 6/42, LG076 6/42, Sidi Haneish 6/42, LG154 6/42-7/42, LG172 7/42, LG85 7/42-8/42, Edku 8/42, LG85 8/42-10/42, Dekheila 10/42, LG172 10/42-11/42, LG101 11/42, El Adem 11/42, Benina 11/42-6/43, Bersis 2/43-6/43, Misurata 6/43-9/43, Bersis 9/43-1/44
Reformed: N/A
Disbanded: N/A
Re-equipped: December 1943 (Spitfire Mk Vb)
Variants Operated: Mk I, Mk IIB & Mk IIC

No.34 Squadron
Code: None
Started Hurricane Operations: St. Thomas Mount 8/43
UK Based: N/A
Foreign Based: St. Thomas Mount 8/43-9/43, Cholavarum 9/43-10/43, Alipore 10/43, Palel 10/43-4/44, Dergaon 4/44-7/44, Palel 7/44-12/44, Yazagyo 12/44-1/45, Onbauk 1/45-4/45
Reformed: N/A
Disbanded: N/A
Re-equipped: April 1945 (Republic Thunderbolt II)
Variants Operated: Mk IIB & Mk IIC

Mk IIC, FT•S of No. 43 Sqn, November 1943 (© RAF Museum P008023)

No.42 Squadron
Code: **AW**
Started Hurricane Operations: Kumbhirgram 10/43
UK Based: N/A
Foreign Based: Kumbhirgram 10/43-11/43, St. Thomas Mount 11/43-12/43, Palel 12-43-5/44, Kangla 5/44-7/44, Tulihal 7/44-11/44, Kangla 11/44-1/45, Onbauk 1/45-3/45, Ondaw 3/45-4/45, Sinthe 4/45, Maida Vale 4/45-5/45, Chakulia 5/45, Dalbumgarh 5/45-6/45, Meiktela 6/45-12/45
Reformed: N/A
Disbanded: N/A
Re-equipped: July 1945 (Republic Thunderbolt II)
Variants Operated: Mk IIC & Mk IV

No.43 Squadron
Code: **NQ** & **FT**
Started Hurricane Operations: Tangmere 10/38
UK Based: Tangmere 10/38-11/39, Acklington 11/39-2/40, Wick 2/40-5/40, Tangmere 5/40-7/40, Northolt 7/40-8/40, Tangmere 8/40-9/40, Usworth 9/40-12/40, Drem 12/40-10/41, Acklington 10/41-7/42, Tangmere 7/42-9/42, Kirton-on-Lindsey 9/42-10/42,
Foreign Based: en route to North Africa 10/42-11/42, Gibraltar 11/42, Maison Blanche 11/42-3/43
Reformed: N/A
Disbanded: N/A
Re-equipped: March 1943 (Spitfire Mk Vc)
Variants Operated: Mk I, Mk IIA & Mk IIB

No.46 Squadron
Code: **PO**
Started Hurricane Operations: Digby 3/39
UK Based: Digby 3/39-11/39, Acklington 11/39-1/40, Digby 1/40-5/40, HMS Glorious 5/40, HMS Glorious 6/40, Digby 6/40-9/40, Stapleford Tawney 9/40-11/40, North Weald 11/40-12/40, Digby 12/40-2/41, Church Fenton 2/41-3/41, Sherburn-in-Elmet 3/41-5/41,
Foreign Based: Skaanland 5/40, Bardufoss 5/40-6/40, en route to Egypt 5/41-7/41, Abu Sueir 7/41-9/41, Kilo 17 9/41-5/42
Reformed: N/A
Disbanded: N/A
Re-equipped: May 1942 (Beaufighter Mk If)
Variants Operated: Mk I, Mk IIA & Mk IIB

No.56 Squadron
Code: **LR** & **US**
Started Hurricane Operations: North Weald 4/38
UK Based: North Weald 4/38-10/39, Martlesham Heath 10/39-2/40, North Weald 2/40-5/40, Digby 5/40-6/40, North Weald 6/40-9/40, Boscombe Down 9/40-11/40, Middle Wallop 11/40-12/40, North Weald 12/40-6/41, Martlesham Heath 6/41, Duxford 6/41-3/42
Foreign Based: Norrent Fontes 5/40
Reformed: N/A
Disbanded: N/A
Re-equipped: March 1942 (Typhoon Mk Ib)
Variants Operated: Mk I & Mk IIB

No.60 Squadron
Code: **MU**
Started Hurricane Operations: St. Thomas Mount 7/43
UK Based: N/A
Foreign Based: St. Thomas Mount 7/43-10/43, Cholavarum 10/43-11/43, Agartala 11/43-7/44, Kumbirgram 7/44-9/44, Kamgla 9/44-1/45, Taukkyan 1/45-2/45, Monywa 2/45-3/45, Thedaw 4/45, Kalaywa 4/45-5/45, Mingaladon 5/45, Thedaw 5/45-6/45
Reformed: N/A
Disbanded: N/A
Re-equipped: June 1945 (Republic Thunderbolt II)
Variants Operated: Mk IIC

No.63 Squadron
Code: None
Started Hurricane Operations: Turnhouse 3/44
UK Based: Turnhouse 3/44-5/44
Foreign Based: N/A
Reformed: N/A
Disbanded: N/A
Re-equipped: May/June 1944 (Supermarine Spitfire)
Variants Operated: Mk IIC & Mk IV

No.67 Squadron
Code: None
Started Hurricane Operations: Alipore 6/42
UK Based: N/A
Foreign Based: Alipore 6/42-4/43, Chittagong 4/43-3/44
Reformed: N/A
Disbanded: N/A
Re-equipped: February 1944 (Spitfire Mk VIII)
Variants Operated: Mk IIB & Mk IIC

No.69 Squadron
Code: None
Started Hurricane Operations: Luqa 1/41
UK Based: N/A
Foreign Based: Luqa 1/41-2/42
Reformed: N/A
Disbanded: N/A
Re-equipped: February 1942 (Bristol Beaufort & Blenheim)
Variants Operated: Mk I & Mk IIB

No.71 Squadron
Code: **XR**
Started Hurricane Operations: Kirton-on-Lindsey 10/40
UK Based: Kirton-on-Lindsey 10/40-4/41, Martlesham Heath 4/41-6/41, North Weald 6/41-12/41, Martlesham Heath 12/41-5/42, Debden 5/42-8/42, Gravesend 8/42, Debden 8/42-9/42
Foreign Based: N/A
Reformed: N/A
Disbanded: N/A
Re-equipped: August 1941 (Spitfire Mk IIA)
Variants Operated: Mk IIB & Mk IIC

No.73 Squadron
Code: **HV** & **TP**
Started Hurricane Operations: Digby 7/38
UK Based: Digby 7/38-/39, Church Fenton 6/40-9/40, Castle Camps 9/40-11/40,
Foreign Based: Le Havre 9/39-10/39, Norrent Fontes 9/39-10/39, Rouvres 10/39-5/40, Reimes/Champagne 5/40, Villeneuve 5/40, Gaye 5/40-6/40, Raudin 6/40, Saumur 6/40, Nantes 6/40, en route to Africa 11/40, Heliopolis 11/40-12/40, Sidi Haneish 12/40-1/41, Amseat 1/41, Gazala West 1/41-3/41, Bu Amoud 3/41-

4/41, El Gubbi 4/41, Sidi Haneish 4/91-9/41, El Gamil 9/41-2/42, El Adem 2/42-5/42, Gambut Main 5/42-6/42, LG115 6/42, LG76 6/42, Qasaba 6/42, El Daba 6/42, Burgh-el-Arab 6/42-7/42, LG39 7/42, LG89 7/42, El Ballah 7/42, Shandur 7/42-8/42, LG85 8/42-10/42, LG89 10/42-11/42, LG21 11/42, LG155 11/42, Gambut West 11/42, El Adem 11/42, El Magrun 11/42-12/42, Merduna 12/42-1/43, Alem el Chel 1/43, Wadi Tamet 1/43, Bir Dufan 1/43-2/43, El Assa 2/43-3/42, Nafatia South 3/43-4/43, Monastir 4/43-5/43, La Seballa 5/43-10/43
Reformed: N/A
Disbanded: N/A
Re-equipped: July 1943 (Spitfire Mk Vc)
Variants Operated: Mk I, Mk IIB & Mk IIC

No.74 Squadron
Code: None
Started Hurricane Operations: Meherabad 12/42
UK Based:
Foreign Based: Meherabad 12/42-5/43, El Daba 5/43, LG106 5/43-8/43
Reformed: N/A
Disbanded: N/A
Re-equipped: August 1943 (Spitfire Mk Vb/Vc)
Variants Operated: Mk IIB

No.79 Squadron
Code: AL & NV
Started Hurricane Operations: Biggin Hill 11/38
UK Based: Bigin Hill 11/38-11/39, Manston 11/39-5/40, Biggin Hill 5/40, Digby 5/40-6/40, Biggin Hill 6/40-7/40, Hawkinge 7/40, Acklington 7/40-8/40, Biggin Hill 8/40-9/40, Pembrey 9/40-6/41, Fairwood Common 6/41-12/41, Baginton 12/41-3/42
Foreign Based: Merville 5/40, Norrent Fontes 5/40, Merville 5/40, en route to India 3/42-5/42, Bombay 6/42, Kanchrapara 6/42-1/43, Dohazari 1/43, Ramu 1/43-5/43, Comilla 5/43-7/43, Ranchi 7/43-10/43, Alipore 10/43-12/43, Chittagong 12/43-1/44, Dohazari 1/44-5/44, Yelahanka 5/44-9/44
Reformed: N/A
Disbanded: N/A
Re-equipped: September 1944 (Republic Thunderbolt II)
Variants Operated: Mk I, Mk IIB & Mk IIC

No.80 Squadron
Code: AP, EY & YK
Started Hurricane Operations: Amriya 6/40
UK Based: None
Foreign Based: Amriya 6/40-7/40, Sidi Barrani 7/40-9/40, Sidi Heneish 9/40-10/40, Abu Sueir 10/40-11/40, Menidi 11/40, Larissa 11/40-12/40, Yannina 12/40-4/41, Argos 4/41, Crete 4/41, en route to Palestine 4/41-5/41, Aqir 5/41-6/41, Haifa 6/41-7/41, Nicosia 7/41-8/41, Aqir 8/41-9/41, Rayak 9/41-10/41, Maaten Bagush 10/41-11/41, Fort Maddelena 11/41-12/41, El Gubbi 12/41, Gazala 12/41, El Adem 12/41-2/42, Mischeifa 2/42, Sidi Heneish 2/42-3/42, Gambut 3/42-5/42, Sidi Barrani 5/42, Fuka 5/42-6/42, Amriya 6/42-9/42, El Bassa 9/442-10/42, LG86 10/42, Burgh-el-Arab 11/42, El Daba 10/42, Sidi Heneish 10/42-11/42, Bu Amoud 11/42-5/43
Reformed: N/A
Disbanded: N/A
Re-equipped: April 1944 (Spitfire Mk Vc)
Variants Operated: Mk I & Mk II

No.81 Squadron
Code: FV
Started Hurricane Operations: Debden 7/41
UK Based: Debden 7/41, Leconfield 7/41-8/41
Foreign Based: en route to Russia 8/41-9/41, Vaenga 9/41-11/41
Reformed: N/A
Disbanded: N/A
Re-equipped: January 1942 (Spitfire Mk V)
Variants Operated: Mk IIB

No.85 Squadron
Code: VY
Started Hurricane Operations: Debden 9/39
UK Based: Debden 9/39, Debden 5/40-6/40, Martlesham Heath 6/40-8/40, Debden 8/40, Croydon 8/40-9/40, Castle Camps 9/40, Church fenton 9/40-10/40, Kirton-in-Lindsey 10/40-11/40, Gravesend 11/40-1/41, Debden 1/41-5/41
Foreign Based: Lille 9/39, Merville 9/39-11/39, Lille/seclin 11/39-4/40, Mons-en-Chaussee 4/40, Lille/Seclin 4/40-5/40, Merville 5/40
Reformed: N/A
Disbanded: N/A
Re-equipped: April 1941 (B.P. Defiant NF Mk I)
Variants Operated: Mk I

No.87 Squadron
Code: LK, 4K & PD
Started Hurricane Operations: Debden 7/38
UK Based: Debden 7/38-9/39, Church Fenton 5/40-11/40, Colerne 11/40-12/40, Charmy Down 12/40-8/41, Colerne 8/41-1/42, Colerne 1/42-11/42
Foreign Based: Boos 9/39, Lille/Seclin 11/39-4/40, Le Touquet 4/40, Glisy 4/40-5/40, Seon 5/40, Lille/Seclin 5/40, Merville 5/40, en route to North Africa 11/42-12/42, Phillipeville 12/42, Djidjelli 12/42-5/43, Tingley 5/43-7/43, Monastir 7/43, Tingley 7/43-8/43, La Sebala I 8/43-9/43, Bo Rizzo 9/43-12/43, Palermo 12/43-3/44
Reformed: N/A
Disbanded: N/A
Re-equipped: March 1944
Variants Operated: Mk I & Mk IIC

No.94 Squadron
Code: GO
Started Hurricane Operations: Ismailia 5/41
UK Based: N/A
Foreign Based: Ismailia 5/41-8/41, El Ballah 8/41-10/41, LG103 10/41-11/41, LG109 11/41, LG124 11/41-12/41, Sidi Rezegh 12/41, Gazala 2 12/41, Mechili

Pilots of B Flight, No. 85 Sqn, in front of a Mk I at Castle Camps in July 1940 (© RAF Museum P010903)

12/41, Msus 12/41-1/42, Antelat 1/42, Msus 1/42, Mechili 1/42, Mariut 5/42-6/42, El Gamil 6/42-1/43, Martuba 1/43-4/43, Cyrene 4/43-5/43, Luigi di Savoia 5/43, Apollonia 5/43-6/43, Luigi di Savoia 6/43-10/43, Bu Amoud 10/43-11/43, El Adem 11/43-4/44, Bu Amoud 4/44-7/44
Reformed: N/A
Disbanded: N/A
Re-equipped: February-May 1942 (Kittyhawk I) & May 1944 (Spitfire Mk Vb)
Variants Operated: Mk I, Mk IIB & Mk IIC

No.95 Squadron
Code: None
Started Hurricane Operations: Freetown 7/41
UK Based: Freetown (Hastings) 7/41-10/41
Foreign Based: N/A
Reformed: N/A
Disbanded: N/A
Re-equipped: October 1941 (Became No. 128 Squadron)
Variants Operated: Mk I
Note: This was the only Short Sunderland squadron to have a flight of Hurricanes!

No.96 Squadron
Code: ZJ
Started Hurricane Operations: Cranage 12/40
UK Based: Cranage 12/40-10/41
Foreign Based: N/A
Reformed: N/A
Disbanded: N/A
Re-equipped: May 1941 (B.P. Defiant NF Mk I)
Variants Operated: Mk I

No.98 Squadron
Code: None
Started Hurricane Operations: Kaldadarnes June 1941
UK Based: N/A
Foreign Based: Kaldadarnes 6/41-7/41
Reformed: N/A
Disbanded: Kaldadarnes 15/7/41
Re-equipped: N/AS
Variants Operated: Mk I
Note: Renumbered as No. 1423 Flight (7/41)

No.111 Squadron
Code: TM & JU
Started Hurricane Operations: Northolt 12/37
UK Based: Northolt 12/37-10/39, Acklington 10/39-12/39, Drem 12/39-2/40, Wick 2/40-5/40, Northolt 5/40, Digby 5/40, North Weald 5/40-6/40, Croydon 6/40-8/40, Debden 8/40-9/40, Croydon 9/40, Drem 9/40-10/40, Dyce 10/40-7/41
Foreign Based: N/A
Reformed: N/A
Disbanded: N/A
Re-equipped: April 1941 (Spitfire Mk I)
Variants Operated: Mk I

No.113 Squadron
Code: AD
Started Hurricane Operations: Yelahanka 9/43
UK Based: N/A
Foreign Based: Yelahanka 9/43-10/43, , St. Thomas Mount 10/43-11/43, Cholavarum 11/43-12/43, Manipur Road, 12/43-3/44, Jorhat 3/44-5/44, Palel 5/44-12/44, Yazagyo 12/44-1/45, Onbauk 1/45-3/45, Ondaw 3/45-4/45
Reformed: N/A
Disbanded: N/A
Re-equipped: April 1945 (Republic Thunderbolt I)
Variants Operated: Mk IIC

No. 116 Squadron
See 'Army - Anti-aircraft Co-operation Units

No.121 (Eagle) Squadron
Code: AV
Started Hurricane Operations: Kirton-in-Lindsey 5/41
UK Based: Kirton-in-Lindsey 5/41-12/41
Foreign Based: None
Reformed: N/A
Disbanded: N/A
Re-equipped: November 1941 (Spitfire Mk IIA)
Variants Operated: Mk IIC

No.123 (East India) Squadron
Code: XE
Started Hurricane Operations: Mehrabad 11/42
UK Based: None
Foreign Based: Mehrabad 11/42-1/43, Abadan 1/43-5/43, Bu Amud 5/43-11/43, Quassassin 11/43, en route to Far East 11/43-12/43, Feni 12/43-1/44, Patharkandi 1/44-6/44, St. Thomas Mount 6/44-9/44
Reformed: N/A
Disbanded: N/A
Re-equipped: September 1944
Variants Operated: Mk IIC

No.126 Squadron
Code: None
Started Hurricane Operations: Ta Kali 6/41
UK Based: None
Foreign Based: Ta Kali 6/41-5/42
Reformed: N/A
Disbanded: N/A
Re-equipped: March 1942 (Spitfire Mk Vb/Vc)
Variants Operated: Mk IIA & Mk IIC

No.127 Squadron
Code: None
Started Hurricane Operations: Habbaniya 6/41
UK Based: None
Foreign Based: Habbaniya 6/41, Haditha 6/41, T1 6/41-7/41, Tahoune Guemac 7/41, Deir-ez-Zor 7/41, Kasfareet 9/41, Hurghada 9/41-2/42, St. Jean 2/42-6/42, Shandur 6/42, Amriya (LG92) 6/42-7/42, LG172 7/42-8/42, LG88 8/42-9/42, Kilo 8 9/42-10/42, LG89 10/42, LG37 10/42-11/42, LG20 11/42, LG08 11/42-1/43, St. Jean 1/43, Ramat David 1/43-3/43, St. Jean 3/43-11/43, Paphos 11/43, St. Jean 11/43-4/44
Reformed: Kasfareet 15/9/41 by re-numbering No. 249 Squadron
Disbanded: April 1944
Variants Operated: Mk I & Mk IIB

No.128 Squadron
Code: WG
Started Hurricane Operations: Hastings (Sierra Leone) 10/41
UK Based: None
Foreign Based: Hastings (Sierra Leone) 10/41-3/43
Reformed: N/A
Disbanded: 8th March 1943
Re-equipped: N/A
Variants Operated: Mk I

Mk I, V7544 of No. 73 Sqn (© RAF Museum P005095)

No.133 (Eagle) Squadron
Code: MD
Started Hurricane Operations: Coltishall 8/41
UK Based: Coltishall 8/41, Duxford 8/41-9/41, Colly Weston 9/41-10/41, Fowlmere 10/41, Eglington 10/41-12/41
Foreign Based: None
Reformed: N/A
Disbanded: N/A
Re-equipped: December 1941 (Spitfire Mk IIA)
Variants Operated: Mk I

No.134 Squadron
Code: GO, GA & GV
Started Hurricane Operations: Leconfield 7/41
UK Based: Leconfield 7/41-8/41, Catterick 12/41-1/42, Eglinton 1/42-2/42
Foreign Based: en route to Russia 8/41-9/41, Vaenga 9/41-11/41, Shandur 1/43-2/43, LG121 2/43-4/43, LG43 4/43, Matariyah 4/43-5/43, Bu Amoud 5/43-6/43, Bersis 6/43-10/43
Reformed: N/A
Disbanded: N/A
Re-equipped: October 1943
Variants Operated: Mk IIB

No.135 Squadron
Code: None
Started Hurricane Operations: Bagington 8/41
UK Based: Bagington 8/41-9/41, Honiley 9/41-11/41, Foreign Based: en route to Burma 11/41-1/42, Zayatkwin 1/42-1/42, Mingaladon 1/42-3/42, Akyab 3/42, Dum Dum 3/42-1/43, George 1/43-5/43, Dohazari 5/43, St. Thomas Mount 5/43-7/43, Yalahanka 7/43-11/43, St. Thomas Mount 11/43-1/44, Minneriya 1/44-9/44, Amarda Road 9/44
Reformed: N/A
Disbanded: N/A
Re-equipped: May 1944 (Republic P-47 Thunderbolt I), ceased Hurricane operations September 1944
Variants Operated: Mk IIA, Mk IIB and MK IIC

No.136 Squadron
Code: HM
Started Hurricane Operations: Kirton-in-Lindsey (20/8/41)
UK Based: Kirton-in-Lindsey 8/41-11/41
Foreign Based: en route to India 11/41-3/42, Alipore 3/42-6/42, Red Road 6/42-8/42, Alipore 8/42-9/42, Dum Dum 9/42-12/42
Chittagong 12/42-6/43, Baigachi 6/43-12/43
Reformed: N/A
Disbanded: N/A
Re-equipped: Baigachi October 1943 (Spitfire Mk Vb)
Variants Operated: Mk IIA, Mk IIB & Mk IIC

No.137 Squadron
Code: SF
Started Hurricane Operations: Rochford June 1943
UK Based: Rochford 6/43-8/43, Manston 8/43-1/44
Foreign Based: N/A
Reformed: N/A
Disbanded: N/A
Re-equipped: Manston January 1944 (Typhoon Mk Ib)
Variants Operated: Mk IV

No.145 Squadron
Code: SO
Started Hurricane Operations: Croydon March 1940
UK Based: Croydon 3/40-5/40, Filton 5/40, Tangmere 5/40-7/40, Westhampnett 7/40-8/40, Drem 8/40-10/40, Tangmere 10/40-5/41
Foreign Based:
Reformed: N/A
Disbanded: N/A
Re-equipped: Tangmere February 1941 (Spitfire Mk I)
Variants Operated: Mk I

No.146 Squadron
Code: NA & LR
Started Hurricane Operations: Dum Dum May 1942
UK Based: None
Foreign Based: Dum Dum 5/42-9/42, Alipore 9/42-5/43, Feni 5/43-6/43, Comilla 6/43-12/43, Baigachi 12/43-3/44, St. Thomas' Mount 3/44-5/44
Reformed: N/A
Disbanded: N/A
Re-equipped: St. Thomas' Mount May 1944 (Republic Thunderbolt I)
Variants Operated: Mk IIB & Mk IIC

No.151 Squadron
Code: DZ & GG
Started Hurricane Operations: North Weald, November 1938
UK Based: North Weald 11/38-5/40, Martlesham Heath 5/40-8/40, Stapleford 9/40-9/40, Digby 9/40-11/40, Bramcote 11/40-12/40, Wittering 12/40-4/43
Foreign Based: N/A
Reformed: N/A
Disbanded: N/A
Re-equipped: Wittering, January 1942
Variants Operated: Mk I & Mk IIC

No.164 (Argentine-British) Squadron

Code: FJ
Started Hurricane Operations: Middle Wallop, February 1943
UK Based: Middle Wallop 2/43-6/43, Warmwell 6/43-8/43, Manston 8/43-9/43, Fairlop 9/43-3/44
Foreign Based: N/A
Reformed: N/A
Disbanded: N/A
Re-equipped: Fairlop, February 1944 (Typhoon Mk Ib)
Variants Operated: Mk IV

No.173 Squadron

Code: None
Started Hurricane Operations: Heliopolis 7/42
UK Based: N/A
Foreign Based: Heliopolis/various LG's 7/42-2/44
Reformed: N/A
Disbanded: Cairo 29 February 1944 (Re-named Middle East Communications Squadron)
Re-equipped: N/A
Variants Operated: Mk I

No.174 (Mauritius) Squadron

Code: XP
Started Hurricane Operations: Manston, March 1942
UK Based: Manston 3/42-7/42, Fowlmere 7/42, Manston 7/42-9/42, Warmwell 9/42, Manston 9/42-12/42, Odiham 12/42-3/43m, Chilbolton 3/43, Grove 3/43, Odiham 3/43-4/43
Foreign Based: N/A
Reformed: N/A
Disbanded: N/A
Re-equipped: Odiham 4/43 (Typhoon Mk Ib)
Variants Operated: Mk IIB

No.175 Squadron

Code: HH
Started Hurricane Operations: Warmwell, 3rd March 1942
UK Based: Warmwell 3/42-10/42, Harrowbeer 10/42-12/42, Gatwick 12/42-1/43, Odiham 1/43-3/43, Stoney Cross 3/43-4/43
Foreign Based: N/A
Reformed: N/A
Disbanded: N/A
Re-equipped: Stoney Cross, April 1943 (Typhoon Mk Ib)
Variants Operated: Mk IIB

Mk IIB, Z3971, SW•S and others of No. 253 Squadron (© RAF Museum P019143)

No.176 Squadron

Code: None
Started Hurricane Operations: Baigachi, May 1943
UK Based: N/A
Foreign Based: Baigachi 5/43-1/44
Reformed: N/A
Disbanded: N/A
Re-equipped: N/A
Variants Operated: Mk IIC

No.181 Squadron

Code: EL
Started Hurricane Operations: Duxford, 1st September 1942
UK Based: Duxford 9/42-12/42
Foreign Based:
Reformed: N/A
Disbanded: N/A
Re-equipped: Duxford, December 1942 (Typhoon Mk Ia)
Variants Operated: Mk I

No.182 Squadron

Code: XM
Started Hurricane Operations: Martlesham Heath, 1st September 1942
UK Based: Martlesham Heath 9/42-12/42
Foreign Based: N/A
Reformed: N/A
Disbanded: N/A
Re-equipped: Martlesham Heath, October 1942 (Typhoon Mk Ia)
Variants Operated: Mk I

No.183 Squadron

Code: HF
Started Hurricane Operations: Church Fenton, 1st November 1942
UK Based: Church Fenton 11/42-3/43
Foreign Based: n/a
Reformed: N/A
Disbanded: N/A
Re-equipped: Church Fenton, February 1943 (Typhoon Mk Ia)
Variants Operated: Mk I

No.184 Squadron

Code: BR
Started Hurricane Operations: Colerne, 1st December 1942
UK Based: Colerne 12/42-3/43, Chilbolton 3/43, Eastchurch 3/43-5/43, Merston 5/43-6/43, Manston 6/43-8/43, 122 A/F 8/43, 125 A/F 8/43-10/43, Detling 10/43-3/44, Odiham 3/44
Foreign Based: N/A
Reformed: N/A
Disbanded: N/A
Re-equipped: Odiham, March 1944
Variants Operated: Mk IID & Mk IV

No.185 Squadron

Code: None
Started Hurricane Operations: Hal Far, Malta, 12th May 1941
UK Based: N/A
Foreign Based: Hal Far 5/41-6/43
Reformed: N/A
Disbanded: N/A
Re-equipped: Hal Far, June 1942 (Spitfire Mk Vc)
Variants Operated: Mk I, Mk IIA & Mk IIC

No.193 Squadron

Code: DP
Started Hurricane Operations: Harrowbeer 1/43
UK Based: Harrowbeer 1/43-2/43
Foreign Based: N/A
Reformed: N/A
Disbanded: N/A
Re-equipped: Harrowbeer 2/43 (Typhoon Mk Ib)
Variants Operated: Mk I & Mk IIC

No.195 Squadron

Code: None
Started Hurricane Operations: Duxford 16 November 1942
UK Based: Duxford 11/42-12/42, Hutton Cranswick 12/42-2/43
Foreign Based: N/A
Reformed: N/A
Disbanded: N/A
Re-equipped: Ludham 5/43 (Typhoon Mk Ib)
Variants Operated: Mk I

No.208 Squadron

Code: RG
Started Hurricane Operations: Qasaba 11/40
UK Based: N/A
Foreign Based:
Qasaba/Gambut/Barce/Heliopolis/Kazaklar 11/40-4/41, Eleusis/Argos/Maleme 4/41-5/41, Gaza/Ramleh 5/41-9/41, Aqir 9/41-10/41, Gerawla/El Gubbi/Tmimi/Acroma/Sidi Azeiz 10/41-3/42, Moascar/LG's/Heliopolis/Burg el Arab 3/42-11/42, Aqsu/K1 1/43-7/43, Rayak 7/43-11/43, El Bassa 11/43-12/43
Reformed: N/A
Disbanded: N/A
Re-equipped: El Basa 12/43 (Supermarine Spitfire)
Variants Operated: Mk I, Mk IIA, Mk IIB & Mk IIC

No.213 Squadron

Code: AK
Started Hurricane Operations: Wittering, January 1939
UK Based: Wittering 1/39-5/40, Wittering 5/40, Biggin Hill 5/40-6/40, Wittering 6/40, Biggin Hill 6/40, Exeter 6/40-9/40, Tangmere 9/40-11/40, Leconfield 11/40-1/41, Driffield 1/41-2/41, Castletown 2/41-5/41
Foreign Based: Merville 5/40, on board HMS Furious 5/41, Abu Sueir 5/41-7/41, Lydda 7/41, Nicosia 7/41-12/41, L.G. 90 12/41-1/42, Edku 1/42-5/42, L.G. 12 5/42-6/42, Sidi Aziz 6/42, L.G.155 6/42, L.G.75 6/42, L.G.76 6/42, L.G.07 6/42, L.G.12 6/42, L.G.05 6/42, L.G.154 6/42-7/42, L.G.172 7/42, L.G.154 7/42-8/42, Kilo 8 8/42, L.G.85 8/42, L.G.172 10/42-11/42, L.G.20 11/42, L.G.101 11/42, El Adem 11/42, Martuba 11/42-1/43, Misurata W. 1/43-7/43, Edku 7/43-2/44, El Gamil 2/44-5/44
Reformed: N/A
Disbanded: N/A
Re-equipped: El Gamil, May 1944 (Spitfire Mk Vc)
Variants Operated: Mk I & Mk IIc

No.225 Squadron

Code: LX & WU
Started Hurricane Operations: Thruxton 1/42
UK Based: Thruxton & Macmerry 1/42-10/42
Foreign Based: Maison Blanche 11/42, Tingley/Souk-el-Arba 11/42-4/43
Reformed: N/A

Mk IIc, KW971, RZ•C of No. 241 Sqn, at Souk el Khemis in 1943 (© RAF Museum P007917/A)

Disbanded: N/A
Re-equipped: Souk-el-Arba 4/43 (Supermarine Spitfire Mk IX)
Variants Operated: Mk I, Mk IIB & Mk IIC

No. 229 Squadron

Code: HB & RE
Started Hurricane Operations: Digby, May 1940
UK Based: Digby 5/40-6/540, Wittering 6/40-9/40, Northolt 9/40-12/40, Wittering 12/40, Speke 12/40-5/41
Foreign Based: en route to Middle east 5/41-9/41, L.G.07 9/41-12/41, Bu Amoud 12/41, Gazala No. 2 12/41, Msus 12/41-1/42, Antelat 1/42, Mechili 1/42, Gazala No. 2 1/42-2/42, L.G.111 2/42, L.GH. 102 2/42, El Firdan 2/42-3/42, Hal Far 3/42-4/42
Reformed: N/A
Disbanded: Hal Far, 29th April 1942
Re-equipped: N/A
Variants Operated: Mk I & Mk IIC

No. 232 Squadron

Code: EF
Started Hurricane Operations: Sumburgh, 17th July 1940
UK Based: Sumburgh 7/40, Castletown 7/40-10/40, Skitten 10/40, Drem 10/40-11/40, Elgin 12/40-4/41, Montrose 4/41-7/41, Abbotsinch 7/41, Ouoston 7/41-11/41
Foreign Based: en route to Singapore 11/41-1/42, Seletar 1/42-2/42
Reformed: N/A
Disbanded: N/A
Re-equipped: Seletar, February 1942 (Spitfire Mk Vc)
Variants Operated: Mk I & Mk IIB

No. 237 (Rhodesia) Squadron

Code: None
Started Hurricane Operations: Benghazi, January 1942
UK Based:
Foreign Based: Benghazi 1/42, Tmimi 1/42, El Firdan 1/42-2/42, Ismailia 2/42-3/42, Mosul 3/42-7/42, Quaiyarah 7/42-9/42, Kermanshah 9/42-12/42, Kirkuk 12/42-1/43, en route to Egypt 1/43-2/43, Shandur 2/43, L.G.106 2/43-6/43, Bersis 6/43-9/43, Edku 9/43-12/43
Reformed: N/A
Disbanded: N/A
Re-equipped: Edku, December 1943 (Spitfire Mk Vb)
Variants Operated: Mk I & Mk IIC

No. 238 Squadron

Code: KC
Started Hurricane Operations: Middle Wallop, June 1940
UK Based: Middle Wallop 6/40-8/40, St. Eval 8/40-9/40, Middle Wallop 9/40, Chilbolton 9/40-1/41, Middle Wallop 1/41-2/41, Chilbolton 2/41-4/41, Pembrey 4/41, Chilbolton 4/41-5/41
Foreign Based: en route to Egypt 5/41-7/41, El Firdan 7/41, L.G.92 7/41, L.G.123 11/41-12/41, Msus 12/41-1/42, Antelat 1/42, El Gubbi 1/42-2/42, Gambut 2/42-5/42, L.G.154 10/43, L.G.172 10/42-11/42, L.G.012 11/42, L.G.101 11/42, L.G.125 11/42, El Adem 11/42, Benuna 11/42, Martuba 11/421/43, El Gamil 1/43-1/44
Reformed: N/A
Disbanded: N/A
Re-equipped: El Gamil, September 1943
Variants Operated: Mk I, Mk IIA, Mk IIB & Mk IIC

No. 239 Squadron

Code: HB
Started Hurricane Operations: Gatwick 1/42
UK Based: Gatwick 1/42-5/42
Foreign Based: N/A
Reformed: N/A
Disbanded: N/A
Re-equipped: Gatwick 5/42 (N.A. Mustang Mk I)
Variants Operated: Mk I & Mk IIC

No. 241 Squadron

Code: RZ
Started Hurricane Operations: Maison Blanche 11/42
UK Based: N/A
Foreign Based: Maison Blanche 11/42, Souk-el-Arba/Souk-el-Khemis/Ariana/Bou Ficha 12/42-10/43, Philippeville 10/43-12/43
Reformed: N/A
Disbanded: N/A
Re-equipped: Philippeville 12/43 (Spitfire Mk VIII/IX)
Variants Operated: Mk IIB

No. 242 (Canadian) Squadron

Code: LE
Started Hurricane Operations: Church Fenton, February 1940
UK Based: Church Fenton 2/40-5/40, Biggin Hill 1/40, Coltishall 6/40-10/40, Duxford 10/40-12/40, Martlesham Heath 12/40-4/41, Stapleford Tawney 4/41-5/41, North Weald 5/41-7/41, Manston 7/41, Valley 9/41-12/41
Foreign Based: Chateaudun 5/40-6/40, Ancevis 6/40, Nantes 6/40, en route to Sumatra 12/41-2/42, Palembang 1/42-2/42, Tjilitang 2/42, Bandoeng 2/42-3/42
Reformed: N/A
Disbanded: Java, approx 10th March 1942
Re-equipped: Turnhouse, 10th April 1942 (Spitfire Mk Vb)
Variants Operated: Mk I, Mk IIB & Mk IIC

No. 245 Squadron

Code: DX & MR
Started Hurricane Operations: Leconfield, March 1940
UK Based: Leconfield 3/40-5/40, Drem 5/40-6/40, Turnhouse 6/40-7/40, Aldergrove 7/40-6/41, Ballyhalbert 6/41-9/41, Chilbolton 9/41-12/41, Middle Wallop 12/41-10/42, Charmy Down 10/42-1/43
Foreign Based: N/A
Reformed: N/A
Disbanded: N/A
Re-equipped: Charmy Down, January 1943
Variants Operated: Mk I, Mk IIB & Mk IIC

No. 247 (China-British) Squadron

Code: HP & ZY
Started Hurricane Operations: Roborough, December 1940
UK Based: Roborough 12/40-2/41, St. Eval 2/41-5/41, Portreath 5/41-6/41, Predannack 6/41-5/41, Exeter 5/42-9/42, High Ercall 9/42-2/43, Middle Wallop 2/43-4/43
Foreign Based: N/A
Reformed: N/A
Disbanded: N/A
Re-equipped: Middle Wallop, March 1943 (Typhoon Mk Ib)
Variants Operated: Mk I, Mk IIA, Mk XII (to Mk IIB configuration) & Mk IIC

No. 249 (Gold Coast) Squadron

Code: GN
Started Hurricane Operations: Church Fenton, 16th May 1940
UK Based: Church Fenton 5/40, Leconfield 5/40-7/40, Church Fenton 7/40-8/40, Boscombe Down 8/40-9/40, North Weald 9/40-5/41
Foreign Based: en route to Malta 5/41, Ta Kali 5/41-11/42
Reformed: N/A
Disbanded: N/A
Re-equipped: Ta Kali, August 1942
Variants Operated: Mk I, Mk IIA, Mk IIB & Mk IIC

No. 250 (Sudan) Squadron

Code: LD
Started Hurricane Operations: Gazala, February 1942
UK Based: N/A
Foreign Based: Gazala 2/42, El Gamil 2/42-4/42
Reformed: N/A
Disbanded: N/A
Re-equipped: El Gamil, April 1942 (Kittyhawk I)
Variants Operated: Mk I & Mk IIC

No. 253 (Hyderbad State) Squadron

Code: SW
Started Hurricane Operations: Northolt, January 1940
UK Based: Northolt 1/40-5/40, Kenley 5/40, Kirton-in-Lindsey 5/40-7/40, Turnhouse 7/40-8/40, Prestwick 8/40, Kenley 8/40-1/41, Leconfield 1/41-2/41, Skeabrae 2/41-9/41, Hibaldstow 9/41-5/42, Shoreham 5/42, Hibaldstow 5/42-6/42, Friston 6/42-7/42, Hibaldstow 7/42-8/42, Friston 8/42, Hibaldstow 8/42-11/42
Foreign Based: en route to North Africa 11/42, Maison Blanche 11/42, Philippeville 11/42-1/43, Setif 1/43-2/43, Jemappes 2/43-3/43, Maison Blanche 3/43-4/43, Jemappes 4/43-6/43, Sousse 6/43-8/43, La Sebala I 8/43-10/43
Reformed: N/A
Disbanded: N/A
Re-equipped: La Sebala I, September 1943
Variants Operated: Mk I, Mk IIA, Mk IIB & Mk IIC

Mk IIB, Z3826, ZT•A of No. 258 Squadron, 1941 *(© RAF Museum P021529)*

No. 255 Squadron

Code: **YD**
Started Hurricane Operations: Kirton-in-Lindsey, March 1941
UK Based: Kirton-in-Lindsey 3/41-5/41, Hibaldstow 5/41-9/41
Foreign Based: N/A
Reformed: N/A
Disbanded: N/A
Re-equipped: Hibaldstow, July 1941 (Beaufighter Mk VIf)
Variants Operated: Mk I

No. 256 Squadron

Code: **JT**
Started Hurricane Operations: Squires Gate, March 1941
UK Based: Squires Gate 3/41-6/42
Foreign Based: N/A
Reformed: N/A
Disbanded: N/A
Re-equipped: Squires Gate, July 1941
Variants Operated: Mk I

No. 257 (Burma) Squadron

Code: **DT** & **FM**
Started Hurricane Operations: Hendon, June 1940
UK Based: Hendon 6/40-7/40, Northolt 7/40-8/40, Debden 8/40-9/40, Martlesham Heath 9/40-12/40, North Weald 10/40-12/40, Coltishall 12/40-11/41, Honiley 11/41-6/42, High Ercall 6/42-9/42
Foreign Based: N/A
Reformed: N/A
Disbanded: N/A
Re-equipped: High Ercall, September 1942
Variants Operated: Mk I, Mk IIB & Mk IIC

No. 258 Squadron

Code: None
Started Hurricane Operations: Drem, December 1940
UK Based: Drem 12/40, Acklington 12/40-1/41, Jurby 1/41-4/41, Kenley 4/41-6/41, Redhill 6/41, Kenley 6/41-7/41, Martlesham Heath 7/41-10/41, Debden 10/41-11/41
Foreign Based: en route to Singapore 11/41-1/42, Seletar 1/42-2/42, P.1 (Palembang) 2/42, P11 2/42, Tjililitan 2/42, Ratmalana 3/42, Racecourse 3/42-2/43, Dambulla 2/43-7/43, Comilla 7/43-11/43, Dohazari 11/43-12/43, Chittagong 12/43-1/44, Hay 1/44, Hove 1/44-2/44, Reindeer I 2/44-5/44, Chittagong 5/44-6/44, Arkonam 6/44-8/44
Reformed: Ratmalana, March 1942. Racecourse (reformed from 'G' Squadron), 30th March 1942
Disbanded: Java, February 1942. Ratmalana (re-numbered No. 131 Sqn) 14th March 1942
Re-equipped: Arkonam, August 1944 (Thunderbolt I)
Variants Operated: Mk I, Mk IIA, Mk IIB & Mk IIC

No. 260 Squadron

Code: **HS** & **HH**
Started Hurricane Operations: Castletown, 22nd November 1940
UK Based: Castletown 11/40-12/40, Skitten 12/40-1/41, Castletown 1/41-2/41, Skitten 2/41-4/41, Drem 4/41-5/41
Foreign Based: en route to Palestine 5/41-8/41, Haifa 8/41-10/41, L.G.115 10/41-12/41, Sidi Rezegh 12/41, Msus 12/41-1/42, Benina 1/42, L.G.109 1/42-2/42, L.G.101 2/42, L.G.115 2/42-3/42
Reformed: N/A
Disbanded: N/A
Re-equipped: Gasr el Arid, March 1942 (Tomahawk II)
Variants Operated: Mk I

No. 261 Squadron

Code: **FJ**, **HA** & **XJ**
Started Hurricane Operations: Luqa, August 1940
UK Based: N/A
Foreign Based: Luqa 8/40-10/40, Ta Kali 10/40-5/41, Habbaniya 7/41-8/41, Shaibah 8/41-9/41, Mosul 9/41-1/42, Haifa 1/42, St. Jean 1/42-2/42, Dum Dum 2/42-3/42, China Bay 3/42-1/43, Dum Dum 1/43-2/43, Baigachi 2/43-6/43, Chittagong 6/43-10/43, Chiringa 10/43-2/44, Baigachi 2/44-3/44, Alipore 3/44-4/44, Yelahanka 4/44-8/44
Reformed: Habbaniya, 12th July 1941 (from No. 127 Sqn)
Disbanded: Ta Kali, May 1941
Re-equipped: Yelahanka, June 1944 (Thunderbolt I)
Variants Operated: Mk I, Mk IIB & Mk IIC

No. 263 Squadron

Code: **HE**
Started Hurricane Operations:
UK Based: Drem 6/40, Grangemouth 6/40-9/40, Drem 9/40-11/40
Foreign Based: N/A
Reformed: N/A
Disbanded: N/A
Re-equipped: Drem, November 1940 (Whirlwind Mk I)
Variants Operated: Mk I

No. 273 Squadron

Code: **MS**
Started Hurricane Operations: Katukurunda, August 1942
UK Based: N/A
Foreign Based: Katukurunda 8/42-9/42, Ratmalana 9/42-2/43, China Bay 2/43-8/43, Ratmalana 8/43-7/44
Reformed: N/A
Disbanded: N/A
Re-equipped: Ratmalana, May 1944 (Spitfire Mk VIII)
Variants Operated: Mk I, Mk IIA, Mk IIB & Mk IIC

Officers and NCO's of No. 257 Sqn in front of a Hurricane at High Ercall in June 1942
(© RAF Museum P000386)

No. 274 Squadron

Code: None
Started Hurricane Operations: Amriya, August 1940
UK Based: N/A
Foreign Based: Amriya 8/40-12/40, Sidi Heneish 12/40-1/41, Bardia 1/41-2/41, Amriya 2/41-4/41, Gerawla 4/41-9/41, Mariut 9/41-10/41, L.G.124 11/41-12/41, Gazala 12/41, Msus 12/41-1/42, Mechili 1/42, L.G.111 1/42-2/42, El Adem 2/42, Gasr el Ayrid 2/42, Gambut 2/42-3/42, Gambut Main 3/42-4/42, Sdid Heneish 4/42-5/42, Gambut 5/42-6/42, El Dawabis 6/42, L.G.07 6/42, El Dawabis 6/42, L.G.105 6/42, L.G.92 6/42-7/42, L.G.173 7/42-8/42, L.G.88 8/42-9/42, Edku 9/42-10/42, L.G.89 10/42, L.G.37 10/42-11/42, Martuba I 11/42-12/42, Benina 12/42, Mellaha 12/42-8/43, Derna 8/43-11/43, Edku 10/43-2/44
Reformed: N/A
Disbanded: N/A
Re-equipped: Edku, November 1943 (Spitfire Mk Vb)
Variants Operated: Mk I

No. 279 (ASR) Squadron

See 'Royal Air Force - Others'

No. 284 (ASR) Squadron

See 'Royal Air Force - Others'

No. 285 (ASR) Squadron

See 'Royal Air Force - Others'

No. 286 (ASR) Squadron

See 'Royal Air Force - Others'

No. 287 (ASR) Squadron

See 'Royal Air Force - Others'

No. 288 (ASR) Squadron

See 'Royal Air Force - Others'

No. 289 (ASR) Squadron

See 'Royal Air Force - Others'

No. 290 (ASR) Squadron

See 'Royal Air Force - Others'

No. 291 (ASR) Squadron

See 'Royal Air Force - Others'

No. 302 (Poznanski) Squadron

Code: **WX**
Started Hurricane Operations: Leconfield, 13th July 1940
UK Based: Leconfield 7/40-10/40, Northolt 10/20-11/40, Northolt 11/40-4/40, Westhampnett 4/41-5/41, Kenley 5/41-8/41, Jurby 8/41-9/41, Church Stanton 9/41-10/41, Warmwell 10/41-11/41
Foreign Based: N/A
Reformed: N/A
Disbanded: N/A
Re-equipped: Warmwell, October 1941 (Spitfire MK IIA)
Variants Operated: Mk I, Mk IIA & Mk IIB

No. 303 (Warsaw-Kosciusco) Squadron

Code: **RF**
Started Hurricane Operations: Northolt, 2nd August 1940
UK Based: Northolt 8/40-10/41, Leconfield 10/40-1/41, Speke 8/41-10/41
Foreign Based: N/A
Reformed: N/A
Disbanded: N/A
Re-equipped: Speke, October 1941
Variants Operated: Mk I

No. 306 (Torunski) Squadron

Code: **UZ**
Started Hurricane Operations: Church Fenton, 28th August 1940
UK Based: Church Fenton 8/40-11/40, Ternhill 11/40-4/41, Northolt 4/41-10/41
Foreign Based: N/A
Reformed: N/A
Disbanded: N/A
Re-equipped: Northolt, July 1941 (Spitfire Mk IIb)
Variants Operated: Mk I & Mk IIA

No. 308 (Krakowski) Squadron

Code: None
Started Hurricane Operations: Baginton, November 1940
UK Based: Baginton 11/40-5/41
Foreign Based: N/A
Reformed: N/A
Disbanded: N/A
Re-equipped: Baginton, April 1941
Variants Operated: Mk I

No. 309 (Ziemia Czerwienska) Squadron

Code: **WC**
Started Hurricane Operations: Drem, April 1944
UK Based: Drem & Hutton Cranswick 4/44-12/44
Foreign Based: N/A
Reformed: N/A
Disbanded: N/A
Re-equipped: Hutton Cranswick, October 1944 (Mustang III)
Variants Operated: Mk IIc

No. 310 (Czechoslovak) Squadron

Code: **NN**
Started Hurricane Operations: Duxford, 10th July 1940
UK Based: Duxford 7/40-6/41, Martlesham Heath 7/41, Dyce 7/41-12/41
Foreign Based: N/A
Reformed: N/A
Disbanded: N/A
Re-equipped: Dyce, December 1941 (Spitfire Mk IIa)
Variants Operated: Mk I, Mk IIA & Mk IIB

No.312 (Czechoslovak) Squadron

Code: **DU**
Started Hurricane Operations: Duxford, 29th August 1940
UK Based: Duxford 8/40-9/40, Speke 9/40-3/41, Valley 3/41-4/41, Jurby 4/41-5/41, Kenley 5/41-7/41,

Martlesham Heath 7/41-8/41, Ayr 8/41-1/42
Foreign Based: N/A
Reformed: N/A
Disbanded: N/A
Re-equipped: Ayr, December 1941
Variants Operated: Mk I & Mk IIB

No. 315 (Deblinski) Squadron

Code: **PK**
Started Hurricane Operations: Acklington, February 1941
UK Based: Acklington 2/41-3/41, Speke 3/41-7/41, Northolt 7/41-4/42
Foreign Based: N/A
Reformed: N/A
Disbanded: N/A
Re-equipped: Northolt, July 1941
Variants Operated: Mk I

No. 316 (Warszawski) Squadron

Code: **SZ**
Started Hurricane Operations: Pembrey, 15th February 1941
UK Based: Pembrey 2/41-6/41, Colerne 6/41-8/41, Church Stanton 8/41-12/41
Foreign Based: N/A
Reformed: N/A
Disbanded: N/A
Re-equipped: Church Stanton, November 1941 (Spitfire Mk Vb)
Variants Operated: Mk I, Mk IIA & Mk IIB

No. 317 (Wilenski) Squadron

Code: **JH**
Started Hurricane Operations: Acklington, 22nd February 1941
UK Based: Acklington 2/41-4/41, Ouston 4/41-6/41, Colerne 6/41, Fairwood Common 6/41-7/41, Exeter 7/41-4/42
Foreign Based: N/A
Reformed: N/A
Disbanded: N/A
Re-equipped: Exeter, October 1941 (Spitfire Mk Vb)
Variants Operated: Mk I, Mk IIA & MK IIB

No. 318 (Gdanski) Squadron

Code: **LW**
Started Hurricane Operations: Detling 4/43
UK Based: Detling 4/43-8/43
Foreign Based: Muqeibila 9/43-10/43, Gaza/LG's 10/43-2/44
Reformed: N/A
Disbanded: N/A
Re-equipped: Egypt 2/44 (Spitfire Mk Vc)
Variants Operated: Mk I & MK IIB

No. 331 (Norwegian) Squadron

Code: **FN**
Started Hurricane Operations: Catterick, 21st July 1941
UK Based: Catterick 7/41-8/41, Castletown 8/41-9/41, Skeabrae 9/41-5/42
Foreign Based: N/A
Reformed: N/A
Disbanded: N/A
Re-equipped: Skeabrae, November 1941
Variants Operated: Mk I & Mk IIB

No. 335 (Hellenic) Squadron

Code: **FG**
Started Hurricane Operations: Aqir, December 1941
UK Based: N/A
Foreign Based: Aqir 12/41, St. Jean 12/41-1/42, El Daba (L.G.20) 1/42-5/42, Gerawla (L.G.10) 5/42-6/42, El Daba 6/42, Idku 6/42-8/42, Dekheila 8/42-9/42, L.G.173 9/42-10/42, L.G.85 10/42, L.G.37 10/42-11/42, L.G.13 11/42, L.G.121 11/42-2/43, Mersa Matruh (L.G.08) 2/43-1/44
Reformed: N/A
Disbanded: N/A
Re-equipped: Mersa Matruh, January 1944 (Spitfire Mk Vb)
Variants Operated: Mk I, Mk IIB & Mk IIC

No. 336 (Hellenic) Squadron

Code: None
Started Hurricane Operations: L.G.219, 25th February 1943
UK Based: N/A
Foreign Based: L.G.129 2/43-4/43, Sidi Barrani (L.G.121) 4/43-1/44, El Adem 1/44-3/44, Bu Amoud 3/44-4/44, Mersa Matruh 4/44-7/44, El Adem 7/44-9/44
Reformed: N/A
Disbanded: N/A
Re-equipped: El Adem, August 1944
Variants Operated: Mk IIC

No. 351 (Yugoslav) Squadron

Code: None
Started Hurricane Operations: Benina, 1st July 1944
UK Based: N/A
Foreign Based: Benina 7/44-9/44, Canne 9/44-2/45, Prkos 2/45-6/45
Reformed: N/A
Disbanded: Transferred to the Yugoslavian Air Force, 15th June 1945
Re-equipped: N/A
Variants Operated: Mk IIC & Mk IV

No. 352 (Yugoslav) Squadron

Code: None
Started Hurricane Operations: Benina, 22nd April 1944
UK Based: N/A
Foreign Based: Benina 4/44-5/44, Lete 5/44-8/44
Reformed: N/A
Disbanded: N/A
Re-equipped: Lete, June 1944 (Spitfire Mk Vc)
Variants Operated: Mk IIC

Mk I, KW•E of No. 615 Sqn, about to land, 1940 *(© RAF Museum P014442)*

No. 401 (Ram) Squadron, RCAF
Code: **YO** & **ZH**
Started Hurricane Operations: Middle Wallop, 20th June 1940
UK Based: Middle Wallop 6/40-7/40, Croydon 7/40-8/40, Northolt 8/40-10/40, Prestwick 10/40, Castletown 10/40-2/41, Driffield 2/41, Digby 2/41-10/41 (inc 3/41 = re-numbered from No.1 Sqn (RCAF) to No. 401 (RCAF) Sqn)
Foreign Based: N/A
Reformed: N/A
Disbanded: N/A
Re-equipped: Digby, September 1941 (Spitfire Mk IIa)
Variants Operated: Mk I (Canadian-built) & Mk IIB

No. 402 (Winnipeg Bear) Squadron, RCAF
Code: **AE**
Started Hurricane Operations: Digby, 11th December 1940 from No. 2 Sqn, RCAF
UK Based: Digby 12/40-5/41 (inc 1/3/41 = re-numbered No. 402 (RCAF) Sqn), Wellingore 5/41-6/41, Martlesham Heath 6/41-7/41, Ayr 7/41-8/41, Rochford 8/41-11/41, Warmwell 11/41-3/42
Foreign Based: N/A
Reformed: N/A
Disbanded: N/A
Re-equipped: Warmwell, March 1942 (Spitfire Mk Vb)
Variants Operated: Mk I, Mk IIA & Mk IIB

No. 417 (City of Windsor) Squadron, RCAF
Code: **AN**
Started Hurricane Operations: Shandur, September 1942
UK Based: N/A
Foreign Based: Shandur 9/42-10/42, Edku 10/42-1/43
Reformed: N/A
Disbanded: N/A
Re-equipped: Edku, January 1943
Variants Operated: Mk IIB & Mk IIC

No. 438 (Wild Cat) Squadron, RCAF
Code: **F3**
Started Hurricane Operations: Bournemouth, 15th November 1943 (from No. 118 Sqn, RCAF)
UK Based: Digby 11/43-12/43, Wittering 12/43-1/44, Ayr 1/44-3/44, Hurn 3/44-4/44
Foreign Based: N/A
Reformed: N/A
Disbanded: N/A
Re-equipped: Hurn, April 1944
Variants Operated: Mk IV

No. 439 (Fangs of Death) Squadron, RCAF
Code: **5V**
Started Hurricane Operations: Bournemouth, 1st January 1944 (moving to Wellingore on the same day)
UK Based: Wellingore 1/44, Ayr 1/44-3/44, Hurn 3/44-4/44, Funtington 4/44, Hurn 4/44-5/44
Foreign Based: N/A
Reformed: N/A
Disbanded: N/A
Re-equipped: Hurn, April 1944 (Typhoon Mk Ib)
Variants Operated: Mk IV

No. 440 (City of Ottawa) Squadron, RCAF
Code: **BV** & **I8**
Started Hurricane Operations: Bournemouth. 1st February 1944 (from No. 111 Sqn, RCAF)
UK Based: Ayr 2/44-3/44, Hurn 3/44-4/44
Foreign Based: N/A
Reformed: N/A
Disbanded: N/A
Re-equipped: Hurn, March 1944 (Typhoon Mk Ib)
Variants Operated: Sea Hurricane Mk X & Hurricane Mk IV

Mk IIC of No. 601 Squadron, 1941 *(© RAF Museum P012507)*

No. 450 Squadron, RAAF
Code: **OK** & **PD**
Started Hurricane Operations: Abu Seir, May 1941
UK Based: N/A
Foreign Based: Abu Seir 5/41-6/41, Amman 6/41-7/41, Damascus 7/41, Haifa 7/41-8/41, El Bassa 8/41, Rayak 8/41-10/41, Damascus 10-41-11/41, Burg el Arab 11/41-12/41, Qassasin 12/41
Reformed: N/A
Disbanded: N/A
Re-equipped: Qassasin, December 1941 (Kittyhawk Mk I)
Variants Operated: Mk I

No. 451 Squadron, RAAF
Code: **BQ**
Started Hurricane Operations: Idku, 12th February 1943
UK Based: N/A
Foreign Based: Idku 2/43-8/43, El Daba 8/43-2/44
Reformed: N/A
Disbanded: N/A
Re-equipped: El Daba, October 1943 (Spitfire Mk Vc)
Variants Operated: Mk IIC

No. 486 Squadron, RNZAF
Code: **SA**
Started Hurricane Operations: Kirton-in-Lindsey, 3rd March 1942
UK Based: Kirton-in-Lindsey 3/42-4/42, Wittering 4/42-9/42
Foreign Based: N/A
Reformed: N/A
Disbanded: N/A
Re-equipped: Wittering, July 1942 (Typhoon Mk Ib)
Variants Operated: Mk IIB

No. 488 Squadron, RNZAF
Code: **NF**
Started Hurricane Operations: Kallang, January 1942
UK Based: N/A
Foreign Based: Kallang 1/42, en route to Batavia 1/42-2/42, Tjililitan 2/42, en route to Australia 2/42
Reformed: N/A
Disbanded: Australia, February 1942
Re-equipped: N/A
Variants Operated: Mk I

No. 501 (City of Gloucester) Squadron, RAuxAF
Code: **SD**
Started Hurricane Operations: Filton, March 1939
UK Based: Filton 3/39-11/39, Tangmere 11/39-5/40, Croydon 6/40-7/40, Middle Wallop 7/40, Gravesend 7/40-8/40, Kenley 8/40-12/40, Filton 12/40-4/41, Colerne 4/41-6/41
Foreign Based: Bethieneville 5/40, Anglure 5/40-6/40, Le Mans 6/40, Dinard 6/40
Reformed: N/A
Disbanded: N/A
Re-equipped: Colerne, June 1941 (Spitfire Mk IIa)
Variants Operated: Mk I

No. 504 (County of Nottingham) Squadron, RAuxAF
Code: **TM**
Started Hurricane Operations: Hucknall, August 1939
UK Based: Hucknall 8/39-9/39, Digby 9/39-10/39, debden 10/39-5/40, Wick 5/40-6/40, Castletown 6/40-9/40, Catterick 9/40, Hendon 9/40, Filton 9/40-12/40, Exeter 12/40-7/41, Fairwood Common 7/41-8/41, Chilbolton 8/41-1/42
Foreign Based: Lille/Marcq 5/40, Norrent Fontes 5/40
Reformed: N/A
Disbanded: N/A
Re-equipped: Chilbolton, November 1941 (Spitfire Mk IIb)
Variants Operated: Mk I & Mk IIB

No. 530 (Turbinlite) Squadron
Code: None
Started Hurricane Operations: Hunsdon, September 1942
UK Based: Hunsdon 9/42-1/43
Foreign Based: N/A
Reformed: N/A
Disbanded: Hunsdon, 25th January 1943
Re-equipped: N/A
Variants Operated: Mk I

No. 531 (Turbinlite) Squadron (No. 1452 Flight)
Code: None
Started Hurricane Operations: West Malling, May 1942
UK Based: West Malling 5/42-10/42, Debden 10/42, West Malling 10/42-1/43
Foreign Based: N/A
Reformed: N/A
Disbanded: West Malling, 31st January 1943
Re-equipped: N/A
Variants Operated: Mk IIC

No. 532 (Turbinlite) Squadron (No. 1453 Flight)
Code: None
Started Hurricane Operations: Wittering, 10th July 1941
UK Based: Wittering 7/41-9/42, Hibaldstow 9/42-3/43
Foreign Based: N/A
Reformed: N/A
Disbanded: Hibaldstow, 1st February 1943
Re-equipped: N/A
Variants Operated: Mk IIC (& Mk XII)

No. 533 (Turbinlite) Squadron (No. 1454 Flight)
Code: None
Started Hurricane Operations: Colerne, 4th July 1941
UK Based: Colerne 7/41-1/42, Charmy Down 1/42-1/43
Foreign Based: N/A
Reformed: N/A
Disbanded: Charmy Down, 25th January 1943
Re-equipped: N/A
Variants Operated: Mk IIC (& Mk XIB)

No. 534 (Turbinlite) Squadron (No. 1455 Flight)
Code: None
Started Hurricane Operations: Tangmere, 7th July 1941
UK Based: Tangmere 7/41-1/43
Foreign Based: N/A
Reformed: N/A
Disbanded: Tangmere, 25th January 1943
Re-equipped: N/A
Variants Operated: Mk IIC, Mk X & Mk XIB

No. 535 (Turbinlite) Squadron (No. 1456 Flight)
Code: None
Started Hurricane Operations: Honiley, 24th Nov 1941
UK Based: Honiley 11/41-6/42, High Ercall 6/42-9/42
Foreign Based: N/A
Reformed: N/A
Disbanded: Renumbered No. 535 Squadron, 2/9/42
Re-equipped: N/A
Variants Operated: Mk IIC

No. 536 (Turbinlite) Squadron (No. 1457 Flight)
Code: None
Started Hurricane Operations: Colerne, 15th Sept 1941
UK Based: Colerne 9/41-11/41, Predannack 11/41-9/42
Foreign Based: N/A
Reformed: N/A
Disbanded: Renumbered No. 536 Squadron, 8/9/42
Re-equipped: N/A
Variants Operated: Mk IIC

No. 537 (Turbinlite) Squadron (No. 1458 Flight)
Code: None
Started Hurricane Operations: Middle Wallop, 9th December 1941
UK Based: Middle Wallop 12/41-1/43
Foreign Based: N/A
Reformed: N/A
Disbanded: Middle Wallop 25th January 1943
Re-equipped: N/A
Variants Operated: Mk IIC, Mk XII

No. 538 (Turbinlite) Squadron (No. 1459 Flight)
Code: None
Started Hurricane Operations: Hunsdon, 20th Sept 1941
UK Based: Hunsdon 9/41, Hibaldstow 9/41-1/43
Foreign Based: N/A
Reformed: N/A

Disbanded: Hibaldstow, 25th January 1943
Re-equipped: N/A
Variants Operated: Mk IIC

No. 539 (Turbinlite) Squadron (No. 1460 Flight)
Code: None
Started Hurricane Operations: Acklington, 15th December 1941
UK Based: Acklington 12/41-1/43
Foreign Based: N/A
Reformed: N/A
Disbanded: Acklington, 25th January 1943
Re-equipped: N/A
Variants Operated: Mk IIC & Mk X

No. 601 (County of London) Squadron, RAuxAF
Code: **UF**
Started Hurricane Operations: Tangmere, February 1940
UK Based: Tangmere 2/40-6/40, Middle Wallop 6/40, Tangmere 6/40-8/40, Debden 8/40-9/40, Tangmere 9/40, Exeter 9/40-12/40, Northolt 12/40-5/41, Manston 5/41-6/41, Matlaske 6/41-8/41, Duxford 8/41-1/42
Foreign Based: N/A
Reformed: N/A
Disbanded: N/A
Re-equipped: Duxford, January 1942 (Bell P-39)
Variants Operated: Mk I & Mk IIB

No. 605 (County of Warwick) Squadron, RAuxAF
Code: **ML**
Started Hurricane Operations: Tangmere, August 1939
UK Based: Tangmere 8/39-2/40, Leuchars 2/40, Wick 2/40-5/40, Hawkinge 5/40, Drem 5/40-9/40, Croydon 9/40-2/41, Martlesham Heath 2/41-3/41, Ternhill 3/41-5/41, Baginton 5/41-9/41, Kenley 9/41-10/41, Sealand 10/41-12/41
Foreign Based: en route to the Far East 12/41-1/42, Palembang 1/42, Seletar 1/42, Tjililitan 1/42-3/42, Andir 3/42, Tasik Majala 3/42, Hal Far 1/42-2/42, Ta Kali 2/42-3/42
Reformed: Hal Far, Jan 1942
Disbanded: Captured by Japanese, 1942. Ta Kali, 27th February 1942
Re-equipped: N/A
Variants Operated: Mk I, Mk IIA & Mk IIB

No. 607 (County of Durham) Squadron, RAuxAF
Code: **AF**
Started Hurricane Operations: Usworth, June 1940
UK Based: Usworth 6/40-9/40, Tangmere 9/40-10/40, Turnhouse 10/40-11/40, Drem 11/40-12/40, Usworth 12/40-1/41, Macmerry 1/41-3/41, Drem 3/41-4/41, Manston 10/41-3/42
Foreign Based: en route to India 3/42-5/42, Alipore 5/42-8/42, Jessore 8/42-12/42, Feni 12/42-1/43, Chittagong 1/43-4/43, Alipore 4/43-10/43, Amarda Road 10/43, Alipore 10/43-11/43, Ramu 11/43-2/44
Reformed: N/A
Disbanded: N/A
Re-equipped: Ramu, December 1943
Variants Operated: Mk I, Mk IIA, Mk IIB & Mk IIC

A group photograph of Officers of No. 504 Sqn in front of Mk I, AW•O *(© RAF Museum P010543)*

No. 610 (County of Chester) Squadron, RAuxAF
Code: **DW**
Started Hurricane Operations: Hooton Park, September 1939
UK Based: Hooton Park 9/39
Foreign Based: N/A
Reformed: N/A
Disbanded: N/A
Re-equipped: Hooton Park, September 1939 (Spitfire Mk I)
Variants Operated: Mk I

No. 615 (County of Surrey) Squadron, RAuxAF
Code: **KW**
Started Hurricane Operations: Virty, April 1940
UK Based: Kenley 5/40-8/40, Prestwick 8/40-10/40, Northolt 10/40-12/40, Kenley 12/40-4/41, Valley 4/41-9/41, Manston 9/41-11/41, Angle 11/41-1/42, Farwood Common 1/42-3/42
Foreign Based: Virty 4/40, Poix 4/40, Abbeville 4/40-5/40, en route to India 3/42-6/42, Jessore 6/42-12/42, Feni 12/42-5/43, Alipore 5/43-11/43
Reformed: N/A
Disbanded: N/A
Re-equipped: Alipore, September 1943
Variants Operated: Mk I, Mk IIA, Mk IIB & Mk IIC

NAVAL HURRICANES

The squadrons of the Royal Navy which used the Sea Hurricane
No. 800 Squadron
No. 801 Squadron
No. 802 Squadron
No. 804 Squadron
No. 806 Squadron
No. 824 Squadron
No. 835 Squadron
No. 877 Squadron (Shore based - Tanganyika)
No. 880 Squadron
No. 881 Squadron
No. 882 Squadron
No. 883 Squadron
No. 885 Squadron
No. 891 Squadron
No. 895 Squadron (Shore based - Stretton)
No. 897 Squadron (Shore based - Stretton)

Other Units which used the Hurricane

ARMY

Anti-aircraft Co-operation and Calibration Units
No. 116 Squadron (Code: **I1**)
Hendon/Heston/Croydon Nov 1941-Jul 1944 (Mk I/IIA)
North Weald/Gatwick/Redhill/Hornchurch Jul 1944-May 1945 (Mk I/IIA)
No. 516 Squadron
Dundonald Dec 1943-Dec 1944 (Mk IIB/IIC)
No. 527 Squadron (Code: **WN**)
Castle Camps/Snailwell/Digby Jun 1943-Apr 1945 (Mk I/IIB)
No. 567 Squadron
Detling/Hornchurch Dec 1943-Jun 1945 (Mk IV)
No. 577 Squadron
Castle Bromwich Dec 1943-Jul 1945 (Mk IIC/IV)
No. 587 Squadron (Code: **M4**)
Weston Zoyland/Culmhead Dec 1943-Jul 1945 (Mk IIC/IV)
No. 595 Squadron
Aberporth Dec 1943-Dec 1944 (Mk IIC/IV)
No. 598 Squadron
Peterhead/Bircham Newton Feb 1944-Apr 1945 (Mk IIC/IV)
No.631 Squadron (Code: **6D**)
Towyn/Llanbedr Mar 1944-Jul 1945 (Mk IIC)
No. 639 Squadron
Cleave Aug 1944-Apr 1945 (Mk IV)
No. 650 Squadron
Cark/Bodorgan Apr 1944-Jun 1945 (Mk IV)
No. 667 Squadron
Gosport Apr 1944-Jul 1945 (Mk I/IIC)
No. 679 Squadron (Code: **3M**)
Ipswich Dec 1943-Jun 1945 (Mk IIC/IV)
No. 691 Squadron
Roborough/Harrowbeer Dec 1943-Aug 1945 (Mk I/IIC)
No. 695 Squadron (Code: **4M**)
Bircham Newton Dec 1943-Aug 1945 (Mk IIC)

ROYAL AIR FORCE - OTHERS

RAF Silloth, Station Flight
RAF Northolt, Station Flight
RAF Cranwell, Station Flight
RAF Coningsby, Station Flight
RAF Waddington, Station Flight
RAF Waterbeach, Station Flight
Empire Central Flying School. Hullavington
No. 1 F.T. Flt., Lyneham
No. 5 (P) A.F.U
No. 9 (P) A.F.U
No. 9 F.T.S.
No. 15 (P) A.F.U
No. 17 (P) A.F.U
No.4 (C) F.PP (Ferry Pool)
No. 23 (Training) Group, Central Flying School
Advanced Training Pool, Andover
No. 11 Group, Andover
No. 55 O.C.U., Aston Down
No. 41 O.T.U.
No. 56 O.T.U., Sutton Bridge
No. 59 O.T.U.
No. 71 O.T.U., Middle East
No. 73 O.T.U.
No. 11 Group Pool, Andover
No. 208 (AC) Squadron
No. 231 Group Communications Flight
No. 279 (ASR) Squadron, Thornaby April 1945-Jun 1945 (Mk IIC & Mk IV)
No. 284 (ASR) Squadron, Tingley/El Aouina Sept 1944-Mar 1945 (Mk IIC)
No. 285 (ASR) Squadron, Woodvale/Andover/North Weald
Jan 1944-Jun 1945 (Mk IIC)
No. 286 (ASR) Squadron, Filton/Lulgate/Bottom/Colerne/Zeals/Locking
11/41-11/43, Weston/Zoyland/Culmhead/Colerne/Zeals 11/43-5/45
(Mk I, Mk IIC & Mk IV) (Code: NW)
No. 287 (ASR) Squadron, Croydon 11/41-2/44 (Mk I, Mk IIC & Mk IV)
(Code: **KZ**)
No. 288 (ASR) Squadron, Digby/Wellingore/Coleby/Grange/Collyweston
12/41-6/45 (Mk I, Mk IIC & Mk IV) (Code: **RP**)
No. 289 (ASR) Squadron, Kirknewton/Turnhouse/Acklington/ Eshott/Andover
12/41-6/45 (Mk I, Mk IIC & Mk IV) (Code: **KZ**)
No. 290 (ASR) Squadron, Newtownards/Long Kesh/Turnhouse
12/43-1/45 (Mk IIC)
No. 291 (ASR) Squadron, Hutton Cranswick 3/44-6/45 (Mk IIC) (Code: **8Q**)
No. 680 (PR) Squadron, Matariya Feb 1943-Dec 1944 (Mk I/IIB)
No. 681 (PR) Squadron, Dum Dum Jan-Sept 1943 (Mk IIB)
No. 2 P.R.U.
No. 518 Squadron (Meteorological Unit) Sept 1945-Oct 1946
No. 520 Squadron (Meteorological Unit) Jun 1944-May 1946
No. 521 Squadron (Meteorological Unit) Aug 1944-Feb 1946
No. 1414 Meteorological Flight
No. 1453 Meteorological Flight
No. 1423 Flight
No. 3 S. of T.T.
T.S.T.U., India
A.F.T.U., India
G.A.T.U., India

**Mk XII, JS290, WN•? of No. 527 Sqn, at RAF Digby
in 1944-45** (© RAF Museum P005008)

MAINTENANCE UNITS

No. 4 M.U.
No. 5 M.U., Kemble
No. 8 M.U., Little Rissington
No. 10 M.U.
No. 13 M.U., Henlow
No. 19 M.U., St. Athan
No. 20 M.U., Aston Down
No. 22 M.U., Silloth
No. 27 M.U.
No. 30 M.U., Sealand
No. 36 M.U.
No. 47 M.U., Sealand
No. 103 M.U.

GOVERNMENT & RESEARCH

T.R.E. Malvern
R.A.E. Franborough
A. & A.E.E. Boscombe Down

RAAF SQUADRONS

No. 3 Squadron
Berka/Benina/Got-es-Sultan/Maraua Feb-Apr 1941 (Mk I)
Martuba/Gaza East/Sdid Mahmoud/LG 79 Apr 1941 (Mk I)
Mersa Matruh/Sidi Haneish/Abourkir/Aqir Apr-May 1941 (Mk I)
Lydda/Nicosia May-Jul 1941 (Mk I)
No. 450 (RAAF) Squadron
Aqir/Amman/Mezze Jun-Jul 1941 (Mk I)
Haifa/El Bassa Jul-Aug 1941 (Mk I)
Rayak Aug-Oct 1941 (Mk I)
No. 451 (RAAF) Squadron
Qasaba/LG's/Sdid Azeiz/Maddalena/Heliopolis Jul 1941-Feb 1942 (Mk I)
Rayak Feb-Mar 1942 (Mk I)
Nicosia Mar-Jun 1942 (Mk I)
El Bassa/Lakatamia/St. Jean Jun 1942-Jan 1943 (Mk I)
Mersa Matruh/Idku/El Daba Jan-Oct 1943 (Mk I/IIC)
No. 2 Communication Flight
No. 3 Communication Flight

RCAF SQUADRONS

No. 1 (F) Squadron (renumbered No. 401 (RAM) Sqn in RAF service)
No. 111 Squadron (renumbered No. 440 Sqn in RAF service)
No. 112 Squadron (renumbered No. 2, then No. 402
(Winnipeg Bear) Sqn in RAF service)
No. 118 Squadron (renumbered No. 438 Sqn in RAF service)
No. 123 Squadron (renumbered No. 439 Sqn in RAF service)
No. 125 Squadron (Home Defence)
No. 126 Squadron (Home Defence)
No. 127 Squadron (Home Defence)
No. 128 Squadron (Home Defence)
No. 129 Squadron (Home Defence)
No. 130 Squadron (Home Defence)
No. 133 Squadron (Home Defence)
No. 135 Squadron (Home Defence)
No. 163 Squadron (Home Defence)

ROYAL EGYPTIAN AIR FORCE

No. 2 Squadron
Almaza/Idku/Mersa Matruh Jan 1944-Jan 1945 (Mk IIC)

ROYAL NEW ZEALAND AIR FORCE

No. 486 Squadron *See entry in Royal Air Force main section
No. 488 Squadron *See entry in Royal Air Force main section

Foreign Service

The following nations operated the Hurricane. Note that many of these
machines were surplus RAF and Canadian stock and they were refurbished
before delivery. Therefore there were a number of changes in the equipment
fitted to all of these machines.

BELGIUM

Belgian Air Force: Mk I (20 Ordered, 15 supplied):
L1918 (1), L1919 (2), L1920 (3), L1993 (4), L1994 (5), L1995 (6), L1996 (7),
L1997 (8), L2040 (9), L2041 (10), L2042 (11), L2043 (12), L2044 (13), L2015
(14), L2016 (15), L2107 (16), L2108 (17), L2109 (18), L2110 (19) & L2111
(20) (Belgian A.F. serial numbers in brackets). At least two others were licence-
built against Contract No. B655029/37
2e Escadrille, Groupe, 2e Regiment

EGYPT

Royal Egyptian Air Force
No.1 (FR) Squadron
No. 2 (FR) Squadron

FINLAND

Twelve machines were released from RAF production and supplied to Finland in
January 1940.
LeLv 22

FRANCE

Free French Air Force
Escadrille de Chasse No. 1
Escadrille de Chasse No. 2
Groupe de Chasse II/3

INDIA

Indian Air Force
No. 1 Squadron
Trichinopoly/Arkonam/Bairagarth.Chharra/Risalpur Sept1942-Jul 1943 (Mk I/IIB/IIC)
Kohar/Sinthe Jun 1943-Mar 1946 (Mk IIB/IIC)
No. 2 Squadron
Arkonam/Ranchi/Imphal/Trichinopoly Sept 1942-Nov 1943 (Mk IIB)
Kohat/Miranshah/Kalyan/Cox's Bazaar/Mambur Nov 1943-Feb 1945 (Mk IIB)
Akyab/Kohat/Samungli/Willingdon/Jodhpur/Raipur/Kohat
Feb 1945-Feb 1946 (Mk IIB)
No. 3 Squadron
Phaphamau/Bairagarh/Ranchi/Kohat/Miranshah Nov 1943-Jul 1944 (Mk IIB)
Bawli North/Dabaing I/Alipore/St. Thomas Mount/Risalpur Jan-Nov 1945 (Mk IIC)
No. 4 Squadron
Phaphamau/Bairagarh/Sulmur/Yelahanka Aug 1943-Feb 1944 (Mk IIC)
Ranchi/Feni/Cox's Bazaar/Madhaibun/Kyaukpyu/Yelahanka
Feb 1944-May 1945 (Mk IIC)
Iwakuni/Mihu Mar-Aug 1946 (Mk IIC)
No.6 Squadron
Trichinopolyu/Bairagarh/Cholavarum/Kajamalai/Kalyan Feb-Nov 1943 (Mk IIB/IIC)
Cox's Bazaar/Ratnap/Risalpur/Kohat Nov 1943-Nov 1945 (Mk IIB/IIC)
No. 7 Squadron
Peshawar/Kohat/Imphal/Sinthe/Magwe Nov 1944-May 1945 (Mk IIC)
Kohat/Hathazari/Samungli/Lahore/Maharajpur May 1945-Mar 1946 (Mk IIC)
No. 9 Squadron
Lahore/Bhopal/Kulaura/Amarda Road Jan-May 1944 (Mk IIC)
Kumbhirgram/Lanka/Dergaon/Comilla May-Jul 1944 (Mk IIC)
Singarbil/Hathazari/Ramu I/Akyab/Dabaing I/Ranchi Jul 1944-May 1945 (Mk IIC)
No. 10 Squadron
Lahore/Risalpur/Chharra Apr-Nov 1944 (Mk IIC)
Ranchi/Ramu/Ranree/Bawli/Kyaukpyu Nov 1944-Apr 1945 (Mk IIC)

IRELAND

Irish Air Corps. Acquired one which crash landed in Eire in 1942 and four
more ex-RAF Mk I's in 1943. A further seven more Mk I's and six Mk IIC's
were also supplied.

PERSIA

18 Mk I's ordered, only two supplied (L2079 (252) was shipped in 1939).
Remainder were supplied post-war (16 ex-RAF Mk IIC's)

POLAND

One ordered in March 1939 and supplied on the 24th July 1939 (L2079). A
further nine (N2322-N2324, N2327, N2349 and N2392-N2395) were ordered,
but Poland was overrun by the Germans before they could be delivered.

PORTUGAL

Fifteen Mk IIB's were supplied in August 1943 and issued to Esquadrilhas BA 2
(Ota) of the Arma da Aeronautica. A further 50 more (including Mk IIB &
Mk IIC's) were supplied before the end of the war.
Esquadrilhas BA 2 (Ota)
Esquadrilhas BA 3 (Tancos)
Lisbon Defence Squadron

ROMANIA

Romanian Air Force (Qty 12) Mk I; L2077, L2078, L2085, L2093 to L2097,
L2014 and L2112 to L2114. Delivery commenced 28/8/39.

RUSSIA

Soviet Naval Air Fleet (72nd Regiment): Mk IIB
Soviet Air Force (VVS): Mk IIA (Qty 210), Mk IIB, Mk XI & Mk XII (Qty 1557),
Mk IIC (Qty 1009) and Mk IV (100)

SOUTH AFRICA

South African Air Force (SAAF)
No. 1 Squadron
Eritrea/Somali/Ethiopia Dec 1940-Apr 1941 (Mk I)
Amriya/Sidi Haneish, South/Maaten Bagush/
SidiBarrini/Fuka Apr - Nov 1941 (Mk IIB)
LG's/Sidi Rezegh/Gazala/Derna Nov 1941- Jan 1942 (Mk IIB)
Gazala III/El Adem/Sidi Haneish/LG's/El Gamil/Idko Jan-Nov 1942 (Mk IIB/IIC)
No. 2 Squadron
No. 3 Squadron
Eritrea/Somali/Ethiopia Dec 1940-Apr 1941 (Mk I)
Khormaksar Jan-Apr 1943 (Mk I)
Helwan/Bersis/Zuara/Nellaha/Savoia/Amriya Apr-Mar 1944 (Mk I/IIB/IIC)
No. 7 Squadron
Amriya/LG's/El Bassa/K8/Sandur/Bernina/Bersis/Derna
May 1942-Aug 1943 (Mk I/IIB/IIC/IID)
No. 40 Squadron
Burg el Arab/LG's/Sidi Azeiz/Qassassin/El Firdan Jan-Nov 1942 (Mk I/IIB)
Sidi Azeiz/El Adem/Gazala II/Martuba/Tmimi/Magrun Nov-Dec 1942 (Mk IIB)
Belandah/Benina/Marble Arch/Alem el Gzina/Hamraiet
Dec 1942-Jan 1943 (Mk IIB)
Sedada/Darragh West/Castel Benito/El Assa/Nefatia/Bu Grara
Jan-Apr 1943 (Mk IIB)
Gabes Town/La Fauconnerie/Goubrine Apr-May 1943 (Mk IIB)
No. 41 Squadron
Almaza/Shandur/Bu Amud/El Adem/Savoia May 1943-May 1944 (Mk IIB/IIC)
No. 43 Squadron

TURKEY

15 Mk I's were ordered and delivered in 1939; L2125 to L2139 inclusive.
Further supplies of Mk IIC's were supplied under the terms of the Allied aid
agreement in 1942.

YUGOSLAVIA

Yugoslavian Air Force
Mk I (Qty 24): First batch of 12; L1751 (1-205), L1752 (2-206), L1837 (3-291),
L1838 (4-292), L1839 (5-0293), L1840 (6-294), L1858 (7-312), L1859
(8-313), L1860 (9-314), L1861 (10-315), L1862 (11-316), L1863 (12-317).
Yugoslavian A.F. serial numbers are shown in brackets.
N2718 to N2729 inclusive (Qty 12) were shipped in February and March 1940
Licence-built: Rogozarski (Qty 40) and Zmaj (Qty 60), only 20 from Zmaj were
delivered before the German invasion.
51st Squadron, 2nd Fighter Regiment
33rd Squadron, 4th Fighter Regiment
34th Squadron, 4th Fighter Regiment

Hurricane Chronology

1933

August

Sydney Camm discussed future RAF fighter requirements with the Directorate of Technical Development.

October

Initial design work for the creation of the Fury as a monoplane fighter were completed.

At the end of this year the Armament Research Division of the Air Ministry sponsored evaluation of various machine guns for service adoption.

1934

The Rolls-Royce Goshawk was replaced by the new P.V.12.

August

Four-gun version of the F.5/34 monoplane tested at the National Physics Laboratory, Teddington, attaining a speed equivalent to 350mph.

17th November

The first drawings of the new F.36/34 Single-Seat Fighter - High Speed Monoplane were with the Experimental Shops at Hawker.

1935

By the beginning of this year the mock-up of the F.36/34 was completed.

10th January

Conference held at Canbury Park Road, Kingston, to view the mock-up.

21st February

First performance data released on the F.36/34.

21st February

Hawker received the Air Ministry manufacturing contract for the prototype (K5083).

April

By the beginning of this month ballast equating to two Vickers Mk V guns (fuselage) and two Colt machine guns (wing) would be installed in the prototype.

July

Changes to the armament of the F.34/36 were brought about by a license agreement between Birmingham Small Arms and Colt.

23rd October

The prototype was moved by road from the Canbury Park plant to Brooklands for assembly.

6th November

Flt Lt P.W.S. 'George' Bulman took the prototype on its first flight.

11th November

The second flight of K5083 took place.

23rd November

Third test flight.

26th November

Fourth test flight.

1936

5th February

Trouble with the engine during test flying this day resulted in the replacement of the 11th Merlin 'C' by the 15th.

7th February

All modifications specified during the initial test flying had been introduced on K5083 by this date. Bulman satisfied that the prototype could undertake service evaluation.

18th - 24th February

Service testing undertaken at A&AEE Martlesham Heath.

March

The Production Drawing Office at Hawkers started work on the drawings for the Hurricane and the Production Planning Department created a draft schedule for an envisaged output of 1,000 machines.

3rd June

Hawker received a contract (527112/36) for 600 aircraft.

8th June

Manufacturing drawings were with the Production Shop.

27th June

The name 'Hurricane' was accepted by the Air Ministry for the Hawker F.36/34 design.

July

Air Defence of Great Britain became Fighter Command under the command of ACM Sir Hugh Dowding.

1937

January

Fighter Command had twenty-six regular regular (or auxiliary) fighter squadrons.

July

Sqn Ldr Anderson flew the prototype to the RAF Pageant at Hendon, where it was shown to the public for the first time.

15th July

The prototype was modified, by the locking of the central flap section, and it was test flown in this new layout on this day.

August

The eight Browning machine guns were installed for the first time in the prototype.

September & October

The Prototype undertook further service trials at Martlesham Heath.

December

Around Christmas No. 111 Squadron at Northolt were the first recipients of the Hurricane.

1938

Early in this year an order for twelve Hurricanes was placed by the Yugoslavian government.

February

By the end of this month No. 111 Squadron at RAF Northolt had received 24 Hurricanes.

10th February

Sqn Ldr John W. Gillan made a high-speed flight from Northolt to Turnhouse and back in just 48 minutes at an average speed of 408.75mph.

April

No.3 Squadron at Kenley were the second unit to receive the Hurricane.

7th March

The 3in extension to the rudder and addition of the ventral strake were incorporated in the production line for all subsequent Hurricanes at this time.

19th April

The first production Merlin II engine delivered to Hawkers and installed in the first production Hurricane Mk I (L1547).

Autumn

The Canadian government ordered twelve Mk Is.

November

Seven production Hurricanes were now flying and service acceptance began.

The South African government requested the release of seven Hurricane Mk Is for use by the SAAF.

The Rumanian government requested the supply of twelve Hurricanes.

15th December

The first aircraft (L1751) was delivered to Yugoslavia.

1939

January

The D.H. Hamilton two-pitch three-blade metal propeller was installed into all machines after L1780 during this month.

24th January

Flt Lt P. Lucas test flew G-AFXX with the new Rotol three-blade propeller installed for the first time.

February

The Air Staff considered tropicalising the Hurricane for the first time during this month.

The first of six Hurricanes sent to Canada were assembled at Vancouver.

March

Production Scheme F of 1936 had called for 500 Hurricanes to be in service by this date.

British and French government agreed to supply aid to Poland.

Mk I's of No. 601 Squadron being re-armed at Tangmere in 1940 *(© C.E. Brown)*

2nd March

The pattern aircraft (L1848) was sent to Canada.

April

The Belgium government placed an order for twenty Hurricanes.

28th April

The first metal wing Hurricane (L1877) was test flown by Flt Lt P. Lucas.

17th May

The first 'tropical' Hurricane (L1669) was test flown by Flt Lt P. Lucas.

July

A Mk I, L1856, was tested during this month with the Merlin VIII (R.M.3S) by Rolls-Royce.

27th August

The first Hurricane was delivered to Rumania.

September

By this time 497 Hurricanes had been delivered to the RAF.

3rd September

War declared.

8th September

No.1 Squadron arrived in France (Le Harve).

10th September

No.1 Squadron flew on to Cherbourg.

15th September

No.1 Squadron arrived at their new base; Vassincourt.

30th October

Plt Off Mould in L1842 attacked and shot down a Do 17 near Toul.

1st November

Fg Off E.J. 'Cobber' Cain scores the first victory for No. 73 Squadron.

1940

Early in this year a number of Hurricanes were delivered to Finland.

January

Increased armament in the Hurricane was proposed by Hawker.

February

The existing TR.9D radio installation in the Hurricane was upgraded to the TR.1133.

The additional twelve machines ordered by the

Yugoslavian government commenced delivery during this month.

March

No. 17 Squadron were the first to re-equip with the TR.1133 Mk Is.

12th March

Finland signed a peace treaty with Russia.

6th April

Germany invaded Yugoslavia.

9th April

Germany attacked Norway.

14th April

The remaining Hurricanes operated by the Royal Yugoslavian Air Force were destroyed on the ground.

May

No. 46 Squadron went to Norway.

10th May

Germany began its invasion of Holland, Belgium and Luxemberg. Hurricane squadrons No. 3, 79 and 504 sent to reinforce the Air Component.

15th May

Holland capitulates.

17th May

Only three squadrons of the Air Component remained fully operational.

21st May

The Air Component returned to England.

26th May

The Dunkirk evacuation began.

June

Hawker's own Hurricane, G-AFXX, was tested with the Merlin 45 (R.M.4S).

3rd June

British forces evacuation from Narvik began.

4th June

The Dunkirk evacuation ended.

5th June

Luftwaffe started attacks on the south-eastern coast of England.

7th June

Evacuation of British forces for Narvik completed.

A Mk I with a pair of Oerlikon cannon in each wing was test flown for the first time by Hawker.

11th June

P3269 fitted with the Merlin XX and Rotol R.X.5/2 propeller.

18th June

All remaining Hurricanes in France were ordered back to the UK.

August

1,373 Hurricanes had been produced since May.

2nd August

HMS Argus with her complement of Hurricanes set out for Malta.

10th August

Adlerangriff (Eagle Attack) set to start on this day.

12th August

The radar station at Ventnor on the Isle of Wight was attacked and remained out of action until the 23rd.

16th August

Flt Lt J.B. Nicholson of No. 249 Squadron was awarded the Victoria Cross.

17th August

The second shipment of Hurricanes on HMS Argus for Malta was a disaster, with most of the aircraft having to ditch short of the island due to lack of fuel.

Mk IIC, V6931, DZ•D of No. 151 Sqn at Wittering in 1941 *(© RAF Museum P002214)*

19th August
The Mk I with four Oerlikon cannons installed was issued to No. 151 Squadron, RAF North Weald.

24th August
Takoradi set up as a sea terminus for the shipment of aircraft to the Middle East.

1st September
No.1 (RCAF) and No. 303 (Polish) Squadrons joined the battle, both flying Hurricanes.

4th September
Deliveries of the first 120 Mk IIA Series 1's commenced to the RAF.

5th September
The first shipment of six Hurricanes arrived at Takoradi.

6th September
HMS Argus arrived at Takoradi with twelve Hurricanes fitted with tropical filters.

15th September
The zenith of the Battle of Britain.

26th September
Hitler cancelled his invasion plans for England.

October
Production of the revised Mk IIA Series 2 began at Langley and Brooklands.

The Directorate of Research and Development (Air) approached Hawker to see if catapult equipment could be added to the Hurricane.

8th October
The first 'Eagle Squadron, No. 71, formed at Kirton-in-Lindsey.

28th October
Italy attacked Greece via Albania.

November
The twelve-gun wing introduced in the production lines, thereby becoming the Mk IIB.

6th November
No. 73 Squadron sent to the Middle East.

December
No. 208 (Army Co-operation) Squadron received its first Tac R Mk I.

5th December
The first flight of the V7360 fitted with new 'cannon wing'.

1941

January
Three Gladiator squadrons (No's. 33, 80 & 112) transferred to Greece.

19th January
Decision made to fit the Hurricane for CAM-ship operations. An order for twenty conversion sets placed from Hawker by the Admiralty.

6th February
First flight of V2461, the prototype Mk IIC.

7th February
Hurricanes allocated to No. 80 Squadron, where they became B Flight under the command of Flt Lt M. St. J. Pattle.

March
A converted Hurricane with arrester hook and catapult spools passed to Farnborough for evaluation.

1st March
Germany invaded Bulgaria.

April
Twelve Mk IIs delivered to No. 261 Squadron on Malta.

6th April
Germany attacks Yugoslavia.

17th April
All allied forces in Greece had retreated to Athens.

18th April
Mk I P2989 fitted with racks to carry two 250lb bombs flew for the first time at Boscombe Down.

19th April
Just 22 Hurricanes remained serviceable in Greece.

20th April
Flt Lt M. St. J. Pattle killed during an air battle over Piraeus, Greece.

22nd-23rd April
All British aircraft ordered out of Greece, to Crete or Egypt.

27th April
More Hurricanes arrived on Malta.

30th April
Power in Iraq seized by Rashid Ali.

30th April - 5th May
Iraqi forces attacked RAF Habbaniyah, Iraq.

May
The Air Ministry approached Hawker to ask if the new 40mm cannon from Vickers could be carried by the Hurricane.

By this time there were twenty-nine squadrons operating 'Rhubarb' sweeps over Europe.

8th May
Another stock of Hurricanes arrived on Malta.

12th May
A new squadron, No.185, formed on Malta.

16th May
RAF Habbaniyah attacked by Luftwaffe He 111's.

17th May
No. 94 squadron and its Hurricanes and Gladiators arrived at Habbaniyah.

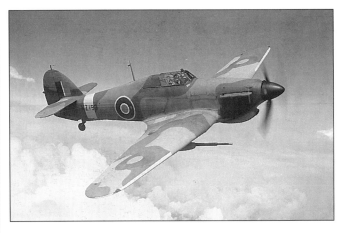

An in-flight shot of Mk V, KZ193 taken near Langley on the 11th August 1943 (© C.E. Brown)

19th May
Just four Hurricanes remained serviceable on Crete.

21st May
Four additional Hurricanes supplied to No. 94 Squadron.

21st May
No. 251 Squadron arrived on Malta.

25th May
Force assembled to eliminate any threat that the pro-Vichy regime in Syria might offer.

31st May
Crete was in German hands.

June
No. 2 Photographic Reconnaissance Unit formed at Heliopolis during this month.

The first Mk IIC arrived on Malta.

First convoy protected by a Fighter Catapult Ship (HMS Maplin) set off.

1st June
The Regent was returned to the capital of Iraq.

8th June
Ground assault against the pro-Vichy regime in Syria began.

18th June
The Hurricat on HMS Maplin was launched on the first interception.

22nd June
Germany attacked Russia.

25th June
Finland declared war on Russia.

July
Four Hurricanes sent to No. 98 Squadron, Iceland. Later these machines became No. 1423 Flight.

10th July
The Allied forces had the pro-Vichy forces in Syria trapped.

14th July
Vichy forces in Syria surrendered.

August
No. 1423 Flight was reinforced with another five Hurricanes.

12th August
No. 81 and No. 134 squadrons were formed into No. 151 Wing at RAF Leconfield.

21st August
No. 81 and No. 134 Squadron embarked and set-sail for Russia on HMS Argus.

28th August
Nos. 81 and No.134 Squadrons arrived on HMS Argus at Murmansk.

7th September
Twenty-four Hurricanes arrived at Vaenga after disembarking from HMS Argus.

12th September
Remaining Hurricanes that had arrived crated at Archangel, were flown into Vaenga from Keg Ostrov.

18th September
Mk II Z2326 flown for the first time with a pair of Vickers 40mm 'S' cannon installed.

November
By the end of this month the pilots and ground crew of No. 81 and No. 134 Squadrons had returned to the UK from Russia.

1st November
First operational launch of a Sea Hurricane from a CAM-ship (HMS Empire Foam).

18th November
Operation Crusader to relieve Tobruk started.

December
Luftflotte 2 moved from Russia to Rome and started operations against Malta.

7th December
Japan entered the war when they attacked the American fleet at Pearl Harbor.

19th December
No. 1423 Flight disbanded.

23rd December
Japanese forces attacked Burma. Hurricanes delivered to support No. 67 Squadron.

1942

January
Rommel counter-attacked in North Africa.

First Sea Hurricane Mk IC joined No. 811 Squadron.

3rd January
Fifty-one Hurricanes had arrived at Singapore.

19th January
The fifty-one Hurricanes at Singapore were eventually uncrated.

28th January
Only twenty of the fifty-one Hurricanes in Singapore were left.

10th February
The remaining seven Hurricanes in Singapore were withdrawn to Sumatra.

11th February
Just fifteen Hurricanes remained in Burma.

10-14th February
No, 226 (F) Squadron formed on Sumatra and thirty-three more Mk IIA's flown off of HMS Indomitable as replacements.

14th February
Japanese attacked Sumatra.

18th February
Only twenty-five Hurricanes remained in Sumatra.

23rd February
Mk IIA Z2415 flew for the first time with full armament and eight rocket projectiles.

March
First Spitfires arrived on Malta.

5th March
Just six Hurricanes remained in Burma.

7th March
Just two Hurricanes remained in Sumatra.

8th March
Rangoon was captured by Japanese forces.

12th March
The remains of No. 67 Squadron flew to Akyab.

20th March
Japanese forces landed 200 miles south of Magwe.

22nd March
Japanese forces attacked Magwe and destroyed it, leaving just five Hurricanes intact. These machines retreated to Akyab.

April
By the end of this month only eighteen Hurricanes remained on Malta.

During this month No. 261 and No. 30 Squadrons returned to Burma off HMS Indomitable.

No. 267 Squadron at Heliopolis was operating at least one Hurricane for communication duties.

26th April
The first Russian route convoy with CAM-ship (HMS Empire Morn) protection set sail.

May
Hawker undertook the first true Sea Hurricane Mk IIC was conversion (BD787).

June
By the end of this month the German advance had been halted by the Eighth Army at El Alamein.

Eleven squadrons re-equipping or formed with the Hurricane in India.

July
By the end of this month all the Hurricanes remaining in the three squadrons on Malta had been replaced by Spitfires.

19th August
Dieppe raid.

September
No. 95 Squadron at Sierra Leone was operating a Hurricane for communications duties.

October
The Eight Army was ready to counter-attack from El Alamein.

8th November
British and American troops landed on the French Moroccan and Algerian coats during 'Operation Torch'.

December
Japanese launched a number of raids on Calcutta.

1943

January
The prototype Mk IV was nearing completion.

14th March
The prototype Mk IV, KX405, flew for the first time.

23rd March
The second prototype Mk IV, KZ193, flew for the first time.

28th April
No. 516 (Combined Operations) Squadron formed at Dundonald.

May
The ground forces in the west of Burma were forced to retreat.

13th May
All enemy action in Tunisia stopped.

July
Two Hurricanes that had landed in Eire were returned to the UK in exchange for three Mk Is.

August
Hurricanes passed to equip No. 6 Squadron, Indian Air Force at Trichinopoly.

No. 1413 Flight at Lydda used Hurricanes on Meteorological duties for the first time.

November
The second assault into Burma was undertaken by XV Corps, supported heavily by Hurricane squadrons.

1944

February
XV Corps assault into Burma was halted.

March
No. 516 Squadron was undertaking reconnaissance work prior to the D-Day landings.

16th March
Japanese forces had laid siege to Imphal.

29th March
No. 6 Squadron used the rocket-armed Mk IV for the first time operationally in Albania.

May
The second Chindit expedition into Burma began.

June
No. 516 Squadron re-equipped with the N.A. Mustang.

October
No. 6 Squadron was joined in the Balkans by No. 351 (Yugoslav) Squadron.

1945

By the beginning of 1945 the Sea Hurricane had been totally replaced in the Naval inventory.

20th March
Mandalay fell to Allied forces.

3rd May
26th Indian Division entered Rangoon.

June 1945
No. 351 (Yugoslav) Squadron transferred to the re-constituted Yugoslav Air Force.

14th August
Japanese forces agreed to unconditional surrender.

1946

October
No. 6 Squadron in Palestine was the last operational RAF squadron operating the Hurricane (Mk IV).

1947

Hurricanes remained in service with the Irish Air Corps until this year.

The two-seat Hurricane Mk IIC conversion was delivered to the Persian Air Force at Doshan Teppeh during 1947.

1951

Hurricanes were operated by the Portuguese Air Force until this time. Later this year these machines came to the Uk to star in the film 'Angels One Five'.

1953

It is possible that a Mk XII remained airworthy with the Indian Air Force until this year.

Hurricane Production

Appendix IX

Prototype
Contract 357483/34 to Air Ministry Specification F.36/34
K5083 (first flown 6th November 1935)

600 ordered 3/6/36 (Hawker Built)
Production Specification 15/36
Mk I L1547-L2146, Contract Number 527112/36.
Merlin II, Watts two-blade propeller, fabric-covered wings. Delivered 15/12/37 to 6/10/39.
L2098 To No.55 O.C.U., Aston Down
L1910 & L2006 To No.56 O.T.U. Sutton Bridge
L2057 To No.71 O.T.U.
L2064, L2069, L2070, L2072-5 To No. 11 Group Pool, Andover
L1652 Crashed 1938 killing Hawker test pilot John Hindmarsh
L1708, L1710 & L1711 To South Africa via No. 36 M.U.
L1751 (l-205), L1752 (2-206), L1837 (3-291), L1838 (4-292), L1839 (5-293), L1840 (6-294), L1858 (7-312), L1859 (8-313), L1860 (9-314), L1861 (10-315), L1862 (11-316), L1863 (12-317) to Yugoslavia (Yugoslavian A.F. serials in brackets)
L2077, L2078, L2085, L2093 to 2097, L2104, L2112 to L2114 to Rumanian Air Force
L1759 (310), L1760 (311), L1761 (312), L1762 (313), L1763 (314), L1878 (315), L1879 (316), L1880 (317), L1881 (318), L1882 (319). L1883 (320) L1884 (321), L1885 (322), L1886 (323), L1887 (324), L1888 (325), L1890 (326), L2021 (327), L2022 (328), L2023 (329). Delivered to Canada, RCAF serials in brackets. L1848 delivered as pattern aircraft and L1884 returned to England, becoming the Hillson F.H.40 Slip-wing prototype.
L1918 (1), L1919 (20), L1920 (3), L1993 (4), L1994 (5), L1996 (7), L1997 (8), L2040 (9), L2041 (10), L2042 (11), L2043 (12), L2044 (13), L2105 (14), L2106 (15), L2107 (16), L2108 (17), 2109 (18), L2110 (19), L2111 (20) to Belgium, Belgian Air Force serials in brackets. 20 Aircraft delivered, of which 15 reached operational service.
L2048 to Poland (24/7/39)
L2079 (252) to Persia
L2125 to L2139 to Turkey (delivered 14/9/39 to 6/10/39)
L1547 performance and handling trials Hawker Aircraft Ltd
L1574 trials, Martlesham Heath
L1582 experimental colour schemes
L1606 returned from No.56 Sqn to Hawker Aircraft Ltd and refurbished as G-AFXX
L1638 hydraulic trials
L1669 tropical aicraft, to Rolls-Royce and then on to the Middle East for trials
L1695 propeller trials A&AEE
L1696 slootted wing trials A&AEE
L1702 trials at RAE
L1713 trials with RAE and later to Rolls-Royce
L1717 trials at RAE
L1750 extra armour and 20mm cannon trials
L1856 used as the Merlin XII trials aicraft
L1887 first Mk I fitted with metal skinned wings

300 ordered (Hawker Built)
Mk I N2318-N2367, N2380-N2409, N2422-N2441, N2453-N2502, N2520-N2559, N2582-N2631, N2645-N2729. Contract Number 751458/38.
Merlin III, de Havilland or Rotol three-blade variable-pitch propellers. The first 80 aircraft were delivered with fabric-covered wings but all subsequent aircraft had metal wings. Delivered 29/9/39 to 1/5/40.
N2322-N2324, N2327, N2349 & N2392-N2395 shipped to Poland (9/39), but these machines were diverted to the Middle East.
N2718 - N2729 to Yugoslavia (Feb/March 1940)
N2365, N2463 & N2469 to No.56 OTU
N2455, N2471 & N2555 to No.59 OTU
N2483 & N2674 to No.71 OTU
N2318 to Rolls-Royce for engine trials
N2359 to No.6 OTU
N2365 to No.9 (P) AFU
N2422 was the first production aicraft fitted with metal wings
N2460 to No.1510 Flight
N2488 to No.6 OTU
N2520 to No.55 OTU
N2541 for de-icing trials at Hawker Aircraft Ltd.
N2599 converted to Sea Hurricane Mk IA
N2646 hydraulic trials with Hawker Aircraft Ltd.
N2530 this machine was to be converted to a two seater under W/O 7522 and Contract Number 29838/39, but cancelled (10/1/40)
N2625 & N2626

500 ordered (Gloster Built)
Mk I P2535-P2584, P2614-P2653, P2672-P2701, P2713-P2732, P2751-P2770, P2793-P2836, P2854-P2888, P2900-P2924, P2946-P2995, P3020-P3069, P3080-P3124, P3140-P3179, P3200-P3234, P3250-P3264. Contract Number 962371/38/C.23a
Merlin III, de Havilland or Rotol three-blade variable-pitch propellers.
P2881, P2887 & P3146 to No.55 OTU
P2630, P2679, P2877, P3089, P3095 to No.59 OTU
P2640, P2641, P2948, P2987 to No.4 (C) FPP
P2638 - P2641, P2643 & P2651 converted to Tropical Mk I and send to Middle East via Takoradi
P2682 (DG641), P2829 (DR355), P2835 (DR353), P2682 (DG641), P2904 (DR357), P29008 (DR369), P2975 (DR372), P3023 (DR342), P3103 (DR340), P3106 (DR370) & P3151 (DR350) converted to Mk II Series I. Subsequent serial numbers in brackets.
P2968 to No.9 (P) ATU and No. 9 FTS
P2617 No.9 FTS
P2968 shipped to Eire to become '107' (2/44)
P3090 converted to Sea Hurricane Mk IA
P3218 No.5 (P) AFU
P3250 to No.71 OTU

A No. 6 Sqn Mk IID on the ground at Shandur in December 1942 *(© RAF Museum P013261)*

519 ordered
Mk I Z4022-Z4071, Z4085-Z4119, Z4161-Z4205, Z4223-Z4272, Z4308-Z4327, Z4347-Z4391, Z4415-Z4434, Z4482-Z4516, Z4532-Z4681, Z4603-Z4652, Z4686-Z4720, Z4760-Z4809, Z4832-Z4865.
Merlin III, de Havilland or Rotol three-blade variable-pitch propellers.
Z4093, Z4102, Z4113, Z4266, Z4380, Z4425, Z4491, Z4837 & Z4855 to No.71 OTU
Z4037 shipped to Eire (became '106') 7/43
Z4576 used to test a modified oil system by Gloster Aircraft Compnay
Z4646 used for modeified filter fairing trials by Gloster Aircraft Company and A&AEE
Z4770 used to test various propeller spinners.
Z4809 used to test various camouflage schemes by RAE
Z4838 used for night flying equipment trials at A&AEE and RAE

481 ordered
Mk IIA Series 2 & Mk IIB Z4866-Z4876, Z4920-Z4969, Z4987-Z5006, Z5038-Z5087, Z5117-Z5161, Z5202-Z5236, Z5252-Z5271, Z5302-Z5351, Z5376-Z5395, Z5434-Z5483, Z5529-Z5563, Z5580-Z5629, Z5649-Z5693.
Merlin XX, de Havilland or Rotol three-blade variable-pitch propellers. 140 completed as Mk IIAs, whilst the remaining 341 were Mk IIBs.
Z4924, Z4933, Z4964, Z5207 & Z5261 to No.71 OTU North Africa
Z5159, Z5210-Z5213, Z5227, Z5236, Z5259, Z5262, Z5263 & Z5480 sent to Russia, 1941-2
Z4866 used for performance and handling trials by Gloster Aircraft Compnay and A&AEE
Z4867, Z4922, Z4931 & Z5440 converted to Sea Hurricane Mk IA & Mk IB configuration
Z4993 & Z5390 used for a number of unspecified trials by RAE (1942-3)

449 ordered (Gloster Built)
Mk IIA, Mk IIB & Mk IIC BG674-BG723, BG737-BG771, BG783-BG832, BG844-BG888, BG901-BG920, BG933-BG977, BG990-BG999, BH115-BH154, BH167-BH201, BH215-Bh264, Bh277-BH296, BH312-BH360.
Merlin XX, de Havilland or Rotol three-blade variable-pitch propellers. 400 sent to Russia, while the remainder went to the Middle East.

500 ordered (Hawker Built)
Mk I P3295-P3279, P3300-P3324, P3345-P3364, P3380-P3429, P3448-P3492, P3515-P3554, P3574-P3623, P3640-P3684, P3700-P3739, P3755-P3789, P3802-P3836, P3854-P3893, P3902-P3944, P2960-P3984. Replacements; P8809-P8818, R2680-R2689, T9519-T9538, W667-W6670. Contract Number 962371/38.
Merlin II, de Havilland or Rotol three-blade variable-pitch propellers and metal wings. Delivered 21/2/40 to 20/7/40.
P3265 used for performance trials at Brooklands (1940)
P3269 this was the prototype Mk II fitted with a Merlin XX and used for tests with rear view hood
P3345 used for tests of various camouflage schemes
P3416 & P3898 used by No.9 (P) AFU P3416 was later shipped to Eire as'108'
P3462 used for tests with long range fuel tanks
P3463, P3524 & P3886 to No. 59 OTU
P3458 & P3459 to No. 55 OTU
P3620 converted by General Aircraft to a Sea Hurricane Mk IA
P3641 used for radio trials at TRE Malvern
P3705, P3723 & P3977 converted to Trop Mk Is and passed to No. 103 MU, North Africa
P3715 to No.17 (P) AFU
P3720 shipped to Iran as '252'
P3736 used for fuel consumption trials by Hawker Aircraft Ltd.
P3811 used for trials with 12 gun wing and various propellers.
P3820 & P3823 used for engine handling trials by Hawker Aircraft Ltd.
P3830 used by Hawker Aircraft Ltd in trials to improve rearward vision.
P3923 used for propeller trials by Hawker Aircraft Ltd.
P3967 & P3970 converted to Trop Mk Is and shipped to Takoradi in 1940.
P3702, P3715 & P3881 to No.4 (C) FPP, June 1940.

500 ordered (Hawker Built)
Mk I V7200-V7209, V7221-V7260, V7276-V7318, V7337-V7386, V7400-V7446, V7461-V7510, V7533-V7572, V7588-V7627, V7644-V7690, V7705-V7737, V7741-V7780, V7795-V7838, V7851-V7862, AS987-AS990. Contract Number 62305/39.
Merlin III, de Havilland or Rotol three-blade variable-pitch propellers and metal wings. Delivered 2/7/40 to 5/2/41.
V7856, V7858-V7862, AS989 & AS990 to RAF Abbotsinch 1st February 1941. AS990 was the last Hawker-built Mk I delivered to the RAF.
V7249 used in de-icing trials by Hawker Aircraft Ltd.
V7260 used for trial installation of four 20mm gun armament in July 1940
V7338 used by the Station Flight, RAF Silloth.
V7299, V7477 & V7482 via Takoradi to Middle East, December 1940.
V7366 & V7462 to No. 59 OTU, December 1943
V7480 used for a number of trials by Boscombe Down, March 1941.
V7504 converted at Speke to catapult launch machine, 14/3/42.
V7540 to Eire, July 1943 (became '105')
V7670 captured by the Germans, intact in March 1941, later recaptured by British troops at Gambut airfield

1,000 ordered (Hawker Built)
Mk II Z2308-Z2357, Z2382-Z2426, Z2446-Z2465, Z2479-Z2528, Z2560-Z2594, Z2624-Z2643, Z2661-Z2705, Z2741-Z2775, Z2791-Z2840, Z2882-Z2931, Z2959-Z2993, Z3017-Z3036, Z2050-Z3099, Z3143-Z3187, Z3221-Z3270, Z3310-Z3359, Z3385-Z3404, Z3431-Z3470, Z3489-Z3523, Z3554-Z3598, Z3642-Z3691, Z3470-Z3784, Z3826-Z3845, Z3885-Z3919 and Z3969-Z4018. Contract Number 62305/39.
Merlin XX, de Havilland or Rotol three-blade variable-pitch propellers and metal wings. Delivered 14/1/41 to 28/7/41.
Presentation Aircraft: Z2661-Z2705 (Z2705 'Bahamas'), Z2791-Z2840 (Z2840 'McConnell's Squadron'), Z2882-Z2931 (Z2899 'McConnell's Squadron')
Z2320/G & Z3092/G used at Boscombe Down for rocket projectile trials, April 1941.
Z2326 used at Boscombe Down for Rolls-Royce BF and Vickers 'S' 400mm cannon trials, 1941-42.
Z2346 used at Boscombe Down for cockpit heating trials.
Z2461 used at Boscombe Down for hood jettison trials, February 1941, Z2885 fited with four Hispano 20mm cannon, 9/3/41.
Z2895 fitted with a modified fuel system at Boscombe Down.
Z2905 trial installation at Boscombe Down of 90 gallon ferry tanks and four-cannon wing, 3/41.
Z3157 used at Boscombe Down for eight-gun wing trials.
Z3451 used at Boscombe Down for a number of trials, May 1941
Z3564 used at Boscombe Down for armament trals in relation to the Mk IIB, 6/41.
Z3888 trials installation work at Boscombe Down for the Mk IIC, 7/41 & 1/42.
Z2308 used for air intake and performance trials by Hawker Aircraft Ltd.
Z2326 external stores trials at Hawker Aircraft Ltd.
Z2399 used for tests with a modified oil cooler by Hawker Aircraft Ltd.
Z2415 high altitude trials by Hawker Aircraft Ltd in December 1940.
Z2457 & Z2691 used for miscellaneous trials by RAE, 1942
Z2589 used for trial installations on Mk IIC wing by Hawker Aircraft Ltd, January 1941.
Z2340 not delivered: cannibalised for spares.
Z2795 used by TRE Malvern for radio trials.
Z2832 force landed in Eire, 1943. Temporarily registered '94' in the Irish Air Corps and returned to the RAF in July 1943., Z2903, Z3036, Z3056 & Z3058 used by the Station Flight, RAF Northolt.
Z3067 damaged during tests. RAF delivery delayed until 24/3/41
Z3078 crashed during delivery, later repaired.
Z3179 to Gloster Aircraft Co., April 1941 for development trials.
Z3429 damaged during air test, RAF delivery delayed until April 1941.
Z3682 the remains of this airframe were ar Waterbeach in 1953 and were used as spare parts for LF363.
Z3687 wfitted with a low-drag A.W.A wing in 1946-7.
Z3919 used by RAE for rocket projectile trials.
Z3981 used by Hawker Aircraft Ltd for miscellaneous trials, July & August 1941.
Z4015 built as a Mk IIB, later converted to Sea Hurricane Mk IC.

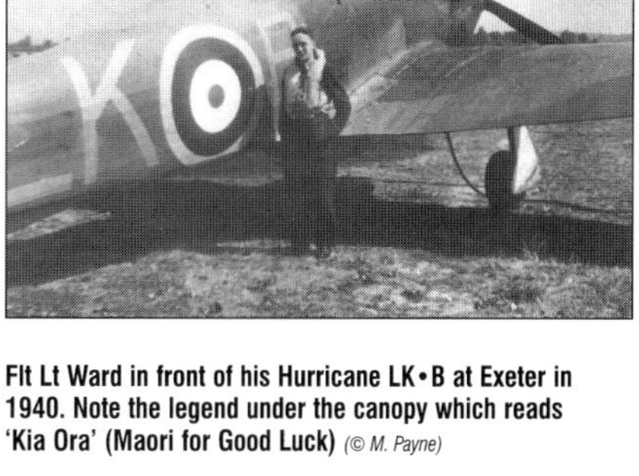

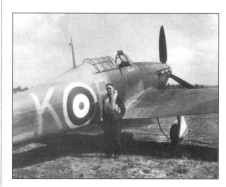

Flt Lt Ward in front of his Hurricane LK•B at Exeter in 1940. Note the legend under the canopy which reads 'Kia Ora' (Maori for Good Luck) *(© M. Payne)*

1,350 ordered (Hawker Built)
Mk II BD696-D745, BD759-BD793, BD818-BD837, BD855-BD899, BD914-BD963, BD980-BD986, BE105-BE117, BE130-BE174, BE193-BE242, BE274-BE308, BE323-BE372, BE394-BE428, BE468-BE517, BE546-BE590, BE632-BE651, BE667-BE716, BM898-BM936, BM947-BM996, BN103-BN142, BN155-BN189, BN203-BN242, BN265-BN298, BN311-BN337, BN346-BN389, BN399-BN435, BN449-BN497, BN512-BN547, BN559-BN603, BN624-BN654BN667-BN705, BN719-BN759, BN773-BN802, BN818-BN846, BN859-BN882, BN896-BN940 and BN953-BN987.
Merlin XX, de Havilland or Rotol three-blade variable-pitch propellers and metal wings. Delivered 24/7/41 to 18/3/42.
BD709, BD731, BD956, BD959, BE470, BN416, BN471,BN481 and BN428 shipped to Russia, 1942 (all Mk IIC's).
BE162 converted from a MK IIB to a Mk IIC and shipped to Russia, 1942.
BD772, BD916, BE157, BE167, BE227 & BN837 tropical conversion Mk IIB's & Mk IIC's, shipped to No. 103 MU, North Africa in 1942.
BD787 converted to a Sea Hurricane MK IA.
BE173/G used for miscellaneous armament trials by Hawker Aircraft Ltd, Langley.
BE329, BE494, BN627 and BN961 tropical Mk IIB's shipped to No. 71 OTU, North Africa in 1943.
BE711 used by Rolls-Royce Ltd. for trials in 1942.
BN114/G, BN526/G & BN571/G used for armament trials by A&AEE from 1942.
BN635 to Field Consolidated Aircraft Services, Hanworth in April 1942.
BN878 for radio trials at TRE Malvern.

1,888 ordered (Hawker Built)
Mk II & Mk IV BN988-BN992, BP109-BP141, BP154-BP200, BP217-BP245, BP259-BP302, BP316-BP362, BP378-BP416, BP430BP479, BP493-BP526, BP538-BP566, BP579BP614, BP628-BP675, BP692-BP711, BP734-BP772, HL544-HL591, HL603-HL634, HL654HL683, HL698-HL747, HL767-HL809, HL828-HL868, HL879-HL913, HL925-HL941, HL953HL997, HM110-HM157, HV275-HV317, HV333-HV370, HV396-HV445, HV468-HV516, HV534HV560, HV577-HV612, HV634-HV674, HV696HV745, HV768-HV799, HV815-HV858, HV873-HV921, HV943-HV989, HW115-HW146, HW167-HW207, HW229-HW278, HW291-HW323, HW345-HW373, HW399-HW444, HW467-HW501, HW533-HW572, HW596-HW624, HW651-HW686, HW713-HW757, HW779-HW808 AND HW834-HW881. Contract number 62305/39/B, Parts 1-9.
Merlin XX, de Havilland or Rotol three-blade variable-pitch propellers and metal wings. Delivered 17/3/42 to 23/11/42.
BP352 presentation aircraft 'Mohlomi'
BP452 presentation aircraft 'Kenya Weekly News'
BP606, HL612, HL628, HL706, HL934, HV369, HV581, HV664, HV673, HV837, HV853, HV854, HV857, HV911 & HW659 (tropical Mk IIB's) to No. 71 OTU, North Africa, 1942-3.
BP657, Mk IIB (converted from Mk IIC) shipped to Russia, 1943.
HL629, HL992, HL994, HV362, HV364, HV840, HV844, HV880, HW117, HW143, HW233, HW347, HW364, HW471, HW551, HW552, HW557 and HW571, Mk IIC's shipped to Russia in 1943.
HL549 & HL665 shipped to Russia and converted to two seaters, 1943.
HV279, HV287, HV293, HV556, HV593, HW168, HW205, HW300, HW357, HW371, HW406, HW715, HW868, HW872 & HW879, tropical Mk IID's, shipped to Russia in 1943.
HW660 presentation aircraft 'Swaziland II'
HW686 shipped to Russia.
HV513, HV551 & HV608, tropical Mk IIC's, supplied to Turkey from Middle East stocks in October/November 1942.
BP173 (later became BP173/G) built as a Mk IIB and delivered to No. 47 MU, RAF Sealand in April 1942. Returned to Hawker Aircraft Ltd amd modified to Mk IV standard, then to A&AEE in July 1942 for various trials.
BP743 to Middle East.
HL673 converted to Sea Hurricane (Tropical) Mk IC.
HL706-HL714, Mk IIB's to No.1 FT Flt, RAF Lyneham in June 1942.
HV366, Tropical MK IIC, used by Cranwell Station Flight in 1942-3.
HV559, Tropical Mk IIB, to AFTU, India in 1944.
HV722 used by No.231 Group Communications Flight in 1944.
HW115 used for production oil system checks in August 1942.
HW182/G used for armament trials by A&AEE in October 1942.
HW187 (and HW187/G) used for armament trials by A&A.E.E in October 1942.
HW203 used for drop tank trials on the universal wing by Hawker Aircraft Ltd.
HW566, Tropical Mk IIB, to TSTU, India in 1943-4.
HW747 used for trials at A&AEW during December 1942.

1,200 ordered (Hawker Built)
Mk II & Mk IV KW696-KW731, KW745-KW777, KW791-KW832, KW846-KW881, KW893-KW936, KW949-KW982, KX101-KX146, KX162-KX202, KX220-KX261, KX280-KX307, KX321-KX369, KX382-KX425, KX452-KX491, KX521-KX567, KX579-KX621, KX691-KX736, KX749-KX784, KX796-KX838, KX851-KX892, KX922-KX967, KZ111-KZ156, KZ169-KZ201, KZ216-KZ250, KZ266-KZ301, KZ319-KZ356, KZ370-KZ412, KZ424-KZ470, KZ483-KZ526, KZ540-KZ582 and KZ597-KZ612. Also Sea Hurricane Mk IIC conversions; NF668-NF703. Contract number 62305/39/C, Parts 1-6.
Merlin XX, de Havilland or Rotol three-blade variable-pitch propellers and metal wings. Delivered 20/11/42 to 19/4/43.
Sea Hurricane Mk IIC delayed for conversion and subsequent registration in barckets; KW770 (NF668), KW774 (NF671), KW791 (NF669), KW792 (NF670), KW799 (NF672), KW800 (NF673), KW804 (NF674), KW807 (NF677), KW808 (NF675), KW809 (NF678), KW810 (NF676), KW816 (NF679), KW817 (NF680), KW827 (NF681), KW828 (NF682), KW849 (NF683), KW850 (NF684), KW860 (NF685), KW862 (NF686), KW868 (NF687), KW870 (NF688), KW878 (NF689), KW880 (NF690), KW897 (NF691(, KW899 (NF692), KW908 (NF693), KW909 (NF694), KW910 (NF695), KW911 (NF696), KW918 (NF697), KW919 (NF698), KW920 (NF699), KW921 (NF700), KW928 (NF701), KW929 (NF702) and KW930 (NF703).
Mk IIC's KW706, KW723, KX113, KX125 (fighter), KX137, KX538 (tropical), KX545 (tropical), KZ234; MK IID's KW777 (tropical), KX177 (tropical), KX181 (tropical) and KZ301; Mk IV's KX813 (fighter), KX865 (anti-tank), KX888, KZ509 (shipped as a catapult Sea Hurricane MK IIC, but not used during voyage). All of these machines were shipped to Russia in 1943.
KW922 presentation aircraft 'Orissa VIII'.
KW942 presentation aircraft 'British Prudence'.
KX180 (Mk IV) used by A&AEE for rocket projectile trials.
KX247 (tropical Mk IV) to AFTU, India in 1944.
KX405 (tropical Mk IV) converted to Mk V prototype with Merlin 32 and sent to A&AEE.
KX412 used for comparative trials with KX405 at Hawker Aircraft Ltd.
KX700 (Mk IIC) used as a training aicraft and not fitted with guns.
KX862 (Mk IV) trials installation aicraft used by A&AEE in 1943.
KX877 (tropical Mk IV) this machine was temporarily modified to Mk V standard and used by Hawker Aircraft Ltd. and A&AEE in March 1943.
KZ138 (tropical Mk IIB) to No. 71 OTU, North Africa in 1944.
KZ193 (prototype Mk V), later converted back to Mk IV standard.
KZ232 used for stability trials by Hawker Aircraft Ltd and A&AEE in 1943.
KZ352 (tropical Mk IIC) at GATU, India in June 1945.
KZ466 used for performance trials by Hawker Aircraft Ltd in April 1943.
KZ569 to TSTU, India in 1944-5.

1,205 ordered (Hawker Built)
Mk II & Mk IV KZ613-KZ632, KZ646-KZ689, KZ702-KZ750, KZ766-KZ801, KZ817-KZ862, KZ877-KZ920, KZ933-KZ949, LA101-LA144, LB542-LB575, LB588-LB624, LB639-LB687, LB707-LB744, LB769-LB801, LB827-LB862, LB873-LB913, LB927-LB973, LB986-LD131, LD157-LD185, LD199-LD219, LD232-266, LD287-LD315, LD334-LD351, LD369-LD416, LD435-LD470, LD487-LD508, LD524-LD539, LD557-LD580, LD594-LD632, LD651-LD695, LD723-LD749, LD772-LD809, LD827-LD866, LD885-LD905, LD931-LD979 and LD993-LD999. Contract number 62305/39/C, Parts 7-12.
Merlin XX, de Havilland or Rotol three-blade variable-pitch propellers and metal wings. Delivered 18/4/43 to 29/9/43.
KZ858 & LD205 (Mk IIC fighter) shipped to Russia in 1943-4.
LB991 (Mk IIC fighter-bomber) shipped to Russia in 1943-4.
KZ819 (tropical Mk IIC) and LB675 (tropical Mk IIB) to No. 71 OTU, Middle East in 1944.
LB891 & LB893, Mk II target tugs to No. 71 OTU, in 1944.
KZ679 (also KZ679/G) used for rocket projectile trials by A&AEE
LB771 later became instructional airframe number 4628M.
LD182 crashed during tested, later deposited at Premier Garage, Bath Road, Slough, 13/9/43.
LD264, LD438 & LD439 to A&AEE for trials in July 1943.
LD412 (tropical Mk IV) to GATU, India in 1944.
LD621 damaaged during test flight.

1,357 ordered (Hawker Built)
Mk II & Mk IV LE121-LE146, LE163-LE183, LE201-LE214, LE247-LE273, LE291-LE309, LE334-LE368, LE387-LE405, LE432-LE449, LE456-LE484, LE499-LE535, LE 552-LE593, LE617-LE665, LE679-LE713, LE737-LE769, LE784-LE816, LE829-LE867, LE885-LE925, LE938-LE966, LE979-LE999, LF101-LF135, LF153-LF184, LF197-LF237, LF256-LF298, LF313-LF346, LF359-LF405, LF418-LF435, LF451-LF482, LF494-LF516, LF529-LF542, LF559-LF601, LF620-LF660, LF674-LF721, LF737-LF774, MW335-MW373, PG425-PG456, PG469-PG499, PG512-PG554, PG567-PG610, PZ730-PZ778, PZ791-PZ835 and PZ848-PZ865. Contract number 62305/39/C, Parts 13-19.
Merlin XX, de Havilland or Rotol three-blade variable-pitch propellers and metal wings. Delivered 29/9/43 to 24/5/44.
LE398, LE502, LE815, LF157 & LF203 (tropical Mk IIC's), LE646 & LE993 (tropical Mk IV's) to GATU, India in 1945.
LF295, LF296, LF322, LF346, LF363, LF366, LF368, LF376, LF379, LF386, LF396, LF680, MW363 & PG476 (Mk IIC's) to No. 41 OTU in May 1945.
LF293 (tropical Mk IIC) and LF366, LF376, LF379 & MW366 (Mk IIC's) to No. 61 OTU in July 1945
LE529 (Mk IIC fighter-bomber), LF463, LF470, LF473, LF481, LF509, LF501, LF592, LF595 & LF596 (Mk IV's) shipped to Russia in 1944.
LF342 (tropical Mk IIB fighter-bomber), LF133, LF360, LF383, LF422, LF425, LF514, LF564, LF565, LF568, LF570, LF586, LF620, LF699, LF706, LF717, LF757, LF772, MW373, PG521, PG535, PG538, PG543, PG599, PG610, PZ735, PZ738, PZ745 & PZ759 (tropical Mk IIC fighter-bombers) sold to Portugal in 1945-6.
LF541 (116), LF624 (118) & PZ796 (120) sold to Eire (subsequent serials in brackets).
LF374, LF382 & LF395 (Mk IIC) used by Coningsby Station Flight.
LF404 & LF421 (Mk IIC) used by Waddington Station Flight.
PG567, PG568, PG571 & PG573 (Mk IIC) used by Empire Central Flying School, Hullavington in 1944.
LE747 (5496M), LF398 (5415M), LF580 (5402M), LF627 (No.5 S. of T.T.), LF674 (5418M), LF680 (No.5 S. of T.T.), LF738 (5405M), LF745 (5406M), LF755 (5419M), MW340 (5463M), MW341 (5311M), MW354 (5321M), PG440 (5462M), PG451 (5420M), PG484 (5422M), PG497 (5417M), PG498 (5421M), PG517 (5407M), PG529 (5408M), PG546, PG570 (5464M), PG593 and PG604 (5416M) used as Ground Instructional Airframes (subsequent serial number shown in brackets).
LE353 (Mk IIC), used without armament by No.231 Communications Flight.
LE525 used for trials by A&AEE in November 1943.
LE796 (tropical Mk IIC) used by D Flight, No.22 AACU, in 1944.
LE806 (MK IIC) crashed during test flight.
LF363 last Hurricane on RAF charge, operated by BBMF, RAF Coningsby until it crash landed. Currently being restored to fly.
LF422 used for trials with Merlin 22 at Hawker Aircraft Ltd., Langley in January 1945.
LF632 guns removed and used as a trainer.
PZ865 purchased by Hawker Aircraft Ltd, named 'Last of the Many' and registered as G-AMAU. Operated by BBMF, RAF Coningsby.

300 ordered (Austin Motor Co. Ltd Built)
Mk II AP516-AP550, AP564-AP613, AP629-AP648, AP670-AP714, AP732-AP781, AP801-AP825, AP849-AP898, AP912-AP936. All except AP516-AP518 were scheduled to go to Russia in 1941-2. Some were sent by PQ convoy, although other aicraft were retained and issued to the RAF.
Merlin XX, de Havilland or Rotol three-blade variable-pitch propellers and metal wings.
AP516 retained by Austin Motor Co., Ltd. for performance and handling trials.
AP517 used for production performance and handling checks by Hawker Aircraft Ltd. and A&AEE in 1941.

Mk IIA, Z2487, FC•T of the Station Flight, RAF Northolt in 1941 *(© RAF Museum P012512)*

FOREIGN PRODUCTION

40 ordered (Canadian Car & Foundry Corporation, Canada)
Mk I P5170-P5209.
Merlin II, de Havilland three-blade variable-pitch propellers and metal wings. Shipped to UK during March to August 1940, although some were retained in Canada.
P5195 to No. 56 OTU, Sutton Bridge in November 1940.
P5170 used for production trials by Hawker Aircraft Ltd., RAE and A&AEE during March to August 1940.
P5176 force landed in Eire in 1942. This aicraft was brought by the Irish Air Corps, becoming '93'.
P5183 converted to a Sea Hurricane Mk IA and sent to Merchant Ship Fighter Unit, Speke in 1941.
P5187 used for catapult trials by RAE, November 1940 to March 1941.

340 ordered (Canadian Car & Foundry Corporation, Canada)
Mk X AE958-AE977, AE945-AG344 and AG665-AG684.
Packard-built Merlin 28, Hamilton Hydromatic three-blade variable-pitch propellers (without spinner) and metal wings. Approximately 100 machines were finished with the eight-gun metal wing, while the remainder had the twelve-gun wing fitted. Some later had four Oerlikon 20mm cannons fitted.
AG277, AG301, AG341, AG344, AG671 & AG680 converted to 12-gun wings at No. 13 MU, RAF Henlow.
AG299 (1378) and AG310 (1379) served with RCAF (serial numbers in brackets).
AG237, AG253 & AG267 (eight-gun wing) with No. 55 OTU in 1941.
AG123, AG212 & AG245 (eight-gun wing) with No. 59 OTU in 1941.

149 ordered (Canadian Car & Foundry Corporation, Canada)
Mk X AM271-AM369 and BW835-BW884.
Packard-built Merlin 28, Hamilton Hydromatic three-blade variable-pitch propellers (without spinner) and metal wings. Originally built with eight-gun metal wing, however many were later converted to twelve-gun and four-cannon armament.
AM271, AM301, AM302, AM349, AM367, BW870 & BW883 converted to 12-gun wing at No. 13 MU., RAF Henlow.
AM367, BW835, BW851, BW878 & BW879 shipped to Russia.

150 ordered (Canadian Car & Foundry Corporation, Canada)
Mk XI BW885-BX134.
Packard-built Merlin 28, Hamilton Hydromatic three-blade variable-pitch propellers (without spinner) and metal wings. Originally built with eight-gun metal wing, however many were later converted to twelve-gun and four-cannon (Oerlikon or Hispano) armament.
BW901, BW906, BW907, BW914, BW919, BW941, BW944, BW948, BW962, BW963, BW967, BX124, BX128 & BX133 converted to 12-gun armament at No. 13 MU., RAF Henlow.
BW920, BW922, BW926, BW984, BX102, BX108-BX111, BX119-BX124 (4-cannon wing) to No. 22 MU, RAF Silloth for shipment to Russia in 1942.

248 ordered (Canadian Car & Foundry Corporation, Canada)
Mk XII JS219-JS371, JS374-JS420 (12-gun wing), JS421-JS468 (mostly converted in the UK to 4-cannon armament).
Packard-built Merlin 28, Hamilton Hydromatic three-blade variable-pitch propellers and metal wings.
JS330 (12-gun armament) with No. 59 OTU in December 1943.
JS220, JS221, JS225, JS227, JS228, JS233, JS240, JS256, JS300, JS391, JS396-JS399, JS405-JS412, JS415 & JS419 (12-gun armament) to No. 22 MU, RAF Silloth and Packing Depot, RAF Sealand for packing and shipment to Russia.
JS219, JS229, JS232, JS235, JS237, JS241, JS257, JS309 & JS317 to No. 13 MU, RAF Henlow and Packing Depot, RAF Sealand for shipment to Russia.

150 ordered (Canadian Car & Foundry Corporation, Canada)
Mk XIIA PJ660-PJ695, PJ711-PJ758, PJ779-PJ813 and PJ842-PJ872.
Packard-built Merlin 29, Hamilton Hydromatic three-blade variable-pitch propellers and metal wings. Most built with eight-gun wings, although many were later converted to 12-gun or 4-cannon armament. Most of these machines were sent directly to Russia or Burma, with a few going to the UK. A small number were also retained in Canada and fitted with deck landing equipment to become Sea Hurricane Mk XIIA's.

Hurricane Aces

The list below gives details of all the pilots who achieved over 10 kills while flying the Hurricane. Each pilot is shown with the highest score he achieved, plus all decorations, the period and theatre of operations in which he achieved the kills listed.

The highest Hurricane ace, Flt Lt M.T. St.J. Pattle DFC*, who acheived 35 kills before his death on the 20th April 1941

Wg Cdr R.R.S. Tuck DSO DFC*, a Hurricane Ace with 15 kills

Gp Capt D.R.S. Bader KBE DSO* DFC*, an Ace with 11 kills, is seen here after having lunch with the Luftwaffe squadron that shot him down in 1940!

Wg Cdr W. Urbanowicz DFC, an Ace with 15 kills is seen here with his Hurricane Mk I (© M. Payne)

RANK	NAME	KILLS	SQUADRONS	PERIOD	OPERATIONAL THEATRE	REMARK
Flt Lt	M.T. St.J. Pattle DFC*	35	80/33	Feb-Apr 41	Greece	KIA 20 Apr 1941
Gp Capt	F.R. Carey DFC* AFC DFM	25	43/3/135/267	May 40-Feb 42	France/BofB/Far East	
Sqn Ldr	J.H. Lacey DFM*	23	501	May-Oct 40	France/BofB	
Wg Cdr	M.N. Crossley DSO OBE DFC	20	32	May-Aug 40	France/BofB	
Sqn Ldr	W. Vale DFC* AFC	20	80	Mar-Jun 41	Greece	
Grp Capt	G.R. Edge OBE DFC	18	605/253	May-Sept 40	BofB	
Flt Lt	K.M. Kuttelwascher DFC*	18	1	Apr 41-Jul 42	England	
Sqn Ldr	A.G. Lewis DFC*	18	85/249	May-Sept 40	France/BofB	
Sgt	J. Frantisek DFM*	17	303	Sept 40	BofB	KIA 8 Oct 1940
Sqn Ldr	A.A. McKellar DSO DFC*	17	605	Aug-Oct 40	BofB	KIA 1 Nov 1940
Fg Off	W.L. McKnight DFC*	17	615/242	May-Sept 40	France/BofB	KIA 12 Jan 1941
Fg Off	L.R. Clisby DFC	16	1	Apr-May 40	France	KIA 14 May 1940
Wg Cdr	H.J.L. Hallowes DFC DFM*	16	43	Apr-May 40	BofB	
Fg Off	E.J. Cain DFC	16	73	Nov 39-May 40	France	Killed 6 June 1940
Wg Cdr	A.C. Rabagliati DFC*	16	46/126	Aug 40-Feb 42	BofB/Malta	KIA 6 Jul 1943
Wg Cdr	M.H. Brown DFC*	15	1	Apr-Aug 40	France/BofB/Malta	KIA 12 Nov 1941
Grp Capt	W.D. David CBE DFC* AFC	15	87/213	May-Oct 40	France/BofB	
Sqn Ldr	E.M. Mason DFC	15	274/261	Dec 40-Aug 41	North Africa	KIA 15 Feb 1942
Sqn Ldr	N. Orton DFC*	15	73	Nov 39-May 40	France	KIA 17 Sept 1941
Wg Cdr	R.R.S. Tuck DSO DFC*	15	257	Sept 40-Aug 41	BofB/UK	
Wg Cdr	W. Urbanowicz DFC	15	145/303	Aug-Sept 40	BofB	
Sgt	J. Dodds DFM	14	274	Dec 41- Jun 42	North Africa	
Flt Lt	R.P. Stevens DSO DFC*	14	151	Jan-Oct 41	UK	KIA 16 Dec 1941
Wg Cmdr.	V.C. Woodward DFC*	14	33	Oct 40-Jun 41	North Africa/Greece	
Sqn Ldr	C.M.B. Czernin MC DFC	13	85/17	May-Sept 40	France/BofB	
Grp Capt	T.F. Dalton-Morgan DSO OBE DFC*	13	43	Jul 40-Oct 41	BofB	
Flt Lt	E.W.F. Hewett AFC DFM	13	80	Feb-Apr 41	Greece	
Wg Cdr	J.I. Kilmartin DFC	13	1/43	Apr-Sept 40	France	
Flt Lt	R.T. Llewellyn DFM	13	213	May-Sept 40	BofB	
Sqn Ldr	J.A.F. Machlachlan DSO DFC*	13	261/1	Jan 41-Jun 42	Malta/UK	KIA 18 Jul 1943
Wg Cdr	R.A. Barton OBE DFC*	12	249	Aug 40-Nov 41	BofB/Malta	
Grp Capt	A.H. Boyd DSO DFC*	12	145	May-Oct 40	BofB	
Air Cdre	P.M. Brothers CBE DSO DFC*	12	32/257	May-Sept 40	France/BofB	
Flt Lt	S.D.P. Connors DFC*	12	111	May-Aug 40	France/BofB	KIA 18 Aug 1940
Flt Ltn	F.W. Higginson OBE DFC DFM	12	56	May-Sep 40	France/BofB	
Flt Ltn	A.E. Marshall DFC DFM	12	73	Jun 40-Apr 41	North Africa	KIA 27 Nov 1944
Wg Cdr	T.F. Neil DFC* AFC	12	249	Sep 40-Jun 41	BofB/Malta	
Sqn Ldr	J.E. Scouler DFC AFC	12	73	Apr-May 40	France	
Wg Cdr	L.C. Wade DSO DFC*	12	33	Nov 41-Sept 42	North Africa	Killed 12 Jan 1944
Flt Lt	G. Allard DFC DFM*	11	85	May-Sept 40	France/BofB	Killed 13 Mar 1941
Grp Capt	D.R.S. Bader KBE DSO* DFC*	11	242	Jul-Sept 40	BofB	
Sqn Ldr	J.A.A. Gibson DSO DFC	11	501	May-Sept 40	France/BofB	
Sgt	H.N. Howes DFM	11	85/605	May-Nov 40	France/BofB	Killed 22 Dec 1940
Air Mshl	J.H. Lapsley KBE DFC AFC	11	80/274	Aug-Dec 40	North Africa	
Wg Cdr	M.M. Stephens DSO DFC**	11	3/232/80	May 40-Dec 41	France/Turkey/N.Africa	
Wg Cdr	J.M. Bazin DSO DFC	10	607	May-Sept 40	France/BofB	
Sqn Ldr	J.R. Cock DFC	10	87	Apr-Sep 40	France/BofB	
Wg Cdr	C.F. Currant DSO DFC*	10	605	Aug-Dec 40	BofB	
Maj	K.W. Driver DFC	10	1 (SAAF)	Dec 40-May 41	Eritrea	
Sgt	W.L. Dymond DFM	10	111	May-Aug 40	France/BofB	KIA 2 Sept 1940
Wg Cdr	I.R. Gleed DSO DFC	10	87	May 40-May 41	France/BofB	KIA 16 Apr 1943
Fg Off	G.E. Goodman DFC	10	1/73	May 40-Apr 41	France/BofB/North Africa	KIA 14 Jun 1941
Flt Lt	K.W. MacKenzie DFC	10	501/247	Oct 40-Sept 41	England	
Fg Off	F.N. Robertson DFM	10	261	Nov 40-Mar 41	Malta	KIA 31 Aug 1943
Sqn Ldr	F.J. Soper DFC DFM	10	1/257	May 40-Sept 41	France/England	KIA 5 Oct 1941
Wg Cdr	J.E. Storrar DFC* AFC	10	145/73	May 40-Apr 41	BofB/North Africa	
Flt Lt	H.C. Upton DFC	10	43	Aug-Sept 40	BofB	
Fg Off	P.P. Woods-Scawen DFC	10	85	May-Aug 40	BofB	KIA 1 Sept 1940

Hurricane Bibliography

The Hawker Hurricane
Francis K. Mason
Macdonald & Co. (Publishers) Ltd. ©1962

Hawker Hurricane
Robert Jackson
Blandford Press © 1987
ISBN 0 7137 1683 5

Hurricane
Edward Bishop
Airlife Publishing Ltd. © 1986
ISBN 0 906393 62 0

The Hawker Hurricane Mk I
Francis K. Mason
Profile Publications Ltd. © 1967
Aircraft in Profile Volume 5

The Hawker Hurricane Mk I
Francis K. Mason
Profile Publications Ltd. © No Date
Profile Number 111

The Hawker Hurricane Mk IIC
Francis K. Mason
Profile Publications Ltd. © 1971
Aircraft in Profile Volume 1

The Hurricane at War
C. Bowyer
Ian Allan © 1974

The Hurricane at War 2
N. Franks
Ian Allan © 1986

The Hawker Hurricane Mk IIC
Francis K. Mason
Profile Publications Ltd. © No Date
Profile Number 24

Hawker Aircraft since 1920
Francis K. Mason
Putnam Aeronautical Books. © 1961, 1971 & 1991
ISBN 0 85177 839 9

Hawker Hurricane - Classic Aircraft No.4
Bruce Robertson & Gerald Scarborough
Patrick Stephens Ltd. © 1974
ISBN 0 85059 124 4

Hawker Hurricane In Action - 'In Action' No 72
Jerry Scutts
Squadron/Signal Publications Ltd. ©1986
ISBN 0 89747 174-1

Hurricane Walk Around - 'Walk Around' No 14
Ron MacKay
Squadron/Signal Publications Ltd. ©1998
ISBN 0 89747-388-4

Hawker Hurricane - Aero Detail 12
Shigeru Nohara & Hajime Ohsato
Art Box Co., Ltd © 1994
ISBN 4 499 22636 8

The Hurricane II Manual edited
Dr. J. Tanner
Arms & Armour Press © 1976
ISBN 0 85368 430 8

Hurricane: The Story of a Great Fighter
F.H.M. Lloyd
Harborough Publishing Co. © 1945

The Hawker Hurricane Described
Francis K. Mason
Kookaburra Technical Publications Ltd. © 1970

Hawker Hurricane
Mr Kit & J.P. de Cock
Editions Atlas © 1978

Hurricane Special
M. Allward
Ian Allan Publishing © 1975

The Hurricane Story
P. Gallico
Michael Joseph © 1959

Hawker Hurricane
Peter Jacobs
The Crowood Press @1998
ISBN 1 86126 126 8

Hurricanes over Burma
Sqn Ldr M.C. Cotton DFC
Grub Street @ 1995

RAF Fighters Part 2 - WW2 Aircraft Fact Files
William Green & Gordon Swanborough
Macdonald & Jane's Publishing Ltd (Pilot Press) © 1979
ISBN 0 354 01234 7

Fight for the Sky
Douglas Bader
Sidgwick & Jackson © 1983

The Hurricats
R. Baker
Pelham Books © 1978

The Catafighters
Kenneth Poolman
William Kimber © 1970

Battle of Britain Memorial Flight
BBMF © 1983

Aeroplanes in Detail (Reprinted from 'The Aeroplane')
J.H. Clark
English Universities Press

Hawker - An Aircraft Album
D.N. James
Ian Allan © 1972

Camouflage & Markings No.3: Hawker Hurricane
James Goulding
Ducimus Books Ltd. © 1966

Flying Wartime Aircraft; ATA Ferry Pilot's Handing Notes for Seven WWII Aircraft
David & Charles © 1972
ISBN 0 7153 53503

Hawker Hurricane Mk I/IV in RAF & Foreign Service
R. Ward
Aircam Aviation Series No. 24
Osprey Publications © 1971
ISBN 85045 029 2

Hurricane - The War Exploits of the Fighter Aircraft
A. Stewart
William Kimber © 1982

Official Publications

Air Publication AP1564A Hurricane Mk I
Air Publication AP1564B Hurricane Mk II/IV
Air Publication AP1564B, C & D Hurricane Mk IIA, IIB, IIC,
Sea Hurricane Mk IIB, IIC & Mk IIB & IIC (with arrestor hook),
Hurricane Mk IID & Mk IV

General Titles

Aircraft of the Royal Air Force since 1918
Owen Thetford
Putnam Publishing Ltd. © 1957, 58, 62, 68, 71, 76, 79 & 1988
ISBN 0 85177 810 0

Action Stations 5
Chris Ashworth
Patrick Stephens Ltd @1982

Action Stations 8
Bruce B. Halfpenny
Patrick Stephens Ltd @1984

Action Stations 9
Chris Ashworth
Patrick Stephens Ltd @1985

The British Fighter since 1912
P. Lewis
Putnam Publishing Ltd. © 1965

British Racing & Record-Breaking Aircraft
P. Lewis
Putnam Publishing Ltd. © 1970

Armament of British Aircraft 1909-1939
H.F. King
Putnam Publishing Ltd. © 1971

British Civil Aircraft since 1919. Volume 2
A.J. Jackson
Putnam Publishing Ltd. © 1973

Royal Air Force - The Aircraft in Service since 1918
C. Bowyer & M. Turner
Hamlyn © 1981

50 Fighters 1935-1945
R. Ward
Aircam Aviation Series No. 517 (Volume 1)
Osprey Publications © 1973
ISBN 0 85045 130 2

Fighter Squadrons at War
A.J. Brookes
Ian Allan © 1980

Fighter Squadrons of the RAF
J. Rawlings
MacDonald & Jane's

Warplanes of the Second World War
William Green
MacDonald & Jane's

Squadrons of the Fleet Air Arm
Ray Sturtivant
Air Britain Publications

Fleet Air Arm at War
Ray Sturtivant
Ian Allan © 1982

Fleet Air Arm: 1939-1945 Portfolio
Roderick Dymott
Ian Allan © 1981

Testing Years
R.P. Beamont
Ian Allan © 1980

Wings of the Navy
Capt Eric 'Winkle' Brown
Pilot Press © 1980

Combat Aircraft of the World edited
J.M.R. Taylor
Edury Press & Michael Joseph ©1969

Warplanes of the World 1918-39
M.J.H. Taylor
Ian Allan © 1981

Aircraft of World War 2
B. Gunston
Octopus Books Ltd. © 1980

Fighting Colours
M.J.F. Bowyer
Patrick Stephens Ltd. © 1969, 1970, 1975
ISBN 0 85059 191 0

Camouflage & Markings; RAF 1939-45
M. Reynolds
Argus Books. ©1992

The World's Fighters
H.F. King
The Bodley Head ©1971
ISBN 0 370 10807 8

The World's Strike Aircraft
H.F. King
The Bodley Head ©1973
ISBN 0 370 01571 1

Aircraft of the Battle of Britain
W. Green
Jane's © 1980

Famous Fighters of the Second World War
W. Green
MacDonald © 1957

RAF Fighters Part 2; World War 2 Fact Files
W. Green & G. Swanborough
MacDonald & Jane's © 1979

War Planes of the Second World War - Volume 2
W. Green
MacDonald © 1961

World Aircraft, WWII. Volume 1
E. Angelucci & P. Matricardi
Sampson Law Ltd © 1978

Les Avions Britanniques Leurs Exploits dans la Guerre Aerienne
Bureau d'Information Allie

I Caccia Della Seconda Guerra Mondiale
C. Barbieri
Ermauno Albertelli © 1971

What Were They Like to Fly?
D.H. Clark
Ian Allan © 1964

In the Cockpit. Flying the World's Great Aircraft
A. Robinson
Orbis Publications © 1981

Famous Aircraft Cockpits 2
H. Seo
Asahi Shimbun © 1981

Combat Aircraft of the Battle of Britain
N. & A. Shennan
Kookaburra Technical Publications © 1970

The Battle of Britain
C. Shores
Osprey Publications © 1968

Aircraft of the Indian Air Force 1933-73
P. Singh
B. Chondhri © 1974

Night Hawk
R. Darlington
William Kimber Ltd. © 1985

Dimensione Cielo Aerei Italiani Nelle 2a Guerra Mondiale Volume 3
Edizioni Bizzarri © 1972

Les Flottes de L'air en 1937
Societe d'Editions © 1937

The Encyclopedia of the Worlds Combat Aircraft
B. Gunston
Hamlyn © 1976

The Illustrated Encyclopedia of Combat Aircraft of World War II
B. Gunston
Salamander Books © 1978

RAF Fighters of WW2 - Airfix Magazine Guide 6
A.W. Hall
Patrick Stephens Ltd © 1975
ISBN 0 85059 204 6

No. 242 Squadron: The Canadian Years
H. Halliday
Canada's Wings © 1981

The War in the Air: More Fighters of the Present War
E. Hawks
Real Photographs © 1944

Combat Aircraft of WWII
C. Weal
Arms & Armour Press © 1977

Periodicals & Journals

Aeronautics, December 1964
Aerospace Historian, September 1979
Aeroplane Monthly, August 1985
Aeroplane Monthly, September 1985
Aerpoplane Monthly, November 1985
Aeroplane Monthly, April 1988
Aeroplane Monthly, January 1991
Aeroplane Monthly, Dcember 1992
Aeroplane Monthly January 1994
Aeroplane Monthly February 1994
Aeroplane Monthly, November 1994
Aeroplane Monthly, August 1995
Aeroplane Monthly, November 1995
Aeroplane Monthly, December 1995
Aeroplane Monthly, January 1996
Aeroplane Monthly, July 1997
Aerospace Historian Vol. 29 No. 3
Air Britian News, March 1995
Aircraft Engineering Vol. 11 (1939)
Aircraft Illustrated, December 1985
Aircraft Illustrated Vol. 23 No. 10 (October 1990)
Aircraft Illustrated, October 1997
Aircraft Modelworld, September 1981
Aircraft Production Vol. 1 No. 14
Aircraft Production Vol. 3 No. 30 (April 1941)
Air Enthusiast No. 23
Airfix Magazine, March 1980
Airfix Magazine, March 1983
Air International, December 1979
Air International, April 1987
Air International, May 1987
Air International, June 1987
Air International, July 1987
Air International, September 1987
Air International, May 1988
Air International Vol. 38 No. 2
Air Pictorial, November 1979
Air Pictorial, September 1995
Airplane Vol. 13 No. 17
Airpower, September 1986
Avaition News Vol. 14 No. 3
Avaition News Vol. 14 No. 14
Avaition News Vol. 17 No. 17
Avaition News Vol. 19 No. 21
Flight, 12th May 1938
Flypast, November 1985
Flypast, August 1988
Flypast, April 1991
Flypast, August 1992
Flypast, September 1995
Flypast, November 1995
Flypast, January 1996
IPMS Qyarterly, Vol. 19 No. 1
Klub 1:72 Skrzydlatej Polski, 1988
Letectvi & Kosmonautika 1981
Pilot, January 1989
Quarter Scale Modeller November 1995
RAF Yearbook 1987
Scale Aircraft Modelling, September 1979
Scale Aircraft Modelling Vol. 12 No. 11 (August 1990)
Scale Aircraft Modelling Vol. 13 No. 6
Scale Aircraft Modelling Vol. 18 No. 5
Scale Models Vol. 11 No. 131, August 1980
Scale Models Vol. 11 No. 132, September 1980
Scale Models Vol. 11 No. 133, October 1980
Scale Models, November 1985
Scale Models, December 1985
Small Air Forces Observer Vol. 19 No. 4
The Aeroplane, 4th December 1935
The Aeroplane Vol. 14 No. 10
Warbirds Worldwide, Spring 1995
Warbirds Worldwide No. 9
Warbirds Worldwide No. 10
Warbird Worldwide No. 11
Warbirds Worldwide No. 31
Wingspan, November 1985
Wingspan No. 68
Wingspan No. 70, November 1990
Wingspan No. 71, December 1990/January 1991
Wingspan, November 1991

Note: The 'Periodicals & Journals' listing is not, and cannot be, complete. The list gives a broad overview of the subject and is offered as a reference guide for all those wishing to build the type. Further research into suitable source material is, however, still recommended.

Index

Please note, this index does not reference the appendices.

Personnel of No. 501 Sqn in front of a Hurricane Mk I at RAF Kenley in 1940
(© RAF Museum P001853)

Mk IIC, PZ865 'Last of the Many' in flight (© Hawker-Siddeley)

Mk IIC's, Z3778 (JX•Y), BN964 (JX•S), HL603 (JX•I), JX•B, JX•H and JX•J of No. 151 Sqn in flight

Mk I, P2627 of No. 274 Sqn, in flight, November 1940

'Last of the Many'

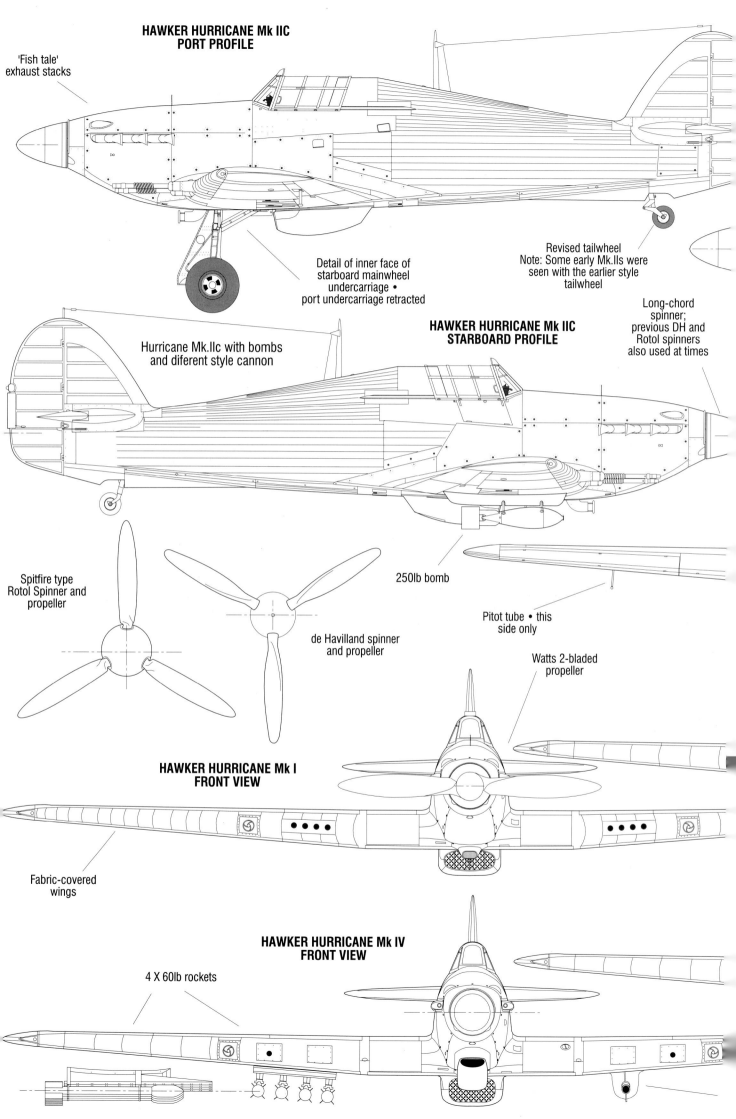

**HAWKER HURRICANE Mk IIC
PORT PROFILE**

'Fish tale'
exhaust stacks

Detail of inner face of
starboard mainwheel
undercarriage •
port undercarriage retracted

Revised tailwheel
Note: Some early Mk.IIs were
seen with the earlier style
tailwheel

Hurricane Mk.IIc with bombs
and diferent style cannon

**HAWKER HURRICANE Mk IIC
STARBOARD PROFILE**

Long-chord
spinner;
previous DH and
Rotol spinners
also used at times

Spitfire type
Rotol Spinner and
propeller

de Havilland spinner
and propeller

250lb bomb

Pitot tube • this
side only

Watts 2-bladed
propeller

**HAWKER HURRICANE Mk I
FRONT VIEW**

Fabric-covered
wings

**HAWKER HURRICANE Mk IV
FRONT VIEW**

4 X 60lb rockets

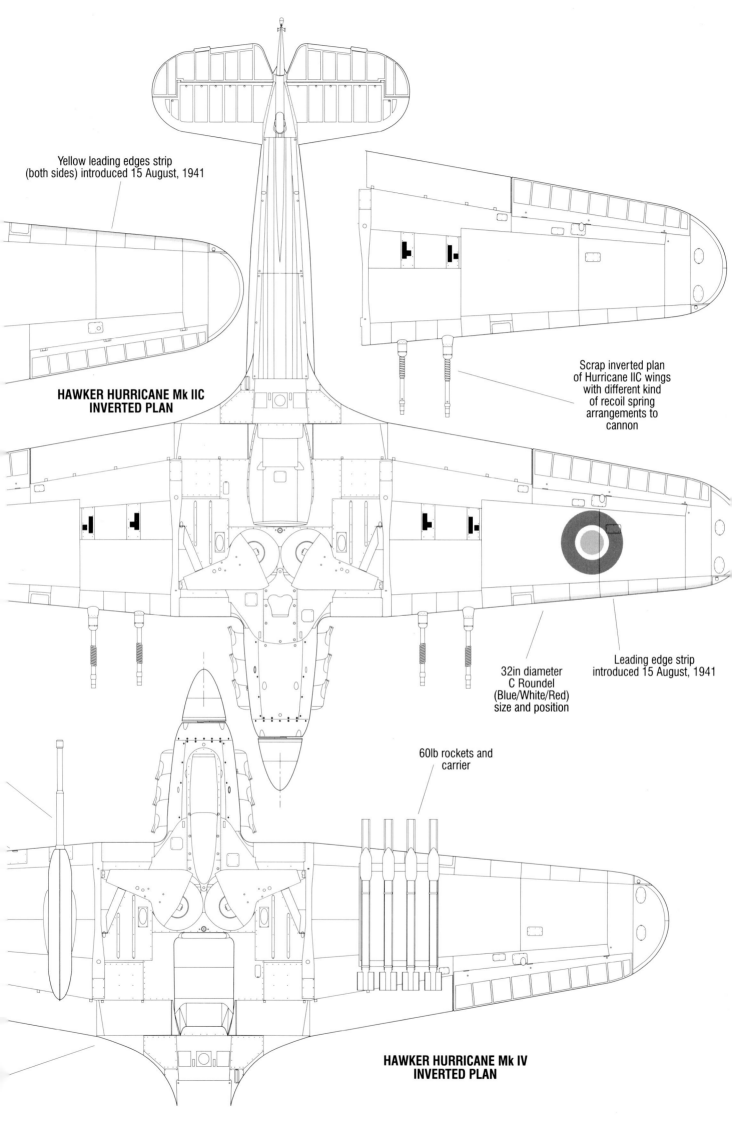

Yellow leading edges strip
(both sides) introduced 15 August, 1941

**HAWKER HURRICANE Mk IIC
INVERTED PLAN**

Scrap inverted plan
of Hurricane IIC wings
with different kind
of recoil spring
arrangements to
cannon

32in diameter
C Roundel
(Blue/White/Red)
size and position

Leading edge strip
introduced 15 August, 1941

60lb rockets and
carrier

**HAWKER HURRICANE Mk IV
INVERTED PLAN**

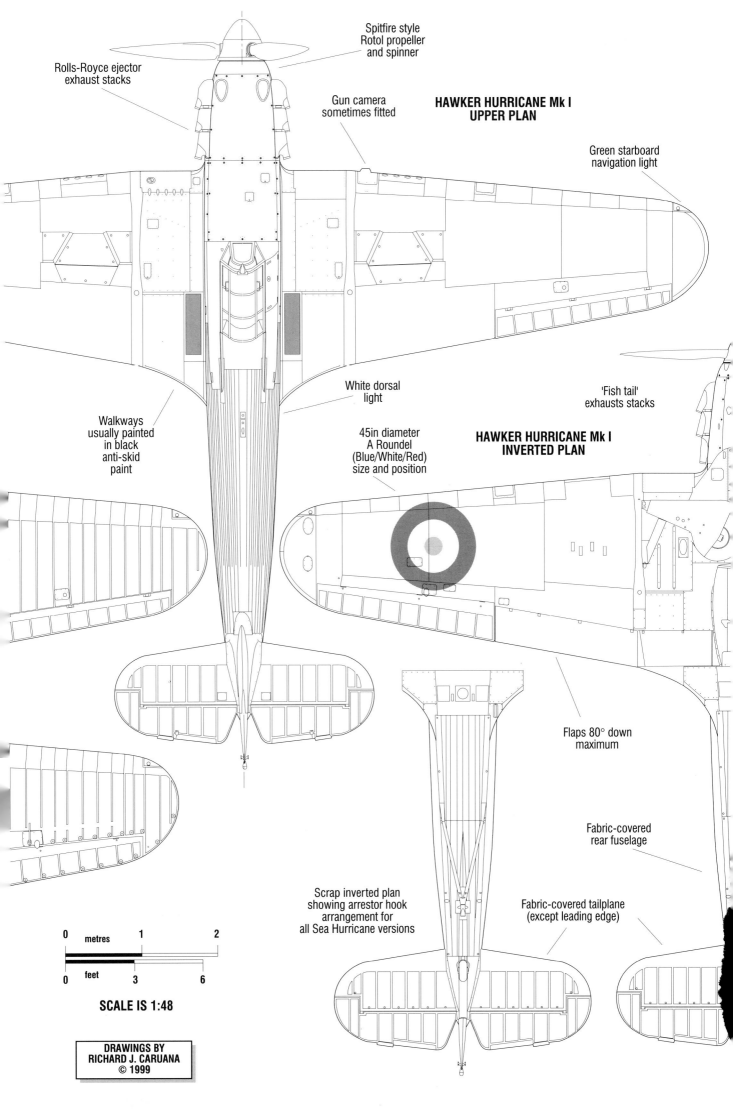

Rolls-Royce ejector
exhaust stacks

Spitfire style
Rotol propeller
and spinner

Gun camera
sometimes fitted

**HAWKER HURRICANE Mk I
UPPER PLAN**

Green starboard
navigation light

Walkways
usually painted
in black
anti-skid
paint

White dorsal
light

'Fish tail'
exhausts stacks

45in diameter
A Roundel
(Blue/White/Red)
size and position

**HAWKER HURRICANE Mk I
INVERTED PLAN**

Flaps 80° down
maximum

Fabric-covered
rear fuselage

Scrap inverted plan
showing arrestor hook
arrangement for
all Sea Hurricane versions

Fabric-covered
tailplane
(except leading edge)

0 metres 1 2
0 feet 3 6

SCALE IS 1:48

**DRAWINGS BY
RICHARD J. CARUANA
© 1999**

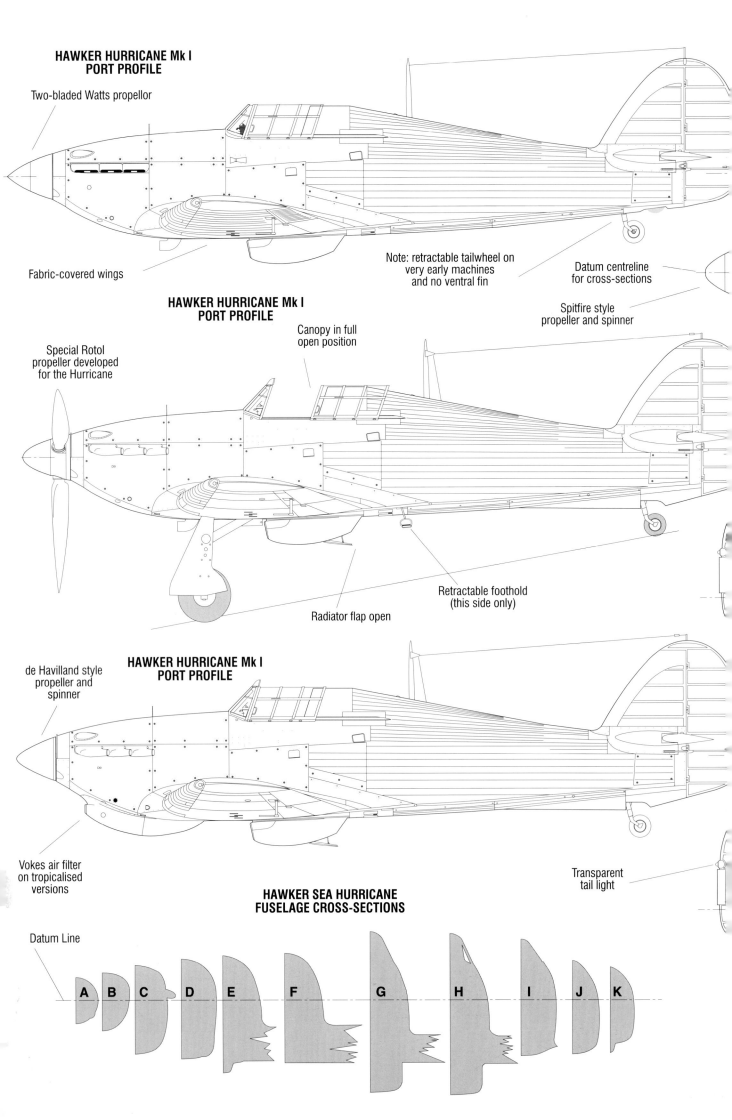

HAWKER HURRICANE Mk I
PORT PROFILE

Two-bladed Watts propellor

Fabric-covered wings

Note: retractable tailwheel on
very early machines
and no ventral fin

Datum centreline
for cross-sections

Spitfire style
propeller and spinner

HAWKER HURRICANE Mk I
PORT PROFILE

Canopy in full
open position

Special Rotol
propeller developed
for the Hurricane

Radiator flap open

Retractable foothold
(this side only)

HAWKER HURRICANE Mk I
PORT PROFILE

de Havilland style
propeller and
spinner

Vokes air filter
on tropicalised
versions

Transparent
tail light

HAWKER SEA HURRICANE
FUSELAGE CROSS-SECTIONS

Datum Line

A B C D E F G H I J K

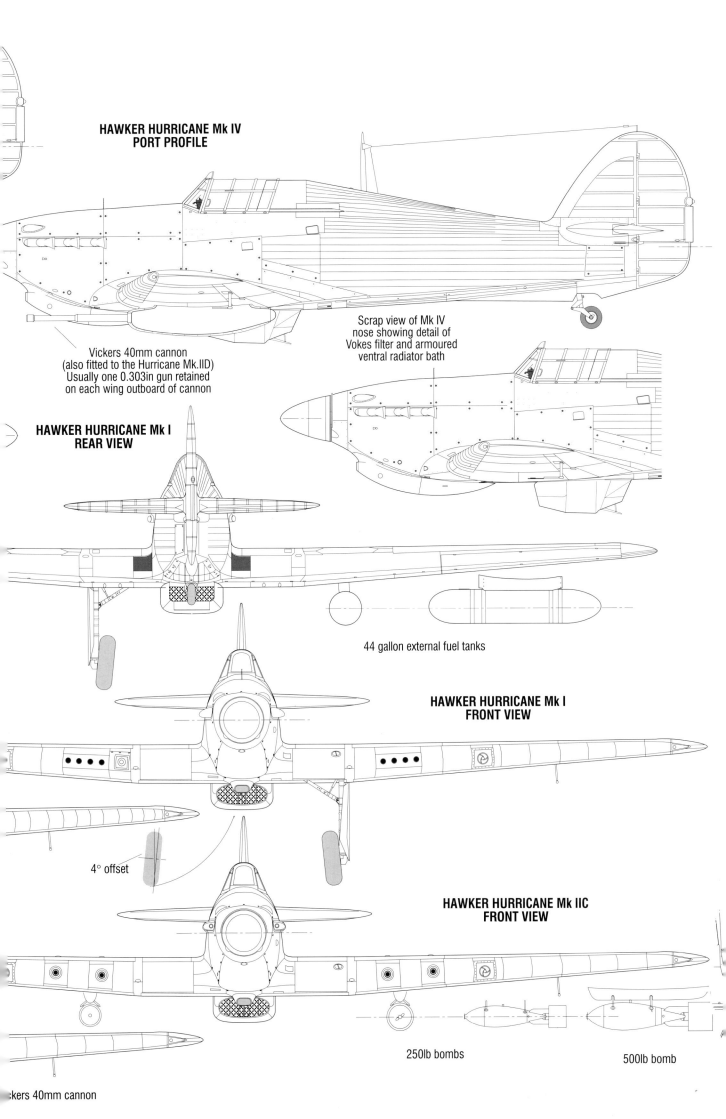

**HAWKER HURRICANE Mk IV
PORT PROFILE**

Vickers 40mm cannon
(also fitted to the Hurricane Mk.IID)
Usually one 0.303in gun retained
on each wing outboard of cannon

Scrap view of Mk IV
nose showing detail of
Vokes filter and armoured
ventral radiator bath

**HAWKER HURRICANE Mk I
REAR VIEW**

44 gallon external fuel tanks

**HAWKER HURRICANE Mk I
FRONT VIEW**

4° offset

**HAWKER HURRICANE Mk IIC
FRONT VIEW**

250lb bombs

500lb bomb

ckers 40mm cannon

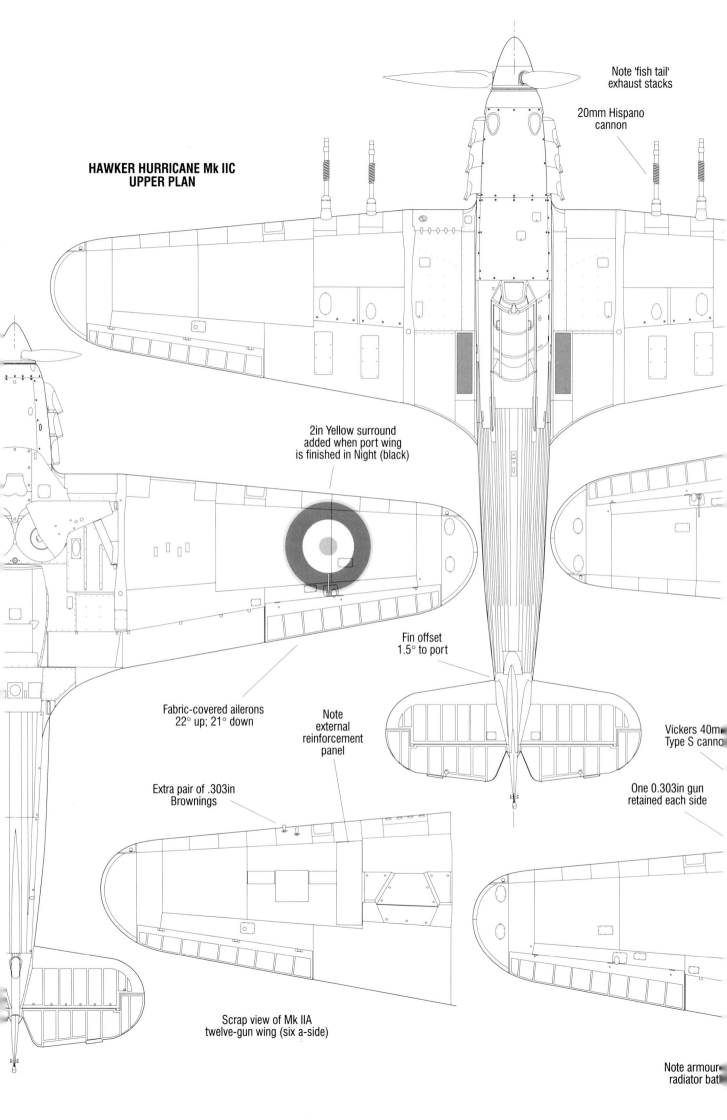

**HAWKER HURRICANE Mk IIC
UPPER PLAN**

Note 'fish tail'
exhaust stacks

20mm Hispano
cannon

2in Yellow surround
added when port wing
is finished in Night (black)

Fin offset
1.5° to port

Fabric-covered ailerons
22° up; 21° down

Note
external
reinforcement
panel

Vickers 40m
Type S canno

Extra pair of .303in
Brownings

One 0.303in gun
retained each side

Scrap view of Mk IIA
twelve-gun wing (six a-side)

Note armour
radiator bat

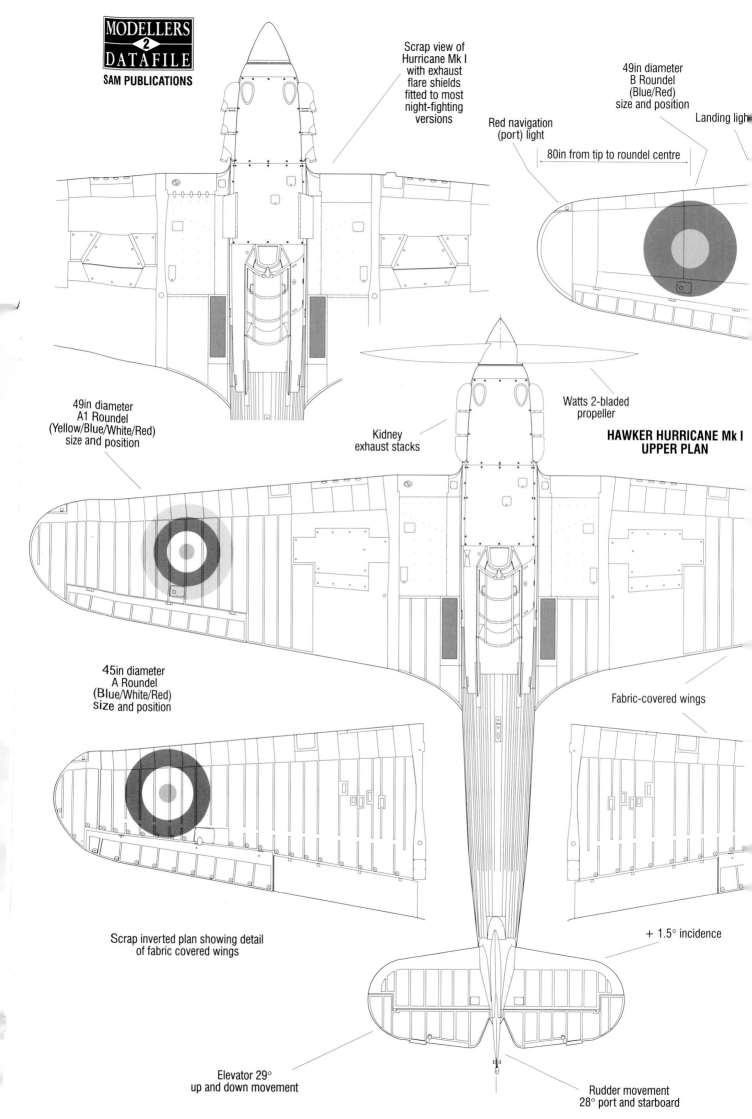

Scrap view of
Hurricane Mk I
with exhaust
flare shields
fitted to most
night-fighting
versions

49in diameter
B Roundel
(Blue/Red)
size and position

Landing ligh

Red navigation
(port) light

80in from tip to roundel centre

49in diameter
A1 Roundel
(Yellow/Blue/White/Red)
size and position

Kidney
exhaust stacks

Watts 2-bladed
propeller

**HAWKER HURRICANE Mk I
UPPER PLAN**

45in diameter
A Roundel
(Blue/White/Red)
size and position

Fabric-covered wings

Scrap inverted plan showing detail
of fabric covered wings

+ 1.5° incidence

Elevator 29°
up and down movement

Rudder movement
28° port and starboard

HAWKER HURRICANE Mk I
PORT PROFILE

Aircraft is shown fitted with
Rolls-Royce ejector
exhaust stacks

A B C D E F G H I J K

DRAWINGS BY
RICHARD J. CARUANA
© 1999

HAWKER HURRICANE Mk I
STARBOARD PROFILE

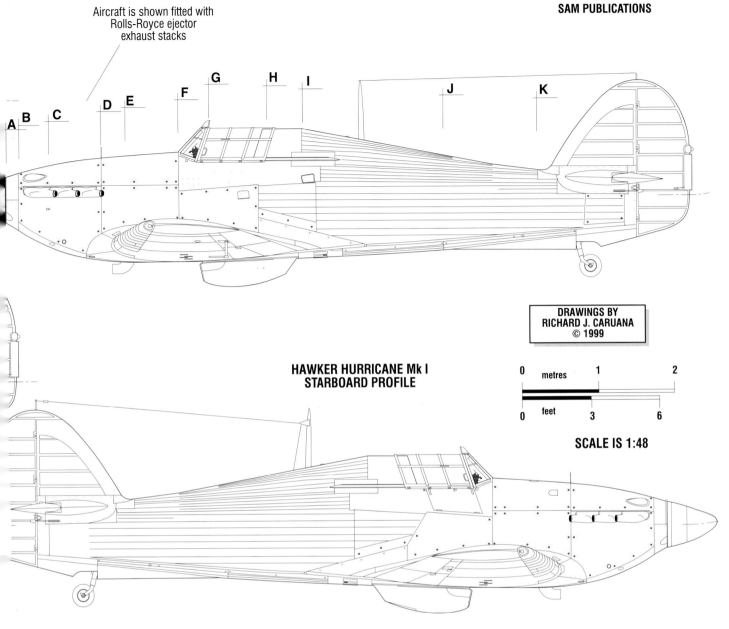

0 metres 1 2

0 feet 3 6

SCALE IS 1:48

HAWKER SEA HURRICANE Mk IC
STARBOARD PROFILE

Note: Sea Hurricanes Mk IA and Mk IB
are navalised versions of Hurricane Mk I
with the eight-gun wing

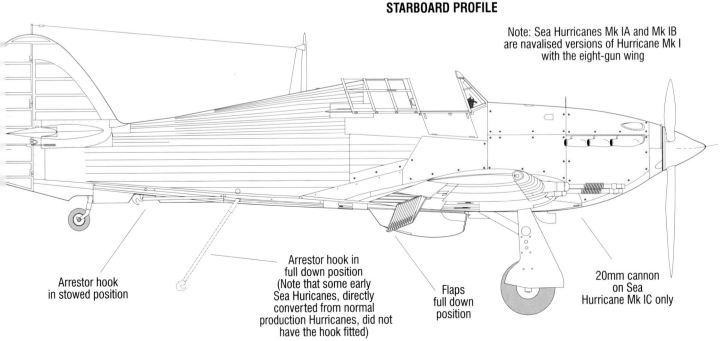

Arrestor hook
in stowed position

Arrestor hook in
full down position
(Note that some early
Sea Huricanes, directly
converted from normal
production Hurricanes, did not
have the hook fitted)

Flaps
full down
position

20mm cannon
on Sea
Hurricane Mk IC only